Class struggles in the USSR

Class struggles in the USSR

by Charles Bettelheim

Translated by Brian Pearce

First period: 1917–1923

THE HARVESTER PRESS

Copyright © 1976 by Monthly Review Press
All rights reserved

Originally published as *Les luttes de classes en URSS*,
copyright © 1974 by Maspero/Seuil, Paris, France.

Library of Congress Cataloging in Publication Data
Bettelheim, Charles.
    Class struggles in the U.S.S.R.
    Translation of Les luttes de classes en URSS.
    CONTENTS: v. 1. The first period, 1917–1923.
    Bibliography: p.
    Includes index.
    1. Russia—Politics and government–1917–
2. Russia—Social conditions—1917– 3. Kommunisti-
cheskaia Partiia Sovetskogo Soiuza. 4. Russia—History
—Revolution, 1917–1921. I. Title.
DK266.B4413   320.9′47′084   76-28986
ISB 0-85345-396-9

Monthly Review Press
62 West 14th Street, New York, N.Y. 10011
21 Theobalds Road, London WC1X 8SL

First printing

Manufactured in the United States of America

Contents

5

6 Contents

Key to abbreviations, initials, and Russian words used in the text

Artel	A particular form of producers' cooperative
Cadet party	The Constitutional Democratic Party
CLD	See STO
Cheka	Extraordinary Commission (political police)
Glavk	One of the chief directorates in the Supreme Council of the National Economy or in a people's commissariat
Gosplan	State Planning Commission
GPU	State Political Administration (political police)
Kulak	A rich peasant, often involved in capitalist activities of one kind or another, such as hiring out agricultural machinery, trade, moneylending, etc.
Mir	The village community
Narkomtrud	People's Commissariat of Labor
NEP	New Economic Policy
NKhSSSRv	National Economy of the USSR in (a certain year or period)
NKVD	People's Commissariat of Internal Affairs
OGPU	Unified State Political Administration (political police)
Orgburo	Organization Bureau of the Bolshevik Party
Politburo	Political Bureau of the Bolshevik Party
Rabfak	Workers' Faculty
Rabkrin	See RKI
RCP(B)	Russian Communist Party (Bolshevik): official

	name of the Bolshevik Party, adopted by the Seventh Party Congress in March 1918
RKI	Workers' and Peasants' Inspection
RSDLP	Russian Social Democratic Labor Party
RSDLP(B)	Russian Social Democratic Labor Party (Bolshevik)
RSFSR	Russian Socialist Federal Soviet Republic
Skhod	General assembly of a village
Sovkhoz	State farm
Sovnarkhoz	Regional Economic Council
Sovnarkom	Council of People's Commissars
SR	Socialist Revolutionary
STO	Council of Labor and Defense
Uchraspred	Department in the Bolshevik Party responsible for registering the members and assigning them to different tasks
Uyezd	County
Volost	Rural district
VSNKh	Supreme Economic Council
VTsIK	All-Russia Central Executive Committee (organ derived from the Congress of soviets)
Zemstvo	Administrative body in country areas before the Revolution

Preface

It seems to me essential to explain to the reader why and how I have written this book and how it relates to my previous writings.

The simplest procedure is undoubtedly to begin by showing how the book began and how what was at first a project of limited scope developed into a more ambitious one.

What gave the immediate impetus to this work was the invasion and occupation of Czechoslovakia by the Soviet forces. Those who claim to be Marxists cannot confine themselves to condemning or deploring political acts; they have also to explain them. Regrets and wishes may help the people to endure their woes, but they do not help them either to perceive their causes or to struggle to get rid of them or to prevent their reemergence. By explaining the reasons for something that does indeed deserve condemnation from the standpoint of the interests of the working people, we can contribute, however, to causing political forces to evolve in such a way that the "regrettable" events do not recur.

In the case of the invasion and occupation of Czechoslovakia, I thought it all the more necessary not to confine myself to expressions of regret because what was at issue was, besides the fate of a people which had already suffered many occupations, the judgment to be passed upon what the Soviet Union has become today, since it was Russian forces, together with their "allies," that carried out this act of violence.

If I felt justified in dealing with the problems of the Soviet Union, this was because I have been studying that country for nearly forty years and because I believe that everything concerning it has worldwide significance and implications. That was my opinion in 1934, when I began to learn Russian; in

9

1936, when I visited the USSR to study Soviet planning; in 1939, when I published a book on the subject; in 1946, when I published another book dealing with the theoretical and practical problems of planning; in 1950, when I published a book on the Soviet economy; and since then, in several visits to the country and in other books on planning[1] and on the transition to socialism.[2]

Basically, my interest in the Soviet Union since the mid-1930s has been determined by identification of what was happening in that country with the first experience of socialist construction. Without being blind to the difficulties and contradictions that marked this process (how could I be, when I was in Moscow in 1936, at the time of the first of the "great trials,"[3] and was able to sense every day the confusion into which the city's inhabitants had been thrown and the fear of voicing their opinions that was felt by the most ordinary people as well as by old members of the Bolshevik Party and the Communist International?), I nevertheless considered, not only that the October Revolution had opened a new era in the history of mankind (which I still believe), but also that the economic and social development of the Soviet Union provided a sort of "model" for the building of socialism. The difficulties and contradictions accompanying this development seemed to me, despite their seriousness, to be due above all to the special historical conditions of Russia. I thought there was no reason why they should reappear elsewhere, or should prevent Russia from continuing to advance toward socialism and communism.

The undeniable economic successes achieved by the USSR, especially in the industrial field (from the five year plans onward), the Red Army's victory over Hitlerism, the rapidity with which economic reconstruction was carried out after the war, the improvement in the Soviet people's standard of living, the help rendered by the government of the USSR to socialist China, all seemed, moreover, to confirm the appreciations and forecasts I have mentioned, even though the social inequalities that developed during the first five year plans were tending not to diminish but rather to intensify.

The Twentieth Congress of the Soviet Communist Party,

although it offered no *analysis* of the difficulties and contradictions that had led to the acts of repression committed indiscriminately and on a large scale during the preceding years, but confined itself to substituting for such an analysis personal accusations against Stalin (who was made solely "responsible" for the "negative" aspects of the past period), seemed to confirm that the Soviet Union, having reached a certain level of economic development, was now about to enter upon a phase of greater socialist democracy, thus opening up vast opportunities for working-class initiative. This congress seemed to show, too, that the party had retained—or rather, had recovered—the capacity for self-criticism that was essential if errors were to be rectified.[4]

Actually this was not at all the case. The contradictory reality of Soviet history and Soviet society was not subject to the least analysis. The aspects of reality which needed to be condemned and transformed were not explained in relation to the inner contradictions of the Soviet Union. They were presented as being "perversions" due to the actions of a certain "personality," namely, Stalin. The acceptance by the Soviet Communist Party of such a pseudoexplanation testified to its abandonment of Marxism as a tool of analysis. This made the party incapable of helping to transform the social relations that had given rise to that which was being condemned in words. The pseudoexplanation given thus fulfilled its task of consolidating the class relations which concentrated economic and political power in the hands of a minority, so that the contradictions engendered by these class relations, far from diminishing, were actually deepened.

Among many other consequences, this deepening of the social contradictions resulted in a worsening of the conditions in which the USSR's economy functioned. The same thing happened in those countries linked with the USSR whose leaders followed the same political line. Instead of an attack being launched on the social contradictions themselves, "economic reforms" were introduced which were attempts to make the economic system "work better" by increasing the powers of factory managers and giving ever-greater scope to capitalist forms and criteria of economic management.

Contrary to the hopes of the leaders of the Soviet Union and the "fraternal countries," the various "reforms" have not radically solved any of the difficulties with which these leaders are faced. To be sure, momentary successes have been obtained in limited fields, but failures predominate: there is greater dependence on foreign techniques, increased foreign indebtedness, a marked reduction in the rate of industrial growth, and difficulties in the field of food supplies. Signs of discontent on the part of the working people with their situation and with the impact of the "economic reforms," become more and more apparent.

The whole world saw what happened in Poland in December 1970, when the workers in the big Baltic coast cities of Gdansk, Gdynia, Szczecin, and Sopot went on strike against a government policy which meant price increases and a lower standard of living for the working people. The repressive measures taken against the struggling Polish workers caused them to counterattack by occupying the offices of the party and of the political police and organizing a strike committee which formed a workers' militia. Although the security forces then resorted to still more intense repression, killing or wounding a number of the workers, the latter resisted, kept up their strike, and compelled the authorities to modify the composition of the ruling group, to negotiate, and to yield on a certain number of the workers' demands.[5]

The events in Poland were a turning point in the relations between the working class in the countries of the Soviet zone and the political authorities of these countries. We know that they produced a profound echo among the working class of the USSR and aroused a wave of fear among the leading circles there—fear which was reflected in the revision of the economic plans for 1971, and also in intensified repression.

In the USSR itself there has indeed been in recent years a tendency to increased repression which has become more and more obvious, as shown in the adoption of new police measures and in what we know of the population of the camps—now, according to available estimates, amounting to about two million.

On the basis of these deepening internal contradictions, the international policy of the USSR is marked by increasing negation of what formerly made up the socialist aspects of Soviet foreign policy. Instead of the aid that once was given to China and Albania, we have seen since 1960 a deliberate attempt, in the name of ideological "divergences," to sabotage the economic development of these countries through unilateral repudiation of signed agreements, cutting off of supplies needed for factories under construction, withdrawal of technicians, etc. The Soviet Union is in this way trying, unsuccessfully, to make use of the economic relations it established with these countries in the past to bring severe pressure to bear upon them and subject them to its hegemony.

In general, the USSR's international policy appears more and more like that of a great power seeking to secure as many economic and political advantages as possible for itself by utilizing the close relations it has formed with other countries. This imperialist type of policy leads the USSR both to collaborate with and to come into contradiction with the USA. These two great powers are both struggling for world hegemony. They are also led to make compromises at the expense of the peoples. They talk about "détente" while engaging in an armaments race exceeding anything previously known to history, and while American imperialism continues to carry on its wars against Third World peoples.

By taking its stand on the same ground as the USA, that is, by entering into competition with that country for world hegemony, the USSR has been led to build offensive armed forces of unprecedented strength, equipping itself with gigantic means for intervention anywhere in the world. So as to be able to wield such a potential, equal or even superior in some fields to that of the USA, the USSR is now devoting 25 to 30 percent of its Gross National Product to military expenditure, as against 7 to 8 percent in the case of the USA. It is increasing year by year the number of divisions it keeps on a war footing on the frontiers of China; but its main military potential is turned toward Western Europe, and is also increasing rapidly.

In order to have at their disposal instruments of an

imperialist-type foreign policy, the Soviet leaders are imposing a heavy burden on the people of the USSR, which hinders
the country's economic development. Ultimately they have
been compelled to seek financial and technical aid from
American imperialism even while constantly clashing with
the latter.

A review of this process of evolution (in which the occupation of Czechoslovakia figures as one moment) caused me to
reconsider also the *past* of the Soviet Union, for it is impossible to suppose that the course being followed by that country
results merely from the "personal responsibility" of a few
leaders. The accession to power of these leaders and their
ability to operate the policy I have described are necessarily
to be explained by the social relations that now prevail in the
USSR, and that took shape over a long preceding period.
Hence the need to analyze these relations.

In the analysis which I was thus led to undertake, I was also
able to draw upon the experience I had had of the economic
and political transformations effected in China and Cuba.

As regards the latter country, this was a very concrete practical experience, as I participated on several occasions in discussion of the problems that arose in planning the Cuban
economy in the years 1960–1966. On the basis of this experience I found myself thereafter questioning a set of conceptions regarding the conditions for working out economic
plans, the significance of planning in the transition to
socialism, and the implications of the existence of commodity
and money relations in social formations in which state ownership of the means of production plays an important role.

So as to clarify the nature of the theses set forth in the
present book and help the reader to situate them better in
relation to those which I expounded in two previous books
(and which were very largely the result of my experience of
Cuba's problems), it is appropriate to recall what were the
limits of my questioning of previously held conceptions.

In *The Transition to Socialist Economy*, which brings together a series of writings produced between 1962 and 1967, I

applied myself to showing the connection between the existence of commodity and money relations, in Cuba as in the USSR, and of units of production which function, de facto, in relative independence of each other (despite the working of an economic plan), thus operating as "economic subjects."[6]

The analysis I then put forward tended to explain the existence of commodity and money relations, and of wage relations, by that of real social relations which function independently of men's will (and which cannot therefore be made to "disappear" merely by proclaiming them to be "abolished"). In the setting of this analysis, therefore, commodity and money relations appear as the manifestation of underlying social relations: they are effects of these relations, and objective requirements for the reproduction of these relations.

Today I consider that the specific form of the analysis I offered in 1962 and 1967 was not satisfactory. I have been induced to modify very seriously the terms of my analysis in the light of further thinking about the conditions under which socialism is being built in China, and in particular about the lessons to be drawn from the Cultural Revolution.

The chief shortcoming of my writings of 1962–1967 lies in the fact that what is there treated as something dictated by objective requirements is essentially related to the level of development of productive forces.[7] Although the concept of "the nature of the productive forces" is mentioned in these writings, the precise significance of the concept is not developed. Consequently, it is not made clear that the main obstacle to a socially unified policy (of which the economic plan can only be the means) consists not in the level of development of the productive forces but rather in the nature of the dominant social relations—that is, both in the reproduction of the capitalist division of labor and in the ideological and political relations which, while being an effect of this division, also constitute the social conditions for this reproduction (by causing individuals and enterprises to "function" as "subjects" which accord priority to their own interests over the collective interest: the latter, moreover, possibly being only momentary or illusory if it is not identified with the demands of a policy that really works to create the conditions for the disappearance of antagonistic class interests).

What therefore fails to come out clearly in the writings collected under the title *The Transition to Socialist Economy* is that the development of the productive forces can never, by itself, cause the capitalist forms of the division of labor, or the other bourgeois social relations, to disappear. What is not said is that only a *class struggle* developing under the dictatorship of the proletariat and correctly led—thanks to scientific experimentation on a mass scale and to theoretical analysis—can bring about the disappearance of capitalist economic relations, by attacking the capitalist division of labor and, at the same time, the ideological and political relations that make it possible for relations of exploitation and oppression to be reproduced.

If in 1962–1967 I did not set out the formulations which I now put forward, this was because I was still strongly influenced by a certain conception of "Marxism" which has been widely prevalent in Europe, and which is nothing but a special form of what Lenin called "economism."[8] It was the lessons to be drawn from the Cultural Revolution in China that enabled me to carry further my break with economism and so to reestablish contact with the revolutionary content of Marxism, a content masked and "overgrown" by the long years of economistic practice that have characterized the European labor movement.[9]

In *Economic Calculation and Forms of Property*, in which I mentioned that I was preparing an analysis of the Soviet social formation, I began to turn away from my previous problematic, in which the disappearance of commodity and money relations and the progress of socialist planning tended to be seen as dependent above all on the development of the productive forces (this development being conceived, moreover, in somewhat unilinear fashion), and not, first and foremost, on the revolutionization of social relations. As I have said, it is in the course of these last few years and, in part, through thinking about the Cultural Revolution and its significance, that I have come to take account more systematically of what is implied by rejection of the "problematic of the productive forces," that is, of a conception which unilaterally subordinates the transformation of social relations to the development of the productive forces.

These were the circumstances in which, between 1968 and the present time, I wrote a number of articles on some problems of socialism,[10] and undertook a fresh analysis of the Soviet Union, with a view to defining better the specific nature of state capitalism and the relations and practices of the classes which dominate that country today.

At the beginning of 1969, I finished writing a first essay (unpublished) setting out the results of this analysis, from which it emerges that, under cover of state ownership, relations of exploitation exist today in the USSR which are similar to those existing in the other capitalist countries, so that it is only the *form* of these relations that is distinctive there. This distinctive form is that of state capitalism; and we have known since Engels's time that state capitalism is merely capitalism "pushed to an extreme."

Nevertheless, when I critically reread the essay I had written, it struck me that what was lacking in it was historical background. It is indeed impossible to understand the Soviet Union's present without relating it to the country's past. It is not enough to show the relations and practices that are dominant today; one must also explain how they have become dominant. One needs therefore to consider how, through what struggles and contradictions, the first country of the dictatorship of the proletariat has become transformed into a country carrying out an imperialist policy, which does not hesitate to send its armed forces into other countries in order to uphold its great-power interests.

Analysis of the transformation that the Soviet Union has undergone is at least as important as analysis of the present situation taken on its own; such an analysis can serve as an invaluable source of instruction, and help other proletarian revolutions to avoid taking the same road and ending up not with socialism, but with a specific form of capitalism just as oppressive and aggressive as the "classical" forms.

The present period demands, despite the difficulties involved, that this task be fulfilled. Even if it falls short of perfection, the effort to accomplish it cannot but help us to understand a past which is also our present, and to grasp how a proletarian revolution can be transformed into its opposite, namely, a bourgeois counter-revolution.

The Soviet experience confirms that what is hardest is not the overthrow of the former dominant classes: the hardest task is, first, to destroy the former social relations—upon which a system of exploitation similar to the one supposed to have been overthrown for good can be reconstituted—and then to prevent these relations from being reconstituted on the basis of those elements of the old that still remain present for a long time in the new social relations.

In our time it is therefore vital that we understand the reasons why the first victorious socialist revolution has ultimately produced the Soviet reality of today. If this is not understood, then, despite the positive and invaluable lessons to be drawn from the successes of the Chinese Revolution, the risks are indeed tremendous that what may begin, here or elsewhere, as a proletarian revolution, could result in the end in something quite different from socialism.

The essay I wrote in 1969 therefore seemed to me inadequate, and before publishing it in updated form I thought it necessary to complete my work by making an analysis of the Soviet Union's past. When I took up this task I appreciated that it was at least as complex as the already tackled one: first, because it covered an historical period that was much longer and richer in events and conflicts, and secondly, because one had to try to discover, through and beyond the particular history of the Soviet Union, the general movement of the contradictions of which this very particularity was the form of existence. By itself, indeed, this particularity might seem accidental or fortuitous and would not enable us to draw the necessary lessons from what has happened in the USSR.

The objective was to arrive at a knowledge of the history of the Soviet Union sufficiently precise to make it possible to write something other than a history of that country: to subject the class struggles in the USSR since the October Revolution to an analysis of sufficiently universal bearing, even though presenting itself in the specific shape of a contemporary history of the USSR. I thus had to analyze the decisive moments through which the Soviet social formation has passed and determine the nature of the social relations that have existed and have been dominant at each of these moments. I also sought to define the nature of the social forces that have contributed to altering the articulation of these relations, even when, as often happened, struggles were carried on that aimed at changes quite different from those which actually ensued. The present volume sets out the first results of this work, the ultimate aim of which is to provide an analysis of present-day Soviet reality—an analysis that would remain to some extent incomprehensible in the absence of an adequate knowledge of the conditions in which today's reality took shape.

These analyses thus continue the work of rectification which I began between 1962 and 1967.

My work of rectification and of concrete analysis of the Soviet Union, of its present and past, caused me gradually to break with a certain congealed and simplistic conception of Marxism and to reestablish contact with what I believe to be the revolutionary content of historical and dialectical materialism.[11]

Only a part of the results of this work is included in the present volume, but I must provide a general survey in this foreword, for what is involved goes far beyond what might be a mere personal itinerary of no great interest to the reader.

As mentioned earlier, the simplified Marxism from which I tried to break free was not something personal to me: it had become that which the European sections of the Third International, departing further and further from Leninism, had caused to prevail in Europe, starting in the early 1930s, at the time when I began to think about the problems of socialism.

This simplified Marxism bore within itself, moreover—if not in germ then at least as a possibility to which it was exposed—the premises of modern revisionism, that is, of a bourgeois ideology which has contributed to consolidating the existence of capitalist social relations in the Soviet Union and also outside it.

It would be futile to claim that I have analyzed all aspects of the congealed Marxism with which I have had to break in order to render intelligible what has happened in the Soviet Union (a reading of the book will reveal the most important of these aspects). It is necessary, however, to set forth and discuss some of the theses, explicit or implicit, of this kind of Marxism, so as to afford a better understanding of the meaning of the rectification being carried out in the pages that follow, and of the significance of the conclusions that will be brought together in the last volume of the work.

Three of the fundamental theses of the congealed Marxism with which one must break in order to restore a true revolutionary character to historical and dialectical materialism concern (1) the basis of class relations, (2) the role of the productive forces, and (3) the conditions for the existence of the state and for its "withering away." I shall say just a few words about these three theses and their objective ideological and political functions.

Class relations and legal forms of ownership

The first thesis with which one has to break is that which makes a mechanistic identification of legal forms of ownership with class relations, particularly where the transition to socialism is concerned.

This thesis was explicitly expounded by Stalin in his report on the draft constitution of the USSR, presented on November 25, 1936, to the Seventh Congress of Soviets of the USSR.[12]

In his report, Stalin summed up the transformation of forms of ownership that had taken place in Russia during the period

1924–1936. He showed that in this period legal private ownership of the means of production and exchange had been practically abolished, and replaced by two other forms of ownership—state property, which predominated in industry, transport, trade, and banking; and collective-farm property, which predominated in agriculture; and he concluded: "The capitalist class in the sphere of industry has ceased to exist. The kulak class in the sphere of agriculture has ceased to exist, and the merchants and profiteers in the sphere of trade have ceased to exist. Thus all the exploiting classes have now been eliminated."[13]

According to this report, there were now only the working class, the peasant class, and the intelligentsia, who "must serve the people, for there are no longer any exploiting classes."[14]

In conclusion, this part of Stalin's report asserted that, as a result, economic and political contradictions between classes (that is, between the peasants, the workers, and the intellectuals) "are declining and becoming obliterated."[15] Acceptance of this thesis obstructs analysis of the contradictions which in fact continued to manifest themselves in the Soviet Union. It makes incomprehensible the idea that the proletariat could lose power to any sort of bourgeoisie, since the latter seems to be incapable of existence unless capitalist private property is reconstituted. Such a thesis disarms the proletariat by persuading it that the class struggle is now a thing of the past.

Life has made it its business to show, or rather to recall, that changes in legal forms of ownership do not suffice to cause the conditions for the existence of classes and for class struggle to disappear. These conditions are rooted, as Marx and Lenin often emphasized, not in legal forms of ownership but in *production relations,* that is, in the form of the social process of appropriation, in the place that the form of this process assigns to the agents of production—in fact, in the relations that are established between them in social production.[16]

The existence of the dictatorship of the proletariat and of state or collective forms of property is not enough to "abolish" capitalist production relations and for the antagonistic classes, proletariat and bourgeoisie, to "disappear." The bourgeoisie can continue to exist in different forms and, in particular, can assume the form of a state bourgeoisie.

The historical role of the dictatorship of the proletariat is not only to change the forms of ownership but also—and this is a much more complex and protracted task—to transform the social process of appropriation and thereby destroy the old production relations and build new ones, thus ensuring the transition from the capitalist mode of production to the communist mode: the transition to socialism meaning this transition, which alone enables bourgeois social relations, and the bourgeoisie as a class, to be eliminated.

The above is nothing new, but quite literally, a return to Marx and Lenin—to Marx, for whom the dictatorship of the proletariat is the necessary point of transition for arriving at the abolition of class differences in general;[17] and to Lenin, who frequently recalled that "classes *still* remain and *will remain* in the era of the dictatorship of the proletariat," adding that *"every* class has undergone a change," so that their *relations* have also altered, and the class struggle, while continuing, "assumes different forms."[18]

It is because the task of the socialist revolution is not confined to transforming legal property relations, and that what is fundamental is to transform social relations as a whole, including production relations, that Lenin comes back so often to the essential idea that it is comparatively "easy . . . to *start* the revolution . . . but it will be more difficult . . . to *continue* the revolution and bring it to its consummation."[19] Thus, the transition to socialism inevitably occupies a long period of history, and cannot be "accomplished" within a few years.[20]

It is clear that if one is to understand the changes in Soviet society and the possibility of the reestablishment of a bourgeois dictatorship in the USSR (without any change in legal property relations), one has to abandon the thesis that exploiting classes have ceased to exist merely because there is a dictatorship of the proletariat (over what class would the proletariat be exercising its dictatorship, in that case?) and because state and collective-farm property predominates; one needs to go back to Lenin's conception of the dictatorship of the proletariat as "the continuation of the class struggle in new forms."

The primacy of the development of the productive forces

A second thesis characteristic of the simplification of Marxism which tended to impose itself during the 1930s in the European sections of the Third International was that of the primacy of the development of the productive forces. This thesis presented the development of the productive forces as the "driving force of history."

For a certain period, acceptance of this thesis gave one the illusion of possessing an "explanation" of the contradictions in the Soviet social formation—an explanation that was no longer to be sought in the class struggle, as this was supposed to be "on its way out," or even to have ceased altogether with the disappearance of antagonistic classes.

In a very general form, the thesis according to which the productive forces are the driving force of history was set forth by Stalin in his essay of September 1938 entitled "Dialectical and Historical Materialism,"[21] in which he wrote: "First the productive forces of society change and develop, and then, *depending* on these changes and *in conformity with them*, men's relations of production, their economic relations, change."[22]

The thesis thus formulated does not deny the role of the class struggle—in so far as there is a society in which antagonistic classes confront one another—but relegates this to the secondary level: the class struggle intervenes essentially in order to smash production relations that hinder the development of the productive forces, thus engendering new production relations which conform to the needs of the development of the productive forces.

Actually, in the passage quoted above, Stalin acknowledges that the new production relations can appear independently of a revolutionary process, when he writes: "The rise of new productive forces and of the relations of production corresponding to them does not take place separately from the old system, after the disappearance of the old system, but within the old system . . . "[23]

One can certainly find passages in Marx which suggest a similar problematic: but his work as a whole shows that, for him, *the driving force of history is the class struggle*, and that, as long as classes exist, it is through conflicts between classes that social relations are transformed; it shows also that socialist social relations can arise only through class struggle. Similarly, Lenin would never have been able to formulate his theory of "the weakest link in the imperialist chain"—the theory which explains why a proletarian revolution could take place *in Russia*—if, like the Mensheviks, he had held to a conception which put the main stress on the development of the productive forces, since, according to this conception, a proletarian revolution could not happen elsewhere than in the most highly industrialized countries.

The thesis of the primacy of the productive forces prevents one from using rigorously the concepts of historical materialism, and leads to incorrect political formulations, such as this one, put forward by Stalin in the above-quoted essay: "If it is not to err in policy, the party of the proletariat must both in drafting its programme and in its practical activities proceed primarily from the laws of development of production, from the laws of economic development of society."[24] The conception of the productive forces developed in this way certainly gave rise to a number of difficulties when it came to fitting it into the theses of historical materialism as a whole; but it was a necessary corollary to the thesis about the disappearance from the USSR of exploiting classes, and therefore also of exploited ones.

The connection between these theses is seen, for example, when Stalin writes that "the basis of the relations of production under the socialist system . . . is the social ownership of the means of production. Here there are no longer exploiters and exploited . . . Here the relations of production fully correspond to the state of productive forces . . . "[25]

One of the difficulties arising from this formulation (according to which there is "full conformity" between productive forces and production relations) is that it does away with any possibility of contradiction between the two elements of the economic basis. This led Stalin in 1952 to make a partial rectification of his earlier formulation, when he reproached A. Ya. Notkin for having taken literally his formulation regarding "full conformity," and said that this referred only to the fact that "under socialism . . . society is in a position to take timely steps to bring the lagging relations of production into conformity with the character of the productive forces. Socialist society is in a position to do so because it does not include obsolescent classes that might organise resistance."[26]

Ideologically and politically, these two theses on the disappearance of exploiting and exploited classes in the USSR and on the primacy of the development of the productive forces, have contributed to blocking any organized action by the Soviet proletariat to transform the production relations, that is, to destroy the existing forms of the process of appropriation, the basis for the reproduction of class relations, and build a new process of appropriation, excluding the social division between the function of management and that of execution, the separation between manual and mental labor, and the differences between town and country and between workers and peasants—in short, to destroy the objective basis for the existence of classes. On the one hand, classes were supposed to have disappeared, and on the other, the production relations were supposed to correspond perfectly to the productive forces, and any contradiction that might seem to exist was supposed to be bound to disappear in good time, thanks to the action of "socialist society."

Under these conditions, the fundamental problem for the Soviet proletariat to solve seemed to be that of increasing production as quickly as possible: in building "the material foundations of socialism" it was "guaranteed" that the corresponding production relations and the appropriate superstructure would also develop. Hence the slogans of the period: "Technique decides everything" and "Catch up with and surpass the most advanced capitalist countries."

It is understandable that the Chinese Communist Party considered itself justified in saying, in the publication *On Khrushchev's Phony Communism and Its Historical Lessons for the World*: "Stalin departed from Marxist-Leninist dialectics in his understanding of the laws of class struggle in socialist society." [27]

Actually, this understanding of the laws of the class struggle was not particular to Stalin. Here, as on many other matters (for example, on how to conceive the relations between struggle and unity within the party), Stalin merely expressed in systematic fashion the views of the leading strata of the Bolshevik Party. Despite appearances, his role was essentially that of transmitting and concentrating orientations which reflected the changes going on within Soviet society and the Bolshevik Party. This role was due to the fact that the party itself was becoming less and less capable of going against the tide, that is, of revolutionizing practice and theory. Even when Stalin, at certain moments, disregarded the fears and reservations of the Central Committee and the Political Bureau, he did not go "against the tide" in the strict sense,[28] but merely deduced the ultimate consequences of the conceptions prevailing in the party's leading circles. It was this will to go through to the end that placed Stalin apparently "above" the party and caused to seem specifically "his" some conceptions which, except in a few cases,[29] were not peculiar to him but acquired exceptional authority through the support he gave them: this was just what happened with the understanding of the laws of the class struggle in socialist society.

The fact is that this "understanding" dominated the ideological and political conceptions of the European sections of the Third International, and thereby helped to conceal the existence of classes and of class struggle in the Soviet Union, thus encouraging people to seek "elsewhere" than in class contradictions the causes of the grave difficulties being experienced by the Soviet Union.

This "elsewhere" was signposted by the thesis on the primacy of the productive forces: it was because those forces were "insufficiently developed" that the USSR had to cope with enormous difficulties and therefore was obliged to take a series of measures that were remote from what the Bolshevik Party's old program thought corresponded with the demands of the building of socialism: increased wage differentials, development of a bonus system, growing privileges accorded to technicians, strengthening of the personal authority of the manager of an enterprise, etc.

For a whole generation, my own generation, the two theses mentioned above enjoyed a sort of "obviousness" which caused us to avoid analyzing the real contradictions and problems: even when these were not ignored, their "solution" was put off till later—it would in due course be provided by the development of the productive forces.

In order to appreciate the "obviousness" of these theses (a quality which they have retained both for modern revisionism and for what is called Trotskyism), one must remember that they expressed the view not only of Stalin personally but also of *the most revolutionary wing of the European Marxist movement of the time.*[30]

It will not be out of place to quote here some of Trotsky's statements regarding these two theses: although his attitude to them was close to Stalin's, it nevertheless caused him to draw very different conclusions.

Like Stalin, Trotsky accepted that, after the collectivization or statization of the means of production, "there are no possessing classes,"[31] since "private property" no longer exists. Explaining his idea, Trotsky added that there were no "possessing classes" in the USSR because the establishment of "state property" prevented any "bureaucrat" from acquiring "stocks or goods" which he could "transmit to his heirs."[32] He also observed that "in civilised societies, property relations are validated by laws,"[33] leaving it to be assumed that production relations belong to the superstructure and do not correspond to the relations established in the social process of production and reproduction.

We also find in Trotsky, although in caricatured form, Stalin's formula according to which the communist program must "proceed primarily from the laws of development of production," as when he writes: "Marxism sets out from the development of technique as the fundamental spring of progress, and constructs the communist programme upon the dynamic of the productive forces."[34]

These similarities render all the more striking the difference between the practical conclusions drawn by Stalin and Trotsky respectively.

For Stalin, socialism had been achieved, in essentials, at the end of the first five year plan. For Trotsky, this conclusion was inacceptable for two main reasons: on the one hand, as he saw it, there could be no question of "socialism in a single country," and, on the other (and this calls for particular notice), "the achieved productivity of labour" was too low in the Soviet Union for it to be possible to talk of socialism having been realized there.[35] Thus, Trotsky acknowledges that the social content of one and the same legal form can vary, but this variation is not related, for him, to different production relations (indeed, the concept of production relations is practically absent from his writings on this subject), but to "the achieved productivity of labour," and this leads him to declare that "the 'root' of every social organization is the productive forces."[36]

Finally, from the standpoint with which we are concerned here, what characterizes Trotsky's conception is that it accepts the thesis of the primacy of the development of the productive forces in its uttermost implications, notably in the two following respects.

First, reference to the level of the productive forces enables Trotsky to bring in the notion of "bourgeois norms of distribution,"[37] which have been dictated to the USSR by the low level of the productive forces, and which could lead to a restoration of private property. The idea of a restoration of bourgeois domination within the setting of state property is thus implicitly rejected by Trotsky, though he is unable to bring forward any genuine arguments to justify this rejection.

Second, the role which Trotsky ascribes to the development of the productive forces goes so far that it completely replaces the class struggle, so that he can write: "The strength and stability of regimes are determined in the long run by the relative productivity of their labour. A socialist economy possessing a technique superior to that of capitalism would really be guaranteed in its socialist development for sure—so to speak, automatically . . . "[38]

I have quoted Trotsky at this length, alongside Stalin, in order to show the extent to which, despite the different conclusions drawn, the two theses (on the disappearance of antagonistic classes in the USSR and on the primacy of the development of the productive forces) were a sort of "commonplace" in "European Marxism" in the 1930s (remaining so until a comparatively recent date), which tended to obstruct analysis of the transformation of society in terms of the class struggle.

I shall endeavor later on to state what, in my view, were the reasons that enabled these two theses to play for so long their particular ideological and political role. Before doing this, however, I must say something about a third thesis which was linked with the two discussed so far.

The existence of the state and the disappearance of exploiting classes

One of the difficulties to which acceptance of the thesis of the disappearance of exploiting classes gives rise relates to the existence of the Soviet state, not as a transitional form becoming transformed into a nonstate, a "commune"—to use the formulation employed by Engels in a letter to Bebel, and taken over by Lenin—but as a state becoming more and more separate from the masses, endowed with an apparatus increasingly jealous to safeguard its "secrets," and functioning in a hierarchical manner, with each "echelon" subordinate to a "higher" one.

From the Marxist standpoint, the form of existence of the Soviet state and the nature of its apparatuses created a problem, since, for historical materialism, this type of state can exist only on the basis of class antagonisms: the strengthening of such a state machine is a symptom of the deepening of these antagonisms, whereas their disappearance is accompanied by the extinction of the state in the strict sense (as an organ of repression) and its replacement by organs of self-administration by the masses.

This problem was considered by Stalin, notably in his report to the Eighteenth Congress of the Soviet Communist Party.[39] In his address Stalin recalled Engels's formulation in *Anti-Dühring*: "As soon as there is no longer any social class to be held in subjection; as soon as class rule, and the individual struggle for existence based upon our present anarchy in production, with the collisions and excesses arising from these, are removed, nothing more remains to be repressed, and a special repressive force, a state, is no longer necessary."[40]

In order to solve the problem thus presented, Stalin was obliged to declare that "certain of the general propositions in the Marxist doctrine of the state were incompletely worked out and inadequate."[41] He then proposed that this inadequacy be repaired by claiming that the Soviet Union needed a state and a vast state machine not because of internal social relations but owing to an external factor, namely, capitalist encirclement. This produced the following formulation:

> The function of military suppression inside the country died away . . . In place of this function of suppression the state acquired the function of protecting socialist property from thieves and pilferers of the people's property. The function of defending the country from foreign attack fully remained: consequently, the Red Army and the Navy also fully remained, as did the punitive organs and the intelligence service, which are indispensable for the detection and punishment of the spies,

assassins and wreckers sent into our country by foreign intelligence services.[42]

Apart from the theoretical difficulty that arises from asserting the need for a huge force specializing in *internal* repression in order to deal with an external danger, when the masses' own organizations ought to be capable of coping with the task of detecting the hostile elements "sent into our country by foreign intelligence services," in a country where, in principle, no class was ready to cooperate with such elements, this thesis on the need to maintain a state machine came up against a more concrete difficulty (the full dimensions of which became apparent only when the scale of the repression became known—using this modest term "repression" to mean the arrest, imprisonment, and deportation of several million persons): how to explain that such numerous measures of coercion needed to be taken if it was merely a matter of striking at elements "sent in," together with "thieves and pilferers of the people's property," or persons who, out of "weaknesses," "vanity," or "slackness of will" had allowed foreign foes "to enmesh them in their espionage nets"?[43] It is hard to answer this question when so formulated. However, the scale of the repression carried out, the forms it assumed, and the contradictions shown in it can be much better understood when we set these facts in relation not mainly to the activity of foreign spies and the "slackness of will" of Soviet citizens but to *a class struggle that was both furious and blind*.

Trotsky, having also accepted the thesis of the disappearance of class oppression, was faced with the same problem in explaining the existence of a state machine. The "solution" he offered was purely economic in character. Taking up the formulation by Engels quoted above, he singled out from it "the individual struggle for existence," and declared that it was because this had not disappeared in the USSR that the state continued to exist—and that it would also exist after a revolution "even in America, on the basis of the most advanced capitalism."[44] It is worth quoting also this curious prognostiçation: "In so far as the social organisation has become socialistic, the soviets [in other words, precisely the organs of self-administration by the masses, the "nonstate"—C.B.] ought to drop away like the scaffolding after a building is finished."[45]

Nevertheless, however unsatisfactory the thesis according to which the form of existence of the Soviet state was explicable by the threat from outside and the "slackness of will" of the citizens of the USSR, acceptance of the first two theses made it almost inevitable.

This flashback should help the reader to understand the quasi-impossibility for those who accepted the theses discussed (and until recently that meant, in Europe at least, the overwhelming majority of all who recognized that the October Revolution had opened a new era in the history of mankind) to carry out a Marxist analysis of Soviet society, since essential to such an analysis would be not to shut one's eyes to class relations and the effects of the class struggle, but on the contrary, to perceive that here are relations and a struggle which are of decisive importance, and destined to remain so until a classless, communist society has been built.

But this review of the past still fails to provide an answer to the following question: why did the economistic problematic, of which the theses discussed above formed parts, play for so long (and why does it still play) its specific ideological role?

I.   The dominance of the problematic of the productive forces

In answering this question it must not be forgotten that the problematic of the productive forces—one of the aspects of the problematic of economism—was historically bound up, in an indissoluable way, not only with the European labor movement of the years 1880–1914 but also, in transformed fashion, with the history of the Russian Revolution, especially from the end of the 1920s onward, during the first attempt ever made to build socialism. The prestige which this attempt acquired in the eyes of the great majority of those who rightly saw in capitalism the "perfected" system of exploitation of man by man—a system which has already produced two world wars and innumerable wars of lesser dimensions—was bound, to some degree necessarily, to cast reflected glory upon the theoretical problematic connected with this attempt.

This is, however, only half an answer, for we still have to ask why this historical link was formed between the first attempt to build socialism and the theses that lie at the heart of the problematic we are discussing.

To this second aspect of the question I shall try, in this preface, to give only some elements of a reply, elements which will themselves be developed in the present volume and its successors (insofar as such development is required for an analysis of the transformation of the Soviet social formation).

(a) *The cessation of the fight against economism in the Bolshevik Party*

The first element of my reply relates to the ideology of the Bolshevik Party itself. This party, despite the far-reaching changes it underwent through the mere fact of its revolutionary activity, and through Lenin's ideological struggle against economism, was far from having rid itself of all economistic conceptions at the moment when, with Lenin's departure, the fight against economism ceased to be a feature of the ideological struggle inside the party.

It should be recalled that the term "economism" was used by Lenin to characterize critically a conception of Marxism which sought to reduce it to a mere "economic theory" by means of which all social changes could be interpreted. Such a conception can assume a variety of forms. When not systematized, it may play only a relatively secondary role, and it is possible then to speak only of a "tendency to economism."

Because economism defines the development of the productive forces as the driving force of history, one of its chief effects is to depict the political struggle between classes as the direct and immediate result of economic contradictions. The latter are thus supposed to be able by themselves to "engender" social changes and, "when the time is ripe," revolutionary struggles. The working class thus appears to be spontaneously urged toward revolution (it is therefore not necessary to form a proletarian party). The same problematic tends to deny that exploited and oppressed classes other than the proletariat are capable of struggling for socialism.[46]

At another level of analysis, economism is characterized by the fact that it tends to identify productive forces with the material means of production, thus denying that the principal productive force consists of the producers themselves: consequently, economism ascribes the major role in the building of socialism not to the initiative of the working people but to the accumulation of new means of production and technical knowledge.

Economism can appear in a variety of forms, even contradictory ones. Depending on the conjuncture of the class struggle, it can appear as rightist or leftist (actually, it is always both). In the Bolshevik Party, economism fostered certain attitudes taken by opposition groups in 1918 and in 1920–1925, including the trade-union oppositions, whose rightwing character was especially clear.[47]

Among the "rightist-leftist" effects of economism in the Bolshevik Party must also be mentioned the positions taken during the "war communism" period by Bukharin, Trotsky, and Preobrazhensky, who contemplated a "direct transition to communism" by way of generalized resort to state compulsion (militarization of labor, discipline imposed from above, requisitioning and rationing of agricultural produce), this being defined as the expression of "proletarian self-discipline," as a result of abstractly identifying the Soviet state with a "workers' state."

This form of economism made of centralized management of the economy the essence of "communism." It can be regarded as rightist in that it subjected the working people to an apparatus of coercion. It seemed thus to stand in opposition to a left-wing economism which declared, implicitly at least, that the unification of the working class and the unity of this class with the other toiling classes can be effected spontaneously through the convergence of the interests of all the working people. In reality these two conceptions both deny the decisive role of the ideological and political class struggle and the necessity (in order to carry this struggle through to victory) of a Marxist-Leninist party guided by a correct political line. The first conception tends to substitute state coercion for political and ideological leadership of the proletariat,[48] while the second tends to replace this leadership by the activity of the trade unions. As will be seen, these two "interpretations of Marxism" led certain Bolsheviks, when "war communism" came to an end, to call for "statization of the trade unions," while others came out in favor of "trade unionization of the state."

If it is necessary to dwell at such length here upon economism, this is not only because it has played an increasingly influential role in the European sections of the Third International, but also because the existence of economism, in one form or another, constantly confronts the labor movement with new problems. It is an illusion to imagine that Marxism and Marxist parties can be "wholly and finally" purged of it. This is in fact the form that bourgeois ideology takes within Marxism, and this ideology has its roots in bourgeois social relations that can disappear only when classes themselves disappear.

Struggle against economism is thus necessarily a part of the life of Marxism, and is even the principal form taken by the ideological class struggle in this field. Marx and Lenin waged this struggle in their writings.

Lenin's activity enabled the Bolshevik Party to shake off the crudest forms of economism, but tendencies to economism continued very strong within it. This was the reason why Lenin often had difficulty in making his views prevail. It also explains why economism marked so deeply the way in which the NEP was implemented, and the conception of collectivization and industrialization that prevailed in the Soviet Union, assigning the most important role to accumulation and treating technique as though it were "above" classes.

What has been said does not yet enable us to understand more than partially the historical link between the first attempt to build socialism and economism. In order to arrive at a fuller understanding of this link, two other series of ideas need to be followed through, concerning, first, the *social foundations* of economism, and secondly, the explicit revival of a number of economistic theses at the time of the five year plans.

(b) The social foundations of economism

Without entering into a debate for which this is not the place, it needs to be recalled that economism is itself a product, within Marxism, of the class struggle. To forget this is to fall into idealism—to suppose that ideas develop by their own motion and affect history independently of social contradictions.

In its original form, economism arose in the Second International, in the German Social Democratic Party. In its rightist variant it was connected with the existence within this party of a powerful political and trade-union apparatus which became integrated with the German state machine. The heads of this powerful apparatus were able to delude themselves that a steady increase in their organizational activity and pressure for workers' demands would eventually create the conditions for capitalism to be overthrown. They were all the more attached to this illusion because, by indulging it, they could strengthen their own positions in the German labor movement without, apparently, having to incur the risks inherent in revolutionary activity. In this way there emerged a bourgeois ideology, decked out with a few seemingly Marxist formulations which exercised a considerable influence on the German labor movement as a whole, insofar as the operations of the movement's political and trade-union apparatus and the strength of German imperialism enabled some strata of the working class to secure an improvement in their living standards. Conversely, in tsarist Russia, where the conditions for the development of a legal labor movement were not present, the Mensheviks' economism found no echo in the Russian working class, apart from a few relatively "privileged" sections such as the railroad workers.

In the Bolshevik Party itself the trade-union leaders proved on a number of occasions to be the principal agents of a right-wing economism, and after the October Revolution, the growth among party members of a stratum of administrators and of business, planning, and financial officials favored the development of economism in new forms. As will be seen, these new forms assumed a rightist or leftist appearance depending on the course of the class struggle and on the characteristics of those strata of the workers that could provide a social basis for them.

In its turn, the economism which had developed in the Communist Party of the Soviet Union found a response in the sections of the Communist International established in those countries where it was possible for the labor movement to develop in forms akin to those of the German labor movement before the First World War.

(c) The explicit revival of economistic theses during the implementation of the five year plans

The explicit revival of economistic theses which was expressed in a particularly systematic way in the writings mentioned above needs to be considered in two aspects—as the result of a profound evolution of Russian society and the Bolshevik Party, and in connection with the new authority acquired by these theses through their having been expounded by Stalin.

The first aspect is clearly the decisive one. It was the many changes undergone by Soviet Russia and by the Bolshevik Party between October 1917 and the beginning of 1929 that made it possible for conceptions to be adopted—at first only implicitly, in practice—which identified the building of socialism with the fastest possible development of the productive forces,[49] and of industry in particular, even at the expense of the alliance between the working class and the peasantry.

The economistic theses, in the form in which they triumphed at the end of the 1920s, were never fundamentally challenged by the various oppositionist trends. What the latter challenged were only particular concrete measures or groups of measures, of a political or administrative character, decided on the basis of a general orientation which they did not challenge fundamentally. Even the objections raised by Bukharin against an industrialization campaign which he thought was being conducted too hastily, were aimed at warning against the long-term negative economic effects of an initial industrial effort which he considered excessive. His argument was essentially that a smaller initial effort would make it possible to accomplish more quickly the same sort of industrialization that was aimed at by the five year plans. He did not question whether this type of industrialization was in conformity with the needs of socialist construction (though he did disagree that the type of collectivization carried through from 1929 onward would really enable socialist relations to be built in the countryside).

While it is true that the economistic conceptions which triumphed with the first five year plans corresponded to deepseated tendencies in the Bolshevik Party of that period, it is no less true, as has been observed, that the explicit assertion by Stalin of the economistic theses in question endowed the latter with exceptional weight, by virtue of the equally exceptional authority attached to his interventions. Here arises one of the aspects of what has been called "the question of Stalin."

In raising this question (which cannot be properly studied until the second volume of this work, in connection with my analysis of the period 1924–1953 as a whole), it must be kept in mind, first and foremost, that Lenin and Stalin had very different attitudes regarding problems of ideological struggle within the party.

Lenin, generally speaking, always put this struggle in the

forefront. He never hesitated to go "against the tide," as a result of which he more than once found himself in a minority in the Central Committee, and this on questions of vital importance—which shows, incidentally (and it is a point I shall return to at some length), how mistaken it is to see the Bolshevik Party as a "Leninist" party.

Stalin saw his leading role in a different way. On major problems he endeavored above all (particularly until 1934) to give expression to profound tendencies existing in the party, for which he thus acted as spokesman. From this standpoint, polemical attacks leveled against Stalin on the grounds that, by means of his "personality," he imposed on the party conceptions that were alien to it, are groundless. They relate to something quite different, namely, that Stalin persevered with inflexible rigor in putting into effect measures called for by conceptions that were not only his but also those of almost all the party members, including most of those who opposed certain of these measures.

Furthermore, the party was constantly changing: the social forces largely operative within it in 1929 were different from what they had been in 1917, and were different again in 1934 and in 1952, these changes being themselves bound up with changes in Soviet society.

However, and this is the second point that needs to be considered, by making himself the spokesman of profound tendencies in the party, Stalin gave additional weight to these tendencies, greatly reinforcing them. This was especially so in the case of the economistic conceptions which prevailed from 1929 onward.

The additional weight conferred by Stalin upon the theses he backed was a consequence of his own authority. This was not mainly due—as some like to imagine—to the fact that Stalin was the General Secretary of the Bolshevik Party (for that fact also has to be explained, without resorting, as is so often done, to anecdotes about Stalin's "personality" which, even when they are true, explain nothing at all). His authority was due to what almost the entire party, from the early 1930s onward, saw as the exceptional twofold merit of Stalin—that he had not given up the idea of building socialism in the USSR, and that he had worked out a policy which, as the party saw it, would successfully bring about that result.

When, after Lenin's death, the other Bolshevik leaders were ready to allow the continuation of a NEP that would have meant development toward private capitalism, or else to advocate certain measures of industrialization which they declined to present as leading to the establishment of socialism, Stalin, taking up a thesis of Lenin's,[50] reaffirmed that it was possible to undertake the building of socialism in the USSR without making this dependent on the victory of the proletarian revolution in Europe or in the rest of the world.

By adopting this line, and then by framing a policy aimed at drawing the logical consequences from it, Stalin intended to give back confidence to the Soviet working class; he provided the party with an objective other than merely trying to keep itself in power while waiting for better days; and in this way he contributed to the inception of a gigantic transformation process, which was to create the conditions needed for defense of the Soviet Union's independence and for intensification of the divisions in the imperialist camp, as a result of which the Soviet Union was able to play a decisive part in the defeat of Hitlerism. The policy of industrialization kept alight the beacon of the October Revolution, sustained the people's confidence in the victorious outcome of their struggles, and thus objectively helped to ensure the success of the Chinese Revolution.

By proclaiming that the Soviet Union could advance to socialism, Stalin, contrary to Trotsky's claims, appeared as heir to Lenin's position, several of whose writings, especially the last, asserted this possibility. This was one of the sources of Stalin's authority, which was linked with the theses he propounded. Actually, the enormous authority that Stalin enjoyed, especially right after the Second World War, was due not only to the theses he had upheld, but also to the efforts, courage, and self-sacrifice of the Soviet people. It was through the toil and heroism of this people that the industry of the USSR had been built and the Hitlerite armies defeated.

Nevertheless, it was Stalin who had directed these efforts and struggles by giving them the right objectives.

True, life has shown that, in respect of the precise path to be followed and the concrete measures to be taken in order to arrive at the objective decided upon, Stalin made serious mistakes, but their exact nature was not immediately apparent at the time.[51] Moreover, in the situation that the Soviet Union and the Bolshevik Party were in at the end of the 1920s, the mistakes made were doubtless historically inevitable.

The fact that these mistakes were made, and that they entailed grave political consequences (especially the blind repression which struck not only at the enemies of socialism but also at the masses and at genuine revolutionaries, while real enemies were spared), has given the world proletariat an exemplary lesson. It has been finally demonstrated that certain forms of attack against capitalism are illusory and only strengthen the bourgeoisie within the machinery of political and economic administration. The lessons drawn by Lenin from the comparable, even though limited, experience of "war communism" have thus been confirmed.

For the moment, however, the fact that the Soviet Union accomplished in a few years changes of extraordinary scope, resulting in the elimination of private capitalism and precapitalist forms of production, gave unprecedented authority to the theses upheld by the Bolshevik Party and formulated by Stalin. This strengthened still further the "obviousness" which these theses were seen as possessing by the great majority of members of the revolutionary movement, not only in the Soviet Union but also in Europe and elsewhere.

(d) Economism in the labor movements and Communist parties of Europe

Another factor helps to account for the role played, outside the Soviet Union, by the economistic conception of the building of socialism. This factor is the circumstance that the economism which Lenin had combated in the Bolshevik Party was much more widespread and lively in the European sections of the Third International than in its Russian section. In Europe—more precisely in Western Europe, and especially in Germany and France—economism had a long history which was largely identical with that of Europe's Social Democratic parties, mainly from the time when European capitalism entered the phase of imperialism. Since economism had not been combated in the rest of Europe as it had been in Russia, it is easy to understand that the revolutionary workers' movement in Europe was quite prepared to accept as "obvious" the economistic theses of the Soviet Communist Party.

Today, the economistic problematic of the building of socialism has been severely shaken (at least with respect to the form it took from the late 1920s onward) for at least two reasons.

The first of these is external to the USSR. It is the Chinese Revolution. What is happening in China proves that a low level of development of the productive forces is no obstacle to a socialist transformation of social relations, and does not necessarily require passing through forms of primitive accumulation, with aggravation of social inequalities, and so on.

China's example shows that it is not necessary (and, indeed, that it is dangerous) to aspire to build *first of all* the material foundations of socialist society, putting off *till later* the transformation of social relations, which will thus be brought into conformity with more highly developed productive forces. China's example shows that socialist transformation of the superstructure must *accompany* the development of the productive forces and that this transformation is a condition for truly socialist economic development. It shows, too, that when the transformations are carried out in this way, industrialization does not require, in contrast to what happened in the Soviet Union, the levying of tribute from the peasantry, a procedure which seriously threatens the alliance between the workers and the peasants.

The second reason why the economistic problematic of the building of socialism has been severely shaken is the actual disappearance of the "facts" from which the economistic theses under discussion claimed to derive their "obvious" character.

As long as the Soviet Union was economically weak, with only a mediocre degree of industrial development, that which seemed, in the economic and political relations obtaining in that country, to be in contradiction with what Marx, Engels, and Lenin had said about socialism could be attributed by economism to this economic weakness of the USSR. The economistic conceptions left room for hope that when the Soviet Union ceased to be weak there would be an end to the restrictions imposed on freedom of expression by the masses, the inequality of incomes would be reduced, the many privileges enjoyed by a minority of cadres and technicians would be abolished, and the repression extended to wide sections of the population would cease. The "negative" features of Soviet society could thus be seen as the "price" that had to be paid in order to build the "material foundations" of socialism, as "transient" phenomena that must disappear automatically when this objective was attained or was being approached. The "facts" thus seemed to justify the economistic problematic and render pointless any analysis of Soviet reality in terms of class struggles that might express the rise of a state bourgeoisie[52] which was taking over all positions of command and setting up the apparatus needed to ensure its domination.

Today the situation is quite different. Although still experiencing great economic difficulties,[53] which have to be explained, the Soviet Union has long since become the world's second industrial power and Europe's first, and in many fields of science and technology it holds the leading position. Furthermore, it is bordered by European countries closely associated with it, which possess a far from negligible economic potential. And yet the phenomena which economism claimed to account for by the "backwardness" of the USSR, and which therefore should have been only transient, far from disappearing, are being maintained and developed. The privileges that, when they arose in the recent past, were regarded as having been imposed by the conditions of the moment, by the needs of accumulation, are today officially recognized elements in the system of social relations within which it is claimed that the Soviet Union is "building the material foundations of communism." For the Soviet Communist Party there is no question of dismantling this system: on the contrary, it seeks to reinforce it. There is no question of allowing the Soviet workers to exercise collective control over the utilization of the means of production, over the way current production is used, or over the activity of the party and its members. The factories are run by managers whose relations with "their" workers are relations of command, and who are responsible only to their superiors. Agricultural enterprises are run in practically similar ways. In general, the direct producers have no right to express themselves—or rather, they can do so only when ritually called upon to approve decisions or "proposals" worked out independently of them in the "higher circles" of the state and the party.

The rules governing the management of Soviet enterprises[54] are to an increasing degree copied from those of the "advanced" capitalist countries, and many Soviet managers go for training to the business schools of the United States and Japan. What was supposed to give rise to increasingly socialist relations has instead produced relations that are essentially capitalist, so that behind the screen of "economic plans," it is the laws of capitalist accumulation, and so of profit, that decide how the means of production are utilized.

The producers are still wage earners working to valorize the means of production, with the latter functioning as collective capital managed by a state bourgeoisie. This bourgeoisie forms, like any other capitalist class, the corps of "functionaries of capital," to use Marx's definition of the capitalist class. The party in power offers to the working people only an indefinite renewal of these social relations. It is, in practice, the party of the "functionaries of capital," acting as such on both the national and international planes.

For anyone who faces the facts, life itself has dispelled any hopes one might have cherished for the consolidation—and, a fortiori, the extension—of the gains of the proletarian revolution in the Soviet Union. Today we need to try and understand why these hopes have been dashed, so as to appreciate what the USSR has become, and by way of what transformations. These are two of the aims of this work, which I have thought it necessary to pursue for several reasons.

II. The need to determine the prevailing social relations in the USSR and the conditions for their formation

The first reason is that there are still many people who do not want to face the facts. They still identify the Soviet Union with socialism. This has important effects on the workers' class struggles, especially in the industrialized countries. In the eyes of the workers of these countries, even those who are most militant and most convinced of the need to do away with capitalism, the lot of the Soviet workers does not seem an enviable one, and they therefore fear that what—with the Soviet Union held up as an example—is offered as an alternative to capitalism is not really an alternative. Accordingly, the leaders of the Western communist parties, while claiming still to see the Soviet Union as "the socialist fatherland," at the same time try to assure the workers of their own countries that the socialism they propose to build will be different from that which, they say, exists in the Soviet Union. Explanations of the how and why of this difference remain rather cursory—related, at best, to the alleged psychology of nations, e.g., "The French are not the Russians"—and have nothing in common with a political analysis. They can therefore convince only those who want to be convinced: for the rest, the equation USSR = socialism serves to put them off socialism.[55]

The second reason why it is of the highest importance to understand why the Soviet Union has become what it is today, and to find an explanation which is independent of the merely

"Russian" aspect of Soviet history,[56] is that this "why" is closely bound up with the "official Marxism" of the communist parties which identify the Soviet Union with socialism, a Marxism that is still burdened with the economistic heritage of the Second International.

One of the essential aspects of the ideological struggle for socialism has always been the struggle against economism (whether of right or left). And when we analyze why the Soviet Union has become what it is today—a capitalist state of a particular type—we see clearly the help that economism has rendered to the bourgeois social forces which were promoting this evolution, for it has disoriented revolutionaries and ideologically disarmed the Soviet workers.

Analysis of the transformations that the Soviet Union has undergone and the struggles through which these have been accomplished is thus extremely topical in its implications. What has been at issue in these struggles is precisely the conceptions that still largely prevail in the labor movement of the industrialized countries (in their inverted form, that is, as leftism in various shapes, they are also often present in the revolutionary movements of the underindustrialized countries). Analyzing as concretely as possible, through the example given by the experience of the Soviet Union, the mistakes to which these conceptions lead thus provides a "negative" lesson that cannot but help those who want to fight for socialism in getting rid of these conceptions.

Analysis of what has happened and is happening in the USSR is of special importance for members and sympathizers of the revisionist parties. These are, indeed, ideologically "paralyzed" by their inability to understand the Soviet Union's past, and therefore its present as well. One expression of this "paralysis" is the resort to empty formulations about the "personality cult," or the attitude that consists in distancing oneself somewhat from the Soviet Union while continuing to proclaim one's fidelity to "the socialist fatherland."

Such formulations and attitudes testify to an ideological crisis which is deeper than it seems, and which may turn out to be the prelude to thinking that will finally challenge reformist and revisionist practice. This thinking needs to be nourished by an attempt to understand the past and the present of the Soviet Union. Without it, one remains more or less doomed to remain imprisoned in schemas that conceal historical truth. The revisionist leaders are clearly frightened of such thinking, which is why, once again, we hear formulas of incantation about anti-Sovietism whenever there is any sign of critical thinking about the concrete history of the USSR. The only purpose of these formulas is to prevent members and sympathizers of the revisionist parties from posing the vital questions, those which could lead the struggles of the proletariat and the people to result in something other than the triad of parliamentary reformism, trade-union struggles allegedly independent of any political organization, and the cult of spontaneity.

Of course, analysis of Soviet reality, past and present, is only one factor that can help to bring about ideological clarification and so contribute indirectly to rescue the labor movement, and especially the sclerotic Marxism that prevails over a large part of the world today, from the circle in which it seems to be imprisoned. Fortunately, however, there are other factors, too.

One of these factors is the worsening of capitalism's own crisis, both on the economic plane (where it has begun in the form of a tremendous international monetary crisis) and on the planes of ideology (shown in the refusal of a large section of the population of the industrialized countries, particularly working-class youth, students, and women, to put up with the forms of subjection previously forced upon them by capitalism) and politics (with the rise of national and revolutionary struggles in many underindustrialized countries).

Another factor contributing to give new life to the people's struggles and their orientation is the positive lessons which, in contrast to the Soviet Union's failure, can be drawn from the building of socialism in China. There, life—meaning the struggle of the masses, led by a genuine Marxist-Leninist party—has shown how to solve the problems presented by the socialist transformation of social relations. Marxism-Leninism has thus found fresh vigor and clarified a series of questions which could indeed be clarified only through social practice. Thereby, too, as has already been observed, we can today understand more clearly the nature of the transformations undergone by the Soviet Union.

More precisely, by rejecting the economistic problematic we can grasp that what has happened to the Soviet Union is the result of a process of class struggle, a process which the Bolshevik Party controlled badly, and even controlled less and less well as time went by, through not being able to unite the popular forces and find at each moment the correct line of demarcation between the forces in society that could give support to the proletarian revolution, those that were inevitably hostile to it, and those that could be neutralized. In the class struggle that went on in Russia and in the Soviet Union the proletariat therefore suffered serious defeats: but the struggle of the proletariat and the peasantry continues, and will inevitably—after delays and through ups and downs about which it is futile to speculate—lead the working people of the Soviet republics to restore their power and resume the building of socialism.

—*January 1974*

Notes

1. *Planification et croissance accélérée.*
2. *La Transition vers l'économie socialiste* and *Calcul économique et formes de propriété.* These two books also bear the marks of two great social and political experiences—the Chinese and Cuban revolutions, which I have followed closely since 1958 and 1960, respectively—and also of the revival of Marxist thought in France. This revival has been connected especially with the increasingly widespread influence of Mao Tse-tung's ideas and has been affected by the break made by L. Althusser and his associates with the "economistic" interpretation of Marx's *Capital.*
3. This was the trial in which the chief accused were Zinoviev and

Kamenev. The Muscovites queued up at the newsstands in the early hours of the morning in order to be sure of buying a paper with a report of the hearings.

4. This was also the opinion of the Chinese Communist Party, as expressed in the articles "On the Historical Experience of the Dictatorship of the Proletariat" and "More on the Historical Experience of the Dictatorship of the Proletariat" which are usually attributed to Mao Tse-tung. *People's Daily*, April 5, 1956, and December 29, 1956.

5. There are detailed accounts of what happened in the Polish ports and of the discussions that followed the armed clashes in December 1970 (see *Gierek face aux grévistes*).

6. Bettelheim, *The Transition to Socialist Economy*, pp. 31 ff. The problem is discussed in particular on pp. 65 ff. and 163 ff.

7. Ibid., pp. 44–71, especially pp. 46–47.

8. The problem of "economism" is discussed later.

9. Cf. Bettelheim, *Cultural Revolution and Industrial Organization in China.*

10. Cf. *On the Transition to Socialism,* by Paul M. Sweezy and Charles Bettelheim.

11. "Reestablishing contact" with the revolutionary content of Marxism obviously does not mean "finding afresh" theses that Marx and Engels allegedly formulated nearly a century ago, before the lessons were available that we can draw today from the class struggles which have taken place since then. "Reestablishing contact" means getting rid of conceptions that are wrong in content (even though they may have seemed true at a certain period) and thus obstruct the development of Marxist theory on the basis of the concrete analysis of class struggles and their effects. As Lenin wrote, discussing the attitude of revolutionary Marxists to Marxist theory: "We do not regard Marx's theory as something completed and inviolable; on the contrary, we are convinced that it has only laid the foundation stone of the science which socialists *must* develop in all directions if they wish to keep pace with life" ("Our Programme," in *CW*, vol. 4, pp. 211–212).

12. Stalin, *Leninism*, pp. 561 ff.

13. Ibid., p. 565.

14. Ibid., p. 567.

15. Ibid.

16. "Classes are large groups of people differing from each other by

the place they occupy in a historically determined system of social production, by their relation (in most cases fixed and formulated by law) to the means of production, by their role in the social organisation of labour, and, consequently, by the dimensions of the share of social wealth of which they dispose and the mode of acquiring it. Classes are groups of people one of which can appropriate the labour of another one owing to the different places they occupy in a definite system of social economy" (Lenin, "A Great Beginning," in *CW*, vol. 29, p. 421). It will be observed that though Lenin observes that the places occupied by different social classes may be "fixed and formulated by law," he mentions this only as a possibility. The existence of a "legal relation" to the means of production does not come into the actual definition of classes.

17. See the first formulation of this idea in Marx's letter to Weydemeyer, March 5, 1852, in Marx and Engels, *Selected Correspondence*.

18. Lenin, "Economics and politics in the era of the dictatorship of the proletariat," November 7, 1919, in *CW*, vol. 30, p. 115.

19. *CW*, vol. 31, p. 64.

20. The pressure that bourgeois ideology exerts upon Marxism (and which is manifested in the struggle between the two lines, bourgeois and proletarian, within Marxism itself) has more than once given rise to the tendency to reduce production relations to mere legal relations. This occurred in Soviet Russia during the civil war, with the illusion that the extension of nationalization and the ban on private trade (which was replaced by measures of requisition and rationing that did not involve the market) were equivalent to "establishing" communist relations—from which came the incorrect description of this period as that of "war communism." As Lenin acknowledged, the illusions which arose at that time resulted in "a more serious defeat on the economic front than any defeat inflicted upon us by Kolchak, Denikin or Pilsudski" (*CW*, vol. 33, p. 63).

21. Stalin, *Leninism*, pp. 591 ff.

22. Ibid., p. 608.

23. Ibid., p. 615. While the thesis that the socialist productive forces, with their corresponding social relations, "arise" within the capitalist mode of production itself contradicts the teachings of historical materialism, it does nevertheless hint at the fact that "the material conditions of production and the corresponding

relations of exchange (*Verkehrverhältnisse*) for a classless society" are already "concealed in society as it is" (Marx, *Grundrisse*, p. 159). Marx is here referring to the fact that capitalism breaks down local particularisms, developing conditions for comparisons and relations on a "universal" scale (ibid., pp. 160–162).

24. Stalin, *Leninism*, p. 608.
25. Ibid., pp. 613–614.
26. Stalin, *Economic Problems of Socialism in the USSR*, p. 57.
27. Mao Tse-tung, *On Khrushchev's Phoney Communism*, p. 15.
28. "Going against the tide" means, for a member of a revolutionary party, whatever position he may hold, *striving*, when he finds himself in a minority, to *persuade* those who do not agree with him of the correctness of his point of view. "Putting into practice" his own ideas by changing the balance of forces in the party through compromises which obscure the differences of view, or through use of whatever power he wields to bring pressure to bear on certain people or to alter the composition of leading bodies, etc., is not really "going against the tide" but carrying on a struggle at the organizational level in order to impose his own view (which may, of course, be a sound one).
29. The rare instances in which Stalin overruled conceptions that were dominant in the party were of immense historical importance, and I shall examine the reasons for them in the next volume, but in these cases the method of *persuasion* played only a small part in his mode of action.
30. There were theoreticians claiming to be Marxist, and even some small organizations, especially in Germany, who, at one moment or another, voiced disagreement with the political conclusions of these theses and with some of their ideological premises, but these theoreticians and movements (which were part of the "leftism" of that time) remained marginal, for, on the most fundamental theoretical questions, they never took their stand on any ground different from that of those whom they were criticizing, this common ground being "economism."
31. Trotsky, *The Revolution Betrayed*, p. 19.
32. Ibid., p. 249.
33. Ibid., p. 248.
34. Ibid., p. 45.
35. Ibid., p. 47.
36. Ibid., p. 64.

37. Ibid., p. 244. Everyone knows that Marx, in his *Critique of the Gotha Programme*, speaks of the "bourgeois limitation" which affects the distribution of goods during "the first phase of Communist society"; however, this "limitation" is not related to the level of the productive forces, but to "the enslaving subordination of the individual to the division of labour" and to the corresponding social relations which hinder the development of the productive forces (Marx and Engels, *Selected Works in Three Volumes*, vol. 3, pp. 18–19).

38. Trotsky, *The Revolution Betrayed*, pp. 47–48.

39. Report presented on March 10, 1939: in Stalin, *Leninism*, pp. 619 ff.

40. Marx and Engels, *Selected Works*, vol. 3, p. 147.

41. Stalin, *Leninism*, p. 687.

42. Ibid., p. 662.

43. Ibid., p. 657.

44. Trotsky, *The Revolution Betrayed*, p. 53.

45. Ibid., p. 64.

46. It will be seen that the term "economism" is here being used not to describe one of the *particular forms* assumed by this conception (for example, the one that Lenin combated at the beginning of the century) but the whole set of forms in which it can appear.

47. The trade-union oppositions called for independence of the trade unions (considered as defending the basic interest of the working class) in relation to the Bolshevik Party. Such independence can give an advantage to the economic demands of the working class, thus placing it in conflict with the other classes whose support is needed for the advance of the proletarian revolution; and that can undermine the *leading role* of the proletariat, a role which implies that the latter shows readiness to sacrifice some of its immediate interests to those of the revolution. The tendency to put in the forefront "immediate demands," even those of particular categories or sections, is inherent in syndicalist and "self-management" conceptions. This tendency was present in the program of most of the "left" oppositions in the Bolshevik Party between 1921 and 1928.

48. This caused Preobrazhensky, for instance, to consider that once the dictatorship of the proletariat had been "established," the party ceased to be of any use, and its role could thenceforth be played by the state machine (see Broué, *Le Parti bolchévique*, p. 129).

49. This identification has often been confused with Lenin's view, expressed at certain precise conjunctures (for example, at the end of "war communism"), according to which, at *certain moments*, the task of rapidly reviving agricultural and industrial production and exchange between town and country had to be seen as the most urgent task.

50. This reaffirmation of Lenin's thesis concerning the possibility of building socialism in the USSR undoubtedly helped to endow Stalin, both inside and outside the party, with a prestige that was enjoyed by no other member of the leadership (this, moreover, for reasons not always connected with defense of the interests of the proletariat, as was shown by the "support" given Stalin's policy by the nationalist section of the Russian bourgeoisie represented by the *Smenovekhovtsy*). Stalin's stand on this question was most explicitly affirmed in his article in *Pravda* of December 20, 1924, entitled "October and Comrade Trotsky's Theory of Permanent Revolution," in which he departed from the much more hesitant line he had still been advocating a few months earlier in *Pravda* of April 30, 1927 (see Stalin, *Works*, vol. 6, pp. 391–392 and 110–111).

51. The reference is to Stalin's mistakes at the end of the 1920s and during the 1930s. Today we can see that these mistakes were connected with a certain number of general political and theoretical positions which had caused Stalin to come into conflict with Lenin on problems of major importance, such as the relations between Soviet Russia and the non-Russian peoples. The fact that Stalin defended these views against Lenin's criticism also has to be related to the position held by Stalin in the Bolshevik Party. By virtue of this position (he was General Secretary), Stalin was subject to pressure from the party and state apparatuses and consequently tended to adopt such measures as were immediately "effective," even when theoretical analysis could show that this immediate "effectiveness" entailed grave dangers for the future (as would have been the case if Lenin had not had his way in the matter of retaining the state monopoly of foreign trade).

52. The concept of "state bourgeoisie" (or state-bureaucratic bourgeoisie) cannot be expanded here. I will merely say that it refers to those agents of social reproduction, other than the immediate producers, who, by virtue of the existing system of social relations and prevailing social practice, have de facto *at*

their disposal the means of production and of their products
which, formally speaking, belong to the state. The economic
basis for the existence of this bourgeoisie is constituted by the
forms of division and unity in the process of reproduction (see
Bettelheim, *Cultural Revolution*, p. 19); its real place in the
process depends on the class struggle which permits (or forbids)
the state bourgeoisie and its representatives to occupy certain
positions in the machinery of state and, given certain circumstances, to change the class nature of the state. The representatives of the state bourgeoisie are not necessarily its "conscious
agents": they are what they are because "in their minds they do
not get beyond the limits" which this class does not "get beyond
in life," so that "they are consequently driven, theoretically, to
the same problems and solutions to which material interest and
social position drive the latter practically. This is, in general, the
relationship between the political and literary representatives of
a class and the class they represent" (Marx, *The Eighteenth
Brumaire*, in Marx and Engels, *Selected Works*, vol. 1, p. 424).

53. These difficulties are illustrated by the way the Soviet leaders
are seeking to obtain capital, technical assistance, and foodstuffs
from the United States, Japan, West Germany, etc. The policy of
"cooperation" with the Western imperialists which is advocated
by the Soviet leaders in another aspect of this search for support.
I shall come back to these points when, in the third volume, I
deal with Soviet revisionism.

54. The management of Soviet enterprises is based on two main
principles: management by a single manager who is responsible
to higher authority, and "financial autonomy," which obliges
each enterprise to try to make a profit. When these two principles
were introduced in 1918 and 1921, Lenin emphasized that they
corresponded to a temporary "retreat" dictated by the circumstances of the time, and that their application brought capitalist
relations into the state sector. Speaking of the "financial autonomy" conferred on state enterprises, Lenin mentioned that to
a large extent it put these enterprises "on a commercial capitalist
basis" (Lenin, *CW*, vol. 42, p. 376). Since 1965 the financial
autonomy of enterprises and the striving for profitability have
made substantial progress.

55. The Soviet leaders try, of course, to safeguard their policy and
the realities of their country from any criticism by translating this
equation into the form: "Anti-Sovietism (meaning analysis of

Soviet reality or of the consequences of the USSR's international policy) = anticommunism."

56. This is not intended to mean that Soviet society does not bear the marks of the tsarist society from which it issued. To the extent that the work of the revolution was not carried through thoroughly, *many social relations characteristic of the old Russia were not smashed* and this explains the astonishing resemblances observable between the Russia of today and "Holy Russia."

Introduction to the "first period"

This volume aims to analyze the principal aspects and effects of the class struggle during the first years of Soviet power, until Lenin's departure from the scene. As will be noticed, the plan adopted is not chronological, because my task is to show the changes that took place in that period in the relations between classes and in economic, political, and ideological relations. These various changes are themselves analyzed as they developed historically, which necessitates frequent references to the main stages through which the Soviet revolution passed during those years. It is only at the end of this overall analysis, however, in Part Five of the present volume, that the significance and implications of these stages will be ready for discussion. For this reason it will be useful briefly to review here the principal subdivisions of the period being studied.

The first stage of the Soviet revolution after its victory was that of the establishment of proletarian power and the initial economic and political changes connected with this—a stage that runs from the insurrection of October 1917 to the beginning of the White rebellions at the end of May 1918. During these months, the Soviet power strove to break the economic power possessed by the bourgeoisie by virtue of its ownership of the principal means of production and exchange, by nationalizing large industrial enterprises, mines, banks, etc., and placing the economy as a whole under supervision by the working class, while not proceeding to widespread measures of nationalization. Lenin called this policy one of "state capitalism,"[1] which was destined to pass on later "to the second step towards socialism, i.e., to pass on to workers' regulation of production."[2] During the first months of 1918, it did not look as though this second step would be taken very soon, for a number of reasons, some of which were connected with the unsatisfactory functioning of the soviets,[3] while others were bound up with the idea, generally accepted in the Bolshevik Party, that only an upsurge of the proletarian revolution in the rest of Europe would enable Russia's march to socialism to be speeded up.[4]

In fact, the outbreak of the White rebellions and the intervention by the imperialist armies led to the development of economic and political practices that were very different from those originally envisaged. These methods, in which the predominant role was played by the state apparatus, and in which coercion by the state, especially in the form of requisitioning agricultural produce, constituted what was called "war communism," prevailed in the period running from June 1918 to March 1921.

At the close of the period of civil war and foreign intervention, Russia was devastated and on the brink of famine. The methods of "war communism" seemed incapable of helping to improve this situation. The New Economic Policy (NEP) was adopted. This policy appeared at first to be a return to the "state capitalism" of the winter of 1917–1918. The NEP conception underwent several changes until it was abandoned in 1929. One of its principal aspects was the reestablishment of freedom of trade in agricultural produce and the end of requisitioning.

If this first volume is largely devoted to analysis of the changes that took place before Lenin's death, the reason is that that event coincided with the actual transition of the Russian Revolution from one phase to another: with the ending of military operations, production began to recover and an active industrial proletariat was reconstituted, while increasing social differentiation began to become apparent among the peasantry. This new phase is clearly distinct from the first years of Soviet power, with special features that necessitate separate analysis. For this reason, the actual consequences of NEP are not examined in this volume, and only the different notions of NEP held by various Bolshevik leaders are discussed, these being expressions of underlying differences about the social and political conditions for the building of socialism.

The analysis of social and political changes in the pages that follow is based on documents of the time (inquiries, censuses, congress reports, etc.), on the works of historians and economists both Russian and non-Russian, and to a very large extent on many of Lenin's writings. The latter are, indeed, of exceptional importance. They not only show the orientations that Lenin endeavored to give to Soviet policy; many of them provide a clear and unembellished analysis of the situation, and where the past is concerned offer a critical evaluation of the policy followed.[5] It is to these writings that I especially refer, for they are exceptionally instructive. The ones that define political orientations are, of course, instructive as well, but not in the same way: they enable us to grasp the political conclusions that Lenin drew from a certain analysis, but we need to take care not to confuse these conclusions, and the measures advocated by Lenin, with the actual changes in, or even the actual policy of, the Soviet state and the Bolshevik Party. The implementing of Lenin's orientations often, in fact, came up against substantial resistance, either because the objective process of the class struggle and the real strength of the classes involved determined changes other than those aimed at, or because the machinery of party and state followed only imperfectly the orientations indicated (this being, as a rule, an effect of the class struggle).

In the first part of this volume I examine the main features of the revolutionary mass movement which developed from the winter of 1916–1917 onward, one of the effects of which was the setting up of Soviet power in October 1917. The dual character of this movement—proletarian in the towns and democratic in the countryside—is analyzed and related to the characteristics of the system of proletarian dictatorship established after October. The specific role played by the Bolshevik Party in the revolutionary movement and in the political relations formed after October is given special attention.

Part Two is devoted to analyzing the changes that took place in class relations between 1917 and 1922, while Part Three seeks to reveal the changes in the main instruments of the proletarian dictatorship during that period. Part Four sets out the ideological and political struggles between various tendencies within the Bolshevik Party, and also relates these struggles to the general movement of class contradictions and the changes in the economic situation and the international conjuncture. Finally, Part Five endeavors to draw up a balance sheet of this period, estimating the actual implications and the real impact of the changes that had been made down to the end of it, so as to bring out the principal tasks facing the Bolshevik Party at the moment Lenin left the stage.

Generally speaking, the analysis that follows tries to break with a certain conception of the history of the Soviet revolution which presents this history as the "outcome" of decisions and "choices" made by the Bolshevik Party, and thus in imagination making the party a demiurge responsible for all the successes and failures of the Russian Revolution. Although this way of conceiving history is completely false to the real movement of events and to historical materialism, which enables us to understand this movement, from the beginning of the 1930s it very soon became characteristic of most Soviet historians, leading them to provide an apologetic picture in which the achievements of the Russian Revolution appeared as the work of the Bolshevik Party and even, more particularly, of Lenin, followed by Stalin. Thereby there vanished the real substance of the movement of history: the development and the shifting of contradictions, and, first and foremost, of class contradictions.

It is this movement that the following pages seek to understand, without always succeeding very well, for it is extremely complex, and has only rarely been analyzed as it should be, namely, as an objective process.

In breaking, or trying to break, with a "subjectivist" conception of the Russian Revolution and the subsequent changes in Soviet society, one has to recognize that what is being analyzed is not the result of the will or the intentions of the Bolshevik Party or of the Russian proletariat. It has to be appreciated that the Russian Revolution and the subsequent changes in Soviet society resulted from an *objective process of conflict between social forces* (which themselves changed in the course of this very process) and from the interventions of their ideological and political representatives.

Consequently, analysis has to be centered on the social classes, the mutual relations in which these were caught, the struggle between the classes, and the effects—political, ideological, and economic—of these struggles. It has to be accepted, in conformity with reality, that the social changes resulting from these struggles were only to a very limited extent anticipated or willed. This way of analyzing the historical process does not mean denying the reality of the activity of the Bolshevik Party, but it does oblige us to situate this activity differently from when the party is imagined to be the "subject of history." It compels us to recognize that the Bolshevik Party, like any other proletarian revolutionary party linked with the masses, participates in the movement of history, but does not *determine* it.

The revolutionary party's participation in the movement of history enables it, in certain definite circumstances, to affect the course of this movement by ensuring that the changes with which the movement is potentially pregnant do in fact take place. This is the meaning of the revolutionary party's intervention in the historical process in which it participates, an intervention which can take a variety of forms, but which is effectual (that is, produces the effects aimed at) only insofar as the revolutionary party finds its bearings correctly amid the contradictions, and helps the masses to act upon the latter through a sufficiently correct line based on the real movement and taking account of its potentialities.

The conditions for an effectual intervention by the revolutionary party in the historical process are extremely variable, but it is only when they have been appreciated that the party really plays a leading role. This was the role that the Bolshevik Party did in fact play in October 1917 and in a certain number of other situations so that its activity had decisive historical significance. Even when this is the case, however, it is the objective process that determines the changes, although the dominant factor in this process is the party's intervention.

The leading role of the Bolshevik Party resulted from the way it was inserted in the movement of history, its relations with the social forces whose actions were decisive, and its capacity to guide them on the basis of a Marxist analysis of the contradictions. This role was shown in striking fashion at the moment of the revolutionary upheaval brought about by the October days of 1917, and also, even if in a less immediately obvious way, in the party's day-to-day work. This is the fundamental work of a revolutionary party, which consists in helping the masses to organize themselves and to transform, through their own practice, their consciousness of their capacity for action, and also to discover the forms this action needs to take. Basically, this is the principal aspect of the party's leading role. Mao Tse-tung gave a remarkable definition of what this role means when he wrote: "Leadership is neither a slogan to be shouted from morning till night nor an arrogant demand for obedience; it consists rather in using the Party's correct policies and the example we set by our own work to convince and educate people outside the Party so that they willingly accept our proposals."[6]

Whenever the conditions for effectual intervention by the Bolshevik Party were not present—because it had not correctly analyzed the contradictions, worked out a sufficiently correct line, or kept to a nonauthoritarian style of leadership, so that its relations with the masses had deteriorated (as frequently happened during the period of "war communism")— the objective process of history developed without the party exerting a positive influence on its course. Consequently, the decisions taken failed to produce the results expected. This is why it is precisely the objective process of class struggle that must be first of all subjected to analysis. It is in relation to the development of this process that we need to examine the party's political line, the measures it adopted, and the struggles carried on within it. This is the type of analysis that has been attempted in these pages.

Notes

1. An analysis of the various conceptions of "state capitalism," "war communism," and NEP will be found in Part Five.
2. Lenin, "The Immediate Tasks of the Soviet Government" in *CW*, vol. 27, p. 255.
3. At the Seventh Congress of the Bolshevik Party in March 1918, Lenin, speaking of the task of building a new type of state "without a bureaucracy, without police, without a regular army," said: "In Russia this has scarcely begun and has begun badly" (ibid., p. 133).
4. The initial weakness of the Bolshevik Party, which took power under the pressure of a rapid upsurge of class contradictions, led Lenin to consider for a certain period that what the Bolsheviks had above all to do was to "hold on" until the revolution spread to the rest of Europe, thereby bringing new strength to the Russian revolutionary movement. When the moment came when the Soviet government had lasted longer than the Paris Commune, this was seen as a tremendous achievement by Lenin and his comrades-in-arms.
5. Lenin constantly stressed the need for a revolutionary party to carry out such analyses and critiques, as this was a vital means whereby the party could help the masses to see clearly. Thus, for instance, when Lenin proposed that high salaries be paid to former engineers and managers, he said: "To conceal from the people the fact that the enlistment of bourgeois experts by means of extremely high salaries is a retreat from the principles of the Paris Commune would be sinking to the level of bourgeois politicians and deceiving the people. Frankly explaining how and why we took this step backward, and then publicly discussing what means are available for making up for lost time, means educating the people and learning from experience, learning together with the people how to build socialism" (ibid., p. 249).
6. Mao Tse-tung, *Selected Works*, vol. 2, p. 418.

Part 1
The October Revolution and the establishment of Soviet power

The Russian bourgeoisie and landlord class lost power on October 25, 1917.[1] On that day the armed workers, together with the soldiers and sailors of Petrograd and Kronstadt, formed the insurrectionary forces of the revolution led by the Bolshevik Party, and went into action. Within a few hours, all the important public buildings in the capital had fallen into the hands of the revolutionary forces. In the early morning of October 26, the Winter Palace, seat of Kerensky's Provisional Government, was occupied and the ministers found there taken prisoner.

On October 25 the Petrograd Soviet had confirmed the removal of the Provisional Government, which had been decreed that morning by the Soviet's Military Revolutionary Committee. In the evening the Second All-Russia Congress of Soviets assembled. The Bolsheviks had a majority. During the night of October 25–26, the congress (from which most of the Mensheviks and Social Revolutionaries (SRs) had withdrawn[2]) also confirmed the downfall of the Provisional Government. It declared that the powers of the previous central executive committee of the soviets had expired, and itself took power. In the hours that followed, the Second All-Russia Congress of Soviets decided to form a provisional workers' and peasants' government, bearing the name of the Council of People's Commissars and made up of leaders of the Bolshevik Party. The congress instructed this government to "start immediate negotiations for a just, democratic peace"[3] and adopted the Decree on Land which abolished the landlords' ownership of land.[4]

The armed insurrection triumphed at almost the same time

in Moscow (then the second capital) and in the other big towns. This victory testified to the former Provisional Government's loss of authority in the eyes of the masses. Though Kerensky escaped from Petrograd, he was no longer obeyed by the bulk of the army. Only a few sections still followed him, and they were so few and so demoralized that the offensive he tried to launch against Petrograd immediately after the October days proved a miserable failure. The test of arms thus confirmed that the bourgeoisie had indeed lost power and that this was now wielded by the soviets under the leadership of the Bolshevik Party.

The succession of events that occurred in the capitals on October 25 and 26, and the leading role played by the Bolshevik Party, the revolutionary party of the proletariat, are not in themselves, however, enough to determine fully the characteristics of the new stage into which the Russian Revolution then entered, or the class character of the new ruling power. These characteristics were also determined by all the class struggles that had taken place between February and October 1917, which were of a specific sort, connected with the interweaving of the democratic and proletarian revolutionary processes that made up the substance of the Russian Revolution. This interweaving was to have, moreover, a great influence on the relations established between the dominant political apparatuses of Soviet power and on the subsequent course of the revolution.

Notes

1. Until February 1918 (according to the calendar in use in Western Europe), Russia used the Julian calendar. All dates between November 7, 1917 (i.e., October 25, 1917, by the Julian calendar) and February 13, 1918 (January 31, 1918) are given here in accordance with the old calendar, and thereafter according to the Western European calendar.
2. The Mensheviks claimed to be Marxists, like the Bolsheviks, but

refused to accept that a proletarian revolution was possible in Russia, and therefore favored a bourgeois government. The SRs were the most important element in a political tendency claiming to unite all the "toilers" under the formal leadership of "the peasantry," and in fact leaving power in the hands of the bourgeoisie. These Trudoviks ("spokesmen of the toilers") were even ready to agree to a "constitutional monarchy." As Lenin wrote in 1906: "The typical Trudovik is a politically conscious peasant . . . His main efforts are concentrated on the fight against the landlords for land, on the fight against the feudal state and for democracy. His idea is to abolish exploitation; but he conceives this abolition in a petty-bourgeois fashion, and therefore, *in fact*, his strivings are converted into a struggle, not against all exploitation, but only against the exploitation practised by the landlords and the big financiers." (*CW*, vol. 11, p. 229). During the revolution the SRs split into "Right SRs" and "Left SRs," and the latter agreed during the winter of 1917–1918 to collaborate with the Bolsheviks.

3. Lenin, *CW*, vol. 26, p. 249.
4. Ibid., p. 258.

1. The interweaving of the revolutionary processes between February and October 1917

From late 1916 onward, the discontent of the masses of workers and peasants, condemned to increasingly difficult living conditions, increased rapidly, together with the anger of the soldiers who were undergoing indescribable hardships in a war the imperialist character of which they realized more and more clearly. In the middle of February 1917, the discontent of the Petrograd workers and of the soldiers stationed in the capital found open expression. Strikes and demonstrations followed each other, partly spontaneous, partly (and increasingly) organized by the Bolsheviks and Mensheviks. They spread to Moscow and the industrial centers. On February 25 the soldiers in Petrograd began to fraternize with the workers of the capital and its outlying districts. On the twenty-sixth mutinies broke out in the garrison, and on the twenty-seventh workers and soldiers joined forces. The Winter Palace was taken, and the tsar abdicated.

So ended the first act of the Russian Revolution. It had occurred in a country whose specific features made it, in Lenin's words, "the weakest link in the imperialist chain."

The Russia of before October 1917 was both an imperialist country and one heavily dependent on world imperialism (mainly on British and French imperialism) which had invested millions of francs in loans to the tsarist state, in the extraction of oil and coal, and in the iron-and-steel and engineering industries.

The dependence of Russian imperialism on British and French capital was one of the sources of its weakness and was itself a consequence of the specific way in which Russian

69

imperialism had developed, with an industrial-capitalist basis that was extremely narrow. Russian imperialism thus bore a dual character: it resulted from a close combination of two forms of imperialism—capitalist and precapitalist. To the first of these corresponded a high degree of capitalist concentration in industry and the existence of bank capital closely linked with industrial capital, so forming a finance capital which pressed toward imperialist expansion in alliance with Anglo-French imperialism. To the second form of imperialism corresponded Russia's essentially "military" expansionism. The economic bases of this expansionism—which was manifested vigorously from Peter the Great's time onward—call for separate analysis. Here, let it merely be mentioned that tsarist expansionism was rooted in the internal contradictions of Russian society, which urged the tsarist state into making a series of moves that prepared the way for Russian capitalism. Once the latter had arisen, the contradictions of the old Russian society and those of nascent capitalism led the tsarist state to go ahead with its military expansion and to support the development of Russian capitalist industry by various means, in particular by the so-called "emancipation" of the serfs, decreed in 1861, which enabled the state to carry out accumulation at the expense of the peasantry.

Russia's expansion, begun seriously under Peter the Great, proceeded thereafter without interruption. In Europe it was directed toward Finland, the Baltic countries, and Poland. To the south it was directed toward Turkey, Persia, Afghanistan and, beyond them, toward India, with Russia aiming to secure access to warm water, in the Mediterranean, the Arabian Sea, and the Indian Ocean. This drive brought Russia into conflict with Britain on more than one occasion.

Eastward, Russia's expansion was directed toward Siberia, China, and even the American continent. Already in the seventeenth century the conquest of Siberia was practically complete, and the Russians continued their thrust to the East, across the Bering Strait, occupying Alaska (which Russia was compelled to "sell" to the United States in 1867).

Toward China, Russia's expansion was marked by a series of clashes followed by treaties which the Russians regularly broke. Of particular importance were the treaties imposed on China by Russia in the second half of the nineteenth century.[1] These operations, carried out in conjunction with the aggressions of France and Britain against China, enabled tsardom to annex from that country nearly 1.5 million square kilometers of territory.

Thus, the tsarist Russia which collapsed in February 1917 had behind it a long past of expansion and colonization,[2] originally commercial-mercantile in character, and later increasingly industrial-capitalist.

The dual character of Russian imperialism corresponded to the weak capacity for accumulation possessed by Russian big capital, a reflection of the relative weakness of the bourgeoisie, which was unable to struggle against tsardom for its own class aims. This incapacity explains the fear that gripped the Russian bourgeoisie whenever the established order was threatened. After the Revolution of 1905, the Russian bourgeoisie knew that it was faced by a working class capable of determined struggle. The power of the Russian proletariat grew steadily.[3] Thanks to its organization, it was increasingly ready to take advantage of every revolutionary change. The bourgeoisie was thus paralyzed and doomed to leave the initiative for revolution to the proletariat and the peasantry,[4] which was what happened in February 1917.

The lack of any real political initiative on the part of the bourgeoisie[5] in relation to tsardom, which granted it hardly any political rights, was also due to its economic dependence on tsardom. The relatively rapid process of industrialization which developed in the last years of the nineteenth century and the years preceding the First World War was, in fact, based only partly on accumulation of industrial profits and expansion of the home market. It depended partly on foreign investment, but also on government money—loans from the state bank, orders from the public services, etc. To a large extent Russia's industrial expansion was still based on a "primitive accumulation" (an increasing expropriation of the peasantry) of which the tsardom was the political and ideological instrument. The lack of real political initiative by the bourgeoisie explains the peculiarities of the February Revolution of 1917, which began by throwing up soviets, whereas the bourgeois Provisional Government was not formed till later.[6]

On February 27, 1917, indeed, there came into being the Provisional Executive Committee of the Council of Workers' Deputies, mainly consisting of leading members of the Socialist and SR parties. This committee called on the workers and soldiers of the capital to choose delegates to a Petrograd soviet, which duly held its first meeting on the twenty-eighth. The committee issued a decree subordinating all the troops in the capital to the soviet. In the days and weeks that followed, soviets of workers, peasants, and soldiers, and also factory committees, were formed all over the country, though the make-up of these bodies varied, as the class struggle of the proletariat and peasantry developed very unevenly from one town or region to another.

At the end of February 1917, the only organ that could speak in the name of the revolution which had just come about was the Petrograd soviet, with behind it the soviets that were being set up all over Russia. This soviet power, backed by the mutinous troops, was seemingly confronted by no other power. The only organ that might have claimed to oppose it, namely the committee derived from the Imperial Duma (tsardom's parody of a parliament) enjoyed no prestige among the revolutionary masses, for it consisted of representatives of the bourgeoisie and the landlords. But the Petrograd soviet, consisting mainly of Mensheviks and SRs, made a pact with the Duma committee on March 1, and by virtue of this a Provisional Government composed of bourgeois politicians was formed, and the soviet undertook to support this government on certain conditions.[7] In this way began the situation which Lenin described as "dual power" (the soviet power and the power of the Provisional Government)[8]—a situation which ended in October 1917 as a result of the development of the soviet organizations, the strengthening of the Bolshevik Party's influence within them, and, finally, the triumph of the October Revolution.

I. The rise of the soviet movement

From March 1917 onward, soviets of workers and soldiers were formed in all the towns of the Russian Empire. The movement began in the big cities and spread to the middle-sized towns. After a time, peasant soviets also came into being. It was estimated that there were 400 soviets in May, 600 in August, and 900 in October.[9] Parallel with this process went the formation of factory committees, and of district soviets in towns of a certain size.

In considering the spread of this movement, it is in practice impossible to distinguish between what was due to "spontaneity" and what resulted from the activity of Menshevik and (especially) Bolshevik militants. The presence of such militants in nearly all the soviets, and the role that they played in them, show that the movement, while certainly corresponding to an aspiration on the part of the revolutionary masses to organize themselves for action, assumed the scale that it did as a result of the work of political activists.

The Mensheviks and SRs did not want to see the soviets as organs of power. For them, the soviets were organs of revolutionary struggle and propaganda, while the factory committees were assigned the task, in the main, of carrying out trade-union functions.

In fact, owing to the loss of authority among the masses suffered by the Provisional Government, and to the persevering activity of the Bolshevik Party, the soviets tended to transform themselves into local organs of power and take on the solving of numerous administrative problems. They also elected delegates to soviets of regions and provinces, and to the All-Russia Congress of Soviets.

At the end of March 1917, the First All-Russia Congress of Workers' and Soldiers' Soviets was held, and on June 3 the First All-Russia Congress of Soviets. From the latter emerged the Central Executive Committee of Russia, in which the SRs had a big majority. This committee sought unsuccessfully to compete with the Petrograd soviet, which enjoyed great authority throughout Russia and became increasingly dominated by the Bolsheviks.

The extremely different level of activity of the soviet organizations in the big towns and in the regions where there was little industry, and the equally very different political composition of these organizations, reflected the very unequal participation of different classes in the soviet movement. The movement excluded the bourgeoisie as such,[10] through the way of electing delegates (workers, peasants, and soldiers) on which it was based. This, of course, did not prevent some of these delegates from speaking for the bourgeois, and especially petty bourgeois, ideological and political tendencies that were influential among sections of the masses. This was the case immediately after the February Revolution, when the SRs were well represented in most of the soviets, and even more so in the excutive committees elected by the latter.

(a) The working class and the upsurge of the soviets

During the months between February and October 1917, the soviet movement was essentially proletarian. It was so first of all in its social basis, and then, increasingly, because the workers' soviets took up revolutionary proletarian positions. While the SRs and Mensheviks lost credit through their collaboration with the bourgeoisie and their support for the continuance of the imperialist war, the influence of the Bolsheviks grew in the workers' soviets.

The radicalization of the working-class soviets developed slowly at first, then with startling rapidity. When, on March 6, 1917, a Bolshevik fraction was formed in the Petrograd soviet, it had only forty members among the two to three thousand delegates (whose numbers varied constantly and rapidly). At the First All-Russia Congress of Soviets, in June, there were still only 105 Bolsheviks out of a total of 1,090 delegates, but the Bolsheviks already dominated the workers' section of the congress, in which a resolution expressing their views was passed by 173 votes to 144. In October the Bolsheviks, based in the working class, had a majority in the Second All-Russia Congress of Soviets, as well as in the Petrograd soviet.

The principal social and organizational basis on which the "bolshevization" of the town soviets developed was provided by the factory committees. These committees increased rapidly after the February Revolution. Although the Bolsheviks were still in a minority in many town and regional soviets, they captured the majority in nearly all the big industrial centers and garrison towns[11] and they were in the majority in the Central Council elected at the First Conference of Factory Committees of the city of Petrograd, held in the spring of 1917. Their ascendancy was still greater at the Second Conference, which met in August. Radicalization proceeded more slowly in Moscow and in the provinces, but speeded up in the course of the summer. On the eve of the October Revolution, the All-Russia Conference of Factory Committees numbered 96 Bolsheviks among its 167 delegates, with only 24 SRs, 13 Anarchists, and 7 Mensheviks.[12]

The main point is that between August and October the slogans of the Bolshevik Party made rapid headway among the working-class masses. A minority party in February, the Bolsheviks thus advanced to become the majority party of the proletariat of Russia. The "craze" Lenin had talked of in April faded away. The proletariat became aware of the blind alley into which the policy of the Mensheviks and SRs was leading them (and some of the SRs themselves broke off to form a left SR tendency). They realized more and more clearly that it was necessary to get rid of the Provisional Government and install a Soviet government led by the Bolshevik Party, which would be able to put an end to Russia's participation in the imperialist war, help the masses in their struggle to satisfy their revolutionary desires, and organize the fight against the forces of counter-revolution.

(b) The soldiers and peasants and the upsurge of the soviets

The peasants and the soldiers (who were mainly peasants, but peasants who had been uprooted from the conditions of village life and who were concerned primarily to bring about a quick peace) formed the other component of the soviet movement.

The soldiers in the rear, the garrison troops, were very directly influenced by the working class, and their delegates to the soviets became radicalized at much the same rate as the workers' representatives. The movement progressed more slowly among the soldiers at the front. Until June they remained under the influence of the SRs and Mensheviks. During the summer the bloody failure of the offensive decided on by Kerensky, and the increasingly well-organized propaganda of the Bolsheviks, quickly transformed the situation, and in October the soldiers at the front, like those in the rear, gave massive backing to the Bolsheviks' policy.

The peasants in the strict sense of the term, however, entered much more hesitantly into the soviet movement, and were far from rallying en masse to the Bolshevik line.

To be sure, the peasantry was already organized in the spring of 1917, but the center of gravity of their organization was not the soviet system but the system of Land Committees, which were set up mainly at the level of provinces, counties, and districts, that is, remote from the villages themselves. These committees worked with the Provisional Government, and were dominated by the rural petty bourgeoisie (agronomists, teachers, Zemstvo representatives, organizers of cooperative societies, etc.). Politically, they were largely under the influence of the SRs, and that situation did not change much between February and October.

Soviets of peasants' deputies gradually arose to confront the

Land Committees. The initiative in forming these came not from within the villages but from peasants in uniform, from soldiers. In fact, the movement for the creation of peasants' soviets remained fundamentally a movement led from above. This too was promoted by the SRs and by the Cooperative Union, which united mainly well-to-do peasants under SR influence. The reason the latter took such an interest in developing peasants' soviets was that they saw them as a means of offsetting the radicalization of the town soviets. Formally speaking, the SRs succeeded well enough: at the First Congress of Peasants, held May 4–28, 537 delegates out of 1,115 were SRs and only 14 were Bolsheviks. On the very eve of the October Revolution the peasant soviets at county and province level were mostly dominated by the SRs. At that time, most of the peasant soviets were opposed to participation in the All-Russia Congress of Soviets.[13] Until October the peasant soviets were, in the main, organs that functioned at county and province level: there were few at district level, and fewer still in the villages.

In fact, between February and October 1917, the activity of the peasant masses hardly took the soviet form at all. The peasant masses remained ideologically under SR influence and did not raise the question of power. Their activity was essentially focused on the agrarian revolution, formulated in terms of expropriating and dividing up the great estates of the landowners, the state, and the clergy. They thus followed the same line as in past peasant struggles: local risings and direct seizure of land.

Nevertheless, between May and October this mass revolutionary activity grew in scope,[14] escaped from control by the SRs, and objectively prepared the way for the October Revolution.

One of the features of the peasant movement between February and October 1917 was thus its indifference to the question of power, and so to the establishing of local organs of power. Left to itself, without the support and leadership of the town proletariat, this movement was doomed to suffer the same defeat as all previous peasant revolts, for it was incapa-

ble of offering organized and unified resistance to repression
by a state acting to protect the interests of the property-owning
classes. Left to itself, unsupported by the movement and the
organization of the proletariat, it was equally incapable of
destroying that state and of building a state that would defend
the interests of the toiling masses.

There were many reasons why the activity of the peasant
masses themselves remained confined within the limits of
direct action in relation to the land, and did not turn toward
organized alliance with the proletariat of the towns. The
ideological and political factors are easily perceived: the
strength of the influence of the SRs and the feeble influence
exercised by the Bolsheviks. But these two aspects of one and
the same political situation need to be explained. If we turn to
the past, however, the explanation is seen to be relatively
simple: the Bolsheviks had done little by way of propaganda
and organization among the peasant masses, whereas the SRs,
operating through the rural intelligentsia, had acquired a certain degree of influence over an entire section of the peasantry. Between February and October the Bolsheviks could
not redress the situation for lack of available forces.

Besides, the very structure of the village, the existence of
traditional village assemblies (the *skhod*[15]) usually dominated
by rich and middle peasants, tended to block the formation of
village soviets and a thorough radicalization of the peasant
movement. Indeed, the old village structure (which combined
legal "common ownership" of the soil with individual exploitation thereof), although undermined by the development of
capitalism, still helped make every village a little world of its
own, more or less self-enclosed, whose problems, it seemed,
could be settled on the spot. This structure—the basis of
autocracy and bureaucratic despotism as well as of revolts,
continually renewed and always unsuccessful, against the exploitation made possible by this order of things—presented a
strong obstacle to penetration of the Russian village by the
revolutionary ideas of the proletariat, and even by bourgeois-
democratic ideas.

Between February and October 1917 many motions were

indeed put forward from rural sources which included "radical" political demands, calling for the establishment of a "democratic republic," universal suffrage, the convening of a constituent assembly, etc.[16] But the circumstances in which these notions were composed—by the rural intelligentsia, in a situation where the peasants themselves were not organized—and the content of the agrarian demands included in them (which hardly mentioned the *obshchina* and rarely called for the abolition of private ownership) give reason to suppose that they expressed not so much the aspirations of the peasant masses, still deeply attached to communal forms of property, as those of the well-to-do peasants, the kulaks, and the landowners who had left the *mir*. These strata of the peasantry were the first to speak up, but the rest soon took practical action, and a section of the well-to-do peasants and kulaks joined them so as to get a share for themselves in the division of the expropriated estates.

II.   The ripening of the conditions for the October Revolution

Throughout the period between February and October the Provisional Government, backed by the Mensheviks and SRs, sought to keep the movement of the masses within the framework of "bourgeois legality," trying to deceive the workers and peasants with promises of concessions that were put off again and again. In this way the contradictions between the aspirations of the masses and the class nature of the Provisional Government become greater and greater.

(a)   The development of a new revolutionary situation between February and October 1917

Between February and April 1917 the mass of the workers and the soldiers were still in the state of having, as Lenin put it, "succumbed to the craze of 'revolutionary' defencism," and he fought against this "craze," calling on the party, then still in the minority, not to "succumb to the general epidemic" on the poor pretext that they wished "to remain with the masses." [17] After April, and especially after June and July, the situation changed rapidly. Experience taught the masses new lessons. The workers and soldiers saw with growing clarity that continuance of the war did not correspond to the interests of the people but to those of the Russian bourgeoisie and of Anglo-French imperialism. They came to realize that the Provisional Government, the Mensheviks, and the SRs upheld the interests of the bourgeoisie, and that the Bolsheviks alone fought against the latter. It was therefore urgently necessary to get rid of the Provisional Government, transfer power to the soviets, and act to ensure that leadership in the latter was held by the Bolsheviks. A revolutionary mass movement had to be developed in order to drive out the Provisional Government, which would not depart of its own accord. Insofar as these ideas took hold of the mass of the workers and of the soldiers—and this happened in the two capitals and in many industrial centers and garrison towns—the conditions for a new revolution, for a proletarian revolution, were maturing.

The confidence that the peasantry still placed in the SRs, even on the eve of October, showed that they had not yet drawn from the experience they had undergone all the lessons drawn by the workers and by the soldiers, especially in the garrison towns. Nevertheless, the bulk of the peasantry gradually moved into action, seizing the land in disregard of the ban placed on such conduct by the Provisional Government and the exhortations of the majority of the SRs. The Bolshevik Party supported the revolutionary movement of the peasant masses. The analysis given by Lenin in April allowed this new situation to be seen as a de facto breakdown in the class collaboration between the bourgeoisie and the peasantry, as the opening of "a new stage in the bourgeois-democratic revolution." [18]

The ripening of the conditions for proletarian revolution in the towns, and the entry into a new stage of the democratic revolution in the countryside, confirmed the analysis made by Lenin, who had shown that Russia was the weakest link in the imperialist chain and that a proletarian revolution could be victorious there through the explosive combination of the exploitation of the masses—by landlords, Russian capitalists, and foreign capital—with state oppression which served both the expansionist tendencies of Russian imperialism and the demands of primitive accumulation. This specific combination of exploitation and oppression was the source of the misery of large sections of the people and of the profound discontent of part of the intelligentsia. The imperialist war intensified to the utmost the contradictions in Russia's situation, and the experience of the Provisional Government proved that the bourgeoisie and petty bourgeoisie were incapable of rescuing the country from the hopeless situation it was in. The increasingly open revolt of the masses—workers, soldiers, and peasants—led the Bolshevik Party—and Lenin in the first place, for several of the Bolshevik leaders hesitated—to decide on the October insurrection.

(b) Insurrection and revolution, October 1917

The overthrow of the power of the bourgeoisie, exercised by Kerensky's Provisional Government, and the establishment of a new ruling power resulted from an armed conflict in the form of insurrection. This armed conflict had to take place in order to consolidate the relationship of forces in favor of the proletarian revolution and demonstrate in practice that real power was now in the hands of the soviets and of the Bolshevik Party.

On October 25, 1917, the Bolshevik Party showed concretely that it was able, by taking the initiative in operations, to sweep away the Provisional Government as a material fact, by making Kerensky take to his heels and by arresting some of his ministers.

It showed also, and especially, through the combination of military and political action, that the forces organized in the soviets could effectively cease to "recognize" the existence of the Provisional Government, thereby compelling the General Staff (made up of former tsarist generals) to bow to the accomplished fact, since, as a result of the political transformation carried out on the initiative of the Bolsheviks, the General Staff had ceased to be able to dispose of the bulk of the forces it had been able to count on the day before.

What happened on October 25 was thus neither the culmination of a people's war nor of a rebellion, but of an insurrection supported by the masses and carried out, in accordance with a preconceived plan, by armed forces. These armed forces[19] were drawn from the working class and the garrisons, and operated so as to achieve precise aims which had been assigned to them by the Bolshevik Party. As Lenin often pointed out, "insurrection is an art."

The insurrectionary form of action was dictated by the course that the class struggle followed between February and October 1917. On the one hand, the extent of the peasant revolt testified to the profundity of the revolutionary crisis into which the country had entered. On the other, the characteristics of this revolt meant that it was in grave danger of being crushed: the peasant movement did not itself raise the question of power, and it was developing in a disunited, localized way, so that it could be suppressed "bit by bit." Under these conditions, survival of the Provisional Government meant danger that the peasants would be defeated, and, with them, the revolution. As Lenin wrote, if the Bolsheviks failed to take the offensive against the Provisional Government, which was crushing the peasants, they would be "traitors" to the peasants and to the revolution, for "to tolerate the suppression of the peasant revolt by [the] government . . . would be to *ruin* the whole revolution."[20]

The peasants' entry into the struggle for land carried the Russian Revolution into a new stage. It signified a de facto breakdown of the alliance between the peasantry and the bourgeoisie, that alliance which had made it possible for the Provisional Government to be formed and had given strength to the bourgeoisie.[21] Thereafter, a clash between the bourgeoisie and the revolutionary masses was inevitable, and it was imperative that the proletariat and the Bolshevik Party act quickly. There could be no question of waiting for the coming congress of soviets to discuss matters "peacefully," or for a mass movement to develop in the towns. Waiting would mean leaving the initiative to the Provisional Government, permitting it not only to put down the peasantry but also to concentrate against Petrograd the troops still loyal to it and take the offensive at the moment and in the conditions of its own choice. Therefore, Lenin called on the Bolsheviks to "launch a *surprise* attack." They must not hesitate, for they were sure of the support of the masses throughout Russia, while in Petrograd they had at their disposal "*thousands* of armed workers in Petrograd who could *at once* seize the Winter Palace, the General Staff building," etc. Lenin added that the Soviet government formed in the course of the insurrection could not be overcome by the bourgeoisie: "Agitational work in the army will be such as to make it *impossible* to combat this government of peace, of land for the peasants, and so forth."[22]

Facts were to show that Lenin's analysis was correct, that it was possible to establish Soviet power through armed insurrection, and that this power, the establishment of which opened a new stage in world history, would be remarkably firmly grounded. Nevertheless, it was only with great difficulty that the Central Committee of the Bolshevik Party agreed to the idea of insurrection and recognized its urgency.[23] The point is important because, together with other similar cases, it shows the gap that often existed—especially on matters and at moments of a decisive character—between Lenin and the majority of the party leadership, a situation that was to have consequences later on.

III. The stages of the Russian Revolution between April and October 1917

In order to appreciate the new stage into which the Russian Revolution entered as a result of the October insurrection and to understand its distinctive features, we must start from the situation existing in April 1917. This situation was marked by the "interweaving" of domination by the bourgeoisie and revolutionary democratic dictatorship of the proletariat and the peasantry, the "dual power" which then constituted the peculiarity of the situation in Russia.[24]

"Dual power" meant that in April 1917 the democratic dictatorship of the proletariat and the peasantry was both realized (for, "actually, in Petrograd, the power is in the hands of the workers and soldiers") and not realized, for, through the SRs, the majority of the people supported a line of class collaboration, so that "the bourgeoisie is in power."[25] This situation of dual power was highly unstable. It implied that Russia was then in "a period of *transition* from the first stage of the revolution to the second."[26]

This peculiarity of the Russian Revolution was itself due to the "interweaving" of two revolutionary processes: that of the proletarian revolution and that of the bourgeois-democratic revolution. After October this "interweaving" did not cease to exist, but assumed entirely new features.

Already in April 1917 Lenin forecast that "there will be a new stage in the bourgeois-democratic revolution," beginning "when the peasantry separates from the bourgeoisie, seizes the land and power despite the bourgeoisie."[27] Things happened, in fact, in a different way from what Lenin expected at that time. To use one of his own expressions in this same article, life, in putting this forecast into practice, "concretized it and thereby modified it."[28]

What actually happened was that the Russian Revolution passed through two distinct and complementary stages.

(a) The revolutionary struggle of the peasants
for the land and the new democratic stage
traversed by the revolution during the
summer of 1917

The first of these two stages resembled the one that Lenin had forecast, although it presented some different features.

From the summer of 1917 onward, the peasantry separated itself in practice from the bourgeoisie, for it began to seize the land; however, ideologically and politically it did not decisively break with the bourgeoisie. The peasantry, in the main, did not withdraw its confidence from the SRs, and did not raise the question of power. It could raise this question, and answer it, only by accepting the leadership of the working class and the Bolshevik Party, which at that time it was not prepared to do. Lenin recognized this on the very evening of October 25 when, in addressing the Petrograd Soviet of Workers' and Soldiers' Deputies, he raised the question of winning the confidence of the peasants, declaring: "A single decree putting an end to landed proprietorship will win us the confidence of the peasants. The peasants will understand that the salvation of the peasantry lies only in an alliance with the workers."[29]

The revolutionary struggle waged by the peasants from the summer through the autumn of 1917 thus marked a new stage in the bourgeois-democratic revolution, for its aims were the division of the land and the development of private exploitation of the soil, aims which remained wholly within the limits of the bourgeois order.

The framework within which the division of the land took place was normally the *mir*. The latter was supposed, in principle, to carry out a periodic redistribution of land among its members. While such a periodic redistribution might delay the development of capitalism in agriculture, it could not prevent this, for the conditions in which it took place were affected by the development of capitalism outside agriculture and by the social inequalities which this development brought about within the *mir* itself.

If, during the summer and early autumn of 1917, the bourgeois power represented by the Provisional Government was repressing the peasantry, this was not because the peasants' activities were destroying the foundations of capitalist development, but because the immediate interests of the Russian bourgeoisie were closely bound up with those of the landlords. It was in order to protect these immediate interests that the Provisional Government resorted to a repression that jeopardized the entire revolutionary process, so that the intervention of the proletariat was needed in order to enable the revolution to proceed and dig deeper.

As a result of this intervention, that is, of the October insurrection, a new stage was reached in the Russian Revolution. The entry of the revolution into this new, proletarian stage did not mean, however, that all the democratic tasks of the revolution had been accomplished. On the contrary, the relations between classes were then such that these democratic tasks could be fully accomplished only in connection with the rise and triumph of the proletarian revolution. This was true of the democratic aims pursued by the peasantry. It was true also of the national aims of the non-Russian peoples of the former tsarist empire. In 1917 these peoples entered into battle to win their national independence. By setting up their own governments they freed themselves from foreign oppression and helped the Russian proletariat to smash bourgeois domination. Lenin understood very quickly the dialectical unity of these revolutionary movements, and succeeded in convincing the Bolshevik Party of this, so that it asserted, in the name of proletarian internationalism, the right of these peoples to "separate" and form their own states. One of Lenin's historical merits is that he grasped the revolutionary implications of the movement of the peoples formerly subjected to Russian domination and the need for the Bolshevik Party to support this movement.[30] It is well known that this need was not understood either by certain Bolsheviks or by the revolutionary wing of the German Social Democrats. Rosa Luxemburg, for instance, saw, in the main, the bourgeois aspect of the national movements and did not realize that the democratic aspect of these movements demanded that they be supported by the proletariat, just as the proletariat must support the movement of the peasants fighting for the land.

(b) The revolutionary struggle of the workers to overthrow the Provisional Government and the new proletarian stage of the revolution begun in October 1917

The rise of the revolutionary peasant movement (with the distinctive features that have just been recalled) and of the revolutionary movement of the non-Russian peoples, combined with a powerful advance of the proletarian forces, determined the possibility and necessity of the October insurrection, in order that the revolution might continue. The victory of the October insurrection radically altered the characteristics of the Russian Revolution, the conditions in which the peasants' struggle for the land went forward, and the nature of the ruling class.

From October onward, the principal aspect of the Russian Revolution was its proletarian aspect. Thereafter, the revolutionary struggle of the peasants proceeded as a democratic revolution. It took place under the political hegemony of the proletariat, but was not actually led by the proletariat and its party, a circumstance that gave rise to some special features in the subsequent course of the Russian Revolution and also to *certain special features of the dictatorship of the proletariat* established by the October Revolution.

Notes

1. The first of these was the Treaty of Aigun (1858), which enabled Russia to take over extensive territories to the north of the river Amur (and some to the south of it), right up to the Pacific. Russia was thus able to found the city of Vladivostok and strengthen its position on the island of Sakhalin. By the Treaty of Peking (1860) Russia seized further territory to the south of the river Amur and in the Ussuri region, so that it had access to "warm water" (free from ice). Later, after invading part of Central Asia, Russia obliged China to cede important territories in that region, thereby

installing itself on the borders of Sinkiang and on the Pamirs, and coming close to India.

2. What is meant here is colonization in the etymological sense of the settlement of *colonists*. By doing this, the tsardom reduced the pressure that increased population in Russia put upon agrarian structures which changed only very slowly, and which the autocracy sought to control, since these structures formed the essential social basis of its existence. Colonization also gave the tsardom fresh means for future expansion, a typical example of this policy being the establishment of "colonies" of Cossacks.

3. It was estimated that in 1913 the Russian proletariat made up 14 percent of the population, but this proletariat was highly concentrated in a few big industrial centers and its wretched conditions drove it to rebellion.

4. In 1913 the peasantry accounted for nearly 67 percent of the population (this percentage and that mentioned in the previous note are taken from *Narodnoye Kh. SSSR v. 1970 g.*, p. 22). Poor and middle peasants constituted the majority of the peasantry.

5. This lack of real political initiative on the part of the bourgeoisie did not, of course, prevent certain political representatives of this bourgeoisie from engaging in various intrigues, some directed against the ruling power. In the period just before the events of February 1917, especially after December 1916, certain generals, encouraged by discontent with Tsar Nicholas II in "liberal" circles, were apparently preparing a coup d'état in favor of his son, with a view to appointing as regent the tsar's brother, who was thought to be more favorable to a parliamentary form of government. The February Revolution put an end to these palace intrigues.

6. It is not possible to give a more detailed analysis here except to mention that the Russian industrial bourgeoisie at the beginning of the twentieth century was clearly divided into two main sections. One section, closely dependent on the state and most intimately linked with French and British imperialism, gave more direct support to tsarist expansionism. The principal center of activity of this section was St. Petersburg. The other section was comparatively more independent of the autocracy, for its own financial foundations were more solid. The principal center of activity of this section of the bourgeoisie was Moscow. The Soviet economic historian N. N. Vanag, in an article published in *Istorik marksist*, no. 12 (1929), described St. Petersburg as "the

incarnation of the 'extra-national' (*nenatsionalnyi*) system of finance capital," while Moscow incarnated the system of national capital (ibid., p. 43). See on this subject, James D. White, "Moscow, Petersburg and the Russian Industrialists," in *Soviet Studies* (January 1973), pp. 414 ff.

7. See O. Anweiler, *Die Rätebewegung*, pp. 127–130 and 158 ff.

8. Among Lenin's writings on the "transitional" nature of the situation that existed in the spring of 1917 and on dual power, should be mentioned his "April Theses" (*CW*, vol. 24, pp. 20–26) and "The Dual Power" (ibid., pp. 38–41).

9. Anweiler, *Die Rätebewegung*, p. 140.

10. Anweiler notes that one of the reasons given by the Mensheviks and SRs for opposing the slogan "All Power to the Soviets!" was that "the Soviets are class organisations which unite only part of the population," so that, they said, if the Soviets took power, "the other social groups—the bourgeoisie first and foremost, but also part of the peasantry—would break with the revolution, and the proletariat, the live force of Soviet power, would find itself . . . reduced to isolation" (ibid., pp. 173–174).

11. Ibid., p. 156.

12. Ibid., especially pp. 156–157.

13. Ibid., pp. 150 and 229.

14. Official statistics recorded 49 "peasant riots" in March 1917, 378 in April, 678 in May, 988 in June, 957 in July, 760 in August, 803 in September and 1,169 in October (S. Dubrowski, *Die Bauernbewegung in der Russischen Revolution 1917*, p. 90, quoted in Anweiler, *Die Rätebewegung*, p. 148, n. 114).

15. The *Skhod* was formally in charge of the land of the *obshchina*, the village community, which was also often called the *mir*.

16. Marc Ferro, *The Russian Revolution of February 1917*, pp. 121–130.

17. Lenin, "First Letter on Tactics," in *CW*, vol. 24, p. 54.

18. Ibid., p. 47.

19. They were the Red Guards. Estimates of their total number in Russia as a whole vary widely. The two extreme figures usually quoted are 75,000 and 200,000. For Petrograd alone, estimates vary between 4,000 and 40,000, the figure of 20,000 being the one most widely accepted. In any case, the numbers involved were not very large. Furthermore, the Red Guards were poorly organized. If their action was decisive, this was because of the political situation—the break-up of the armed forces of the Pro-

visional Government. As regards their social origin, the indications available show that the Red Guards were *mostly workers in large-scale industry*. (On these points see D. N. Collins, "A Note on the Numerical Strength of the Red Guards in October 1917," in *Soviet Studies* [October 1972], pp. 270 ff., an article which includes an extensive bibliography.)

20. Lenin, "The Crisis has Matured," in *CW*, vol. 26, p. 81.
21. The repression of the working class and of the Bolshevik Party by the government after the popular demonstrations of July 1917, and the fact that the Bolshevik Party then had to go more or less underground, showed that, at the same time the masses had been becoming radicalized, the bourgeoisie and its government had made use of the months that had passed since February to organize their forces and acquire the power to launch a counter-revolutionary offensive. The attempted coup d'état by General Kornilov in August, which was frustrated through the activity of the Bolsheviks, also testified to a regrouping of some of its forces by the bourgeoisie.
22. Lenin, *CW*, vol. 26, pp. 83–84.
23. It was on October 10, after several weeks of hesitation, that the Central Committee declared in favor of insurrection. Until then it had left unanswered the appeals from Lenin, and had even "censored" some of his articles, as a result of which Lenin had offered the Central Committee his resignation, so that he might "campaign among the rank and file of the Party and at the Party Congress" for his views (ibid., p. 84).
24. Lenin, "Letters on Tactics," in *CW*, vol. 24, p. 46.
25. Ibid., p. 46.
26. Ibid., p. 43.
27. Ibid., p. 47.
28. Ibid., p. 45.
29. *CW*, vol. 26, p. 240.
30. Thanks to this internationalist attitude the Bolshevik Party recruited many non-Russian members, who came to constitute a considerable proportion of the party leaders, and this helped to give a proletarian character to many of the national movements in the old Russia, which accepted Bolshevik leadership. (The introduction to G. Haupt and J.-J. Marie, *Makers of the Russian Revolution*, p. 26, gives details of the national origin of the Bolshevik leaders of 1917: out of the 246 leading party members whose biographies are included in this book, only 127 were Russian by nationality.)

2. The dictatorship of the proletariat and class relations on the morrow of October

The October insurrection put an end to the dictatorship of the bourgeoisie and established the dictatorship of the proletariat in Russia. It thus enabled the proletariat to form itself into the dominant class in order to continue the revolution, carry out the tasks of the democratic revolution, and take the first steps toward socialism.

The October insurrection made it possible to smash the power of the bourgeoisie because it constituted a moment in an overall revolutionary process which at that point reached a certain degree of maturity.

It was, of course, not the occupation of a few public buildings or the arrest of a few ministers (whom the bourgeoisie could easily have replaced if it had had the capacity) that enabled the proletariat to substitute its rule for that of the bourgeoisie. What made possible this world-historic change was the new relations of forces between classes which the October insurrection *revealed,* at the same time as it helped to consolidate this, for *power is precisely a relation between classes,* and not an "object" which is "seized."

If the October insurrection was able to *reveal* and at the same time consolidate the existence of a new relation between classes, the reason was that this event demonstrated that it was no longer the bourgeoisie but the proletariat, together with its party, "which was in command of the guns." It revealed that the new dominant class had acquired, and the old dominant class had lost, decisive military power.[1]

In October 1917 the proletariat possessed decisive military power because *the armed forces which were in a position to decide the fate of the revolution were no longer prepared to*

91

fight for the bourgeoisie.[2] They had rallied to the revolution for ideological and political reasons, because they could not escape the pressure and activity of the masses. The latter were urged forward by the hopeless situation in which the Russian bourgeoisie was holding the country. The thrust of the working-class masses became irresistible thanks to the Bolshevik Party, which helped these masses to grasp the character of the situation, and to act unitedly and at the right moment.[3] It was thus the combination of overall revolutionary conditions and the action of the Bolshevik Party which made possible the victory of the October insurrection and the establishment of the dictatorship of the proletariat.

Of the various factors that facilitated the October victory—the hopelessness of the situation, the exasperation of the masses, the pressure they exerted which caused a decisive section of the armed forces to come over to the camp of revolution, the leading role played by the Bolshevik Party, etc.—it was the party's leadership of the urban masses, and first and foremost of the working-class masses of Petrograd, Moscow, and the other main industrial centers, that determined the proletarian character of the ruling power resulting from this victory. For the class content of the October Revolution and the ruling power emerging from it, what was decisive was the leading role played by the Bolshevik Party.

All revolutions are due to the resolute action and heroism of the masses, and in particular, when this class is present, of the working class. That was so in the case of the revolution of February 1917, in which the working classes of Petrograd, Moscow, and other towns played the determining role, and yet this revolution did not lead to the establishment of proletarian rule. The October Revolution was unlike all previous revolutions, except the Paris Commune, by virtue of the fact that it was carried through under the guidance of proletarian ideas.

The Bolshevik Party was the organized carrier of these ideas, and it was this that enabled the Russian proletariat to make itself the dominant class. Thanks to the ties of confidence established between it and the most combative sections of the proletariat, the party served as the instrument of the dictatorship of the proletariat. It remained such as long as it maintained these ties and also continued to be the carrier of proletarian ideology and practice: the second condition being always the decisive one, for a party may possess an extensive base in the working class and yet be only a "bourgeois labor party," through failing to uphold proletarian ideology and practice.

I. Characteristics and limitations of the leading role of the Bolshevik Party in 1917 and immediately after October

The leadership exercised by the Bolshevik Party in the revolutionary process bore two aspects, the ideological and the political. Of these the ideological was the dominant one, although this was itself the product of the party's political activity, its work in organizing and uniting mass struggles, for it was this work that enabled the party to enrich its theoretical conceptions, define its political line, and spread this line among the people.

The leading ideological role of the Bolshevik Party corresponded to the ideological leadership of the revolution by the proletariat, whose party concentrated the most combative forces and revolutionary initiatives. This leading ideological role was one of the conditions for the *hegemony of the proletariat*[4] in the revolution.

Proletarian hegemony and the leading ideological role of the proletariat must obviously not be confused with the dominance of proletarian ideology. The latter can be achieved only as the result of a protracted class struggle carried on under the dictatorship of the proletariat and bringing about a revolutionary transformation in social relations.

The leading ideological role of the proletariat and its party constitutes a necessary point of transition on the road to political power. The Bolshevik Party's activity had succeeded in reaching this point on the eve of October through the political and ideological work carried out by its militants.

What marks the conquest of a leading ideological role by the proletariat and its party is that a certain number of revolutionary ideas concerning the immediate situation, the contradictions in the situation, and the way to resolve them, have seized hold of the masses to a sufficient degree to become "material forces" and shake the dominance of bourgeois ideology. This was one of the results achieved by the Bolshevik Party's activity on the eve of October, a result that expressed itself in the fact that the masses ceased to bow before the existing order and the soldiers refused to use their weapons against those who were pointed out to them as targets by the beneficiaries of this order. Having reached that point, the leading ideological role of the proletariat could be transformed into proletarian hegemony, which enabled the political power of the proletariat to be established, as was done by the October Revolution.

In October 1917 the leading role of the Bolshevik Party was subject to a certain number of limitations which must be mentioned here, as they had important effects on the subsequent course of the revolution and on relations between the different parts of the state machine.

The first of these limitations, which was a specific feature of the revolutionary situation of that time, has already been indicated. This was the fact that at the moment of the October insurrection the leading role of the Bolshevik Party was mainly established in relation to the working-class masses, whereas it was still comparatively weak where the peasantry was concerned. The consequences of this limitation were to be all the more important because it would be very difficult thereafter for the Bolshevik Party to effect any radical change in the situation. True, during the civil war a decisive section of the peasantry came to accept the political leadership of the Bolshevik Party (especially in the military sphere). It fought under the party's leadership and thereby enabled the Soviet power to defeat the White Guards and the foreign interventionists; but this rallying to the Bolshevik banner did not mean that the peasant masses had, in the main, accepted the ideas propagated by the party, either in the field of revolutionary Marxism or even in that of immediate measures.

The second limitation on the leading role of the Bolshevik Party was that, even among the workers, the leading ideological role of the party was principally political. What had to a large extent penetrated a decisive section of the working-class masses were not the fundamental ideas of revolutionary Marxism—those which light up the path to socialism and reveal what is necessary for the march to communism—but those that corresponded to what Lenin called "immediate tasks."[5]

As a result of these various limitations on its leading role, and of the immediate tasks of the revolution, the Bolshevik Party could not set itself the aim, once Soviet power had been established, of tackling the tasks of socialist transformation straight away. In 1917 and at the beginning of 1918, the party rightly considered that to try to rapidly attain socialist objectives, except in relation to certain points, would be utopian and therefore extremely dangerous.

This necessary momentary restriction of the party's tasks was the theme of many reminders issued by Lenin and other Bolshevik leaders. In Lenin's "April Theses," for instance, he declared: "It is not our *immediate* task to 'introduce' socialism, but only to bring social production and the distribution of products at once under the *control* of the Soviets of Workers' Deputies."[6]

He reaffirmed this conception shortly before the October Revolution,[7] proclaimed it afresh on the very day of the insurrection,[8] and repeated it with emphasis six months later.[9] As we see, Lenin in those days stressed consistently that Russia was only at the beginning of the transition to socialism, pointing out that what had been done in October 1917, and then between October 1917 and April 1918, though essential, was still only enough to allow the first steps to be taken in the direction of socialism.

From most of Lenin's writings we get the impression that

the main reason he thought it was not possible to go faster and farther toward socialism was the economic situation—the breakdown of industry, the general disorganization, famine, etc. But this main reason was itself dependent on a more fundamental one, connected with the type of leadership that the Bolshevik Party was then in a position to exercise, that is, with the limitations restricting the party's leading role at that time. Thus we observe that the party thought it would be easy to "pass directly into communism" from the second half of 1918 onward, when economic conditions had become still worse, but when it seemed that the political and ideological conditions were greatly improved, with the peasant masses united around the Soviet power in order to resist the White Guards and the imperialist forces.

In this period of civil war the leading role of the party was indeed considerably enlarged, but not to the point of allowing it, without grave danger, to advance beyond the line it had drawn in 1917.[10] The party recognized this in 1921, and came to see the problems of the conditions for progress toward socialism in terms essentially similar (though modified on some important points) to those which had been established nearly four years earlier.

It is in the light of what has been said of the leading role of the Bolshevik Party, its characteristics and its limitations, in October and in the period immediately after October, that we can examine the problem of the forms of proletarian power and its specific features in that period.

II.   *The forms of proletarian power in October 1917 and its specific features*

The revolutionary struggle of the workers in the large towns, led by the Bolshevik Party, thus brought into being a proletarian hegemony, an ideological and then a political power of the proletariat. *This power was first and foremost a relation between classes.* It cannot be identified with a *par-*

ticular political institution: the same class power may, depending on concrete circumstances and conditions, be "accomplished in reality" in a variety of "political institutions."[11]

After October 1917 the power of the proletariat, its organization as the dominant class, was wielded through the Bolshevik Party. It was this party that "accomplished in reality" proletarian power, which concept included state power but was not confined to it: indeed, proletarian power dominated state power. We must therefore distinguish between political power and the Bolshevik Party which "accomplished in reality" this power; state power, through which coercion of the bourgeoisie and the counter-revolutionary elements was exercised; the forms assumed by this power; and the machinery and organizations which concretely enabled this power to carry out particular actions (but could also obstruct the power of the proletariat insofar as, under the pressure of other classes or as a result of mistakes made by the party, they separated themselves from the proletariat and became "independent").

(a) The system of the dictatorship of the proletariat

The power of the proletariat, the dictatorship of the proletariat, constitutes a *system*: Lenin calls it, indeed, "the system of the dictatorship of the proletariat."

In this system, the proletariat and the classes with which it is allied, the class organizations, and the class machinery occupy different places, and these are not immutable. They can alter as a result of the class struggle and its effects on social relations as a whole, relations between classes, and more especially, the ideological relations prevailing between the proletariat, the proletarian party, and the classes allied with the working class.

During the years following the October Revolution, the system of the dictatorship of the proletariat presented a certain number of characteristics which Lenin described in his address, already quoted, on "The Trade Unions, the Present Situation and Trotsky's Mistakes."

In the system as it then existed the party held the leading place because, as Lenin put it, "the Party, shall we say, absorbs the vanguard of the proletariat," and "this vanguard exercises the dictatorship of the proletariat," which placed it higher than state power.[12]

Between the latter and the party Lenin placed the trade unions as organizations embracing all the workers in industry and capable of forming "a *link* between the vanguard and the masses."[13] This must be a two-way link: from the "leading circles" to the rank and file, and from the rank and file to the "leading circles." In fact, the place thus assigned by Lenin to the Soviet trade unions was never really occupied by them, and the question remains open: can the trade unions, given their structure, which reproduces a certain division in the working class, occupy this place, and, if so, under what conditions?

As regards state power, it did not possess, in the circumstances then obtaining, a truly proletarian character; from which followed, according to Lenin, the need "to protect the material and spiritual interests of the massively organised proletariat from that very same state power."[14]

The reasons why the proletariat in power needs to be protected from state power are not clearly stated in the passage quoted, nor indeed in any other statement by Lenin or the Bolshevik Party.

Lenin offered two explanations in this passage. The first related to the class alliance which the proletariat had had to conclude with the peasantry in order to be able to wield its dictatorship in a country with a peasant majority. (As Lenin said, "Ours is not actually a workers' state but a workers' and peasants' state.")[15] The second explanation put forward by Lenin related to what he calls the "bureaucratic twist"[16] which had been given to the Soviet state. This distortion affected the machinery of the state. It needs to be related to what Lenin observed as early as the beginning of 1918 (and it had not got any better between then and December 1920), namely, that within the system of the dictatorship of the proletariat, "there is much that is crude and unfinished in our

Soviets," so that, as regards the functioning of the system as a soviet system, "this has scarcely begun and has begun badly."[17]

The indications Lenin gave so frankly and plainly between 1918 and 1920, and which he continued to give right down to his last writings, concerning the characteristics of Soviet "state power" are of great importance. They contrast with the apologetic style that was to prevail later on, and help us to understand better the "crude and unfinished" quality of the Soviet system of that period. At the same time—and there is no reason to be surprised at this, given the lack of sufficiently protracted experience, which would have made it possible to acquire a more thorough knowledge of the relations underlying these characteristics—Lenin's formulations do not always provide real explanations, but rather a series of observations.

One of the aims of this book is, indeed, to endeavor, as is possible today with the advantage of hindsight, to provide a fuller characterization of the system of the dictatorship of the proletariat as it existed in Russia between 1917 and 1923 and subsequently. This should also make it possible to appreciate better the nature of the social relations and class struggles which determined the characteristics of the system and contributed to its later evolution. In this connection, we must turn back to Lenin's previously quoted formulation: "Ours is not actually a workers' state, but a workers' and peasants' state."

(b) "State power" and the worker-peasant alliance

If it is not clarified, this formula raises more problems than it explains. Lenin returned to it in what he called a "correction," accompanied by a brief commentary.

The "correction" was made in an article published in *Pravda* of January 21, 1921, under the title "The Party Crisis." In the course of this article Lenin replied in a few sentences to a comment made by Bukharin at the meeting on December 30, 1920, at which Lenin had spoken of a "workers' and peasants' state." Bukharin had interrupted Lenin, exclaiming: "What kind of state? A workers' and peasants' state?" In "The Party Crisis" Lenin wrote: "I was wrong and Comrade Bukharin was right. What I should have said is 'A workers' state is an abstraction. What we actually have is a workers' state, with this peculiarity, firstly, that it is not the working class but the peasant population that predominates in the country, and, secondly, that it is a workers' state with bureaucratic distortions.' "

In expressing himself like this Lenin was using, as he himself wrote, terms that were closer to those he had used during the discussion at the Eighth Congress of Soviets, but he virtually maintained what he had said before, as he emphasized in his conclusion: "This correction makes no difference to my reasoning or conclusions."[18]

Actually, this "correction" made Lenin's idea more precise, since it enabled him to point out something that certain Bolsheviks tended to forget, namely that the concrete reality of the Soviet state was necessarily affected by the nature of the relations that the peasant population—the determining social force in a country with a peasant majority—maintained with the proletariat, the leading social force operating through its party.

The problem here presented is twofold—that of the contradiction between the massive presence of nonproletarian popular forces (mainly the peasants) and the proletarian and democratic character of the ruling power,[19] and that of the correct handling of this contradiction.

In the given circumstances, this was a necessary condition: while the system of the dictatorship of the proletariat must be led by the proletariat and its party, this system had also to be based on the broad masses of the people, even if these were nonproletarian, and these masses must therefore find a place, and a substantial one, in the organs of the proletarian power—first and foremost in its organs of self-administration and government, namely, the soviets.

This contradiction is more or less acute depending on the characteristics of the ideological and political leadership exercised by the proletariat and its party over the popular masses themselves. It becomes especially acute when, insofar as a section of the masses is concerned, this leadership, this leading activity, is weak, or comparatively so. This was the case in Russia, apart from a few rather short periods, where the peasants were concerned.

As is known, the weakness of the leading activity of the party in relation to the peasantry was connected with the apparently independent form assumed by the revolutionary activity of the peasantry and its success. Actually, this success was won and consolidated only because the working-class masses and the Bolshevik Party had ensured the victory of the proletarian revolution in the towns and so protected the revolutionary movement of the peasantry,[20] but the close connection between the proletarian revolution in the towns and the democratic revolution in the countryside was not fully apparent to the peasants, as the Bolshevik Party was not there on the spot or present among them. Hence the need, reasserted again and again, to convince the peasant masses of the identity between their fundamental interests and those of the proletariat. Hence, too, the tension that frequently developed between the Soviet power and wide sections of the peasantry.[21]

Thus, Lenin's formulation, "a workers' and peasants' state," referred primarily to the effects on the life of the soviet organs (in the villages, districts, counties, etc.) which were an integral part of the system of the dictatorship of the proletariat that might be produced by a numerous peasantry liable to develop political activity independent of the dictatorship of the proletariat. There was thus a danger that the soviet organs might take a line of action that would weaken the proletarian dictatorship.

This danger could not be banished by simply excluding the peasant masses from the soviets. That would only reduce the popular foundation on which the dictatorship of the proletariat had to base itself. It would weaken the indispensable bonds of alliance between proletariat and peasantry, hinder the fulfillment of the democratic tasks of the revolution, and render it impossible to develop the party's leading role. This role can, indeed, be developed only insofar as the party of the proletariat itself shows confidence in the masses and so enables them, *through their own experience*, to rally ever more closely around the proletarian party.

If the party departs from this path, if it does not handle correctly the contradiction between the proletarian character of the ruling power and the necessary involvement of broad nonproletarian masses in the organs of power, it runs into another danger, namely, that of the management of public affairs becoming concentrated in the hands of a small number of persons. Such concentration reinforces the *state* aspect of the organization of the ruling power, the separation of the machinery of government from the masses, and leads to nondemocratic forms of centralization. It leads to the spread, rather than the contraction, of bourgeois political relations, and so compromises the proletarian character of the ruling power. We know that the latter is *not only* a state power, for the political power of the proletariat does not mean the existence of a "state in the strict sense" but a power which is "no longer a state in the proper sense of the word."[22]

It can be seen that Lenin's formulation about the workers' and peasants' state also points to the need for correct handling of the contradictions revealed by this formulation. History has shown the mistakes that were made in Russia in the handling of this contradiction.

At the level of the functioning of the organs of power, the existence of a numerous peasantry among whom the leading activity of the proletariat was exercised to only a slight degree gave rise, shortly after the October Revolution, to a certain number of measures and decisions. Formally, the most significant of these was the fixing of peasant representation at the ratio of 1 deputy for every 125,000 inhabitants and the representation of townsfolk at 1 deputy for every 25,000 *electors*.[23] As Lenin saw it, the difference thus established was justified by the fact that the organization of the proletariat had progressed more rapidly than that of the peasantry, and this gave the workers a real advantage.[24]

The adoption of this measure of discrimination against the

peasantry was not unconnected with the results of the elections to the Constituent Assembly, which was dissolved almost as soon as it met, on the night of January 5–6, 1918. These elections, organized under Soviet rule, gave only 175 seats of a total of 707 to the Bolsheviks, as against 410 to the SRs, 17 to the Cadets, [25] 16 to the Mensheviks, and 84 to various national groups.[26]

The same considerations led the Bolsheviks first to restrict to a serious degree, and then practically to ban, the activity of parties other than their own, including the SR Party, which was closely linked with the well-to-do strata in the countryside.

It is hard to determine the effects of these various measures on the attitude of the peasants to the soviets. In any case, at the level of the county soviets (those in which the peasantry could best make themselves felt, and about which we have adequate information), the proportion of Communist delegates, which was nearly 61 percent in 1918, fell steadily, to 43 percent in 1920 and 44 percent in 1921. The disappearance of delegates belonging to the other parties was not accompanied by any increase in the numbers of Communist delegates but only by an increase in "non-party" delegates. In 1920 and 1921, these even outnumbered the Communist delegates.[27]

The most important political effect of the contradiction between the proletarian ruling power and the predominance of a peasant population subject to only a rather slight degree to proletarian leadership was, of course, not only in the electoral sphere, but in the unsatisfactory functioning of the soviets.[28]

This situation was not the outcome of a long historical process: it was present from the very proclamation of Soviet power. It corresponded to the "transitional form," as Lenin put it, then assumed by the dictatorship of the proletariat. The effects of this situation are clearly revealed when we analyze the characteristics and relations of the two main elements in the system of the dictatorship of the proletariat in Russia: namely, the organization of the soviets, as established after October, and the dominant element in the system of proletarian dictatorship, the Bolshevik Party, the party whose ideology, political line, style of leadership, capacity to develop the alliance between the working class and the peasantry and, consequently, relations with the masses, constituted the ultimate guarantee of the proletarian character of the ruling power.

III.   The establishment of the soviet organs and of the Soviet government

The place occupied immediately after October by the soviet organs, and in the first place by the central soviet organs which issued from the Second Congress of Workers' and Soldiers' Soviets, resulted from the actual movement of the revolution and the leading role that the Bolshevik Party had played in the insurrection.

Actually, it was not the soviet organs, many of which were still dominated by the SRs and Mensheviks and had even refused to take part in the Second Congress, that had overthrown the Provisional Government, but the working-class masses led by the Bolshevik Party. As Stalin said some years after October, "the Congress of Soviets merely *took over* power from the Petrograd Soviet,"[29] that is, from the hands of the Bolshevik Party, which presided over its decisions.[30]

As has been said, power, being a relation between classes and not a "thing," cannot be "handed over." The very dynamic of the revolution and its own initiative at the head of the working-class masses invested the Bolshevik Party, and not the soviets, with effective power, and if part of the state power was indeed wielded, under conditions which we shall examine, by organs which emerged from the Second Congress of Soviets and from subsequent congresses, this resulted from the policy followed by the Bolshevik Party itself.

The relations thus established between the soviet organs and the party corresponded both to the real relation of forces between the classes and to the conception that the Bolshevik Party, and especially Lenin,[31] had formed of what the respective positions of the party and the soviets should be in the system of the dictatorship of the proletariat.

Lenin never held a "fetishist" conception of the role of the soviets. When, in the course of the year 1917, the danger loomed that domination of the soviets by the petty bourgeois chauvinist parties which were ready to follow an anti-Bolshevik policy might become more or less consolidated, Lenin withdrew the slogan "All Power to the Soviets!"— pointing out that the latter could become transformed "into mere fig-leaves of the counter-revolution."[32] During the summer of 1917 he explained that "the slogan 'All Power to the Soviets!' was a slogan for peaceful development of the revolution which was possible in April, May, June, and up to July 5 9 . . . This slogan is no longer correct, for it does not take into account that power has changed hands and that the revolution has in fact been completely betrayed by the S.R.s and Mensheviks."[33]

Lenin then put in the forefront (though without renouncing legal *combined* with illegal activity, and while advising against any rashness) the slogan of armed insurrection, with as its aim "to transfer power to the proletariat supported by the poor peasants with a view to putting our Party programme into effect."[34]

During September, the defeat of Kornilov's attempted coup d'état and the strengthening of Bolshevik representation in the soviets led Lenin again to advocate the slogan: "All Power to the Soviets!"

The Bolshevik Party's policy with regard to the soviet organs thus consisted in recognizing that they had a place in the system of proletarian dictatorship, but were not to be identified with the latter. They could therefore not occupy the dominant position in it, the less so because the peasant soviets were undifferentiated, and the agricultural workers and poor peasants did not play a preponderant role in them.

The relations which developed between the Bolshevik Party and the soviet organs, and, more particularly, between the Council of People's Commissars and the All-Russia Central Executive Committee of the Soviets, the two central or-

gans of government, become clearer in the light of the foregoing.

(a) The Sovnarkom

In the evening of October 26, 1917, the All-Russia Congress
of Workers' and Soldiers' Soviets, at its second and last session, approved the formation of a Council of People's Commissars (in Russian, for short, "Sovnarkom")—"the first workers' and peasants' government." This first Sovnarkom was
composed exclusively of Bolsheviks, its members being
nominated by the party.

During a short period between the end of November 1917
and the summer of 1918, some left SRs were included in the
Sovnarkom, that is, the government, but the growing hostility
of the left SRs to the Bolshevik Party's policy (in particular, to
the signing of the peace treaty of Brest-Litovsk with Germany)
led to their removal. Thereafter, the Sovnarkom was composed exclusively of Bolsheviks. Lenin was its chairman until
his death.

(b) The VTsIK

The All-Russia Central Executive Committee of the Soviets
(VTsIK, using the Russian initials of its title) was, legally, the
supreme organ of power. It was elected by the Congress of
Soviets.

The VTsIK that emerged from the Second Congress of
Workers' and Soldiers' Soviets was made up of sixty-two Bolsheviks, twenty-nine left SRs, and ten other socialists, thus
reflecting the composition of the congress after the withdrawal
of the right SRs and delegates of other parties who refused to
continue to participate in the congress, as a protest against the
insurrection.

After this congress, the membership of the VTsIK was enlarged by the addition of peasant delegates elected by the
Congress of Peasants' Soviets, in numbers equal to those of
the workers' delegates who had been elected by the Congress

of Workers' and Soldiers' Soviets, together with one hundred delegates from the army and navy and fifty delegates from the trade unions. The new VTsIK, formed on November 15, 1917, consisted of over 350 members and was officially called the Central Executive Committee of the Soviets of Workers', Peasants' and Soldiers' Deputies. The first Soviet Constitution, that of the Russian Socialist Federal Soviet Republic (RSFSR), approved in July 1918 by the Fifth Congress of Soviets, ratified the same proportions for urban and rural representation, but fixed the number of members of the VTsIK at "not more than 200." The Constitution provided that the VTsIK was to carry out the functions of the congress between its sessions, and to "appoint" the Sovnarkom. In theory, the VTsIK was supposed to sit more or less continuously, but in fact an organ which it elected from among its members, the Presidium of the VTsIK, carried out its functions for most of the time. As a result of a resolution adopted by the Eighth Congress of the Bolshevik Party in 1919, the Congress of Soviets confirmed this practice.

(c) Relations between the VTsIK and the Sovnarkom

De jure, the Sovnarkom was thus subordinate to the VTsIK. The Constitution also stated (Chapter 5, Article 12) that promulgation of decrees, orders, and instructions was effected by the VTsIK, that "supreme authority" in the RSFSR was to be vested in the All-Russia Congress of Soviets, and during the period between congresses, in the VTsIK, while the Sovnarkom was responsible for the "general direction of affairs" (Chapter 7, Article 35).

The practice was quite different. On October 30, 1917, the Sovnarkom passed a decree giving it legislative powers. In principle, this decree was to remain valid only until the meeting of the Constituent Assembly, but in fact it continued in force after the assembly had been dissolved. By the time the Constitution of the RSFSR was adopted the situation had been settled: the Sovnarkom had taken precedence over the VTsIK, which was thereafter merely an organ for ratifying decisions or proposals which it had, as a rule, not initiated. Governmental power was concentrated in the Sovnarkom. The left SRs having been removed from the latter, this meant that governmental power was concentrated in the hands of the Bolshevik Party—to an increasing degree, in those of its Central Committee (CC), and eventually of its Political Bureau, which considered the majority of important decisions at the same time as the Sovnarkom, or even, more often than not, before they were considered by that body.

The process which deprived the VTsIK of effective governmental power, to the advantage of the Sovnarkom and of the CC of the Bolshevik Party, is of considerable importance. This process decided the question of where the supreme political authority was to lie in favor of the Bolshevik Party, and against the VTsIK—that emanation of the soviet organs.

Before the victory of the October Revolution the idea of forming an organ of government like the Sovnarkom, constituting an organism distinct from the soviet organization, had never actually been discussed. It had seemed that all power would be concentrated in the soviet organs in the strict sense. At the conclusion of the process just described, the situation was a different one. It was the Sovnarkom, whose members were chosen by the Bolshevik Party, and which did not issue directly from the soviet organs, as the VTsIK did, that wielded governmental power. What had resulted, therefore, was a power structure different from that which had been contemplated before the October Revolution—by the Bolshevik Party as well as by others.

It is possible to think that the process whereby this structure of government became constituted and consolidated is to be explained mainly by the specific constellation of political forces at the time of the October Revolution: in particular the still far from negligible influence enjoyed by the Mensheviks and SRs in the soviet organizations as well as elsewhere. According to this view, it was for "conjunctural" reasons, so as to "safeguard" the power of government from all possible direct interference by representatives of bourgeois and petty bourgeois parties, that the Sovnarkom, formed by the Bolsheviks and on the initiative of the Central Committee of the Bolshevik Party, was created and set de facto in a dominant position in relation to the VTsIK.

While this view takes account of the concrete historical process, it does not go to the root of the matter, remaining concerned with the succession of events, and considering only the most external aspect of class relations, which were what was fundamentally involved here.

The establishment of the dictatorship of the proletariat means that the proletariat sets itself up as the ruling class, and this cannot be done through organs of the soviet type, which are mass organizations, or through state organs exclusively derived from these. The constitution of the proletariat as ruling class is necessarily effected through an apparatus that is specifically proletarian in ideology and aims, and in the role of leadership and unification that it plays in relation to the masses: in other words, through a proletarian party that plays this leading role, politically and ideologically, and plays it, too, in relation to the machinery of state issuing from the mass organizations.

This being so, the concrete forms of articulation between the state machinery of the proletarian dictatorship and the party of the proletariat, the instrument of this dictatorship, can be very diverse. This diversity reflects the extreme diversity of the possible relations between classes and of the effects of the class struggle, including its effects inside the proletarian party.

In the case of Soviet Russia there can be no doubt that the specific forms of articulation between the state machinery and the proletarian party were largely determined by the weakness of the Bolshevik Party's direct influence among important sections of the masses, in the first place among the peasants, and also by a certain tendency on the part of the party to seek to solve problems of leadership by resorting to organizational rules rather than ideological struggle. This tendency was reinforced, moreover, by the urgency of the tasks that the party was obliged to carry out in order to consolidate the proletarian dictatorship.

(d) The central government and the local authorities

Consideration of the way the Soviet form of government was organized also brings up the problem of relations between the central soviet organs and the local ones, and of their respective powers. The Constitution of the RSFSR did not really settle these questions. It declared at one and the same time that "all authority within the Russian Republic is invested in the entire working population of the country, organized in the urban and rural soviets" (Chapter 5, Article 10), and that "supreme authority in the RSFSR is vested in the All-Russia Congress of Soviets, and during the period between the Congresses, in the VTsIK" (Chapter 5, Article 12). The first formulation implies that every local soviet is "sovereign," whereas the second subordinates the local soviets to the authority of the central bodies.

In practice, listing the powers of the central organs and, still more, day-to-day practice, quickly led to the local soviets becoming subordinate to the central organs on all important questions. Together with this, the leading role of the party was also asserted on the local level, this being reflected in the preeminence of the party committees over the local administrative organs at the different territorial levels—though this situation was not really firmly established in Lenin's lifetime. At the end of the civil war, indeed, the basic organizations of the party were very weak, did not exist everywhere, and where they were present did not always possess effective capacity to guide the administrative machinery of the state, which retained and sometimes even strengthened its independence in relation to the central organs of the party.

(e) The administrative machinery of the state

When it was formed, the Sovnarkom tried to establish its own administrative machinery on new foundations, but this attempt came to very little. The various People's Commissariats were in practice obliged to use, or try to use, a large part of the old administrative machine, which underwent only relatively minor internal changes.

This was a very important fact, to which I shall return. It must be pointed out at once, however, that owing to the class composition of the state administrative machinery, and, more profoundly, to the nature of its relations with the masses, its internal hierarchy, and to its relations with the leading organ of the proletarian dictatorship (the Bolshevik Party), this machinery strongly resisted orders coming from the highest source of power. There was therefore frequently a quite deep divergence between the policy formally adopted by the Central Committee, the policy that the Sovnarkom tried to apply, and the actual conduct of the state administration. Moreover, this administration tended to erect a screen between the Soviet power and the masses. Consequently, when the rank and file of the party were not in a position to inform the Bolshevik leaders directly, the latter were out of touch with what was happening, especially in the country areas, and also, of course, within the state machine itself.

The Bolshevik Party sought to remedy this state of affairs on many occasions. Its first attempt was made in March 1918, with the establishment of a People's Commissariat for Control of the state. This had little real effect, which was not surprising, since it aimed at bringing the machinery of state under the control of the highest authority through the medium of another piece of state machinery.

There were three exceptions to this difficult situation: the Commissariat of Foreign Affairs, the Red Army, and the new political police, the Cheka.[35] I shall return to the subject of what became of the latter; for the moment, I shall confine myself to considering the Red Army.

(f) The Red Army

In the military sphere, the Soviet power did not at first have at its disposal an apparatus which it had developed for its own purposes before the revolution and in which the Bolshevik Party organically played a leading role. The conditions in which the October Revolution took place did not allow for such a development.

To be sure, the Bolshevik Party had, since 1905, possessed a "military organization," but this was in no sense an army, even in embryo. Its role was to coordinate the work of Bolshevik propaganda in the tsarist army. Between February and October 1917 this "military organization" played an active role in creating Bolshevik organizations in the army of the Provisional Government, and began publishing a paper, *Soldatskaya Pravda*. Shortly before October it helped set up the Petrograd Military Revolutionary Committee, which prepared the insurrection.

On the other hand, shortly before October the workers of Petrograd and other cities began to organize themselves in a military way, with the Bolsheviks' help, and so the Red Guard came into being. It played a considerable role between October 1917 and March 1918 in combating counter-revolutionary attempts by various groups of officers. In fact, Red Guards, assisted by the peasant partisans and workers' militias, formed at first the only armed force proper at the disposal of the proletarian power. The old tsarist army was still formally in existence after October, and a large part of it was theoretically under the orders of the Soviet power, but it was in a state of utter disintegration, and in March 1918 the Soviet power decided to dissolve it. In that same month the decision was taken to form a Red Army, and Trotsky was entrusted with the task of organizing it. Initially, the new army was to be based on voluntary service, but already in April 1918 this was replaced by conscription. We shall see the characteristics of this army later on, especially as regards relations between officers and the ranks.

If, as the facts show, the Red Army, formed in this way, was an instrument of great efficacy in the struggle against the White Guards and the imperialist armed forces, this was essentially due to the heroism, spirit of sacrifice, and abnegation of the workers and peasants who defended the revolution; but this army was not and could not become an apparatus that helped revolutionize ideological relations and develop proletarian practices. On the contrary, bourgeois, and even feudal, practices were retained in it. Already in 1918, "external forms of respect" (the military salute and special formulas for addressing one's "superiors") were reintroduced, and officers were accorded various privileges, notably as regards their quarters. Later, the officers' training schools, although recruiting their students from among the workers and peasants (as well as from among the old intelligentsia and scions of the former officer class who had come over to the Soviet power), reproduced the hierarchical and ideological relations characteristic of bourgeois armies.

IV.   The Bolshevik Party and its leading role

The leading role played by the Bolshevik Party in the October Revolution and in the establishment of the proletarian dictatorship in Russia was not merely the result of "the luck of history." It corresponded to a profound necessity: to be victorious, the proletarian revolution needs to be led by a party which is guided by revolutionary Marxism. This is a fact constantly confirmed by experience and which Lenin summed up in the phrase: "Without revolutionary theory there can be no revolutionary movement." [36]

Lenin directly associated the revolutionary proletarian movement's need for theory with its need for a party armed with Marxism when he added: "The role of vanguard fighter can be fulfilled only by a party that is guided by the most advanced theory." [37]

The leading role of the Bolshevik Party did not cease with the establishment of the dictatorship of the proletariat; quite the contrary. After October, as before, the party fought to maintain its leading ideological and political role. To do this it had to draw upon revolutionary theory and work out its political line by learning the lessons taught by the activity of the masses.

In 1917 and 1918 the strength of the Bolshevik Party and its leading role were not based mainly on the use of force, but resulted from its capacity to produce correct theoretical analyses and to translate these into a political line, measures, and slogans which ensured for the party close relations with the most combative elements of the masses. In the last analysis, the leading role of the Bolshevik Party was bound up with its revolutionary development of Marxism in relation to the struggles of the proletariat and peasantry.

The role played in 1917 by the Bolshevik Party must not, however, make us forget that it had existed as such for only five years; it had been born at the conference held in Prague on January 5–17, 1912, as the Russian Social Democratic Labor Party (Bolshevik). This conference was able to launch a party which was not just a mere grouping of a few militants or a few revolutionary intellectuals because its foundation had been preceded by over ten years of theoretical and organizational activity, in which Lenin was one of the principal workers, especially in the theoretical field.

In order, therefore, to understand the leading role played by the party in October 1917 and subsequently, as well as the way in which this party coped with the problems that confronted it after October, it is essential to recall the principal stages in the struggle waged by Lenin and the Bolsheviks, the struggle that enabled the party to win the position it occupied in 1917.

*(a) The theoretical struggle for the primacy of
    revolutionary Marxism in the Russian
    labor movement*

It was in 1894 that Lenin, the future founder and leader of the Bolshevik Party, entered the theoretical struggle for the first time. He was then twenty-four years old and had been politically active for six years. He had already stated his position publicly on many occasions, especially against Narodism.[38]

At that time the struggle of Marxism against Narodism had been in progress for several years, mainly on Plekhanov's initiative. In 1883 he had founded, along with Vera Zasulich and others, the group called "Emancipation of Labor," and helped to make Marxism known in Russia both through his own writings and by translating several of the works of Marx and Engels.

In his essay of 1894, "What the 'Friends of the People' Are and How They Fight the Social Democrats,"[39] Lenin carried the critique of Narodism farther than Plekhanov had taken it, and at the same time showed the role that the peasantry, in alliance with the proletariat, could play in the coming Russian revolution.

Arrested in December 1895 and sent to Siberia (for his activity as organizer of the group he founded, called the "League of Struggle for the Emancipation of the Working Class"), then in exile abroad from 1900 onward, Lenin carried on the ideological struggle, first against Narodism and then against economism and "legal Marxism." The latter doctrine claimed that Russia should "go to school under capitalism," and that, given the country's low level of industrialization, the Russian proletariat should wage only economic struggles, while supporting the bourgeoisie's "democratic demands."

In the ideological fight against these conceptions, Lenin's decisive intervention, which opened the way for the Bolshevik movement to emerge, was *What Is to Be Done?*, published in 1902.[40] In this book he defined the principles that would govern the formation and working of the Bolshevik Party (and which in its essentials continue to govern the working of those Communist parties which have not forsaken revolutionary Marxism). He exposed the errors of economism and of the "cult of spontaneity" with which it is linked. Thus, he wrote: "*All* worship of the spontaneity of the working-class movement, all belittling of the role of 'the conscious element', of the role of Social-Democracy, *means quite independently of whether he who belittles that role desires it or not, a strengthening of the influence of bourgeois ideology upon the workers.*" [41]

The publication of *What Is to Be Done?* and the assimilation of its contents by the revolutionary militants signified a major defeat for economism and the cult of spontaneity in the form that these tendencies assumed in Russia at that time.

In 1904, with the publication of *One Step Forward, Two Steps Back*,[42] Lenin developed and perfected the organizational principles of the future Bolshevik Party. In this work he defined the relations between class and party, stressed the decisive role of organization, the necessity for a close link between the party and the masses, and for democratic centralism, discipline and unity (this unity and discipline are not to be confused with a factitious unanimity, since they presuppose an open discussion such as alone can enable Marxism to advance).

With the publication in July 1905 of *Two Tactics of Social Democracy in the Democratic Revolution*,[43] Lenin developed his fight against Menshevism, which then represented the chief form of opportunism in Russia. In this pamphlet Lenin stressed as the main question the participation of the peasantry in the democratic revolution, with the latter taking place under the leadership of the proletariat, and not, as the Mensheviks proposed, under that of the bourgeoisie. He wrote on this subject: *"The proletariat must carry the democratic revolution to completion, allying to itself the mass of the peasantry in order to crush the autocracy's resistance by force and paralyse the bourgeoisie's instability. The proletariat must accomplish the socialist revolution, allying to itself the mass of the semi-proletarian elements of the population, so as to crush the bourgeoisie's resistance by force and paralyse the instability of the peasantry and the petty bourgeoisie."* [44]

Two Tactics distinguishes clearly between two stages in the revolution, while indicating the possibility of a transition from the first stage to the second and defining the corresponding class alignments.[45] It shows the leading role to be played by the proletariat in relation to the masses, and the significance of the slogan of the revolutionary democratic dictatorship of the proletariat and the peasantry.

It was then that Lenin laid the foundations on the basis of which he was able, taking account of the changes in the situation introduced by the February Revolution, to formulate his theses of April 1917 (the theory of the transformation of the democratic revolution into the socialist revolution was present from that time onward). The Bolshevik Party was thus in a position to work out the essential features of the political line it was to follow after October.

In *Two Tactics* Lenin set forth the theory of the socialist revolution led by the proletariat exercising hegemony and playing a leading role. This theory broke with the conceptions, inherited from Lassalle, which were prevalent at that time in Western Europe and which saw the proletariat as the *only* revolutionary class.

The revolution of 1905 provided a striking confirmation of Lenin's analysis in *Two Tactics*, in particular as regards the role that could be played by mass political strikes at the beginning of an insurrection and during its course. The role of such strikes was confirmed afresh in 1917.

During the revolution of 1905 Lenin returned to Russia for a short time. He continued to lead the theoretical struggle that the Bolsheviks were waging on two fronts: against the "liquidators," who, under the blows of the reaction headed by Stolypin, were ready to wind up the Russian Social-Democratic Labor Party as a whole, and against the *otzovists* (those who advocated *recalling*[46] the Social-Democratic deputies from the 1906 Duma). In 1909 *otzovism* was formally condemned by the Bolsheviks.

At the same time he was fighting these battles, Lenin was also carrying on a struggle on the philosophical front, by writing *Materialism and Empirio-criticism*, which was published in 1909. This book attacked antimaterialist conceptions which are presented in the guise of Marxism, and which Lenin denounced as a "subtle falsification" of Marxism, a falsification characteristic of revisionism, "in political economy as in problems of tactics and in philosophy in general."

Thus, when the Bolshevik Party was formed in 1912 it

possessed a number of theoretical writings which constituted an ideological armament incomparably better than what was possessed at that time by the other working-class parties claiming to be Marxist.

The Bolshevik Party's ideological armament was subsequently completed, as far as the main problems were concerned, by the publication of two other works from Lenin's pen: *Imperialism, the Highest Stage of Capitalism*,[47] and *The State and Revolution*.[48]

The first of these gave a concrete analysis of the development of capitalism in that period and showed what its contradictions and characteristics were. This analysis guided a whole aspect of the activity of the Bolshevik Party, and of the Third International during the first years of its existence.

The second developed further the theory of the state and of the dictatorship of the proletariat, and made a radical break with certain Kautskyist conceptions that still prevailed in the Bolshevik Party.

Armed ideologically in this way, the Bolshevik Party was able to guide the Russian proletariat so as to enable it to win a series of victories of historic significance. It was inevitable, however, that where problems were concerned to which no previous experience was relevant, the theory at the disposal of the Bolshevik Party should show gaps. These caused the party to intervene in mistaken ways in the revolutionary process. Some mistakes were later corrected, but others were not, or the corrections made theoretically were not translated into corresponding practice, and this resulted in grave difficulties for the Russian Revolution.

(b) The political struggle for the building and development of the Bolshevik Party

The Bolshevik Party was constructed essentially on the basis of the principles and theories expounded by Lenin in his books, pamphlets, articles, speeches, letters, etc. These principles and theories were themselves developed in the day-to-day political and organizational activity of the Bolsheviks. Especially after 1905, the latter carried on intense political activity and accomplished a great deal of work in the field of organization: organization of the members themselves and of their newspapers and periodicals, and organization of the ever larger masses who were turning toward the revolutionary movement.

This organizational work was closely linked with the intensification of the contradictions in Russian society and with the economic and political class struggles which, with periods of advance and retreat, accompanied the deepening of the social contradictions. One important stage in these struggles was the rise of the mass movement which culminated in the revolution of 1905. Other large-scale struggles took place between 1912 and 1914. Finally, after the confusion caused by the war, there began, toward the end of 1016, a new upsurge which resulted in the great flare-ups of the February and October revolutions of 1917.

One of the characteristic features of the Bolshevik Party and of Lenin's activity was that theoretical analyses constantly accompanied mass struggles, sometimes preceding and guiding them, sometimes following them, so as to draw lessons from them. The development of Marxism thus did not take the form of a mere accretion of new ideas and theories, but of a dialectical development proceeding by breaks which, on the basis of what was taught by life itself, made it possible to reject and correct whatever had proved to be mistaken. This process of breaking and correcting, of dialectical development, made possible the formation of a revolutionary party without precedent in history, stoutly armed theoretically and closely linked with the masses. It was this party that enabled the Russian proletariat in 1917 to organize itself as the ruling class. This party, as it existed in October, was the outcome of an uninterrupted struggle, first to establish the party itself, and then, from 1912 onward, to accomplish its development and consolidation.

1. The struggle to build the party

The struggle to establish the Bolshevik Party was waged within the Russian Social Democratic Labor Party (RSDLP), and took the form of a struggle to transform it into a party guided by revolutionary Marxism.

The RSDLP held its first congress in March 1898, when Lenin was in Siberia. This was only an abortive first attempt. The congress adopted neither program nor rules, and no leadership came out of it capable of organizing a link-up between the Marxist groups which had existed in Russia for several years, and which, with few exceptions, were not involved in a practical way in the workers' movement for immediate demands. One of the first mergers between the Marxist groups and the labor movement had, however, been effected by Lenin, in 1895, with the formation in Petersburg of the League of Struggle for the Emancipation of the Working Class, which, as Lenin himself put it, was "the embryo of a revolutionary party based on the labour movement."

The real beginning of the formation of a revolutionary party came with the foundation in 1900 of the newspaper *Iskra* (The Spark), which was launched by Lenin jointly with Plekhanov's group. *Iskra* had correspondents all over Russia. Despite its illegal status it managed to circulate more or less regularly. It expounded essentially the same themes as those discussed in *What Is to Be Done?* and had decisive influence in the preparation of the Second Congress of the RSDLP.

This Second Congress was held in July 1903, first in Brussels and then in London. During its discussions the supporters of the *Iskra* line not only came into conflict with the opponents of this line, but were themselves divided on a number of questions. On the whole, however, the line upheld by Lenin secured the majority (*bolshinstvo* in Russian), from which came the term "Bolsheviks," used to describe the supporters of this line, and "Mensheviks" for the members of the minority (*menshinstvo*) who were opposed to it.

After the congress, however, Plekhanov and his group joined forces with the Mensheviks and took over *Iskra*. The Bolsheviks fought against the splitters by carrying on organizational work and by launching a paper of their own called *Vpered* (Forward) in January 1905. Thus, at the time when the mass struggle was about to experience a great upsurge, the

Bolsheviks had a new paper and had begun to form a Bolshevik faction in the RSDLP.

At the beginning of 1905 the Bolsheviks numbered about 8,000, but they did not aim to increase their numbers too rapidly. They were, and wished to be, militants who devoted their lives to work for the revolution. The Third Congress of the RSDLP took place in January 1905. As the Mensheviks had practically broken away, this was de facto a Bolshevik congress.

The upheaval of the revolution of 1905 made possible a considerable increase in the influence of the Bolsheviks. Legal activity became momentarily possible. Consequently, the Bolsheviks altered some of their forms of work, as they were to do again after February 1917. They kept their underground apparatus in being, of course, but their propaganda work was carried on practically openly. They recruited new members, and elected the leaders of their organization at various levels, something which had been almost impossible while the party had had to work underground.

The revolutionary upheaval was accompanied among some members, especially those who had joined recently, by an urge for unity aiming at fusion of the Bolshevik and Menshevik organizations. The Menshevik leaders, especially Martov (with whom Trotsky had been cooperating since the Second Congress), made some formal concessions, and as a result the Fourth Congress of the RSDLP was held in Stockholm in April 1906, reuniting the two organizations. At that stage the Bolsheviks had 14,000 members and the Mensheviks (whose conditions of membership were less demanding) 94,000. The Bolsheviks were in the minority in the new Central Committee elected by this congress.

This reunification remained a formality. The Bolsheviks fought to recover their majority in the RSDLP. They were organized as a faction and had a paper, *Proletary*, the organ of the St. Petersburg Party Committee, headed by Zinoviev.

At the Fifth Congress of the RSDLP, held in London in May 1907, the delegates had been elected by 77,000 members of the party in Russia (to whom were added the Polish and

Lettish delegates and those of the Jewish Bund). The Bolsheviks had been very active and their membership had been swelled by many new working-class cadres who had participated in the soviets of 1905, and so they were in the majority at the congress and in the new Central Committee, which included Lenin, Rykov, and Zinoviev. The congress adopted the principle of democratic centralism, which implies submission by the minority to decisions taken by the majority after a broad discussion.

The Bolsheviks continued to be organized as a faction, with their own elected leadership. The latter consisted of fifteen members, and was responsible for maintaining the unity of the Bolsheviks so that they could operate as a bloc applying a single tactical line within the party.

After the middle of 1907 the labor movement declined, and this decline became serious when Stolypin's repressions began. The membership of the RSDLP shrank (in 1910 it was less than 10,000) and divisions within it intensified, both between Mensheviks and Bolsheviks and among the Bolsheviks themselves. Lenin fought against a series of negative tendencies within Bolshevism, in particular against *otzovism* and the idealistic tendencies of Gorky and Bogdanov. The leaders of the Bolshevik faction had to take drastic measures.[49]

After this period of division, Lenin agreed to a new attempt at unity with the Mensheviks, which was made in January 1910. He expressed his views about this unity move in a letter to Maxim Gorky in April 1910:

There have been deep and serious factors leading to Party unity: in the ideological field—the need to purge Social-Democracy from liquidationism and otzovism; in the practical field—the terribly difficult plight of the Party and of all Social-Democratic work, and the coming to maturity of a new type of Social-Democratic worker. At the C.C. plenum . . . to these serious and deep-lying factors . . . were added . . . a mood of "conciliation in general" (without any clear notion with whom, for what, and how); hatred of the Bolshevik Centre for its implacable ideological struggle; squabbling on the part of the Mensheviks, who were spoiling for a fight, and as a result—an infant covered with blisters.[50]

In fact, the attempt at reunification failed. In face of the revival of the labor movement (once more, strikes and demonstrations took place on a very large scale), Lenin considered it necessary to consolidate the unity of the Bolsheviks, retain their press organs, and establish a school for cadres. This last was set up in France, at Longjumeau, in 1911, under the direction of Zinoviev. Many Bolshevik cadres were trained there, to return secretly to Russia.

In January 1912 the situation was ripe for taking a decisive step forward. The Bolsheviks could now form themselves into a separate party. This was done at a national conference held in Prague. The conference expelled the Mensheviks and thereafter functioned as a party congress. It adopted a minimum program including such immediate slogans as: a democratic republic, an eight-hour day, and the confiscation of all the land of the landlords. The congress decided that the Bolsheviks would take part in the electoral campaign for the Fourth State Duma, and elected a Central Committee in which, along with Lenin, sat Ordzhonikidze, Stalin, and Sverdlov. Thus the RSDLP (B), the Bolshevik Party, came into being.

2. *The struggle to develop the party*

The newborn party developed rapidly between 1912 and 1914, in keeping with the upsurge of working-class struggle that marked that period, but the outbreak of the First World War at first weakened it considerably, both on the plane of organization and on that of ideological unity. Repression, which was already severe, became unprecedentedly harsh during the war. In November 1914 the police raided a conference of the Central Committee's "Russian bureau" and of the Bolshevik Duma deputies; all the participants were imprisoned or sent to Siberia. Not until a year and a half later was it possible to form a new "Russian bureau," with Molotov and

Shlyapnikov among its members. Throughout the country the Bolshevik organizations, which had at first been seriously affected by the wave of repression, began to re-form, especially during 1916, but contact between them amounted to very little.

The war also brought new ideological divisions, and only gradually was a certain degree of unity created around the slogans put forward by Lenin in 1914: transform the imperialist war into civil war, defeat one's own government in the imperialist war. At the Zimmerwald Conference, where Bolsheviks and "internationalist" Social Democrats like Trotsky met, Lenin's slogans were rejected, and in Russia some of the imprisoned Bolshevik deputies, together with a few of the Bolshevik leaders who were at liberty, took a stand for "national unity for the duration." The party's confusion at the time of the February Revolution, when Stalin came out at first for support of the Provisional Government, was typical of the situation that prevailed. This was not put right (and then only with difficulty) until Lenin himself took a hand, especially after his return to Russia, when he set forth his "April Theses."

It remains true that, even during the most difficult years of repression, a certain number of groups and individuals who considered themselves Bolsheviks carried on activity in the factories, especially the war industries, and in the armies. In February 1917 the party had about 40,000 members.[51] Its influence was weaker than that of the Mensheviks (who continued to call their organization the RSDLP), but it developed rapidly and ended by greatly surpassing the Mensheviks in influence in the second half of 1917.

In April 1917 the party had 80,000 members, and by August 240,000. From a party of militants it was becoming a mass party. At the time of the October insurrection its membership stood at about 300,000.

Lenin was not, however, in favor of too rapid an increase in membership, which meant an influx of persons with little political experience, and at its Eighth Congress, in March 1919, the party still had only a little over 300,000 members.[52]

While, as regards discipline, the Bolshevik Party was usually united firmly around its leaders, that is, its Central Committee, this did not mean that its decisions were taken unanimously. In fact, as will be seen later, a number of divergences occurred. Lenin certainly played a preeminent part in it, but he was far from always able to make his view prevail, and he often came up against strong resistance when he considered it necessary to correct the line previously followed, or some analysis that had until then been accepted. The Bolshevik Party can be called "Leninist" only in the sense that it acknowledged Lenin as that one of its leaders who was best equipped theoretically, and the one to whom the party was most indebted for being what it was. The term "Leninist" is inappropriate if understood to mean that the Bolshevik Party rallied "spontaneously" or easily to the new directions indicated by Lenin at certain moments, or that Lenin's analyses were the "expression" of what the party or its leadership was already thinking, more or less.[53] This was far from being the case, and that fact needs to be kept in mind if one is to understand some of the problems that arose between 1918 and 1923.

Nor must it be overlooked that, in October 1917 and in the years immediately following, the Bolshevik Party still had extremely weak roots in many localities and factories, not to mention villages. In many localities there were no members capable of explaining on the spot what the party line was and transforming it into living reality or, what was at least equally important, bringing to the notice of the party leadership the concrete problems that arose and the way in which the party's policy was received by the masses. In this respect the Bolshevik Party was still young and inexperienced, and this is another consideration which helps us to understand the difficulties encountered in consolidating the proletarian dictatorship in Russia.

To this it should be added that the support given to the Bolshevik Party by the masses was based mainly on coincidence between the party's immediate political slogans and the desire of the masses for peace and of the peasants for land. A section of the masses, however, especially among the peasants, did not in the least support the socialist aims of the party. Accordingly, the latter, at least until the summer of 1918, did not consider that the situation was ripe for doing more than taking a few steps "in the direction of socialism." After the summer of 1918, though, as a result of the outbreak of civil war and the beginning of foreign intervention, the policy followed by the Bolshevik Party changed, and the revolution entered the period of "war communism." During this period the pressure of the exigencies of war, the place accorded to state centralization, and the significance attributed by the party to this centralization altered the conditions of the class struggle in Russia, together with the relations between classes. It is this process of transformation that must now be analyzed.

Notes

1. The proletariat, of course, possessed no "army" in the strict sense of the word.
2. In the lecture he gave in Zurich in early 1917 to a gathering of young Swiss workers, Lenin, speaking of the 1905 revolution, mentioned that, already at that time, "the revolutionary ferment among the people could not but spread to the armed forces," but that what was lacking was, "on the one hand, persistence and determination among the masses—they were too much afflicted with the malady of trustfulness—and, on the other, organisation of revolutionary Social-Democratic workers in military uniform—they lacked the ability to take the leadership into their own hands, march at the head of the revolutionary army and launch an offensive against the government." Lenin added this remark aimed against petty bourgeois antimilitarism: "It is not sufficient simply to denounce, revile and 'repudiate' militarism . . . it is foolish peacefully to refuse to perform military service. The task is to keep the revolutionary consciousness of the proletariat tense and train its best elements, not only in a general way, but concretely, so that when popular ferment reaches the highest pitch, they will put themselves at the head of the revolu-

tionary army" (*CW*, vol. 23, pp. 236–253). It was precisely this that happened in October 1917, which had not happened in 1905 or in February 1917, despite the rallying of the army to the revolution, for the latter was not on those occasions being led by the proletariat.

3. In July the Bolshevik Party succeeded in preventing a premature uprising by the proletariat of Petrograd. If this uprising had taken place at that time, at a moment when the revolutionary movement of the peasantry had hardly begun, it would have been crushed, and the chances of victory for a proletarian revolution would have been considerably reduced.

4. This term was employed by Lenin in one of his writings which is of fundamental importance for understanding the problems discussed here, namely, his address to the Eighth Congress of Soviets on December 30, 1920, published under the title "The Trade Unions, the Present Situation and Trotsky's Mistakes" (*CW*, vol. 32, pp. 19 ff.). Lenin said that the transition from capitalism to communism "cannot be achieved without the [hegemony] of that class which is the only class capitalism has trained for large-scale production" (ibid., p. 21). ("Hegemony" renders more accurately than "leadership" [the word used in the official English translation] the meaning of Lenin's own Russian word *glavenstvo*, which includes the idea of preponderance, primacy, supremacy.)

5. It is not possible here to detail the reasons why the leading role of the Bolshevik Party was limited in this way. A few observations may, however, be made.

(a) In any case, before a revolutionary proletarian party has political power at its disposal, such a party's leading role is necessarily subject to limitations. What changes, in accordance with concrete conditions, is the nature of these limitations, the classes in regard to which they are most felt, the forms they assume, etc.

(b) As regards the Bolshevik Party in 1917, the limitations on its leading role were all the greater because it was a relatively young party (the first conference of the Bolshevik groups had been held only thirteen years before, and Bolshevism was subject to the heavy ideological pressure of the petty bourgeois conceptions of the Second International, which it combated under very difficult conditions), and because it had to cope, with only a handful of experienced militants, with a situation which was evolving at prodigious speed: each week of the imperialist war was equivalent, for the masses, to several ordinary years.

(c) Finally, where the Bolshevik Party's activity among the peasants was concerned, this was restricted by the nature of the social relations existing in the Russian countryside, by the predominant influence which the petty bourgeois ideology of the SRs had acquired there, and by the party's own underestimation of the determining role that the revolutionary movement of the peasantry was to play.

It is easy to see how different the leading role played by the Chinese Communist Party could be in 1949—with twenty-eight years of activity behind it, including twenty years at the head of the Red bases and liberated areas, where it had been able to carry on mass activity in the political, military, ideological, and economic spheres.

6. "The Tasks of the Proletariat," in *CW*, vol. 24, p. 24.

7. "From a Publicist's Diary," in *CW*, vol. 25, pp. 298–300.

8. Lenin told the Petrograd Soviet of Workers and Soldiers that it was "in the end" that the new stage of the revolution would "lead to the victory of socialism" (*CW*, vol. 26, p. 239).

9. "The Immediate Tasks of the Soviet Government," in *CW*, vol. 27, pp. 243–244.

10. In China, where the ideological and political conditions in 1949 were more favorable to rapid development on socialist lines than they had been in the Russia of 1917, it was only from 1956 onward that such development was undertaken on a large scale.

11. See on this point, Lenin's remark in the first of his "Letters on Tactics," in *CW*, vol. 24, pp. 44–45.

12. *CW*, vol. 32, p. 20.

13. Ibid., p. 20.

14. Ibid., p. 24.

15. Ibid.

16. Ibid.

17. Lenin's report on the revision of the party program, presented to the Seventh Party Congress (March 8, 1918), in *CW*, vol. 27, pp. 132–133.

18. *CW*, vol. 32, p. 48.

19. It should perhaps be pointed out that in almost all countries the proletariat, in the strict sense, forms a minority, and that what was specific to Russia at this time—but is the case in all countries where little industrialization has taken place—was that, among

the nonproletarian masses, the predominant element consisted of peasants.

20. It is a historical fact that the peasant movement, left to itself, is incapable of mobilizing forces that are sufficiently united to win a decisive victory over the forces of a centralized state machine. Even in China it was the presence among the peasantry of the Chinese Communist Party and of working-class militants that enabled a real army to be formed. In the period of the first Red bases, Mao Tse-tung emphasized this point: "The existence of a regular Red Army of adequate strength is a necessary condition for the existence of Red political power. If we have local Red Guards only but no regular Red Army, then we cannot cope with the regular White forces, but only with the landlords' levies. Therefore, even when the masses of workers and peasants are active, it is definitely impossible to create an independent regime, let alone an independent regime which is durable and grows daily, unless we have regular forces of adequate strength" (Mao Tse-tung, *Selected Works,* vol. 1, p. 66). In Russia, between October 1917 and May 1918, the revolutionary peasant movement did not need a regular army to protect itself against counter-revolution, but the situation changed when the latter went over to the offensive with the backing of the imperialist powers. The peasant masses then appreciated their need of the Bolshevik Party's leadership (even when they disagreed with some particular measure taken by the party). For lack, however, of adequate roots in the countryside, the party's leading activity among the peasants was exercised only in a relatively superficial way, it assumed to only a slight extent the character of an ideological leadership, and it tended to weaken as soon as the need for it ceased to be immediately felt.

21. As will be seen, this tension was kept up because of mistakes committed by the Bolshevik Party in its policy toward the peasantry, especially during the period of "war communism."

22. See Lenin in *The State and Revolution,* in *CW,* vol. 25, especially p. 457, and in a number of his other writings, e.g., in *CW,* vol. 24, p. 85. Lenin was here only repeating the conclusions of Marx and Engels, who, after the experience of the Paris Commune, proposed that in the party program the word "state" be replaced by "commune" when the political power of the workers was referred to (Marx and Engels, *Selected Works,* vol. 3, p. 35).

23. It is necessary to speak here of "townsfolk" rather than "work-

ers" because all inhabitants of the towns had the right to vote, except "those who employ others for the sake of profit," "private businessmen," "those who live on income not arising from their own labour," and "monks and priests," as well as criminals and imbeciles. Intellectuals and members of the professions had votes, and also the specialists and office staff employed by the government. (See E. H. Carr, *The Bolshevik Revolution*, pp. 152–153.)

24. See Lenin's report to the Eighth Congress of the RCP(B) on the party program, in *CW*, vol. 29, especially pp. 184–185. It was in this report that Lenin summed up the constitutional measures taken regarding the franchise by saying: "Our constitution recognises the precedence of the proletariat in respect of the peasants and disfranchises the exploiters." He mentioned that the latter measure was determined by specific circumstances: "We do not at all regard the question of disfranchising the bourgeoisie from an absolute point of view, because it is theoretically quite conceivable that the dictatorship of the proletariat may suppress the bourgeoisie without disfranchising them" (ibid., p. 184).

25. The Cadet party (from the letters KD, standing for the Russian words for "Constitutional Democratic") was a typical bourgeois party. As Lenin put it: "the Cadet is a typical stockbroker. His ideal is to perpetuate bourgeois exploitation in respectable, civilised, parliamentary forms." ("An Attempt at Classification of the Political Parties of Russia," in *CW*, vol. 11, p. 229.) This description, made in 1906, was still valid in 1917.

26. Carr, *The Bolshevik Revolution*, vol. 1, p. 120.

27. See the statistical table in Anweiler, *Die Rätebewegung*, p. 324.

28. Lenin, *CW*, vol. 29, p. 183.

29. Stalin, *Works*, vol. 6, p. 362.

30. When, on October 26, Trotsky announced to the Congress of Soviets that the Provisional Government had been overthrown, in order that this congress might take power, he added: "We as a party considered it our task to create a real chance for the Congress of Soviets to take power into its hands . . . . To achieve this task, what was needed was a party which would wrest the power from the hands of the counter-revolutionaries and say to you: 'Here is the power and you are obliged to take it!' " (*Leon Trotsky Speaks*, p. 80).

31. On this point as on others the party was far from unanimous. Some of the Bolshevik leaders, like Zinoviev and Kamenev, who

had not been in favor of the launching of the October insurrection, were also against the preeminent position taken by the party in the period after it.

32. See Lenin's article, "The Political Situation," in *CW*, vol. 25, p. 177.

33. Ibid., pp. 177–178.

34. Ibid., p. 178.

35. The Cheka, or "Extraordinary Commission," was the first political police established by the Soviet power. It was derived from the Military Revolutionary Committee of the Petrograd Soviet. When this committee was dissolved, a decree of the Sovnarkom dated December 7, 1917, retained the "Extraordinary Commission."

36. "What Is to Be Done?" in *CW*, vol. 5, p. 369.

37. Ibid., p. 370. Lenin recalled in this connection that in his book on *The Peasants' War in Germany* Friedrich Engels stressed the importance of theory, mentioning that the Social Democrats, the organized political movement of the proletariat of that period, must wage a struggle not in two forms only, political and economic, but in three forms, "placing the theoretical struggle on a par with the first two." Engels even saw its "indifference to all theory" as "one of the main reasons why the English working-class movement crawls along so slowly," applying the same notion in the cases of France and Belgium as well (ibid., p. 371). See Engels, preface to *The Peasants' War in Germany*, pp. 32–33.

38. Narodism, the movement of the Narodniki, was a Russian revolutionary movement which came into being in the nineteenth century. It emphasized the potentialities of a peasant revolution which would be faithful to Russia's national traditions and take account of the country's peculiar features. The Narodniki tried to make propaganda among the peasants, and when this failed they turned to terrorism. In the twentieth century, the SRs were their de facto successors, but with a real base in the petty bourgeoisie and the rural intelligentsia.

39. Lenin, *CW*, vol. 1, pp. 129–332.

40. *CW*, vol. 5, pp. 347–529.

41. Ibid., pp. 382–383.

42. *CW*, vol. 7, pp. 203–425.

43. *CW*, vol. 9, pp. 15–140.

44. Ibid., p. 100.

45. In "Social-Democracy's Attitude Toward the Peasant Movement" (*CW*, vol. 9, pp. 230–239), Lenin returns to this question and writes (p. 237): "We stand for uninterrupted revolution."
46. *Otzovat'* is Russian for "to recall."
47. *CW*, vol. 22, pp. 185–304.
48. Ibid., vol. 25, pp. 381–492.
49. Lenin's correspondence enables us to follow the "non-public" part of the disputes among the Bolsheviks. See *CW*, vol. 34, especially the correspondence of the years 1907–1910.
50. Ibid., pp. 419–420.
51. See the estimated figures given in the *Bulshaya Sovyetskaya Entsiklopedia*, p. 531, and T. H. Rigby, *Communist Party Membership*, p. 61. According to earlier sources, the Bolshevik Party had only between 10,000 and 20,000 members in January 1917.
52. *Entsiklopedichesky slovar'*, vol. 1, p. 521.
53. The term "Leninist" used in relation to the party must not cause one to ignore, either, the fact that when the Bolshevik Party led the October Revolution it was a party very different from the one that Lenin had headed in 1914. On the one hand, many of the old militants had disappeared during the war and been replaced by new ones with a less solid training. On the other, at the level of the leading cadres, there had been a merger between the old Bolshevik leaders (who, moreover, were far from being all "Leninists," as their many disputes with Lenin showed) and leaders who had come from other revolutionary organizations. The latter, indeed, made up about half of the "Bolshevik" leaders in October 1917. See G. Haupt and J.-J. Marie, *Makers of the Russian Revolution*, p. 22.

Part 2
Soviet power and the transformation of class relations between 1917 and 1921

After October 1917 a process of extremely complex revolutionary changes began as a result of the proletariat having become the ruling class and of the struggle being waged by the masses under the leadership, or with the aid, of the proletariat and its party. As has been shown, the changes that then took place were twofold in character: democratic in the countryside, where the peasant masses were on the move, and socialist in the towns, where the working class was attacking domination of the means of production by their capitalist owners. These changes proceeded by stages and affected to varying degrees the different social relations and their component elements. They caused class relations to alter.

Before taking a general view of the principal changes undergone by economic and legal relations during the first years of the Russian Revolution, we must examine how relations altered between the proletariat and the bourgeoisie as a result of the establishment of the dictatorship of the proletariat.

1. The transformation of relations between the bourgeoisie and the proletariat under the dictatorship of the proletariat

The establishment of the dictatorship of the proletariat not only represented a profound upheaval in relations between classes, but changed the classes themselves. As Lenin wrote in *Economics and Politics in the Era of the Dictatorship of the Proletariat:*

> Classes cannot be abolished at one stroke. And classes still *remain* and *will remain* in the era of the dictatorship of the proletariat. The dictatorship will become unnecessary when classes disappear. Without the dictatorship of the proletariat they will not disappear. Classes have remained, but in the era of the dictatorship of the proletariat *every* class has undergone a change, and the relations between the classes have also changed. The class struggle does not disappear under the dictatorship of the proletariat; it merely assumes different forms.[1]

If classes remained, even though changed and with changed interrelations, this was because the former social relations and, in particular, capitalist production relations were not "abolished" but only changed by the dictatorship of the proletariat.

In the same article, Lenin said that during the period of transition between capitalism and communism a struggle would be fought out between the former, "which has been defeated but not destroyed," and the latter, "which has been born but is still very feeble."[2]

The existence of "defeated" capitalism obviously implies also that the bourgeoisie and the proletariat still exist: these two classes continue to confront each other, even though their social conditions of existence have been greatly altered.

The primary and basic change in the conditions of existence

of these classes is bound up with the fact that the bourgeoisie has lost power. This means, concretely, that the bourgeoisie no longer dominates the old machinery of politics and administration, which has been smashed, broken up, and more or less completely replaced by apparatuses and organizations linked with the revolutionary masses and led by the proletariat and its vanguard, the proletarian party, a class apparatus which thereafter plays the dominant role. Concretely, this means also that the capitalists and landlords have, in the main, lost their power to "dispose freely" of the means of production. In industry, the activity of factory committees, workers' control, expropriations, etc., profoundly upset the conditions governing use of the chief means of production, which are no longer directly subject to the requirements of the process of valorization of capital. However, these requirements are not "abolished" but only transformed by the exercise of the dictatorship of the proletariat.

If the bourgeoisie and the proletariat continue their struggle under new conditions, this is precisely because the bourgeois social relations which underlie the existence and practices of these classes have not been "abolished" but only transformed. Although the social reproduction process is no longer dominated by the bourgeoisie, the capitalist character of this process is at first only partially modified by the dictatorship of the proletariat: the basic structure of this process has not yet really been broken. In each unit of production the producers continue to be involved in the same type of division of labor, which implies the separation of mental from manual work and that of administrative tasks from performance tasks. What is new is that those who direct the immediate process of production must carry out their role under control by the proletariat, the workers' mass organizations, and the new machinery of the proletarian state and of the proletarian party.

Nationalization of the means of production by a proletarian state results first and foremost in the creation of *politico-juridical conditions favorable to the socialist transformation of production relations* and, to the *socialization* of the means of production but *it is not to be identified with this transformation.*

We know that production relations are determined relations into which "men inevitably enter" and which are "independent of their will." People form these relations among themselves in the course of what Marx calls "the social production of their existence."[3] These relations are imposed upon the agents of production by the structure of the processes of production and circulation, that is, by the real process of social production. This structure is itself embodied in the division of labor and in the instruments of labor (which Marx calls the "indicators of social conditions"). Of course, the specific forms assumed by the division of labor and the instruments of labor do not drop from heaven, but are the effect of previous class struggles and of the character that these struggles have imposed upon the development of the productive forces. In every age, these class struggles (which always take place on determined *material foundations*) make the domination of the production process and the distribution of the labor force among different tasks "the basis of special social functions performed within the production relations by certain of their agents, as opposed to the direct producers."[4]

The embodiment of the production relations in the division of labor and in the instruments of labor signifies that it is not enough for a new class to acquire political domination over the other classes for it to transform the existing production relations straight away. It can do this only by breaking up and restructuring, that is, by "revolutionizing," the real production process.

The capitalist character of the production relations that exist on the morrow of the establishment of proletarian power is obviously also embedded in the very structure of the production process.

Thus, when it establishes its rule and nationalizes some factories, the proletariat acquires the possibility—but only the possibility—of revolutionizing the real process of production and of causing new production relations to appear, with a new social division of labor and new productive forces. Insofar as this task has not yet been accomplished, the former capitalist production relations continue, together with the forms of representation and the ideological forms in which these relations appear. Insofar as this task is in course of being accomplished, the former relations are partly transformed, the socialist transition is under way, and it is possible to speak of a "socialist society."

Socialism thus does not mean—it is particularly necessary to stress this in view of the confusion caused by ideological discourses about the "socialist mode of production"—the "abolition" of capitalist production relations. It means—given certain definite ideological and political conditions that hardly existed in the Russia of 1918–1922—the transformation of these relations, their destruction and reconstruction of *transitional* relations which can be analyzed as a combination of capitalist elements and socialist or communist elements. The advance toward socialism means the growing domination of the latter over the former, the "dying out" of the capitalist elements and the consolidation of the increasingly dominant socialist elements.

This advance requires a long historical period: it corresponds to a revolutionization of the conditions of production which is itself the result of a protracted class struggle, guided by a correct political line, that is, a line that determines, at each stage, objectives which make possible an actual socialist transformation of the production relations. The elaboration of such a line presupposes the existence of a proletarian party armed with revolutionary theory and competent to play its leading role. This role is vital, for it is not the party or the state of the dictatorship of the proletariat that can "directly bring about" a socialist transformation of the production relations, but only the struggle waged by the classes that were formerly dominated and exploited. Such a struggle alone, by revolutionizing the processes of production and social relations as a whole, can put an end to what were formerly the "special functions" fulfilled by the dominant classes.

As long as capitalist relations have been transformed only partially, the *forms* in which these relations manifest themselves continue to be reproduced, so that money, prices, wages, profit, etc., continue to exist and cannot be "abolished" by mere decrees. Only the socialist transformation of the relations of production can bring about the withering away of these forms—a transformation which implies that the socialization of production results increasingly from the coordinated action of the workers, who become a "collective laborer" on the social scale. The process of constituting this "collective laborer" is a long-term one, passing through *stages* and calling for the revolutionization of social relations as a whole—economic, ideological, and political—for the different aspects of this revolutionization are mutually dependent in a complex way.

As long as bourgeois elements persist in the various social relations, then, until the coming of communism, there is room for the existence of a proletariat and a bourgeoisie, and it remains possible for the latter—if the proletarian class struggle fails to follow a correct line—to develop the bourgeois elements in social relations, consolidate the bourgeois aspects of the ideological and political machinery, and ultimately restore capitalism (in the specific forms dictated by those of the previously transformed social relations which the bourgeoisie cannot destroy).

It is in particular because the development of state ownership, even under the dictatorship of the proletariat, leaves in being elements of capitalist relations which are only partly modified, that *the expropriation of the bourgeoisie is not equivalent to its disappearance.* As long as capitalist elements persist in the production relations, there also persists the possibility of *capitalist functions,* and the bourgeoisie can continue to exist in a modified form through the state apparatus and assume the form of a *state bourgeoisie.*

This becomes clearer in the light of Lenin's definition of social classes in his pamphlet *A Great Beginning:* "Classes are large groups of people differing from each other by the place they occupy in a historically determined system of social production, by their relation (in most cases fixed and formulated by law) to the means of production, by their role in the social organisation of labour, and, consequently, by the dimensions of the share of social wealth of which they dispose and the mode of acquiring it."[5]

This passage brings out some vital points: (1) Relations of distribution are only a *consequence* of relations of production (of the place occupied in production and in relation to the means of production.) Therefore, analysis of relations of distribution (of the "mode of acquiring" a certain share of social wealth, and of the dimensions of this share) can help reveal the nature of the production relations and the class relations that these determine, but cannot, by itself, give knowledge of either.

(2) The "fixing" by law of certain relations to the means of production may "formulate" these relations, but the latter exist independently of the "law." Indeed, the law may serve to disguise real relations that differ from those which it "formulates." Thus, in capitalist society, the means of production which are "state owned" belong in reality to the capitalist class: they are a part of the latter's "collective" capital.

(3) Classes are distinguished both by the relations of their members to the means of production (and so by the place occupied by these members) and by the "role" which they play in the "social organization of labor."

The distinction between the "place occupied" by the agents of production and their "role"—and consequently also the *class practices* in which they engage—assumes very special importance when we come to analyze a social formation in which the proletariat is in power. The existence of the dictatorship of the proletariat modifies differentially the place and role of both the bourgeoisie and the proletariat, and the excercise of this dictatorship makes it possible to modify further this place, this role, and the system of dominant social practices. Thus, the initial change which establishes the proletarian power but leaves in being various forms of separation between the proletariat and the means of production, can be followed by other changes. If the class struggle is waged correctly, the proletariat, by revolutionizing social relations, gradually takes over the management of the economy and of the units of production, guidance of transformations in the system of productive forces, the direction of the educational apparatus, and so on.

These changes result from revolutionary struggles which enable the proletariat to become less and less a proletariat—to abolish itself as a proletariat by appropriating all the social forces from which the capitalist mode of production had separated it. During this process of revolutionary transformation, all the "places" and roles that corresponded to those of the bourgeoisie are transformed, and the agents of production and reproduction occupying those places and playing these roles also become less and less a bourgeoisie—although constantly liable to develop, in these places and roles, bourgeois social practices which may cause the proletariat to lose the positions it has already won.

All those who, in the system of social production and reproduction, occupy a place corresponding to that of the bourgeoisie, and who in that system develop *bourgeois social practices* despite the existence of the dictatorship of the proletariat, constitute a bourgeoisie.

After the October Revolution and in the early 1920s in Russia the bourgeoisie was widely represented in the state's economic apparatus; it occupied leading positions in the units of production and in the management of the economy as a whole, and also in the administrative and educational machinery. Historically, this situation was due to the class origin of the majority of those who staffed these organizations, but, over and above this origin, what was decisive was the bourgeois practices of those who occupied the leading positions, and the actual structure of the state machine. These practices and this structure tended to consolidate capitalist relations, and therefore also the existence of a bourgeoisie which took the form of a state bourgeoisie.

This situation was obviously bound up with the stage the Russian Revolution had reached at that time. The revolution was only beginning to carry out some of its socialist tasks. For these tasks to go on being carried out, it was necessary that there should be revolutionary action by the proletariat organized as the dominant class. This required the elaboration and application of a revolutionary political line, and, therefore, the presence of a leading proletarian party.

In order to analyze the transformations that occurred in the place and role of the different classes in the period immediately after October 1917, we must distinguish between the effects of the revolutionary process in the towns and in the countryside.

Notes

1. *CW*, vol. 30, pp. 114–115.
2. Ibid., p. 107.
3. *Contribution to the Critique of Political Economy*, p. 20.
4. *Capital*, vol. III, p. 857.
5. *CW*, vol. 29, p. 421.

2. The transformation of class relations in the towns

The transformation of class relations in the towns resulted first from the leadership of the workers' class struggles by the Bolshevik Party, and then, when the new state machine had been set up, from the operation of this machine as well.

Fundamentally, the changes carried through between October 1917 and the beginning of 1923 resulted in eliminating the bourgeoisie (and the landlords) *from the dominant positions they had previously occupied,* but this elimination as we have seen, was not, and could not be, total and immediate. Although the *private* bourgeoisie was largely eliminated, this period also saw the formation of a state bourgeoisie which was mainly determined by the small extent to which the social process of production and reproduction had been transformed, this being due to the actual conditions of the class struggle, the degree of urgency of the different tasks which the proletariat had to carry out, and the way in which the Bolshevik Party analyzed and handled the contradictions.

The changes affecting the various social classes during this period were numerous, and only the main ones can be examined here. I shall first examine the changes which occurred immediately after the establishment of the proletarian power, and then those which took place in subsequent years.

I. The immediate measures affecting industry and trade

In the period immediately following the establishment of Soviet power there was no question, either for the working-

143

class masses or for the Bolshevik Party, of "introducing socialism." Their chief preoccupation was the consolidation of proletarian power by effecting such changes as would make it possible to "gain time," by developing a "state capitalism" that would permit certain steps to be taken toward socialism, although these transformations were not as yet socialist in character.

Changes of this sort took concrete form in certain decisive measures concerning industry and trade. Of these, the most important were the decree on workers' control, published on November 19, 1917, the decree on the formation of the Supreme Council of National Economy (VSNKh), the decrees on the nationalization of the banks (December 28), the decree on consumers' organizations, placing consumers' cooperatives under the control of the soviets (April 16), and the decree on the monopoly of foreign trade (April 23).

(a) Expropriations

While taking these measures, the Soviet government also decided to expropriate a certain number of enterprises, mainly industrial or commercial. However, these expropriations in no way constituted the principal aspect of the policy then being followed, which was characterized by Lenin as "state capitalism."

Between October 1917 and May 1918, the Bolshevik Party's policy was not at all aimed at extending nationalizations and expropriations. In contrast to the illusions and demands of the "left Communists," among whom Bukharin was prominent, the majority of the party leaders understood very well that multiplying nationalizations and expropriations does not bring one closer to socialism in the absence of the political and ideological conditions which can enable these nationalizations to bring about effective socialization. Lenin explained this when he wrote: "One may or may not be determined on the question of nationalisation or confiscation, but the whole point is that even the greatest possible 'determination' in the world is not enough to pass *from* nationalisation and confiscation to socialisation."[1] A few lines farther on, he pointed out that "the difference between socialisation and simple confiscation is that confiscation can be carried out by 'determination' alone, without the ability to calculate and distribute properly, *whereas socialisation cannot be brought about without this ability.*"[2]

This "ability"—a necessary condition for the socialization of the means of production—was one that the proletariat and its party had to acquire in order to utilize the means of production in a coordinated way on the social scale. The expropriations were aimed, above all, at weakening the bourgeoisie economically and politically and smashing its attempts at sabotage. They were measures of class struggle.

From the spring of 1918 onward, the Soviet power was increasingly compelled, as a result both of pressure from the workers and of the hostility of the industrial capitalists, to employ this weapon on a scale that did not correspond to existing capacity to organize production on new foundations. This entailed a growing degree of disorganization in industry. The establishment, side by side, of workers' control and the VSNKh seemed at the time to provide the two means by which the Soviet power could acquire the "ability" that was indispensable for the coordinated social utilization of the means of production.

(b) Workers' control

Workers' control was effected by a set of measures aimed at enabling the working class to supervise the way in which the means of production were being employed, through organs emanating from the working class and intended to function both in the factories still belonging to private capital and in those which had been expropriated.

The role which Lenin in 1918 attributed to workers' control was essentially that of a preliminary measure aimed at preparing the working class to advance toward socialism. In *The Immediate Tasks of the Soviet Government* he wrote: "Until workers' control has become a fact . . . . it will be impossible to pass . . . to the second step towards socialism, i.e., to pass on to workers' regulation of production."[3]

The actual development of the class struggle during 1917 had led to the problem of workers' control arising in the form of a development of the factory committee movement. This movement had boomed between February and October, and the Bolshevik Party had given it resolute support.

In the weeks following the October insurrection, the Bolshevik Party strove to transform the dispersed and anarchical activity of hundreds and thousands of factory committees into a coordinated system of workers' control, in conformity with the needs of a proletarian policy. This was no easy task, for as the number of factory committees grew, each tended to multiply the prerogatives it claimed and to treat each factory as an independent unit of production, the collective property of its own workers, deciding for itself what should be produced, and to whom it should be sold and at what price—all this when the social domination of the working class over the means of production required that the atomized and contradictory powers of the factory committees be subordinated to a common political end.

Social coordination of production was particularly essential in industry, where each unit of production carried out only a limited number of transformation processes, constituting merely one link in a total production process that was highly socialized. The survival of Soviet industry, and the struggle against market forces and against the predominance of the separate interests of the different factories, therefore called for a certain minimum of prior coordination of the activities of the various production units. In the absence of such a priori intervention, coordination takes place a posteriori, somehow or other, through the market, or else results from the relation of forces between different branches of industry or different factories. In practice, it is possible that it may not even take place at all, in which case production becomes increasingly paralyzed. And this is what actually happened during the winter of 1917–1918.

The Bolshevik Party consequently sought to solve the problem of coordinating the activities of the factory committees by introducing "workers' control." This was to function on a wider scale than that of the individual factory committee, substituting, for the divided and fragmentary (and therefore illusory) "authority" exercised by the collectives of the separate factories, a coordinated and unified class control.

The conditions existing immediately after October did not make it easy to go over to a unified form of control. The workers were not spontaneously convinced of the need for the powers of their factory committees to be limited by subordination to an outside authority. In the eyes of many of them, the establishment of more or less centralized control looked like a "confiscation" of the power which they had just succeeded in wresting from the bourgeoisie and which they wished to retain at the level of their own factory. This way of looking at the matter was encouraged by the opponents of the dictatorship of the proletariat, especially by the Mensheviks, who incited the trade-union organizations in which they had influence to defend the independence of the factory committees and even of the railroad "station committees."

Before the October Revolution Lenin had already foreseen the need for workers' control on a national scale, and the difficulty there would be in implementing it. For example, in *Can the Bolsheviks Retain State Power?* he had written: "The chief difficulty facing the proletarian revolution is the establishment on a countrywide scale of the most precise and most conscientious accounting and control, of *workers' control* of the production and distribution of goods."[4]

Transition to workers' control in this sense, and abandonment of the type of "decentralized" and anarchical control favored by the factory committees, came up against especially strong resistance from the bourgeois and petty bourgeois ideology, still deeply rooted in the masses, of "everyone for himself," of "individual enterprise egoism," and of an abstract notion of "freedom." In this connection Lenin wrote: "The petty-bourgeoisie oppose every kind of state interference, accounting and control, whether it be state capitalist or state socialist."[5]

Despite the political influence exercised by the Bolshevik Party over the most militant sections of the workers, its ideological influence and its foothold in the units of production were still very slight in relation to the task of persuasion that was required in order to transform the factory committees into organs of workers' control. In the period immediately after October this transformation faced great difficulties which were aggravated by the reluctance shown even by some Bolsheviks regarding the restrictions imposed by "countrywide" workers' control on the powers of the factory committees. However, the most serious resistance encountered was due to the influence of the Mensheviks and of some anarchist tendencies among a section of the masses, which they used to obstruct Bolshevik policy as much as possible.

This resistance and reluctance account for the delay that occurred in adopting decisions concerning workers' control, and also for the magnitude of the controversy aroused by these decisions. Here are some facts by way of illustration.

Originally it had been expected that the Second Congress of Soviets would proclaim the establishment of workers' control at its session held on the very day following the insurrection. The decrees on workers' control and on land were to have been promulgated simultaneously. However, this did not happen, and the congress broke up without adopting any measure concerned with workers' control. Again, though *Pravda* of November 3 published a draft decree on the subject, which Lenin had prepared, the decree itself was not immediately submitted to the organs of government (nor was it ever submitted to them in its original form). Finally, it was only on November 14 that a revised version of Lenin's draft was considered by the VTsIK and adopted with a few amendments.

The decree contained the principal provisions of Lenin's draft,[6] in particular as regards the binding character of the decisions taken by the workers' representatives and the responsibility toward the state of these representatives and of the factory owners. Workers' control was made part of the soviet system, factory committees and councils were placed under the supervision of higher bodies which functioned at the level of the locality, province, or region, and an *All-Russia*

Council of Workers' Control, was to head this entire apparatus.

One of the problems the decree had to solve was that of the respective places to be occupied, in the organization of workers' control, by the factory committees and by the trade-union apparatus. This problem was not unimportant, for the factory committees emanated directly from the workers in each enterprise, whereas the trade unions (which were far from embracing all the workers) had a centralized structure which made them especially well-adapted for helping in the establishment of a centralized form of control, but which also meant that they were not under direct influence from the rank and file. The decree dealt with the problem by giving an important place to the trade unions in the organization of workers' control, but this solution caused discontent among some workers who saw it as a kind of tutelage established over them. On the other hand, some of the Bolsheviks in the trade union movement thought that the decree did not go far enough. They considered that the problem had not been settled with sufficient sharpness in favor of the trade unions, and that the decree tended to perpetuate the division of the enterprises into independent units. Thus, for example, Lozovsky, the trade unions' spokesman in the VTsIK, said: "It is necessary to make an absolutely clear and categorical reservation that the workers in each enterprise should not get the impression that the enterprise belongs to them."[7]

At the beginning of 1918 the wording of the November 1917 decree was more or less repeated in the "Declaration of Rights of the Working and Exploited People." This declaration was drafted by Lenin and adopted on January 3 by the VTsIK. It stated that workers' control was confirmed "as a first step towards the complete conversion of the factories, mines, railways and other means of production and transport into the property of the workers' and peasants' state."[8]

This document shows that the Bolshevik Party then accepted that state ownership of the means of production cannot be social ownership until control by the workers themselves of the factories, mines, railways, etc., has been realized.

Shortly before drafting it, Lenin had pointed out that "the accounting and control essential for the transition to socialism can be exercised only by the people."[9]

In March-April 1918 Lenin was to stress again, and more than once (especially in *The Immediate Tasks of the Soviet Government*), that the control by the masses which he had in mind was something different from what the factory committees tended toward in seeking to run their enterprises "each for itself." Workers' control, he said, meant control by the Soviet state, not a multitude of scattered controls. A form of control which would take care of the interests of all would be possible, Lenin added, "only if the proletariat and the poor peasants display sufficient class-consciousness, devotion to principle, self-sacrifice and perseverance"; only then would "the victory of the socialist revolution be assured."[10]

As a result of the various decisions, the uncontrolled initiatives that might be taken at the level of each separate unit of production were, in principle, considerably reduced. To the extent that these decisions were actually applied, the factory committees practically lost their independence: ceasing to possess real powers of their own, they were integrated into the system of central workers' control.

In all the enterprises of a certain size (described as those "of national importance"), the factory committees were made responsible to the state for "the maintenance of the strictest order and discipline and for the protection of property."[11] This responsibility was laid upon the elected representatives of the workers and staff appointed to exercise workers' control.

These measures aroused the discontent of the anarchists and anarcho-syndicalists, who wanted to turn the factory committees into independent committees of management, perhaps organized in a federation, but without any responsibility to the state. Those opposed to the measures said, in particular, that the workers' control regulations extended so far the concept of an enterprise "of national importance" that application of the official rules for workers' control meant the complete subjection of the factory committees to an authority external to themselves.

This authority was made up of the various organs to which the basic organizations of workers' control (principally the former factory committees) were subordinated, namely, the regional councils and the All-Russia Council of Workers' Control. The representatives of the basic organizations of workers' control were in a minority in these bodies. Thus, in the All-Russia Council of Workers' Control there were only five representatives appointed by the All-Russia Council of Factory Committees, whereas there were five representatives of the VTsIK, five from the Central Trade-Union Council, five from the Association of Engineers and Technicians, two from the Association of Agronomists, two from the Petrograd Trade-Union Council, one representative of each trade union with fewer than 100,000 members, and two representatives of each union with more than that number.[12] In the higher organs of workers' control, the representatives of the basic organizations were thus outnumbered by the representatives of the trade unions.

Even transformed in this way, the structure of workers' control proved incapable of ensuring the coordination required by large-scale industrial production. And Russia was in a situation where supplies for the towns and the villages (and soon, for the front as well) made it indispensable that production should be regular and, above all, as closely as possible in accordance with needs which could only be estimated on the basis of an overall view of the situation.

The Bolshevik Party decided to "reinforce" the system of workers' control by establishing other forms of coordination and direction of production as well. The most important of these was the VSNKh.

In fact, in the conditions that developed when the civil war began and when the slogan "Everything for the Front!" prevailed, it was these forms of coordination and direction that took precedence over workers' control.[13] The latter ended by disintegrating, along with the old factory committees.

This breakup seems to have been connected with the shortage in the factories of working-class organizers capable of tackling factory problems. In turn, the lack of working-class organizations at the base is to be seen in relation to the relative numerical weakness of the Bolshevik Party and the absorption (which was doubtless unavoidable) of a growing proportion of the most active workers in organizational tasks in the party, the state machine, and, especially, the army. The lack of any systematic impulsion from the party, and the increasing indifference shown by the workers to the factory committees, also played their part. Eventually, workers' control, as conceived in the first months of the Soviet regime, fell asleep, never to awake. It was on other foundations that the direction and coordination of industrial production came to be ensured.

(c) The VSNKh and the coordination of the production processes

The first mention of the forthcoming establishment of a Supreme Economic Council was made on November 17—three days after the publication of the decree on workers' control. This mention appeared in the decree dissolving the Economic Council, and the Chief Economic Committee which had been set up by the Provisional Government: these bodies were to be replaced by a new Economic Council. Bukharin was given the task of preparing the necessary documents, and the decree he drafted was published on December 5.[14]

The task assigned to the "Supreme Economic Council" (or VSNKh, using the Russian initials of the title) was to "organize the economic activity of the nation and the financial resources of the Government," and to "direct to a uniform end the activities of all the existing economic authorities, central and local," including those of the All-Russia Council of Workers' Control. It actually duplicated the functions of the latter, which also included ensuring "the planned regulation of the national economy." Furthermore, the decree integrated workers' control into the VSNKh, for it stipulated that the latter should include the members of the All-Russia Council of

Workers' Control, and this body was subordinated to the VSNKh.

The subordination of workers' control to the system of economic councils prepared the way for its disappearance. Lenin himself, reviewing the decisions taken during the first months of Soviet power, noted that, after beginning with workers' control, they had advanced to the creation of the Supreme Economic Council.[15]

Some of the concrete arrangements concerning the organization of the VSNKh and the relations it was to maintain with the units of production were strongly marked by the specific conditions of the period in which the VSNKh was set up. These conditions favored administrative centralization rather than democratic centralism. However, the arrangements made under those conditions were, in the main, retained in the subsequent period, and were found in the organization of the *State Planning Commission*, or *Gosplan*, formed on February 22, 1921 (as a development of the All-Russia Electrification Commission, or *Goelro*, established on February 21, 1920). The Gosplan was at first only a minor "technical organ," with the task of carrying out studies with a view to preparing a plan of economic development. Only much later, in February 1925, did the Gosplan, having been equipped with "decentralized" organs, replace to some extent the VSNKh.[16]

During the years 1918–1923, the system of economic councils, of which the VSNKh was the supreme body, became the instrument for the centralization and centralized management of industry. The powers conferred on the VSNKh were considerable: it could confiscate, acquire, or sequester any enterprise or any branch of production or business, and was responsible for directing the work of all the economic organs and for preparing laws and decrees concerning the economy, preparatory to submitting these to the Council of People's Commissars. It was placed directly under the latter.

The VSNKh was made up chiefly of representatives of the various people's commissariats, assisted by experts who were appointed for their technical ability. The VSNKh had a twofold structure, consisting of central organs, the *glavki* (directing the various branches of industry) and regional organs, the local economic councils *(sovnarkhozy)*.

Technically, the decree setting up the VSNKh and the other measures subsequently introduced were to ensure, in principle, the coordination by the state of the work of the various factories. At the same time, these measures conferred a great deal of authority on the stratum of engineers, specialists, and technicians, who occupied dominant positions in the VSNKh and the organs attached to it. By the decree, this "bourgeois section of the population" [17] was restored to positions of leadership, though it held them by virtue of decisions taken by the Soviet power which could, in principle, take away its authority at any moment.

The role played by this "bourgeois section" was enhanced by the economic disorganization against which the Soviet power had to fight in order to prevent the collapse of the proletarian dictatorship. The situation was described in a resolution of the Fourth All-Russia Congress of Soviets (March 1918), which placed on the agenda "a relentless struggle with the chaos, disorganisation and disintegration which are historically inevitable as the consequence of a devastating war, but are at the same time the primary obstacle to the final victory of socialism and the reinforcement of the foundations of socialist society." A congress resolution called for "the creation everywhere and in all directions of strong, solid organisations covering as far as possible all production and all distribution of goods." [18]

In keeping with this resolution, the leadership of VSNKh was recast and Bukharin and some other "left Communists" were removed. Among the new heads of the council were Milyutin, an old Bolshevik, and Larin, a former Menshevik who favored centralized state control of industry and planning.

A system of economic and political relations thus came into being which formed one aspect of what Lenin called "state capitalism," a system which, he said, was not feared by the workers because they knew that it was "the organisers . . . of

really large-scale and giant enterprises, trusts," men belonging to the capitalist class, who had to be hired, "as technicians," and whose services could be obtained only in return
"for higher salaries."[19]

Lenin defended this view in a particularly clear-cut way in
The Immediate Tasks of the Soviet Government, in which he
explained that the Soviet state's recruitment of "bourgeois
specialists" was a "compromise" with the bourgeoisie, and
one the magnitude of which went beyond what had originally
been foreseen, but which had been made necessary by the fact
that the workers' councils, the soviets, and the factory committees had not proved able to organize production on a national
scale: "Had the proletariat acting through the Soviet government *managed* [my emphasis—C. B.] to organise accounting
and control on a national scale, or at least laid the foundation
for such control, it would not have been necessary to make
such compromises."[20]

(d) The appointment of heads of units of production and the question of one-man management

One of the first decisions taken by the VSNKh related to the
conditions governing the management of the units of production and the procedure for appointing heads of enterprises
which had been expropriated. A decree dated March 3, 1918
provided that each "chief directorate" (*glavk*) was responsible
for appointing, in the enterprises within its field, a commissar
representing the government, and two managers (one technical, the other administrative). Only decisions taken by the
administrative manager could be challenged by the factory
committees or whatever bodies took their place: the technical
manager was accountable solely to the chief directorate of the
industry to which the enterprise belonged. In nationalized
enterprises the decisions of the factory or workshop committees must be submitted for approval to an administrative economic council in which the workers (including office workers)
were not to have a majority.[21] The managers appointed by the

glavki were usually engineers and former managers, and among them were former capitalists.

Without anticipating my account of the ideological conflicts which arose within the Bolshevik Party, some brief pointers must be given at this stage as to the attitudes of certain of the Bolshevik leaders to the appointment of factory managers by a central administrative authority. Such appointments were sharply criticized not only by some of the Bolshevik trade-union leaders but also by those who were known as "left Communists." The latter, who included Bukharin, were very active in the spring of 1918 (their group broke up later). They opposed the appointment of factory managers, the power given to these managers, and the relatively high salaries paid to them. For the "left Communists" all this was a violation of the principle proclaimed in the "April Theses," according to which officials ought not to receive a salary higher than the average worker's wage, and were to be both elected and subject to recall by their electors.

Lenin did not, of course, deny that the decree on factory management contradicted some of the principles set forth in his "April Theses," but he stressed that it was a matter of *provisional measures* imposed by the necessity of getting the enterprises to work and not letting this task be hindered by "the practice of a lily-livered proletarian government." [22]

For Lenin these measures were "a step backward," temporary but unavoidable in the existing circumstances, which, he said did not yet allow socialism to advance "in its own way . . . by *Soviet* methods." [23] The "step backward" of which Lenin spoke was defined by him as a strengthening of *capital* (even though there was no reestablishment of legal ownership of the nationalized enterprises by the capitalists), *"for capital is not a sum of money but a definite social relation."* [24] Lenin's principled attitude was thus clear, and so it is all the more important to note that the "step backward" and the strengthening of capitalist relations were not put right later on by the adoption of measures conforming with "Soviet methods" [25] and the "April Theses."

In his article, already quoted, on " 'Left-Wing' Childish-

ness," published in May 1918, Lenin returned to the question
of the appointment of factory managers and to the fact that
sometimes former capitalists were given these posts:

> "Management" is entrusted by the Soviet power to capitalists
> not as capitalists but as technicians or organisers, for higher
> salaries. And the workers know very well that ninety-nine per
> cent of the organisers and first-class technicians of really large-
> scale and giant enterprises, trusts or other establishments belong
> to the capitalist class. But it is precisely these people whom we,
> the proletarian party, must appoint to "manage" the labour pro-
> cess and the organisation of production for there are *no* other
> people who have practical experience in this matter . . . The
> workers . . . are not afraid of large-scale "state capitalism," they
> prize it as their *proletarian* weapon which *their Soviet* power
> will use against small-proprietary disintegration and disorganisa-
> tion.[26]

This quotation shows that Lenin viewed the appointment of
"specialist technicians" to manage state enterprises, where
they enjoyed considerable power and received high salaries,
as an aspect of what he called "state capitalism."

Subsequently, between 1918 and 1920, the conditions of
civil war and foreign intervention caused the Soviet power to
enlarge the scope allowed to experienced administrators and,
correspondingly, to restrict the functions of the factory committees. The resolutions of the Ninth Congress of the Bolshevik Party confirmed this tendency. Speaking at the congress, Lenin emphasised that "for the work of administration,
of organising the state, we need people who are versed in the
art of administration, who have state and business experience," and added that "there is nowhere we can turn to for
such people except the old class."[27]

The congress also made it clear that the factory committees
were to devote themselves mainly to questions of labor discipline, propaganda, and workers' education.[28]

Trotsky and Bukharin (the latter breaking with the line he
had taken in 1918) were among those who tried to "give
theoretical significance" to organizational forms that were established in this period. They strove to ascribe a general

"socialist" implication to measures which, in fact, were above all the result of a very special situation.

Bukharin saw in these measures a direct transition to communism. In an endeavor to reconcile the attitude he had taken as a "left Communist" (in March-April 1918) with his present attitude in favor of extreme centralism and one-man management, he wrote that, in a period when "the emphasis of proletarian tasks is transferred to the area of economic construction," it was necessary to effect a restructuring of the economic apparatus that resulted from the first phase of the workers' struggle—"a restructuring which moves in the direction of the decrease of comaraderie, and in some cases (in individual factories, etc.) to the introduction of the individual administration [i.e., one-man management—*Translator*]. The latter signifies neither a curtailment of the rights of the class nor a diminishing of the role of its organisation. This is the form of proletarian administration of industry, compressed and consolidated . . ."[29]

Bukharin went on to say that, since "one no longer needs to concentrate . . . on the problem of stabilisation of the class position of the proletariat—this question is essentially solved"—at present

> the emphasis does not rest on the principal change of relations of production but in the discovery of such a form of administration which guarantees maximal efficiency. The principle of far-reaching eligibility from below upward (usually even by the workers within the factories) is replaced by the principle of painstaking selection in dependence on technological and administrative personnel, on the competence and the reliability of the candidates. At the top of the factory administrations appear responsible persons—workers or specialists . . . Within this system no engineer may fulfil a different function from that required of him by the proletariat.[30]

The problem of transforming production relations, and the problem of the possibility that managers alien to proletarian ideology might not be subject to direct control by the basic organizations of the party and the workers, were thus "settled" as if by the waving of a magic wand.

The evolution of Bukharin's ideas should not surprise us. It testifies to the profound unity between rightist and leftist attitudes, which is such that one is justified in calling them "rightist-leftist."[31] Lenin severely condemned the "rightist-leftist" extremism of Trotsky and Bukharin, especially in his speech of December 30, 1920, which was published as *The Trade Unions, The Present Situation and Trotsky's Mistakes*.[32] He mentioned that contradictions might develop between workers and managers, and subsequently indicated that in certain circumstances resort to the strike weapon might be justified, even under the dictatorship of the proletariat.[33]

The same "rightist-leftist" mistakes that were committed by Trotsky and Bukharin reappeared during the five year plans in certain statements by Stalin,[34] even though the latter had, in the controversy of the winter of 1920-1921, supported Lenin against Trotsky and Bukharin. Conceptions were thus emerging which were in conflict with revolutionary Marxism. These conceptions found one of their completest expressions in the textbook of political economy issued by the USSR Academy of Sciences.[35] Only one more step needed to be taken in order to arrive at revisionism.

II. The situation of the urban bourgeoisie and petty bourgeoisie at the end of "war communism"

The changes in the situation of the bourgeoisie which had been initiated in the first months of Soviet power went ahead at a faster rate as soon as the White revolt and foreign intervention began. The gradual prohibition of almost all private economic activity, which was a feature of the new period, also affected the urban petty bourgeoisie, especially the small traders. Actually, what was going on was a dual process: the elimination of the activities of the private bourgeoisie, and the development of a state bourgeoisie.

(a) Elimination of the activities of the private bourgeoisie

After the establishment of the VSNKh and its subsequent reorganization, the increasing sabotage of production by the bourgeoisie led, between April and June 1918, to a certain increase in the rate at which factories, mines, etc., were expropriated, and soon after the civil war began, expropriations became general. A decree of June 28, 1918, provided for the rapid nationalization of all large enterprises, i.e., those with a capital of one million roubles or more.[36]

The decree laid down the principle of nationalization, but the actual application of this principle had to be decided from one case to the next. In practice, the expropriation of large-scale enterprises took place quickly, so that the number of state-owned industrial enterprises increased from fewer than 1,000 in May 1918 to between 3,000 and 4,000 in the autumn of that year.[37]

The implementation of these measures and the decision to prohibit practically all activity by private factories and commercial firms had the result that by the end of the civil war period, at the beginning of 1921, the Russian bourgeoisie had lost most of the positions in industry and trade it had still held in the spring of 1918. Henceforth, it no longer possessed the material and social base which made it a part of the imperialist world bourgeoisie: its powerful links with international banking and financial capital had been broken, just as the old state whose economic and military policy corresponded to its interests had departed from the scene.

Many members of the former bourgeoisie, like many former landlords, had emigrated: this was the case especially with those who had formerly been the richest among them.

Nevertheless, despite these upheavals, the prerevolutionary bourgeoisie had not purely and simply "disappeared." A part of the rural bourgeoisie, the kulaks and other rich peasants, had managed more or less to get by, as we shall see in the next chapter. A fairly large proportion of the bourgeois intelligentsia (doctors, academicians, lawyers, engineers, technical specialists, teachers, etc.) had remained in Russia. To be sure, they mostly lived very modestly, having lost almost everything except their "professional income" (and even some of that too), but they tended to fit themselves into the new Soviet society, carrying on the same sort of activity as before. Their influence was not negligible, as may be seen, for instance, from the discussions on the school system and from the nature of the changes made in this system. Some of the members of this intelligentsia obtained posts in the state administration, especially in the economic apparatus, in the new judiciary that was being formed, in the political police, and in the *Prokuratura*.[38]

At the economic level the activity of the bourgeoisie was carried on both "legally" and "illegally." Illegally, first of all, for the bourgeoisie possessed, in Lenin's words, "the 'art' of administration,"[39] and it continued to maintain close relations with the state machine. Even during "war communism" a part of the bourgeoisie continued to participate actively in profitable economic operations through illegal trade involving amounts that were certainly substantial, even though impossible to estimate. These operations enabled the bourgeoisie to retain a degree of economic power that was by no means trivial; this explains why after the end of "war communism," when the NEP period began, a private urban bourgeoisie, the "Nepmen," proved able to "rise from the dead" with comparative ease. However, this element was never to constitute a social force that directly threatened the dictatorship of the proletariat, though its existence and its connections with the state machinery certainly contributed to the subsequent reinforcement of the state bourgeoisie.

(b) The weakening of the private petty bourgeoisie and the position of the administrative petty bourgeoisie

The largest element in Russia's petty bourgeoisie was the middle peasantry, whose problems will be examined later.

Here I shall confine myself to a few remarks concerning the other petty bourgeois elements.

Their numerical importance is very hard to estimate, but it may be assumed that before the revolution they made up about 15 percent of the population, one-fifth of them being office workers.[40] By early 1920 a large proportion of this petty bourgeoisie, especially the small traders, had been declassed: some went in for illegal trade during "war communism," others found more or less secure jobs in the administration and in the cooperative societies, while yet others went to work in the factories.

The situation of the craftsmen also worsened greatly during "war communism": the control of transport and the rationing of raw materials compelled most of them to suspend their activities. A few managed to get work in industry, and some formed producers' cooperatives (*artels*) in order to secure at least a minimum of raw material.

The political attitude of these two sections of the petty bourgeoisie was far from friendly to the Soviet power. The NEP caused them gradually to go over to an attitude of (non-benevolent) "neutrality."

The position of the administrative petty bourgeoisie (small and medium officials, office workers in industry, commerce, banking, etc.) was not very different. At the outset, their enmity toward the Soviet power was even manifested in an "administrative strike." When the people's commissars took over the ministries, they found the offices empty of officials and clerks, and sometimes the files in disorder. Gradually, however, since they needed their salaries, these officials and clerks went back to work. At the start of the NEP their number seems to have been no smaller than before the revolution. Deeply influenced by bourgeois ideology, these petty bourgeois elements continued hostile for a long time. They appear to have often practised a sort of "bureaucratic sabotage" by aggravating administrative delay and routine. Everything suggests that these practices, to some extent inherited from the past, continued to be characteristic of the administrative petty bourgeoisie even after (having been partly renovated by recruitment) it had at last "accepted" the Soviet power.

The technicians, specialists, and engineers of middle rank also belonged to the petty bourgeoisie, and at first their enmity toward the Soviet power (apart from individual exceptions, here as elsewhere) was no less marked than that of the other petty bourgeois groups. Their "neutrality" seems, however, to have been won sooner than that of the others, through the material advantages granted to them, as a result of which their incomes were considerably greater than those of the administrative petty bourgeoisie whose lower stratum received very poor pay, sometimes less than the wages of manual workers.

(c) The development of a state bourgeoisie

The process by which a part of the former bourgeoisie penetrated into the administrative and economic state machinery continued during the period of "war communism." At the same time, the operation of this machinery ensured the reproduction of bourgeois practices and bourgeois relations of distribution. The latter are, as Marx put it, the "reverse side" of capitalist production relations, which also continued to be reproduced,[41] though in a form that was partly transformed by the dictatorship of the proletariat. As we know, these practices and relations create the conditions for the development of a state bourgeoisie.

The development of the state bourgeoisie was thus the counterpart of objective social relations which could not be "abolished" or "destroyed" in a short period, all the less so because the class struggle and the nature of the contradictions needing to be dealt with (the chief of which confronted the Soviet power with the landlords and capitalists of Russia and world imperialism, a contradiction that took the form of armed struggle) did not allow priority to be accorded to the tackling of these relations.

At the same time as a state bourgeoisie began to emerge (still only at the embryonic stage), relations of distribution developed which were favorable to the factory managers, organizers of branches of industry, and highly qualified engineers and technicians. A part of the surplus value produced in industry was thus appropriated by this new bourgeoisie.

A decree of February 21, 1919, consolidated a general scale of wages and salaries with a "spread" which was much wider (that is, which implied much greater inequality) than had been considered acceptable in the period immediately after October, although narrower than the pre-1914 differentials. The decree fixed the minimum wage at 600 roubles and the maximum salary for "highly-qualified administrative personnel" at 3,000 roubles. This applied to Moscow and environs; elsewhere the same coefficients of inequality were to apply, but the basic wage would vary in accordance with local conditions. In fact, salaries exceeding 3,000 roubles could be approved for "very highly qualified" administrative and technical staff.

The payment of such salaries aroused a certain amount of discontent in the working class and disagreement within the party.[42] Consequently, Lenin returned more than once to the problem of the "specialists" and their salaries. He said that it was not possible to get industry to function without them, and also impossible simply to force these men to work for the Soviet power. "To compel a whole section of the population to work under coercion is impossible . . . "[43]

The high salaries paid to the specialists were thus clearly recognized as a *compromise dictated by circumstances of the class struggle* and not, as in the current formulations of the Soviet revisionists, as an application of the principle "to each according to his work."

In his report on the CC, presented to the party congress on March 18, 1919, Lenin stressed that many of the decisions taken by the Soviet government had been forced upon it by the pressure of facts, and he recalled that "Marx once said that it is to the credit of the Paris Communards that they carried into effect decisions which were not borrowed from some pre-conceived theories, but were dictated by actual necessity."[44]

In practice, the measures taken with regard to the salaries of "bourgeois specialists" were fairly soon extended to other "responsible workers," and gave rise to inequalities that were not confined to differences in money received. In April 1919 a decree fixed the salaries of "responsible political workers," providing that the people's commissars, the members of the VTsIK, and certain high officials were to be paid 2,000 roubles per month—which meant partially abandoning the *partmax,* that is, the rule by which no party member must be paid at a rate exceeding a worker's wage.

As a result of the increase in prices in 1919 and 1920, wages and salaries were increased several times. These increases were accompanied by a slight tendency to narrow the "spread," but to a growing extent during these years, money wages lost their significance owing to the general shortage of goods, rationing, and the sharp rise in prices, especially on the black market.[45]

The depreciation of money wages was accompanied by the development of inequality in other forms. The bourgeois engineers, specialists, and administrators were granted various material advantages, and a similar process took place in the Red Army, in which the officers (many of whom came from the old tsarist army) received a number of privileges, not only in respect of payment but also in the form of special quarters, meals differing from those served to the soldiers, and so on.

In 1920 it was practically impossible to evaluate the "average" differences between the wages and salaries of different categories. Individual variations were becoming very important, and there were also "bonuses in kind" which could not be translated into a unified price system, for prices themselves varied a great deal and very quickly. These "bonuses in kind" were paid either in foodstuffs (though this type of payment was not used much, owing to the inadequacy of the supply of provisions at the state's disposal) or in the actual products of particular factories (including such products as transmission belts for machinery, pieces of metal, small tools, etc.). Such products were not, of course, directly consumed by those who received them in this way, but went into the black market, where they were exchanged for other goods.[46]

A part of the workers' wages was also paid in the same

manner, but it was the "bourgeois specialists" who were the chief beneficiaries of the system. For the period in which these wages in kind bulked large, it is impossible to measure the size of the gap between the payment of the producers and that of the specialists, engineers, etc. Nevertheless, there are many indications that the administrators and technicians gave themselves the lion's share of the "deductions in kind" which were made from the factories' production, and that they participated extensively in illegal trade.

Later on, the NEP was to consolidate these distribution relations by confirming the wage spread laid down by the decree of February 21, 1919, together with the many bonuses which were now paid in money to the managers, chief engineers, etc.

The state bourgeoisie being formed during these years was as yet small in numbers. Its size cannot be estimated with any exactness, for there are no relevant statistics, but it cannot have exceeded a few thousand. In fact, it was only gradually that the system of the single manager appointed by the VSNKh came into force and that engineers and technicians also came to be appointed in the factories, trusts, and *glavki*. Thus, at the end of 1920, out of the 2,051 important enterprises for which we have statistics, 1,783 were operating on the basis of one-man management.[47]

In some parts of the state economic machinery especially in certain organs of the VSNKh, penetration by the bourgeoisie was considerable. It was described by a "White" university professor who arrived in Omsk during this period: "At the head of many of the centres and *glavki* sit former employers and responsible officials and managers of business. The unprepared visitor to the centres who is personally acquainted with the former commercial and industrial world would be surprised to see the former owners of big leather factories sitting in Glavokozh, big manufacturers in the central textile organizations, etc."[48]

In this way a state bourgeoisie was formed which was at that stage mainly composed of members of the old bourgeoisie.[49]

This embryonic state bourgeoisie took shape in the first

place in the towns and constituted the mainspring of the organs of state capitalism. It was emerging also in the countryside, where the managers of the *sovkhozy* (state farms) usually ensured a privileged situation for themselves. At the Seventh Congress of Soviets, in December 1919, the *Sovkhozy* were accused of attracting specialists to their service by paying them high salaries, and some of their managers were denounced for living luxuriously in the former homes of the landlords; it even happened quite often that it was the latter who contrived to reestablish themselves in the guise of "managers of state farms." A delegate at the congress went so far as to claim that state farms "have been turned into instruments of counter-revolutionary agitation against the Soviet power."[50]

The merely embryonic condition of the state bourgeoisie during "war communism" and at the beginning of the NEP was due to several circumstances. The class had been formed only recently; some of the same kind of posts that were occupied by "bourgeois specialists" were held by Bolshevik Party members who, inspired by the ideas of revolutionary Marxism, were models of proletarian practice who put first the common interests of the revolution and worked closely with the workers and the organizations of the working class, the party, and the trade unions; finally, the very acuteness of the class struggle to some extent restricted the possibilities for action by members of the former bourgeoisie within the state's economic machinery. They were far from being able to cause the bourgeois practices of which they were the carriers to prevail generally, owing to the suspicion in which they were held by the workers and to the resistance of the latter to the consolidation of certain relations of hierarchy and authority.

The workers' resistance was one of the obstacles limiting the possibilities for the consolidation of a state bourgeoisie. Proofs of such resistance are plentiful. The exasperation felt by the workers led them quite often to refuse to "cooperate" with the bourgeois elements managing the factories, to carry out searches in their homes, and seize their stocks of provisions. These events found an echo in the Soviet press and in Lenin's writings—for example, in his "Reply to an open letter by a bourgeois specialist," published in *Pravda* of March 28, 1919.[51] These forms of workers' resistance to the policy of integrating bourgeois specialists and technicians into the state economic apparatus were never to cease; they continued including during the NEP period, in more or less acute forms.[52]

However, this was an elementary form of class struggle which could not by itself modify the production relations or really prevent those who held posts of leadership in the economic machinery from developing bourgeois practices and becoming a state bourgeoisie.

In any case, it would be quite wrong to assume that all who at that time held leading positions in industry or in the economic and administrative machinery formed part of the state bourgeoisie. Actually, some of these positions were held by Communists who developed proletarian practices to the greatest possible extent, doing all they could to help the workers free themselves from bourgeois relations and find scope for their initiative. These leaders, whose principal function was revolutionary-proletarian in character (and who usually refused, in accordance with the rules of the Bolshevik Party at this time, to draw a salary higher than a worker's wage), did not belong to the state bourgeoisie but to the proletariat, in which they were ideologically and materially integrated and from which in very many cases they themselves stemmed.

(d) The educational system and the subsequent consolidation of the bourgeoisie

A far from negligible role (even though secondary in importance to the reproduction of the hardly transformed capitalist production relations) in the subsequent consolidation of the bourgeoisie was played by the old educational system, which underwent practically no revolutionary transformation. This system remained a bastion of the bourgeois intelligentsia and bourgeois ideology, and increasingly imposed this ideology on the children of workers and peasants who passed through the Soviet schools and in growing numbers filled leading positions.

The old educational system inherited from tsardom and the Provisional Government had strongly subjected its own agents to bourgeois ideology: for several years after October 1917, the teachers and the educational bureaucracy in the main refused to "recognize" Soviet power. As Daniel Lindenberg writes, "the Narkompros (People's Commissariat of Education), established on 22 November 1917, with Lunacharsky as commissar, took over no files or statistics, and the former educational bureaucracy . . . practised sabotage by desertion; as for the great majority of the teachers, they remained deaf to the Bolsheviks' appeals, refusing for years on end to apply the party's recommendations—a form of sabotage by passivity."[53]

After October, the state of affairs in the educational system was as follows: primary education was dominated by the union of primary school teachers, which was led by the Mensheviks and SRs, while the secondary schools were dominated by an association of secondary school teachers which was closely linked with the Cadet party, the situation in higher education being similar.[54]

After the civil war, a modus vivendi was arrived at between the Soviet power and the ideological and political forces that actually dominated the educational system, but it was realized on the basis of bourgeois educational ideology, not on that of proletarian ideology.

In 1917, moreover, the Bolshevik Party did not have a unified conception of what its line in the field of education should be: on this point, as on others, several conceptions clashed. The most influential were those of Krupskaya and Lunacharsky.

On the question of the relations between the educational system and the state administration, Nadezhda Krupskaya's ideas were faithful to those of Marx, being opposed to any direct interference by the state administration in educational matters. She saw it as the task of specific soviets, the "school councils," to take charge of basic education: these councils were to elect the teachers and run the schools, with participation by the schoolchildren themselves.[55] In principle, the content of teaching was to be profoundly altered by the establishment of the "single labor school," the basis of which "must be productive labor, conceived not as being devoted to the material conservation of the school or merely as a method of teaching, but as a productive and socially necessary activity."[56]

As a result of noncooperation by the teachers, the economic and financial chaos resulting from the imperialist war, the civil war, and foreign intervention, and the Bolshevik Party's concentration on other problems, the practical effect of these ideas remained extremely limited; when the schools really got going again at the beginning of the NEP, it was in concrete conditions very different from those which had been envisaged by Krupskaya. Her revolutionary notions had, besides, constantly conflicted with the centralizing and statist notions of an important section of the Bolshevik Party, represented by Lunacharsky, who upheld the conceptions of bourgeois humanism. These conservative ideas made themselves clearly felt after 1917 where secondary and higher educational institutions were concerned.

In fact, at the level of secondary and higher education, nothing changed after October. The system of *gymnasia* remained practically intact until 1928, and the same was true as regards access to the universities, which in practice remained more or less closed to the workers and peasants.

During the summer of 1918 (August 6), at a moment when the civil war had in fact already begun, an attempt was made to modify this state of affairs by opening "workers faculties" (*rabfak*), in which the period of study was relatively short and teaching related mainly to industrial techniques and political work. These *rabfaks* had great success, but after the end of 1918 their role was modified so as to increase the production of specialists. For the same reason the universities reintroduced the old rules for selection: although, in principle, those candidates who held *rabfak* diplomas were exempt from the entrance examination, the content of the final examination was such that university graduates of working-class origin were few and far between, and these rare birds were usually persons who had assimilated the bourgeois ideology reproduced by the university system.

Thus, on the morrow of October, the Soviet power had in practice *not* revolutionized the educational system, and had changed it only to a very limited extent. Fundamentally, the system remained bourgeois, by virtue of what it taught, how this was taught, and the type of relation between theory and practice which it fostered. Apart from a few abortive attempts, this situation was to persist. The functioning of the educational apparatus and its reproduction of bourgeois relations and ideological practices thus played a considerable role in the steady rise of bourgeois forces in the USSR.

III. The situation of the proletariat at the end of "war communism"

The situation of the Soviet proletariat at the end of "war communism" was profoundly contradictory. On the one hand, it wielded state power and, along with the peasantry, it had won victories that were remarkable, given the difference in the material forces involved, over capitalism, the landlords, and foreign imperialism. Furthermore, its material situation, though miserable because of the general shortage of goods was relatively "privileged."[57] On the other hand, its numbers had been reduced and it had been penetrated by alien elements of bourgeois and petty bourgeois origin. A part of the old working class was deeply demoralized and was often kept at work only by a system of rigorous discipline.

This contradictory situation, together with some of the stages that had led to it, needs to be examined fairly closely if we are to understand the specific place of the proletariat in the system of class relations at the end of "war communism."

(a) The "physical" weakening of the Soviet proletariat and its partial "disintegration"

By the beginning of the 1920s the Russian proletariat had suffered a terrible bloodletting. It had literally melted away during the civil war, and this process was continuing at the outset of the NEP. Thus, in 1922, the number of employed workers was less than half the prewar figure—4.6 million instead of 11 million in 1913, within the same frontiers, and of these 4.6 million, only 2 million were employed in industry, 1.2 million being agricultural laborers.[58]

The active working class was not only reduced numerically but also greatly altered in its composition. Many of the most militant workers had fallen at the front. Others had been absorbed into the machinery of the party, the trade unions, and the state. Others, especially in the big industrial centers, had left the ranks of the working class, owing to unemployment or the food shortage, and gone back to their native villages. At the same time, men and women of bourgeois and petty bourgeois origin, who were usually hostile to the dictatorship of the proletariat, had made their way into the ranks of the working class so as to take advantage of the higher rations available to manual workers, or to conceal their class origin.

Amidst a population of 136 million, of whom about half were of working age, the number of those who made up the active nucleus of the new ruling class were thus small; and this was so even if one adds to the workers actually employed in 1922 the former workers who were ready to go back to their old places in production. The solidity of the proletarian dictatorship was not mainly determined by the relative weight of the working class, but, above all, by its class organization and by its ability to exercise ideological and political leadership of the masses.

(b) The standard of living of the working class and the problem of wages

Immediately after October the conditions of the working class improved greatly. The principal changes concerned the abolition of the fines which the capitalists deducted arbitrarily from the workers' wages on all sorts of pretexts, and the maintenance of the same wage level for a shorter working day, this being reduced to eight hours instead of the ten or twelve hours that had previously been worked in many cases. These changes were in line with those which the workers' economic struggle since February 1917 had been able to wrest from the employers before October.

However, the economic disorganization caused by the war and the civil war soon reduced the workers' level of consumption. True, wages were frequently readjusted so as to take account of official price increases, especially where rationed goods were concerned, but rations became increasingly scanty and unavailable. In 1919 consumption was covered only to the extent of 50 percent by purchases made at official prices, the rest being accounted for by the black market, where prices were high and fluctuating.

The problem of wages—the way to determine them and the differentials to be maintained—was the subject, all through "war communism" and at the beginning of the NEP, of many discussions in the trade unions and in the Bolshevik Party. The decisions taken were largely determined by a situation marked by the departure from the active working class of its best elements and the influx of many petty bourgeois and bourgeois. This situation, together with the general economic conditions, led to a catastrophic fall in productivity and in industrial production, a great deal of absenteeism, and the disorganization of industry.

The Labor Code of the RSFSR, adopted on October 10, 1918, confirmed the regulations for the protection of labor adopted after the October Revolution, and charged the trade unions with responsibility for fixing wages in consultation with the managers of enterprises and subject to rectification by the Commissariat of Labor.[59]

In April 1918 the Central Trade-Union Council had declared itself for the extension of piece rates. The labor code provided that wages might be "differentiated" in such a way as to take account not only of the arduousness of the work performed but also of the "degree of responsibility" and the "skill" involved. Piece rates and bonuses were treated as the "normal" form of wages.

The payment of wages on a piece work basis was in fact widespread in Russian industry, and its retention was relatively advantageous to long-established workers, as compared with newcomers to the working class. The majority of the Bolshevik leaders favored this way of calculating wages, seeing in it, in the conditions then prevailing, one of the ways of reestablishing production and the productivity of industrial labor. On this point Lenin wrote: "We must raise the question of piece-work and apply and test it in practice; we must raise the question of applying much of what is scientific and progressive in the Taylor system; we must make wages correspond to the total amount of goods turned out or the amount of work done by the railways, the water-transport system, etc., etc."[60]

This declaration gave rise to a wide discussion in the Bolshevik Party, in which a section of the party, the "left Communists," including leading figures such as Bukharin, Radek, and Osinsky, denounced what they saw as a move in the direction of restoring "capitalist management of the enterprises."

In " 'Left-Wing' Childishness' "[61] Lenin sharply attacked the position of the "left Communists," which, he said, coincided with that of the Mensheviks, who also protested against the introduction of piece wages and of arrangements borrowed from the Taylor system, and against the reorganization of the management of the enterprises and branches of industry under the direction of "industrial trusts." For Lenin, these measures were dictated by the conditions, objective and subjective, of the moment: they were part of the system of "state capitalism" under the dictatorship of the proletariat, the only form of production that could be developed immediately and rapidly.

The orientation advocated by Lenin prevailed. It was maintained throughout "war communism" and during the NEP, though with a tendency, in 1918 and at the beginning of 1919, to narrow the spread of wages as compared with the pre-1914 situation.[62]

The February 21, 1919, decree on wages, already mentioned, divided wages into a large number of groups, each of which was subdivided into twelve categories. Within each group, the ratio of the highest wage to the lowest corresponded to a coefficient of 1.75. Piece wages and bonuses were made general. Only where piece rates were impossible to apply was payment on a time basis treated as admissible, but in such cases "production norms" had to be fixed.

In April 1920, at the Third All-Russia Trade-Union Congress, it was decided to widen the spread of wages somewhat. Within each group the coefficient of differentiation was increased from 1.75 to 2. Actually, since money wages were at that time losing much of their practical significance (owing to the shortage of products purchasable at official prices), it was decided to vary the rations distributed by the state in accordance with workers' levels of skill and output. In practice, this system was fairly widely replaced by payment of wages in kind, with levels also fixed in relation to "output" and "skill."

Eventually, then, along with the growing difficulty in obtaining supplies and the depreciation of the currency (which steadily reduced the significance of wages paid in money), an orientation was established which favored wage differentials, piece rates, and bonuses. With the development of the NEP, the differentiation in money wages and bonuses was to assume its full importance.

In order to appreciate the meaning of the measures described, and those about to be mentioned, it must not be forgotten that when they were adopted most of them were, in principle, transient in character: they were intended to cope with what appeared as an immediate and crying need, in view of the demands of the front, to maintain and increase the quantity of industrial products available, at a time when labor discipline was so gravely compromised that interruptions in production were frequent. Study of the problems presented by labor discipline cannot be separated from consideration of a number of facts relevant to the ideological class struggle.

(c) *The ideological class struggle and labor discipline*

Industrial production, as highly socialized production, calls for strict coordination of the elementary labor processes and the carrying out of these processes in accordance with strict qualitative norms. Genuine labor discipline is necessary for the fulfillment of these requirements, but this discipline always possesses a class character. It may be imposed from above upon workers who try to "dodge" exploitation or administratively fixed rules by reducing their productive effort: this is bourgeois discipline. It may be freely agreed upon by workers who get together and themselves coordinate their efforts: labor discipline is then proletarian in character. The first kind of discipline is despotic and ensures the reproduction of capitalist social relations, of *capital* and *labor*. The second is inherent in socialist cooperation, which does not mean that the task of coordination is not assumed by one particular worker who plays the part of the conductor of the orchestra: "An orchestra conductor need not own the instruments of the orchestra,"[63] he is only the executant of the collective will of the workers.

The transition from one type of discipline to the other, however, even when most of the means of production belong to the state of proletarian dictatorship, cannot be "instantaneous." It forms part of the process of transition from capitalism to communism, and passes through stages in which factory discipline offers contradictory features which express the birth of communist relations and the withering away of capitalist relations. Like the transition process as a whole, this transition is no spontaneous affair, but depends on ideological and political class struggle. It is a revolutionary process with objective and subjective aspects and, like every such revolutionary process, it has to be guided by a revolutionary theory by means of which the lessons of experience and of mass initiative can be drawn.

The subjective side of this revolutionary process is essential, for the agents of production need to free themselves from the ideological relations to which capitalist exploitation has forced them to submit, and from the social practices corresponding to this exploitation. As Marx noted: "This revolution is necessary, therefore, not only because the *ruling* class cannot be overthrown in any other way, but also because the class *overthrowing* it can only in a revolution succeed in ridding itself of all the muck of ages and become fitted to found society anew."[64]

The revolution through which the former exploited class "rids itself of all the muck of ages" is obviously more than a political revolution: it is an ideological revolution such as, we know now, can be accomplished only through several "cultural revolutions." Insofar as the proletariat is not free from bourgeois ideology, it develops practices which contradict its own class interests and tend to consolidate the capitalist elements in the production relations.

At the time of the October Revolution and in the following years, the ideological foundations of the bourgeoisie's political dominance had been sufficiently shaken for that class to lose power and fail to reconquer it, for the Russian workers were ready to fight against it, arms in hand, and make the greatest sacrifices in order to ensure military victory over the class enemy. However, the ideological revolutionization of the Russian proletariat (then extensively penetrated by petty bourgeois and bourgeois elements) and the Bolshevik Party's ability to advance this process (in the extremely complex conditions of the time) were insufficient for mainly proletarian forms of discipline to become predominant in industry.

Immediately after October, the Bolshevik Party made a certain number of attempts to move in the direction of proletarian discipline, drawing upon "practical organizers among the workers and peasants," whom the party tried to get to play a leading role by leaving them the widest scope for initiative. Lenin stressed the decisive importance of the workers' own spontaneous initiative. In his essay "How to Organise Competition" he wrote:

> There are a great many talented organisers among the peasants and the working class, and they are only just beginning to become aware of themselves, to awaken, to stretch out towards

great, vital, creative work, to tackle with their own forces the task of building socialist society. One of the most important tasks of today, if not the most important, is to develop this independent initiative of the workers, and of all the working and exploited people generally, develop it as widely as possible in creative *organisational* work. At all costs, we must break the old, *absurd,* savage, despicable and disgusting prejudice that only the so-called "upper classes", only the rich, and those who have gone through the school of the rich, are capable of administering the state and directing the organisational development of socialist society.[65]

He added that the generalized, universal accounting and control needed for socialism could be carried out only by the masses, and that, in endeavoring to bring it about, "every attempt to establish stereotyped forms and to impose uniformity from above, as intellectuals are so inclined to do, must be combated. Stereotyped forms and uniformity imposed from above have nothing in common with democratic and socialist centralism . . . The Paris Commune gave a great example of how to combine initiative, independence, freedom of action and vigour from below with voluntary centralism free from stereotyped forms."[66]

However, as we have seen, at the very moment Lenin was writing these lines, measures were being taken which cut down the powers of the factory committees and subjected workers' control to central administrative organs. In Lenin's eyes, these measures were justified by the urgent need to establish centralization in the form of state capitalism, and also by the "timidity" with which the working-class masses were approaching the problem of control.[67]

Lenin also justified these measures by reference to the influence of bourgeois and petty bourgeois ideas, together with the fact that "poverty and want forced thousands and thousands on to the path of rowdyism, corruption and roguery, and caused them to lose all human semblance,"[68] which made it necessary to establish strict discipline and strictly centralized control.

In December 1917 Lenin seemed to think that the principal aspect of the situation was the enormous drive of the masses to free themselves from bourgeois and petty bourgeois ideas, to overcome their "timidity" and so to develop their self-confidence and self-discipline. He considered that what would best help the masses to advance in that direction was the class struggle:

> As their enemies, the exploiters, step up their resistance, the exploited mature and gain in strength; they grow and learn and they cast out the "old Adam" of wage-slavery. Victory will be on the side of the exploited, for on their side is life, numerical strength, the strength of the mass, the strength of the inexhaustible sources of all that is selfless, dedicated and honest, all that is surging forward and awakening to the building of the new, all the vast reserves of energy and talent latent in the so-called "common people" the workers and peasants. Victory will be theirs.[69]

A few months later, in March-April 1918, faced with the increasing disorganization of Russia's economy, and with the development of anarchist or anarcho-syndicalist tendencies, which constitute one of the most dangerous forms of penetration by petty bourgeois ideology, Lenin considered that the Soviet proletariat had not succeeded, owing to lack of initiative, resolution, and unity, in developing the capacity to organize accounting and control of production on a countrywide scale, or in establishing its own factory discipline; from this followed the need to give more scope to capitalists and bourgeois specialists in the central organs directing the economy and in the administration and management of the enterprises.

In his speech of April 29, 1918, to the VTsIK, Lenin connected the inadequate level of discipline with the petty bourgeois ideas of those workers who had not been through the school of trade unionism, and denounced the illusions of the "left Communists" who thought it possible to get rid of the capitalists without replacing bourgeois discipline by proletarian discipline. It was in this connection that he observed that the most difficult task was not overthrowing the bourgeoisie but maintaining the dictatorship of the proletariat, and ensuring thereby "the establishment of order, discipline, labour productivity, accounting and control by the proletarian Soviet power."[70]

At that time Lenin thought that the principal danger threatening the Soviet power was not open counter-revolution (as became the case a few weeks later), but the bourgeois and petty bourgeois ideas present among the masses. He developed this theme in his April 23, 1918, speech to the Moscow Soviet: "We have one extremely dangerous secret enemy, more dangerous than many open counter-revolutionaries; this enemy is the deadly enemy of the socialist revolution and the Soviet power . . . The enemy of whom I have spoken is the anarchy of the petty proprietors, whose life is guided by one thought: 'I grab all I can—the rest can go hang.' This enemy is more powerful than all the Kornilovs, Dutovs and Kaledins put together."[71]

He took up the idea again in *The Immediate Tasks of the Soviet Government:*

> Yesterday we were menaced by the restoration of bourgeois exploitation, personified by the Kornilovs, Gotzes, Dutovs, Gegechkoris and Bogayevskys. We conquered them. This restoration, this very same restoration menaces us today in another form, in the form of the element of petty bourgeois laxity and anarchism, or small-proprietor "it's-not-my-business" psychology, in the form of the daily, petty, but numerous sorties and attacks of this element against proletarian discipline. We must, and we shall vanquish this element of petty bourgeois anarchy.[72]

It was thus a whole complex set of reasons that led Lenin and the Bolshevik Party to introduce a series of measures aimed at imposing "from above" as strict a system of labor discipline as possible.

Clearly, it is possible to wonder whether these measures may not have contributed to restrict still further the initiative of the working-class rank and file, to reduce what confidence it may have had in its own powers, and to cause it to resume a passive attitude hard to reconcile with the exercise of its role as the ruling class. Such questions can indeed be asked, but there is, of course, no possibility of answering them. We do know, however, that given the disorganized state of the economy and the disintegration of the working class, and in the absence of a sufficient degree of discipline in the enterprises and coordination of their activities, Soviet industry would have been unable to go on functioning.

We know, too, that the policy of "state capitalism" did make possible a partial reactivation of industry so that the latter was able to sustain the war effort which was forced upon the Soviet power from May 1918 onward.

(d) Labor discipline and the role of the trade unions

The appointment of former capitalists and bourgeois specialists to managerial posts in the factories, the Soviet trusts, the *glavki*, and the VSNKh, which led to the reestablishment of capitalist discipline and methods of management in industry, often gave rise to serious discontent among the workers. From the second half of 1918 onward, this discontent frequently expressed itself in acts of violence and even of revolt, which were echoed in the Soviet press and trade-union congresses of the period. At the same time, as a result of the shortage of foodstuffs in the towns, there was growing absenteeism and migration to the countryside. The factories and mines were thus deprived of workers whose regular presence was essential if production was to be maintained at a level adequate to servicing the hard struggle being waged on many fronts by the workers and peasants who were defending Soviet power.

In the face of this situation the Bolshevik Party was led to take measures resulting in a thorough transformation of trade-union functions. This began during the second half of 1918, when military operations were becoming widespread and the nationalization of enterprises was developing. The trade unions were increasingly called upon to cooperate administratively with the People's Commissariat of Labor (Narkomtrud) and with the managers of nationalized enterprises, especially in fixing labor conditions and disciplinary rules binding on the workers.

The Second All-Russia Congress of Trade Unions (January 1919) ratified the principle of what was then officially called the "governmentalization" of the trade unions, that is, their de facto subordination to the central state administration through the Narkomtrud.

The principle of subordination of the administrative apparatus, a principle not to be identified with the leading ideological and political role of the party, was formulated by the Bolshevik Party[73] itself and submitted by the Bolshevik fraction in the congress for ratification by the Second All-Russia Congress of Trade Unions.

The effects of this subordination might seem limited, seeing that the central collegium at the head of the Narkomtrud was itself made up of trade-union representatives. The task of these representatives in the Narkomtrud was twofold—deciding on rules for labor discipline, and checking that the bourgeois managers, engineers, specialists, etc., did not misuse their power. In principle, therefore, it was a question of endowing the trade unions, as a mass organization of the wage workers, with the formal right to supervise the activities of the "bourgeois specialists" and administer labor discipline themselves.

Actually, in the concrete conditions existing, the presence of trade-union representatives in the central collegium of the Narkomtrud did not mean much, as effective local control of bourgeois factory managers, specialists, etc., was in practice entrusted to the local organs of the Narkomtrud, that is, to a body of officials inherited from the previous regime and organized in the same administrative structures as of old: moreover, the local organs of the Narkomtrud were not subordinated to the local trade-union organizations so that it was an apparatus free from effective control by the workers that increasingly tended to decide questions of working conditions and labor discipline.

The "governmentalization" of the trade unions resulted in their de facto fusion with the state administrative apparatus and the transfer to this apparatus of a part of the tasks which were supposed to be delegated to the trade unions. This was the case with the mobilization of labor that took place throughout 1919.

The development of this mobilization led the Ninth Party Congress (March 1920) to adopt several resolutions, one of which concerned the trade unions. This resolution[74] laid down a number of important principles, some of which were of a general character while others corresponded to concerns of the moment. One of the statements of principle dealt with the tasks of the trade unions. It was said that under the dictatorship of the proletariat the trade unions did not have as their principal task to act as organs of workers' struggle, but rather to contribute to "economic organisation and education." The same resolution said that the trade unions were to carry out their functions "not self sufficiently and in isolation, but as one of the essential instruments of the Soviet state, led by the Communist Party." The resolution defined the trade unions as "schools of communism" and as "the link binding the most backward masses of the proletariat . . . to the proletarian vanguard, the Communist Party." It added that, to this end, they "must educate and organise the masses culturally, politically and administratively."

Furthermore, the resolution stated that the trade unions must carry out their administrative functions as subordinate parts of the state machine as a whole, and must not intervene directly in the management of enterprises. They might put forward candidates for the management of the enterprises, but the principle of election was set aside in favor of that of "selection on the basis of a practical probationary period enabling estimation to be made of the candidate's technical competence, firmness, organisational ability and efficiency."

The principal functions of the trade unions were set forth as follows: "Improvement of labour discipline by all methods, up to and including comradely disciplinary tribunals [elected by a general meeting of workers in the enterprise—C.B.], propaganda for productive labour . . . ; educating the workers and arousing their interest in understanding the role of their factory . . ."

In describing "the current tasks of the trade unions," the

resolution stressed that they must participate in the organization of "work conducted on a war basis."

Those trade-union leaders who refused to follow the path laid down by the resolution could be relieved of their functions and replaced by a directly appointed (and no longer elected) "political leadership." This was in fact done in certain sectors, such as the railroads, where far-reaching disorganization had to be remedied. The old leadership of the railroad workers' union, which was hostile to the Bolshevik Party, was replaced, on Trotsky's initiative, by a "political leadership of transport" which was regarded as a temporary organ of the party and of the Soviet power.

Another resolution, also adopted by the Ninth Party Congress, on "The Immediate Tasks of Economic Construction," stipulated (Article 12) that decisions of this kind *were "exceptional, emergency measures."*[75]

The resistance of the old trade-union leaders to the line laid down by this resolution was clearly inspired by a variety of motives. For some (in particular, the Mensheviks) it was a question of sabotaging the war effort; for others, what mattered was to resist measures that developed in a one-sided way the administrative and disciplinary role of the trade-union organizations. This resistance was all the greater because parts of the congress resolution on "The Immediate Tasks of Economic Construction"[76] were not easily acceptable to a large section of the workers.

These resolutions (which the trade unions had the task of implementing) aimed at introducing a series of measures of a coercive character: compulsory labor, militarization of the economy, obligation of party and trade-union organizations to register all skilled workers (so as to assign them to production with the same strictness "as was and is being shown towards officers in relation to the army's needs"), mobilization of the workers as a whole, including the unskilled, in labor units, with a staff of "technically competent instructors," and establishment of a system of "scientific organization of production."

The role to be assigned to the bourgeois specialists and the administrative and technical personnel, and the basis for their remuneration were provided for as follows:

> Individual calculation of labour productivity and the system of individual bonuses are to be applied, in appropriate forms, to the administrative and technical staff. The best administrators, engineers and technicians must be placed in the most favourable conditions for the full deployment of their capacities in the interest of the socialist economy . . . The prejudice against admission of the higher technical personnel of the enterprises and institutions to membership of the trade unions must be finally uprooted. By welcoming the engineers, doctors, agronomists and other such workers, the trade unions will help them, through fraternal collaboration with the organised proletariat, to partici pate actively in Soviet construction and will acquire workers with specialised scientific knowledge and experience such as the trade unions have very great need of.[77]

These resolutions testify to the great difficulties then being experienced by Soviet industry, and also reflect the existence of contradictory tendencies within the Bolshevik Party. These contradictions, which burst forth at the end of 1920 in the "trade union discussion" in which Lenin opposed Trotsky and Bukharin, related to the significance—were they to be seen as mere conjunctural decisions or as matters of principle?—of some of the resolutions of the Ninth Party Congress, and also to the role to be played by coercion where the workers were concerned. Such coercion was in fact applied until the end of 1920 as a result of economic disorganization and the need to furnish supplies to the armed forces of the revolution.

(e) Resort to measures of coercion against the workers

From the second half of 1918 onward, there developed a growing contradiction between what the war effort demanded from the various industries and the actual amount of work that many workers were disposed to put in "spontaneously." Given the Bolshevik Party's lack of sufficient capacity to undertake the task of persuasion of the masses, coercive measures were adopted.

In the first place, employment was subjected to regulation, so as to prevent workers from moving too often from one enterprise to another, and oblige them to accept whatever jobs were offered to them. This was, for example, the purpose of a decree of September 1918, forbidding unemployed workers to reject the jobs offered them on penalty of losing their right to unemployment pay. At the end of October 1918 the "employment services" were transformed into local organs of the Narkomtrud: thereafter, the conclusion of any contract of employment[78] had to be authorized by these organs, which thus became an obligatory intermediary for workers and employers alike.

In March 1919 the Eighth Congress of the Bolshevik Party took an important step in the same direction. The program it then adopted stated:

> For the purposive development of economic life it is essential to utilise to the utmost all the labour power at the disposal of the state. Its correct assignment and reassignment as between the various territorial areas and as between the various branches of economic life is the main task of the economic policy of the Soviet power. It can be fulfilled in no other way than by an intimate association between the Soviet power and the trade unions. The general mobilisation by the Soviet power of all members of the population who are physically and mentally fit for work (a mobilisation to be effected through the instrumentality of the trade unions), for the discharge of definite social duties, must be achieved far more widely and systematically than has hitherto been the case.

By virtue of these decisions of the Eighth Party Congress, the role of *planned direction of labor, attributed to the trade unions, was exercised in practice by the state administrative system* into which the trade unions were integrated, but because of the place formally assigned to the trade unions, the direction of labor planned in this way was identified with the introduction of "a new socialist discipline."[79]

A month after the Eighth Congress, the Sovnarkom adopted

a "general mobilization order" and gave the trade unions the task of selecting those workers who were to be sent to the front. In practice, this selection was made by the managers of enterprises, who chose the men they considered they could best do without. At the same time, the STO (Council of Labor and Defense), which was headed by Trotsky, published a decree mobilizing at their workplaces those miners who had not been sent to the front.

Other measures were gradually added so as to ensure better control over the way the country's labor force was being used. In June 1919 the workers of Moscow and Petrograd were made to carry *workbooks* containing full details of their work record. It was hoped by this means more effectively to prevent unauthorized moves by workers from job to job: this shifting about, usually inspired by a desire to find more attractive conditions, was indeed occurring on a scale that endangered the functioning of industry and the war effort. This measure was gradually extended to other towns. As the trade unions proved unable to control the workers, this task was taken out of their hands in November 1919. Thereafter, the power to mobilize the workers and direct them to particular factories or tasks was wholly transferred to the Narkomtrud and its local organs. This power to mobilize the labor force was also made applicable to the peasants.

In January 1920 the Sovnarkom proclaimed that it was necessary to "supply industry, agriculture, transport and other branches of the national economy with labour power on the basis of a general economic plan."[80] A system of general labor service was organized, dependent no longer on the Narkomtrud but on the STO. The latter set up its own local organs for the purpose of conscripting workers for urgent tasks. Workers who tried to dodge assignments they did not like by going back to their native villages could be sought out, arrested, and treated as deserters.[81] In April 1920 a report to the Third Congress of Trade Unions went so far as to regret the destruction by the revolution of "the old police apparatus which had known how to register citizens not only in the towns but in the country."[82] In fact, the Narkomtrud and the STO proved able to cope with the needs of the situation: in the forestry industry alone, they mobilized nearly six million persons through the labor service in the first half of 1920.[83]

In the spring of 1920, when the army's need for manpower was slackening off, Trotsky decided not to demobilize that part of the army which was no longer required at the front, but instead to transform it into a "labor army" to be employed in particularly arduous tasks.

The Ninth Congress, in its resolution on"The Present Tasks of Economic Construction," systematized and developed a number of measures which had been adopted during the preceding months, dealing with the formation of "labor armies" and with the introduction of the crime of "labor-desertion," which was to be severely punished. Point 15 of this resolution declared, among other things, that

> given that a considerable number of workers, in search of better food supplies, and often desiring to engage in speculation, are voluntarily leaving the enterprises and moving about from place to place . . . the Congress considers it to be one of the urgent tasks of the Soviet power and the trade unions to struggle in a planned systematic way, persistently and with strictness, against labour-desertion, in particular by the publication of black lists of deserters, the formation of penal labour-detachments made up of deserters and, finally, the internment of deserters in concentration camps.[84]

(f) The principal aspect of the proletariat's situation: its constitution as the dominant class

The necessity under which the Soviet power found itself to resort—in a situation of extreme want and general physical misery, when it had to face an international coalition of counter-revolutionary forces—to severe coercion not only against the enemy classes but also against the vacillating elements in the working class and the peasantry, must be put in its right context. This resort to coercion was only the secondary aspect of a situation whose principal aspect was the constitution of the proletariat as the dominant class. If this is not appreciated, one slips into the empty phrasemongering of the Mensheviks, SRs, and anarchists who, like other ideologists of the petty bourgeoisie and the bourgeoisie, assert that what then existed in Russia was not the dictatorship of the proletariat but a dictatorship over the proletariat. Being incapable of making an overall analysis of class relations, the ideological opponents of the Soviet power are obviously likewise incapable of explaining what class, according to them, was then exercising its dictatorship over the proletariat.

Whoever fails to undertake an overall analysis of class relations and merely isolates certain aspects of reality—like the use of coercion against some sections of the working class and the peasantry—remains unable to explain the actual course of history. The latter is indeed incomprehensible to whoever tries to ignore the fact that the strength of the Soviet power— its capacity to resist and overcome foes who possessed material force that was infinitely greater than its own—was based on its class character, on the fact that it was the power of the broad masses of the toilers. It was because it was *their power*, that the workers and peasants fought for it with a fury and heroism unequalled in previous history.

One must be standing outside the real movement of history to allege that the Soviet power, issued from the *struggle of the masses* against the social and political forces of the bourgeoisie, the landlords, and imperialism, and continuing to wage a fight to the death against those forces (which at that time were leagued against it on a world scale), *had suddenly changed its character*, so that, while still fighting against its former enemies, it became transformed into an organ of oppression of the masses. It is not possible to argue that, because coercion was used against certain elements of the working class and the peasantry, the power using this coercion was not the power of the workers and peasants, when the activity of this power as a whole and its very capacity for action testify to its being thoroughly rooted in the masses, and to the leading role being played by the proletariat, organized as the dominant class, in alliance with the peasantry.

The victories won by the Soviet power over the bourgeoisie, the landlords, and world imperialism were possible only because it was then *a proletarian power concentrating the will of the masses*. If this is not seen, it is impossible to understand the outcome of the battles waged by the Soviet army, badly equipped and supplied, against the White armies backed by the imperialist great powers, to understand how and why Soviet Russia got the better of its powerful enemies although it was gripped by famine and disease. Apart from any abstract considerations, the actual course of events *showed in practice* the existence of the dictatorship of the proletariat, the realization of the fundamental unity of the masses, guided by the Bolshevik Party and revolutionary Marxism.

This proletarian dictatorship, like every historical reality, was complex and contradictory. Through the work of the Bolshevik Party, through the fact that this party was deeply rooted in the working class and that it applied Marxism, which enabled it to carry out at every stage essential revolutionary tasks, the proletarian dictatorship realized the fighting unity of the proletariat and the peasantry. At the same time, for lack of a long ideological and political struggle waged on a large scale before the establishment of the proletarian power, and for lack of previous experience, the unity of the masses thus realized was not completely adequate to the tasks that had to be accomplished. A part of the peasantry and even of the working class continued to be strongly influenced by bourgeois and petty bourgeois ideas and practices, and so gave precedence to personal interests over the interests of the revolution and allowed itself temporarily to be influenced by ideological tendencies that weakened the revolutionary unity of the masses—the SRs, the Mensheviks, and various forms of anarchism. This was only a secondary aspect of the situation, for these trends never succeeded in wielding more than a limited and unstable influence, and as a rule they did not even operate openly. This secondary aspect of the situation explains some particular features of the dictatorship of the proletariat during these years—the low level of activity of some of the mass organizations (the local soviets and, up to a point, the trade unions) and the relatively large proportion of acts of indiscipline which—in a situation of extreme tension—compelled the Soviet power to use coercion against unstable elements.

In these circumstances, the proletarian character of the ruling power was essentially determined by the bonds uniting the Bolshevik Party with the revolutionary masses, by its practice of a mass line of revolutionary Marxism, and by the merging of this party, the vanguard of the proletariat, with the most militant section of the working class.

Whatever may have been the role played by coercion of part of the workers—a coercion that was often exercised, moreover, by workers' detachments and not by a specialized body—power was wielded at that time above all by virtue of the confidence placed in the Bolshevik Party by the broadest masses. The latter saw in the party the victorious leader of the October Revolution, the party that had identified itself with their own desire to get out of the imperialist war, with the peasants' desire to become masters of their own land, and that had shown itself able to unite them to fight the enemies of the revolution. Furthermore, this confidence was based not only on the party's capacity to respond to fundamental popular aspirations and adopt the appropriate decisions, but also on the carrying out of the mass line, for this is essential for consolidating the dictatorship of the proletariat.

(g) *The dictatorship of the proletariat and the mass line*

Lenin frequently expounded some of the conditions needed for the practice of a mass line and emphasized that this practice distinguished a revolutionary proletarian party from the Social Democratic parties of the Second International. Thus, in *One of the Fundamental Questions of the Revolution*, he wrote:

> Don't be afraid of the people's initiative and independence. Put your faith in their revolutionary organisations, and you will see *in all* realms of state affairs the same strength, majesty and in-

vincibility of the workers and peasants as were displayed in their unity and their fury against Kornilov. Lack of faith in the people, fear of their initiative and independence, trepidation before their revolutionary energy instead of all-round and unqualified support for it—this is where the S.R. and Menshevik leaders have sinned most of all. This is where we find one of the deepest roots of their indecision, their vacillation, their infinite and infinitely fruitless attempts to pour new wine into the old bottles of the old, bureaucratic state apparatus.[85]

Lenin came back to the same principles and ideas on the most varied occasions. For instance, in *"Left-Wing" Communism, an Infantile Disorder*,[86] he brought out with particular vigor the significance of the principle of keeping contact with the masses, and dwelled on the conditions for doing this. He also showed that proletarian discipline, in contrast to bureaucratic discipline, a discipline imposed from above, can only be based on "ability to link up, maintain the closest contact, and—if you wish—merge, in certain measure, with the broadest masses of the working people—primarily with the proletariat, *but also with the non-proletarian masses* of working people."[87]

In the same work Lenin writes about another, closely related principle, namely, that the party's role is *not to force* a political line on the masses, but to convince them of the correctness of this line by reference to *"their own experience."*[88] Given these conditions, Lenin adds, proletarian discipline can be achieved, but "without these conditions, all attempts to establish discipline inevitably fall flat and end up in phrasemongering and clowning."[89]

As for the conditions that enable the party to convince the masses, Lenin stresses that they cannot be improvised, that they "cannot emerge at once. They are created only by prolonged effort and hard-won experience. Their creation is facilitated by a correct revolutionary theory which, in its turn, is not a dogma, but assumes final shape only in close connexion with the practical activity of a truly mass and truly revolutionary movement."[90]

This last remark obviously has important implications. It

means that the existence of a revolutionary party linked with the masses can only be the historical product of correct theory and practice. It means, too, that if the product of such theory and practice, that is, a party which has confidence in the masses and in which the masses have confidence, is destroyed because it has committed a certain number of mistakes, only very protracted work can bring about the rebirth of such a party, and without this work all appeals to discipline, confidence, etc., amount merely to "phrasemongering."

Inherent in respect for this principle of maintaining a close link between the party and the masses, their relative "merging," or internal relations to each other, is the party's capacity for "watching the mood of the masses" [91] and learning from experience. [92]

One of the conditions of existence of the dictatorship of the proletariat was respect by the Bolshevik Party for the fundamental requirements of the mass line. This does not mean, of course, as has already been shown, that at every moment and in all circumstances, the Bolshevik Party was able to respect these requirements. The rapidity with which it came to power, its composition, its lack of experience, and the features of the ideological struggle that developed within it meant that a mass line could be followed only to a partial extent: hence the real tensions that developed at certain moments between the Soviet power and some sections of the masses, especially in the countryside. But, however much the Bolshevik Party's practice may at times have departed from the requirements of a mass line, the *dominant aspect* of this practice was respect for these requirements. Had it been otherwise, the Bolshevik Party would not have been able to remain at the head of the Soviet power and ensure its triumph.

(h) The dictatorship of the proletariat and the "merging" of the Bolshevik Party with the advanced elements of the working class

The Bolshevik Party was able to play the role of instrument of the dictatorship of the proletariat by rapidly increasing its membership and merging with the advanced elements of the working class.

Until the end of 1920, the evolution of the party's numbers largely reflected its increasing implantation among the masses, which entailed a profound change in its composition. From 24,000 in January 1917,[93] membership increased to 612,000 in March 1920 and 732,000 in March 1921. From 1921 onward, the numbers were greatly reduced by purges. In 1923 they amounted to 499,000.

Of these members, the number of workers[94] increased from 14,000 in 1917 to about 270,000 in 1920, and 300,000 in 1921. Between 1917 and 1920, the number of peasant members rose from 1,800 to over 200,000 (on January 1, 1921).[95] While the party's peasant membership (or, more precisely, it would seem, its membership of peasant, or even only rural, origin) was slight in a country that was more than 70 percent peasant, the worker members represented in 1921 a considerable percentage of the active working class. From the standpoint of the role of the working class in the state machine, the size of the Bolshevik Party's proletarian membership is all the more significant in that in this period (1919), 60 percent of the members were working in the administrative services of the state and the party, and a quarter in the Red Army, very often in posts of political or military responsibility.[96] Thus, the presence of Communist workers in the principal organs of the state was considerable.

During the years 1919 and 1920, joining the Bolshevik Party was, generally speaking, an act of undoubted political significance. True, the party was in power, and that attracted careerists, but purges were frequent and, above all, the power wielded by the party often seemed gravely threatened by the military offensives of the White armies, who massacred party members in the areas they occupied. Besides, members had to fulfill heavy obligations.

The merging of the party with the advanced workers was at that time real and deep. It was one aspect of the proletarian character of the ruling power. In the long run, however, the incorporation of a large number of workers in administrative functions, in a period when the proletariat was not very numerous and, especially, when its ranks were being thinned and were even being penetrated by bourgeois and petty bourgeois elements, had a negative side to it. After a few years, there was danger of these workers becoming transformed into officials, and their proletarian origin gradually ceasing to mean anything. In 1919, apparently, only 11 percent of the party members were working in factories.[97] At that time, however, the party members in official positions who came from the working class had left its ranks too recently for their class origin to have ceased to be significant. The danger of "deproletarianization" was nevertheless felt to be a real one. Three years later, Lenin was to draw the party's attention sharply to its existence. In 1919 the Eighth Party Congress stipulated that worker-members engaged in full-time administrative work must go back to their factories for at least one month in four.[98]

In the conditions of civil war this obligation does not appear to have been fulfilled, and later it appears to have been "forgotten." The negative consequences of this "forgetting" may subsequently have been all the greater because about 30 percent of the party members were neither workers nor peasants and, in the administration, Communist workers worked alongside many officials taken over from the old regime, to whose ideological influence they gradually succumbed, a process referred to as "bureaucratization," though it would be more correct to call it "bourgeoisification." During the civil war and immediately after, however, the class struggle was too intense for the Communist workers holding responsible posts to be "bourgeoisified" on any large scale by the functions they were carrying out. By their numbers, energy, and devotion they constituted one of the safeguards of the dictatorship of the proletariat.

It is just this merging of the party with the advanced elements of the working class, together with the acuteness of the class struggle, that explains why, as a result of the initiative of the masses during the civil war, entirely new (even though, of course, as yet embryonic) production relations began to arise.

IV.   The emergence of new socialist and communist production relations

The Communist Saturdays *(subbotniki)* are an especially significant aspect of the proletarian character of the Soviet revolution, as they show the close attachment of the most militant workers to the tasks of the dictatorship of the proletariat. During 1918–1921 the ideological revolutionization of these workers gave rise, locally and transiently, to production relations of a new type, Communist relations. This resulted from the ideological intervention of the Bolshevik Party, and in particular of some of its rank and file, in an acute process of class struggle.

(a) The "Communist Saturdays"

One of the first writings in which Lenin dealt explicitly with the concrete appearance of new production relations, Communist relations, was his pamphlet *A Great Beginning*.[99] It is important because in it he shows in a striking way the historic significance of the "Communist Saturdays." It illustrates also Lenin's ability to grasp whatever was really new and revolutionary, and which remains incomprehensible to the bourgeois and petty bourgeois philistines for whom there exists a "human nature" of which the "perfected" manifestation is the egoistic and calculating petty bourgeois.

The "Communist Saturdays" were a form of voluntary mass labor. They were usually aimed at the rapid completion of certain productive tasks, especially, though not exclusively, in the domain of repairing or constructing communications (mainly railroad lines). This is how Lenin evaluates the significance of this initiative taken by the workers themselves:

> The *communist subbotniks* organised by the workers on their own initiative are really of enormous significance. Evidently, this is only a beginning, but it is a beginning of exceptionally great importance. It is the beginning of a revolution that is more difficult, more tangible, more radical and more decisive than the overthrow of the bourgeoisie, for it is a victory over our own conservatism, indiscipline, petty-bourgeois egoism, a victory

over the habits left as a heritage to the worker and peasant by accursed capitalism. Only when *this* victory is consolidated will the new social discipline, socialist discipline, be created; then and only then will a reversion to capitalism become impossible, will communism become really invincible.[100]

A few pages later, Lenin further explains the importance of the Communist Saturdays as he sees it:

The first communist *subbotnik* . . . was of greater historical significance than any of the victories of Hindenburg, or of Foch and the British in the 1914–1918 imperialist war. The victories of the imperialists mean the slaughter of millions of workers for the sake of the profits of the Anglo-American and French multimillionaires, they are the atrocities of doomed capitalism, bloated with over-eating and rotting alive. The communist *subbotnik* organised by the workers of the Moscow-Kazan railway is one of the cells of the new, socialist society, which brings to all the peoples of the earth emancipation from the yoke of capital and from wars.[101]

Lenin is not unaware of the fragility of the social relations which are beginning to emerge in this way, but he knows that the main thing is not this fragility, that it is the novelty of these relations that deserves attention: "Jeering at the feebleness of the young shoots of the new order, cheap scepticism of the intellectuals and the like—these are, essentially, methods of bourgeois class struggle against the proletariat, a defence of capitalism against socialism. We must carefully study the new shoots, we must devote the greatest attention to them, do everything to promote their growth and 'nurse' them."[102]

Nor does Lenin fail to realize that some of these "shoots" are doomed to perish and that this will perhaps be the fate of the "Communist Saturdays," since, in the prevailing circumstances, it is not certain that they will play an especially important role, but, as he says, "that is not the point. The point is to foster each and every shoot of the new; and life will select the most viable."[103] In order to overcome capitalism, Lenin repeats, one needs to have the perseverance to "try hundreds and thousands of new methods, means and weapons of struggle in order to elaborate the most suitable of them."[104]

This is the very language of *antidogmatism,* the language of confidence in the revolutionary initiative of the masses, the language of a proletarian political leader who knows that, as Mao Tse-tung was to say later, "correct ideas do not fall from heaven," but emerge from social practice. It is also the language of a Marxist theoretician who realizes that the building of a new world proceeds necessarily by way of hundreds of attempts, only some of which are destined to bear the fruits that they seem to promise.

For Lenin, the historic significance of the "Communist Saturdays" lies in the fact that they originated from genuine mass initiative, in particular from the initiative of workers, and workers whose own situation was among the *most difficult*. It lies also in the fact that when the workers agree, as they did in the case of the "Communist Saturdays," to work "without remuneration," the transition to communism *has already begun*. This is why Lenin says:

> Communist *subbotniks* are extraordinarily valuable as the *actual* beginning of *communism*; and this is a very rare thing, because we are in a stage when "only the *first steps* in the transition from capitalism to communism are being taken" (as our Party Programme quite rightly says). Communism begins when the *rank-and-file workers* display an enthusiastic concern that is undaunted by arduous toil to increase the productivity of labour, husband *every pood of grain, coal, iron* and other products, which do not accrue to the workers personally or to their "close" kith and kin, but to their "distant" kith and kin, i.e., to society as a whole . . .[105]

In this essay so rich in ideas, Lenin also tackles the problem of the liberation of women and the emergence, in this sphere too, of "exemplary Communist work," freed from "profit-making enterprises."[106]

(b) Communist work and socialist discipline

One of the essential concepts in this essay is that of "Communist work," by which Lenin means work performed "without remuneration in the interests of society, in the interests of all the working people,"[107] work into which it is possible to lead "the whole mass of the working and exploited people, as well as all the petty-bourgeois groups, on the road to new economic development, towards the creation of a new social bond, a new labour discipline, a new organisation of labour." [108]

The new forms of discipline and organization of labor of which Lenin speaks are the basis of communist production relations, beginning a process of revolutionization of the labor process itself, in which the separation between executive tasks and performance tasks tends to disappear, *particular work becomes transformed into general work,* and there is a withering-away of wage labor, "the *essential* form of mediation [of capitalist production], continually reproduced by the capitalist production-relation." [109]

About eight months after the publication of his pamphlet *A Great Beginning*, Lenin returned to the theme of Communist labor in his article *From the Destruction of the Old Social System to the Creation of the New*, in which he expressed the following ideas:

> We can, and should, get right down to the problem of communist labour, or rather, it would be more correct to say, not communist, but socialist labour; for we are dealing not with the higher but the lower, the primary stage of the new social system that is growing out of capitalism.
>
> Communist labour in the narrower and stricter sense of the term is labour performed gratis for the benefit of society, labour performed not as a definite duty, not for the purpose of obtaining a right to certain products, not according to previously established and legally fixed quotas, but voluntary labour, irrespective of quotas; it is labour performed without expectation of reward, without reward as a condition, labour performed because it has become a habit to work for the common good, and because of a conscious realisation (that has become a habit) of the necessity of working for the common good . . .[110]

Here, too, Lenin returns to the close link between the flowering of Communist work and the development of new social relations. He stresses that this flowering is a long-term process which will be spread over decades, for it is a process bound up with a mass ideological revolution, leading to work performed without expectation of any particular payment.

A few days after the publication of this article, on the occasion of May 1, 1920, Lenin declared that, with the victory over the White insurrection and foreign intervention, "the ground is being cleared for the actual building of socialism, for the development of new social links, a new discipline of work in common and a new national (and later an international) system of economy of world-historic importance." [111] He added that, to win this ground, it was necessary to overthrow "the old economic relationship," which also implied "the transformation of all labour habits" and being ready to "make every sacrifice" and "do away with . . . the habit of looking upon work merely as a duty, and of considering rightful only that work which is paid for at certain rates." [112]

(c) "War communism" and Communist work

Lenin's writings on the subject of Communist work are not numerous, but most of them have great theoretical significance. This is true of what he says about the connection between the *transformation of habits* and *the building of new economic relationships*. We are here a long way from the view that it is necessary to wait for a change in economic relationships to take place through pressure from the development of the productive forces.

This is also true of the observations he makes when he shows that the real "constructive task," following the revolutionary overthrow of the exploiters, is that of "establishing new economic relations." [113]

Among his few writings that deal with this question must also be mentioned the *Report on the Tax in Kind*, delivered at a meeting of secretaries and responsible representatives of the RCP (B) cells of Moscow city and Moscow Gubernia on April 9, 1921. This is especially significant because it is subsequent to the "war communism" period. Here Lenin offers a more general definition of socialist economic relations: "In no circumstances must we forget what we have occasion to see very often, namely, the socialist attitude of workers at state factories, who collect fuel, raw materials and food, or try to arrange a proper distribution of manufactured goods among the peasants and to deliver them with their own transport facilities. That is socialism."[114]

However, the new relations which arose between 1918 and 1921 on the initiative of the masses gradually faded away, for a variety of reasons. Among these was the development of administrative centralism, the multiplication of rules and constraints imposed by the state (not propitious for initiatives from below), and the penetration of "bourgeois specialists" into the state machine, with the resulting "bureaucratization." One of the effects of the last-mentioned development was the appearance of "Communist Saturdays" which were no longer "Communist" except in name, as they were made obligatory. This practice (which even received indirect encouragement from certain formulations in the resolution of the Ninth Congress on "The Present Tasks of Economic Construction")[115] tended to destroy the "germs of the new" that were contained in the "Communist Saturdays." It expressed the contradiction between two types of discipline—collective self-discipline, inherent in the genuine "Communist Saturdays," and imposed discipline, inherent in the establishment and development of a centralized machine using coercion in dealing with the masses.

Nevertheless, the "excesses" of centralization and regulation cannot by themselves account for the withering away, after 1920–1921, of Communist work.[116] Actually, once the extremely acute civil war period of class struggle came to an end, Communist work faded away because of the very limited character of the transformation effected in overall social relations. This limitation was dictated by *the phase in which the Russian revolution then found itself.*

In industry, the capitalist division of labor had not been shaken (and, in the transitional stage of the proletarian dictatorship as it then was, matters could not have been otherwise), so that Communist work was only "marginal," appearing in the main outside the process of industrial production.

202 *Charles Bettelheim*

Correlatively with this, the system of bourgeois ideological relations was also only very partially shaken: in the countryside, the stage of the democratic revolution had not been surpassed, and this situation did not constitute favorable ground for the development of socialist relations or Communist work.

There were therefore objective reasons for the narrow limits within which at that time a few fragile "islets" of Communist work could develop. The expansion and even the consolidation of these "islets" would have required a broad transformation of social relations as a whole, in both town and country— and at the opening of the NEP period no such transformation was on the agenda.

Notes

1. " 'Left-Wing' Childishness and the Petty-Bourgeois Mentality," in Lenin, *CW*, vol. 27, pp. 323–354; the passage quoted is on p. 333.
2. Ibid., p. 334.
3. *CW*, vol. 27, pp. 254–255.
4. Ibid., vol. 26. pp. 104–105.
5. " 'Left-wing' Childishness," in *CW*, vol. 27, p. 336. It will be observed that in this passage Lenin employs, unusually for him, the expression "state socialist," which is a contradiction in terms. He does this for the sake of contrast with "state capitalist" in the sense which was previously current, that is, referring to state capitalism under the dictatorship of the bourgeoisie. In alluding to what here appears as "state socialism" Lenin usually employs the expression "state capitalism under the dictatorship of the proletariat." We shall see later on the significance of this expression and some of the ways in which Lenin uses it.
6. On this point, see *CW*, vol. 26, pp. 264–265.
7. Lozovsky, *Rabochy Kontrol'*, p. 21: quoted in E. H. Carr, *The Bolshevik Revolution 1917–1923*, vol. 2, p. 74.
8. *CW*, vol. 26, pp. 423–424.
9. "How to Organise Competition," in ibid., p. 410.

10. *CW*, vol. 27, p. 241.
11. *CW*, vol. 26, pp. 264–265.
12. See Maurice Brinton, *The Bolsheviks and Workers' Control*, p. 18.
13. Carr, *The Bolshevik Revolution*, vol. 2, p. 78.
14. Ibid., pp. 79 ff.
15. See Lenin's speech at the Third Congress of Soviets in *CW*, vol. 26, pp. 453 ff., especially p. 468.
16. *Malaya Sovyetskaya Entsiklopediya*, vol. 2, article on "Gosplan," p. 599.
17. Lenin had no doubt whatever that, on the whole, the engineers, technicians, administrators, and other "specialists" inherited from the old regime constituted a "bourgeois section of the population," as he said, for example, in "All Out for the Fight Against Denikin!", *CW*, vol. 29, p. 418.
18. Quoted in Carr, *The Bolshevik Revolution*, vol. 2, p. 90.
19. " 'Left-Wing' Childishness," in *CW*, vol. 27, p. 349.
20. *CW*, vol. 27, p. 256.
21. Information about the measures mentioned, and some others, will be found in the appendices to volume 22 of the 3rd edition of Lenin's works, published in Russian in 1935 (pp. 549–572); in Carr, *The Bolshevik Revolution*, vol. 2, pp. 73 ff.; in the minutes of the sessions of the VTsIK in the collection (*Sobranie*) of decrees and decisions concerning the economy published in Moscow (in Russia) in 1918, and covering the period between October 25, 1917, and October 25, 1918 (see especially, pp. 171–172 and 311–315); and in an article by D. L. Limon, "Lénine et le contrôle ouvrier." The measures taken by the Soviet government in the spheres of workers' control and economic management in 1917–1921 are summarized in M. Brinton. See also Raoul Labry, *Une Législation communiste*, especially pp. 131–136.
22. "The Immediate Tasks of the Soviet Government," in *CW*, vol. 27, p. 259.
23. Ibid., pp. 248–249.
24. Ibid., p. 249 (my emphasis—C. B.).
25. Some aspects of this problem are discussed (in connection with the changes brought about in China during the Cultural Revolution) in Bettelheim, *Cultural Revolution and Industrial Organisation in China*, pp. 91–103.
26. *CW*, vol. 27, p. 349.

27. *CW*, vol. 30, p. 458.
28. *K.P.S.S. v rezolyutsiyakh,* vol. I, pp. 476 ff.
29. Bukharin, *Economics of the Transformation Period*, p. 129.
30. Ibid., pp. 129–130.
31. Bukharin's change of line between 1918 and 1920 reveals, throughout, a "mechanistic," undialectical conception of Marxism. According to this conception, the economic basis and the superstructure do not possess relative independence, do not form a contradictory whole, but are a totality each part of which expresses the structure of the whole. In 1918 this conception caused Bukharin to claim that the existence of capitalist discipline in the factories was equivalent to a negation of the proletarian dictatorship. In 1920 the same conception made him claim that the existence of the proletarian dictatorship guaranteed the socialist character of the management of the factories. Similarly, his lack of a dialectical conception of what is meant by a contradictory unity prevented Bukharin from grasping, in his discussion with Lenin at the end of 1920, that the Soviet state of that time was "a workers' and peasants' state": for him it had to be *either* a workers' state *or* a peasants' state.
32. *CW,* vol. 32, pp. 19 ff.
33. *CW*, vol. 33, p. 187.
34. In 1936, in his report on the new Soviet constitution, Stalin claimed that exploiting classes no longer existed in the USSR, and in 1935, in his address to graduates from Red Army academies, he proclaimed, as a principle, that "cadres decide everything" (Stalin, *Leninism*, pp. 565, 543).
35. See *Political Economy: A Textbook.*
36. Dobb, *Soviet Economic Development*, p. 95. According to Dobb, this decree was especially aimed at effecting immediate nationalization of large-scale enterprises in the Ukraine, so as to ensure that in regions occupied by the German army it would not be possible for German capital to "purchase" these enterprises from the Russian or Ukrainian capitalists.
37. Ibid., p. 96.
38. This was, among other things, the public prosecutor's office, which supervised the working of the courts. Quite a number of Menshevik former lawyers (such as Vyshinsky, the future public prosecutor in the trials of the 1930s) entered it. In the political police it was more a question of former SRs.
39. *CW*, vol. 30, pp. 107 ff., especially p. 115.
40. *Narodnoye Kh.SSSR v 1970 g.,* p. 22.

41. This was what Lenin pointed out when he reminded his listeners that capital is not a sum of money but "a definite social relation." In this case, it was a question of the social relations implicit in the division of labor.
42. See Lenin's report to the Eighth Party Congress, in *CW*, vol. 29, especially pp. 178–179.
43. Ibid., p. 180.
44. Ibid., p. 152.
45. For more details on this point, see Carr, *The Bolshevik Revolution*, vol. 2, pp. 205–206.
46. In 1919 and 1920 Lenin denounced this situation several times. It was in May 1918 that distribution in kind of part of factory production began to be practised. See ibid., pp. 243–245.
47. See ibid., p. 194, n. 5. During the 1920s, an attempt was made to limit the authority of the manager by requiring him to consult the secretary of the party committee in the factory and the secretary of the trade union on all important questions. This was called the "triangle system." It did not work satisfactorily, and at the beginning of the period of the five year plans, the authority of the manager (now increasingly a party member of working-class origin) was again predominant, although in many cases the secretary of the party committee in the factory might possess at least equivalent authority.
48. Gins, *Sibir', soyuzniki i Kolchak*, vol. 2, p. 429.
49. While the class origin of the members of this state bourgeoisie played at first an important role in the formation of the class, this was not so later on. When the state bourgeoisie became consolidated, the class origin of its members ceased to be significant: thereafter, what was decisive was the place occupied by this new class in relation to the means of production, its role in the social division of labor, the share of the wealth produced that it took, and the class practices that it developed.
50. Quoted in Carr, *The Bolshevik Revolution*, vol. 2, p. 170, n. 1.
51. *CW*, vol. 29, pp. 228 ff.
52. *CW*, vol. 33, pp. 194–195.
53. Lindenberg, *L'Internationale Communiste*, p. 289.
54. On the Soviet educational system immediately after October, see also Lindenberg's article, "Sur la préhistoire de l'école soviétique," pp. 57 ff. On the place of "the school" in the reproduction of bourgeois relations and ideological practices, see Baudelot and Establet, *L'Ecole capitaliste en France*.
55. See Lindenberg, *L'Internationale Communiste*, pp. 306–307.

56. Ibid., p. 304.
57. Thus, from August 1918 on, a differential rationing system applied in Moscow and Petrograd. The population was divided into three categories: manual workers doing heavy work; other workers, and the families of all workers; and members of the former bourgeoisie. The rations allowed to the first category were four times larger, and those of the second category three times larger, than those allowed to the third category. A system that was similar, but often more complex, was gradually extended to all the urban centers. Actually, the rations allowed soon became inadequate for all categories: on the eve of the introduction of the NEP the workers in receipt of the largest rations were getting only 1,200-1,900 calories per day, when their minimum allowance should have been 3,000. See Carr, *The Bolshevik Revolution*, vol. 2, pp. 233 and 243.
58. *Narodnoye Khozyaistvo SSSR 1922–72 gg*, pp. 345 and 346.
59. Carr, *The Bolshevik Revolution*, vol. 2, p. 201.
60. "The Immediate Tasks of the Soviet Government," in *CW*, vol. 27, p. 258.
61. *CW*, vol. 27, pp. 323 ff.
62. See Carr, *The Bolshevik Revolution*, vol. 2, p. 205.
63. Marx, *Capital*, vol. III, p. 379.
64. Marx and Engels, *The German Ideology*, p. 86.
65. *CW*, vol. 26, p. 409.
66. Ibid., p. 413.
67. He wrote, for example, that "the workers and peasants are still 'timid'; they must get rid of this timidity, and they *certainly* will get rid of it" (ibid., p. 412).
68. Ibid., p. 411.
69. Ibid., p. 403.
70. *CW*, vol. 27, p. 300.
71. Ibid., p. 232. Kornilov, Dutov, and Kaledin were commanders of counter-revolutionary forces.
72. Ibid., pp. 271–272. Kornilov, Dutov, and Bogayevsky were White generals: Gotz and Gegechkori—the former an SR, the latter a Menshevik—were politicians who engaged in counter-revolutionary activities.
73. See Lenin's report to the Second All-Russia Congress of Trade Unions, in *CW*, vol. 28, pp. 412 ff., especially p. 419. It will be observed that Lenin uses the expression "governmentalizing," whereas the passing of industrial enterprises into state owner-

ship is called "nationalization." The original Russian terms are, respectively, *ogosudarstvlenie* [better rendered as "statization" than, as in the official translation, "governmentalizing"— Trans.] and *natsionalizatsiya*.

74. *K.P.S.S. v rezolyutsiyakh*, vol. 1, pp. 490–494.
75. Ibid., p. 486.
76. Ibid., pp. 477–490.
77. Ibid., pp. 485–486.
78. *Sobranie uzakonenii, 1917–1918*, no. 64, art. 704, and no. 80, art. 838, quoted in Carr, *The Bolshevik Revolution*, vol. 2, p. 202, n. 1 and 2.
79. See *K.P.S.S. v. Rezolyutsiyakh*, vol. 1, p. 422 (Eng. trans. from appendix to *The ABC of Communism*, ed. E. H. Carr, p. 448).
80. Quoted in Carr, *The Bolshevik Revolution*, vol. 2, p. 211, note 1.
81. Ibid. In April 1919 forced labor camps were set up. In principle, these camps, which were at first administered by the Cheka and later by the People's Commissariat for Internal Affairs (NKVD), were intended for counter-revolutionary elements who had been sentenced by a tribunal. See Carr, *The Bolshevik Revolution*, vol. 2, pp. 212–213.
82. Quoted in ibid., p. 212, n. 2.
83. Kritsman, *Geroichesky period*, p. 106.
84. See appendices to volume 25 of the 3rd edition of Lenin's works (in Russian), p. 556. It was at this time that, alongside the labor camps already mentioned, concentration camps were established. As Carr points out, the concentration camps of 1920 did not have the importance or the economic role they acquired later on, in the period of the five year plans and after.
85. *CW*, vol. 25, pp. 366–373; quotation from p. 370.
86. *CW*, vol. 31, pp. 17 ff.
87. Ibid., pp. 24–25.
88. Ibid., p. 25.
89. Ibid.
90. Ibid.
91. Ibid., p. 44.
92. *CW*, vol. 31, pp. 408 ff., particularly pp. 425–426.
93. Except where otherwise stated, the figures are those for January 1 of each year. They are quoted by Rigby, *Communist Party Membership*, pp. 52–53. From 1919 onward, there was a category of "candidate members" undergoing probation, who do not appear as such in the statistics until after 1922. In principle

they are not included in earlier figures, but this seems contrary to what is said in other estimates, such as those given in the first edition of the *Bolshaya Sovyetskaya Entsiklopediya*.

94. The question of the social composition of the Bolshevik Party and of the significance of the statistics available on this subject is considered later.

95. See Rigby, *Communist Party Membership*, p. 85, for the class composition of the party. The percentages are calculated in accordance with various Soviet sources.

96. Ibid., p. 81.

97. Ibid.

98. In ibid., p. 82.

99. *CW*, vol. 29, pp. 409 ff. The pamphlet was first published in Moscow in July 1919.

100. Ibid., pp. 411–412.

101. Ibid., p. 424.

102. Ibid., p. 425.

103. Ibid., pp. 425–426.

104. Ibid., p. 426.

105. Ibid., p. 427.

106. Ibid., pp. 429–430.

107. Ibid., p. 431.

108. Ibid., p. 423.

109. Marx, *Un Chapitre inédit du "Capital,"* p. 263. In the *Grundrisse* (pp. 158–159), Marx points out that "the very necessity of first transforming individual products or activities into *exchange value* . . . proves two things: (1) that individuals now produce only for society and in society; (2) that production is not *directly* social, is not 'the offspring of association,' which distributes labour internally. Individuals are subsumed under social production; social production exists outside them, as their fate; but social production is not subsumed under individuals, manageable by them as their common wealth." This leads him to observe that "there can therefore be nothing more erroneous and absurd than to postulate the control by the united individuals of their total production, on the basis of *exchange value,* of *money,* as was done . . . in the case of the time-chit bank" (and, we may add today, as is done in present Soviet economic practice). A few pages further on, Marx notes that it is only with collective production, when production has a "communal character," that labor is not "particular" but "general," so that

what the individual "has bought with his labour is not a specific and particular product, but rather a specific share of the communal production" (ibid., pp. 171–172). It was to this type of relation that the "Communist Saturdays" gave birth.

110. *CW*, vol. 30, pp. 516 ff.
111. *CW*, vol. 31, pp. 123 ff.
112. Ibid., p. 124.
113. "Our Foreign and Domestic Position," in *CW*, vol. 31, pp. 408 ff., especially p. 417.
114. *CW*, vol. 32, p. 296.
115. See appendices to volume 25 of the 3rd edition of Lenin's works, pp. 548–558.
116. Even today "Communist Saturdays" are still held in the Soviet Union, but they have nothing in common with the Communist Saturdays that sprang from the initiative of the masses. They are an imposed ritual which serves as a means of getting extra work out of the workers.

3. *The transformation of class relations in the countryside*

The transformation of class relations in the Soviet countryside between 1917 and 1923 was also the outcome of a revolutionary process, but *this* process was basically democratic, resulting from the alliance between the proletariat and the peasantry. It took place through the activity of the peasant masses, protected and consolidated by the dictatorship of the proletariat, which gave support to the democratic revolution in the countryside.

One of the first and most important steps taken by the Soviet power on the very morrow of its establishment was the "decree on land" (ratified on October 26, 1917, by the Second All-Russia Congress of Soviets). This decree annulled all private ownership of land: the estates of the landlords, of the state, and of the church were placed at the disposal of the district committees and peasants' soviets. By this decree the Soviet government proved concretely that it was a workers' and peasants' government. The Soviet state thus showed clearly that, unlike the previous state, it did not protect the interests of the landlords and bourgeois, but, on the contrary, deprived them of their lands. Furthermore, the Soviet power told the peasants that it was encouraging them to take the land *themselves* and to *organize themselves* in order to regulate the use they made of it.

The implications of the October decree were enormous. By confirming in practice that the new ruling power was not that of the exploiting classes, it helped to tip the balance in favor of the Soviet revolution among the still hesitant sections of the peasantry for whom the question of the land (like that of peace, which the Soviet power announced its willingness to conclude immediately) was absolutely vital. The proletarian

210

revolution in the towns thus ensured that the revolutionary movement of the peasants would develop in a new way.

The actual content of the "decree on land," and of the documents accompanying and following it which dealt with its practical application, did not correspond to the Bolshevik Party's previous program, but coincided almost exactly with the first draft of a decree drawn up in August 1917 by the All-Russia Peasants' Congress, which was largely dominated by the Socialist-Revolutionary Party. To those Bolsheviks who protested against their party's approval of arrangements which it had previously stigmatized as being bourgeois-democratic, not socialist—in that, instead of abolishing private exploitation of the land and favoring the development of large, socialist units of production, it favored the multiplication of small-scale units—Lenin replied that these arrangements gave expression to "the absolute will of the vast majority of the class-conscious peasants of Russia."[1]

One of the most remarkable aspects of the October decree—and, to a hardly lesser extent, of the law promulgated on February 19, 1918, which was called the law on "socialization of the land"[2]—was that it did not seek to impose upon the peasants from above any strict rules about what was to be done with the land. The Bolshevik Party was, of course, in favor of collective forms of exploitation of the land, but it wished the peasants to adopt such forms on the basis of their own experience. In this sphere, too, Lenin called on the Bolsheviks to *have confidence in the peasants*. In his address to the Second All-Russia Congress of Soviets, for example, he said:

> In the fire of experience, applying the decree in practice and carrying it out locally, the peasants will themselves realise where the truth lies . . . Experience is the best teacher, and it will show who is right. Let the peasants solve this problem from one end and we shall solve it from the other. Experience will oblige us to draw together in the general stream of revolutionary creative work, in the elaboration of new state forms. We must be guided by experience; we must allow complete freedom to the creative faculties of the masses.[3]

The decisions taken at the end of 1917 and the beginning of

1918 by the Soviet power were thus far from being mere "legislative documents." They were appeals to the masses. They showed confidence in the experience and patient work of the Bolsheviks who would help the peasants to understand what form of social organization would be best for them. They opened the way to something more than a mere legal transfer of ownership—to an upheaval in production relations. It was the mass movement that, given the prevailing objective and subjective conditions, would determine the new production relations emerging from the class struggle that developed in the countryside. Since these new relations emerged from the destruction of the old ones, it is impossible to understand the nature of the revolutionary process then under way in rural Russia unless account is taken of the concrete conditions of the struggles and the specific character of the social relations which were formerly dominant there, and which, moreover, were only partly destroyed during the period 1917–1922.

I. The specific character of the former social relations in the countryside

The social relations and class relations in Russia's rural areas on the eve of the revolution were highly complex and are not well-known. The bulk of the "documentation" about rural realities in prerevolutionary Russia comes from bourgeois specialists—the *zemstvo*[4] statisticians and the rural economists: both described that fraction of the countryside with which they were concerned from the standpoint of their class practice and in terms of their own ideology. Hence the great difficulty experienced by the Bolsheviks in "translating" the "information" provided by these specialists into the terms of production relations.

Lenin was undoubtedly the Bolshevik leader who had most systematically worked over the available documentation. He had brought out in a striking way the importance of the tendencies to capitalist development that existed in the countryside of tsarist Russia. His very earliest writings were devoted to analyzing this problem: *New Economic Developments in Peasant Life, On the So-Called Market Question,* etc.[5] One of his principal economic works, *The Development of Capitalism in Russia,* dealt with it, and he wrote about it in his many polemics with the Narodniks and SRs.

Lenin showed that the complexity of the social relations in the Russian countryside, and the plurality of forms assumed by capitalist development there at the end of the nineteenth and the beginning of the twentieth centuries, were due to the existence of a dynamic stratum of capitalist peasants who had left the old village communities, and to the transformation of some big landlords into capitalist agriculturists. He showed, too, how capitalism was emerging within the peasant communities themselves.

The peasant community, the *mir,* is one of the specific features of Russian rural life which has given rise to many illusions and much discussion. The *mir* was a community that functioned at village level. It controlled the peasants' land,[6] and shared it out among its members in accordance with various criteria which were supposed to maintain a certain "equality" among the various peasant households. After the last quarter of the nineteenth century, the law forbade shareouts at intervals of less than twelve years.

The unit for allotment of a share of the land was the household, and the area of land received by each household was, in principle, a definite proportion of the land of the village to which this household belonged (leaving aside the forests and pastures which made up the common land not subject to distribution). This proportion was decided by taking account of the "number" of members in each household: but, depending on the particular village, this "number" might correspond to the number of "mouths" that the household had to feed or the number of persons in it who were capable of work, and it could also be decided in accordance with the means of production at the household's disposal, in particular the number of draft animals in its possession. Inquiries carried out at that time showed that rich households (which were usually the most numerous, as they frequently practiced adoption) were often the ones most favored when the land was redivided. Moreover, the poor households (those which were inadequately provided with instruments of production) were often obliged to lease out the land assigned to them, and their able-bodied members had to take jobs as wage laborers. Thus, a small group of rich families might dòminate a village.

The inequalities which developed in this way were due to the fact that, behind the "communal" facade of the *mir,* the basic reality was fragmented labor, individual cultivation and stockbreeding, and private ownership of the instruments of production, especially draft animals. As Marx had observed as far back as 1881, the *mir* was breaking up from within because "labour on one's own lot" was "a source of private appropriation," making possible "the accumulation of movable goods,"[7] in other words, a social differentiation. This inevitably affected the functioning of the peasant assembly which regulated "common concerns" and the redistribution of the land. From having been "egalitarian," the *mir* gradually became a means of consolidating and reproducing economic and social inequalities. At the end of the nineteenth and the beginning of the twentieth century, this development was fostered by the landlords, to whom the *mir* was in practice subordinate, and by the general progress of capitalism.

The Narodniks and SRs sought to deny that this evolution was taking place, and interpreted in a one-sided way the 1882 preface to the Russian translation of the *Communist Manifesto,* in which Marx and Engels wrote: "If the Russian Revolution becomes the signal for a proletarian revolution in the West, so that both complement each other, the present Russian common ownership of land may serve as the starting-point for a communist development."[8]

Here we find what Marx had written a year earlier in a letter to Vera Zasulich. In that letter, however, Marx emphasized the forces disintegrating the *mir* from within and also those which were attacking it from without. In 1881 Marx already noted that "the 'village community' is reduced almost to its last gasp."[9]

Thirteen years later, in 1894, Engels remarked that, in the period that had elapsed, "the development of capitalism and the dissolution of the village community in Russia have both taken enormous strides forward."[10]

Lenin, in showing the effects of the development of capitalism in Russia, carried forward in the form of a concrete analysis the comments made by Marx and Engels. At the same time, he warned (for example, in his article of 1905, "From Narodism to Marxism") against the illusions of the Narodniks who thought that the old peasant communities could be revived by means of various "reforms." On this point he wrote: "The 'bourgeois-proprietary' (and at the same time labouring) peasantry has already made good use of the socialist phrases of the Narodnik, democratic intelligentsia which harboured illusions of sustaining 'the toiler traditions and modes of life' by means of its *artels*, co-operatives, fodder-grass cultivation, ploughs, Zemstvo warehouses and banks, but which actually promoted the development of capitalism within the commune."[11]

To the many figures quoted by Lenin which show the development of capitalism in the countryside, it is perhaps worth adding others taken from writers who would like to "prove" that the *mir* did really operate as a leveling device, and yet, in fact, prove the contrary. This is the case with T. Shanin, who shows that in the province of Kaluga in 1897 the area of land *per head* varied in the proportion of 1 to 26 (or of 1 to 3 if the category of landless peasants is excluded), and that it was the most numerous households—those of the *rich peasants* (enlarged, as we know, through the practice of adoption)—that held *the largest amount of land per head.*[12]

Statistics regarding the history of households, though usually also compiled with a view to proving that the latter passed through a "cycle of successive dimensions" (as a consequence of redistributions of land among households), show that in fact this did not happen. Thus, one such set of figures reveals that after thirty years (between 1882 and 1911), 75 percent of the households that originally possessed less than six desyatins were still in the same category and that this was likewise true of about two-fifths of the households possessing more than nine desyatins.[13]

Analysis of social differentiation in the Russian village shows that the *mir* presented no real obstacle to the development of capitalism, but that its existence did give rise to a certain number of problems, as it *ensured the reproduction of specific social relations* which need to be taken into account if one is to appreciate the forms that the class struggle could assume in the countryside of Russia before and after the revolution. Although seriously undermined by inner contradictions, the *mir* still existed in February 1917, and it affected to a considerable extent the way in which the revolution developed in the countryside and also, subsequently, the functioning of the NEP.

The *mir* furnished a political and ideological apparatus that enabled the peasants to act in a relatively "independent" fashion. After October 1917, owing to the absence of a strong representation of the Bolshevik Party in the rural areas, this relative "independence" enabled the village rich to dominate the poor and middle peasants more easily. It must not be forgotten that at the end of 1917, the Bolshevik Party had only 203 peasant branches with 4,122 members, and in 1918 only 2,304 branches with 14,792 members.

Even at that time the "peasant" branches were thus very few in number, and their members (who were largely rural civil servants, such as primary school teachers) made up hardly 5 percent of the party's total membership.

The effects of the *mir*'s existence and of the specific social relations corresponding to it are all the more worthy of attention because the illusion that the *mir* constituted a distinctive "mode of production" and an instrument of social "leveling" continues to be fairly widespread. Briefly, these are the main points to be noted:

(1) The *mir* was not a mode of production (a definite way of producing) but a political apparatus for carrying out redistribution of the land, which ensured not collective but individual cultivation. Consequently, producers "did as they

liked" with what they produced, being free to sell it and to accumulate "freely." The *mir* did indeed impose certain rules on its members, but these were intended to facilitate individual cultivation of the separate holdings and had nothing to do with collective cultivation. The sole "residue" of a former communal mode of production was limited to a few practices of mutual aid between neighbors, and even these amounted to little, being often transformed by the development of exchange, which led to *payment* being required for the services rendered.

(2) The *mir*, being a political apparatus, was of course, not "neutral." It was the battlefield of a class struggle that was fought out within it, and it felt the effects of the class struggle taking place on the scale of society as a whole. Generally speaking, the *mir* was dominated by the better-off peasants, who were often elected village heads or members of the permanent organs of administration, and they profited by their position of advantage to perpetuate their privileged situation. Their advantageous position also made itself felt in the redistribution of the land, despite the "egalitarian principles" which were supposed to govern its procedure. The relatively limited effects of the division of the land carried out between 1917 and 1922, seem to confirm that the domination of the *mir* by the well-to-do peasants was maintained even during those years of acute class struggle.

(3) The *mir* and the *skhod* (the general assembly of peasants) nevertheless took the form of a village community, tending to make of every village a little world of its own, cut off from the rest, with its own local authorities. Historical experience shows that this form fosters a "village patriotism," a local egoism, which has as its counterpart a profound indifference to whatever is happening outside. Historically, the *mir* was the foundation on which the tsarist autocracy developed. Tsardom was the instrument "unifying," in a largely formal way, all the village communities. By ensuring their "military defense," tsardom established an external link between them which enabled it to enslave them. It is significant that most

peasant revolts in Russia were directed against the landlords, not against the tsar. Until the imperialist epoch, the tsar seemed to the peasants to be someone to whom they could "appeal" against the landlords. When the peasants were drafted, they thought of themselves as going to fight not "for Russia" but "for the tsar." The *mir*, based as it was on the household as unit of production, strengthened petty bourgeois individualism. This individualism, combined with the local egoism engendered by the workings of the *mir*, accounts for the relative indifference shown by the peasants, during the period of "war communism," toward the hardships then being suffered by the towns, which were without food.

(4) While substantial inequalities were reproduced on an expanded scale under the prevailing egalitarian forms (which, moreover, were concerned in practice only with land), these forms did nevertheless help, at the ideological level, to reinforce petty bourgeois egalitarianism and individualism. Both of these obtained on a very large scale, to the detriment of the peasants' own interests, leading as they did to "miniparcellization" of the land, in order that each peasant might have a piece of each quality of land—an arrangement which meant that some peasants had to travel huge distances, and also that considerable tracts of land were lost to cultivation. It also contributed to "freezing" for centuries (and even after the revolution) the methods of cultivation, and was thus one of the factors in the low yields and famines that afflicted the peasantry.

It is not wholly out of the question that if the Bolshevik Party had been more effectively present in the countryside, and had been able to make use of what survived of communal traditions in the *mir*, the latter might have been made the point of departure for collective farming. However, if Marx and Engels felt doubtful on the point at the end of the nineteenth century, there is even more reason to doubt whether such a possibility existed at the time of the October Revolution. The *mir*, having undergone still further decomposition, had become a form concealing a reality quite different from what appeared on the surface.

II. *The democratic agrarian revolution and the hope of a socialist agrarian revolution*

The "decree on land" and the subsequent documents issued by the Soviet power gave an extra stimulus to the movement that the peasants had themselves undertaken, from 1917 onward, to seize the estates of the landlords.

(a) *The democratic agrarian revolution of the winter of 1917–1918*

During the winter of 1917–1918 and the succeeding months, the peasants—now backed by the Soviet power—took over (mainly acting through the *mir*) most of the land[14] belonging to the landlords, the state, and the church. The land thus acquired constituted a substantial area, for in 1916 the big landlords held 40 percent of all the cultivable land in Russia.[15]

At the same time, the peasants also took over (again, usually through the *mir*) a part, which has not been estimated, of the land of the rich peasants who had broken away from the *mir* after the reforms of 1861 and 1906. We have inadequate information regarding the land held by these peasants on the eve of October,[16] and we know still less about how much of it was taken from them after October.[17] In any case, these "recoveries" considerably improved the situation of part of the peasantry.[18]

Each *mir* distributed the lands it recovered among the peasant households of the village, for them to cultivate individually. Individual cultivation was thus preserved, for the encouragement being given to joint cultivation by the Bolshevik Party and the Soviet government had little effect at that time.

A quantitative estimate of the results of this process of revolutionary transformation launched by the mass movement of the peasants backed by the Soviet power, becomes possible only in 1919. At that time, according to Soviet statistics (which were doubtless highly approximate), 96.8 percent of the land under cultivation was held by peasants who worked it individually (either within or outside the framework of the *mir*), 0.5 percent was held by agricultural cooperatives, and 2.7 percent was held by state farms.[19] The agrarian revolution had thus indeed been a *democratic, not a socialist transformation.*

This agrarian revolution did not change very deeply the way the *mir* functioned. The sharing-out of land continued to be effected on the basis of the "household" (the peasant "hearth"), and according to the same criteria as before. The scanty information available suggests that, when the land was being divided, the "authority" of the rich peasants (who owned animals and equipment) continued to make itself felt. On the whole, however, because of the acuteness of the class struggle and the reappropriation of the bulk of the land that had been taken out of the *mir,* the proportion of poor peasants was reduced, together with social inequality. Nevertheless, a considerable body of poor peasants continued to exist, and it was on them that the Bolshevik Party sought to rely, in the period from June 1918 onward, in stimulating the class struggle in the countryside, fighting against the rich peasants (kulaks) and their influence, both economic and political.

(b) The attempt to develop an independent movement of poor peasants in the summer of 1918

The Bolshevik Party's desire to base itself, in the countryside, first and foremost upon the agricultural laborers and poor peasants (the rural semiproletariat) was expressed in its program, and was recalled in Lenin's "April Theses." In June 1918 the party thought that the time had come to help these two groups fight directly for socialism. It thought indeed that the democratic agrarian revolution was essentially completed, so that preparation of the socialist stage was now on the agenda. At the same time, the party sought to mobilize in the villages those specific social forces on which it considered the proletarian power must rely in order to cope with economic disorganization: above all, the poor peasants, who were most directly interested in socialism.

During the summer of 1918 the decline in agricultural production assumed very serious proportions, just at the time when the White forces and the interventionist armies were beginning to go into action. The feeding of the towns was gravely jeopardized, for the peasants no longer had any but small quantities of produce available for exchange and were unwilling to sell what they had: the inflation that had developed meant that they could easily pay their taxes (as the phrase then went, "the villages were awash with money") and they had practically nothing to buy in the towns in any case.

In these circumstances the Bolshevik Party and the Soviet government endeavored to break with the policy followed up to that time with regard to the peasantry, a policy which treated the peasantry "as a whole," as an "undifferentiated" ally of the proletariat, an ally within which class differences were as yet of secondary importance and which was fighting to carry through its own task—the democratic agrarian revolution.

A decree of June 11, 1918, gave concrete form to this move. It provided for the setting up of organs of power distinct from the peasant soviets and made up exclusively of poor peasants. This decree officially committed the Bolshevik Party and the Soviet government to systematic *differential treatment* of the different classes of the peasantry. A document of July 11, 1918, stipulated that only peasants who did not employ wage workers and who had no surpluses of grain available for collection could belong to the poor peasants' committees. On July 15 it was decided that the poor peasants' committees were to be one of the instruments of Soviet policy in the countryside, in particular, by helping in the seizure of grain from the kulaks: the poor peasants would be allowed to keep for themselves a proportion of the grain thus confiscated.[20]

For Lenin, at least in 1918, the formation of the poor peasants' committees signified the development of the class struggle in the countryside, the split at last effected between the agricultural laborers and poor peasants on the one hand, and the well-to-do strata of the peasantry on the other. It seemed to him that now an alliance between the town proletariat and the poor peasants had become possible, with the former helping the latter to organize themselves and according them a specific leading role in the villages.

In his address of November 8, 1918, to the delegates of the poor peasants' committees of the central gubernias, Lenin said: "We decided to split (the peasants) . . . The workers have been helping the poor peasants in their struggle against the kulaks. In the civil war that has flared up in the countryside the workers are on the side of the poor peasants, as they were when they passed the S.R.- sponsored law on the socialisation of the land."[21]

He added that Russia must be covered with poor peasants' committees which would become transformed into soviets, that is, into fully recognized organs of the Soviet power. At the same time he stressed the transition to collective work, to communes, that is, to the socialist transformation of production relations in the countryside. In the same period, in October–November 1918, in his pamphlet on *The Proletarian Revolution and the Renegade Kautsky*, Lenin declared that, with the formation of the poor peasants' committees, the revolution could at last transcend in the countryside the bourgeois limits beyond which it had not hitherto been able to advance. In the same pamphlet he described the situation until June 1918 as having been one of "proletarian revolution in the capitals" and "bourgeois democratic revolution" in the countryside.[22]

At that time most of the Bolshevik leaders thought that the class struggle among the peasants themselves had reached a level such that abandonment of individual cultivation and going over to "the real work of building socialism" had now become possible and necessary.[23] As Lenin saw it, "the ruination left by the war simply does not allow us to restore the old small-scale peasant forms." Furthermore, this same war had given the masses the idea that the wonders of technique which had served for destruction could be put at the service of production, on the basis of collective labor. From this Lenin concluded that "the majority of the working peasants are striving toward collective farming," and that it was therefore now possible to develop collective forms of cultivation, agricultural communes, and state farms.[24]

Lenin emphasized in all his speeches that the socialist transformation of production relations must be the work of the peasants themselves. It was not enough, he said, for the revolutionary leaders to be convinced of the necessity for such a change for the latter to become possible, nor was propaganda alone sufficient to win over millions of peasants: *the latter could become convinced only through practical experience.*[25]

In very explicit terms, Lenin thus connected the socialist transformation of economic relations in the countryside not only with the abolition of private property in land (which, he said, inevitably remained "a paper revolution" as long as "the poor peasants, the working peasants" did not themselves take up the struggle against capitalism,[26] but also with the transformation of political relations within the rural community itself (by the formation of poor peasants' committees) and with the transformation of ideological relations which would enable the mass of the peasants to go over to collective farming.

Lenin's and the Bolshevik Party's hopes for a rapid transition to a socialist agrarian revolution were not borne out by the facts. The majority of the working peasants were not really ready to take that path, and the poor peasants' committees were found to be lacking in vitality. They were not established everywhere, and those that did come into being often represented only a minority of the poor peasants, which, moreover, was not always made up of the most militant elements of that class. The committees sometimes included declassed elements who were attracted by the idea of grabbing some of the produce seized from the rich peasants, and who were not at all interested in setting up collective farms.

The ideological and political differentiation in the peasantry was thus not so advanced as had been supposed in the middle of 1918. The division of the estates had somewhat reduced the proportion of poor peasants and increased that of middle peasants. Above all, because of the lack of an adequate presence of the Bolshevik Party in the rural areas, it had led to a relative revitalization of the *mir,* owing to the role the latter played in the sharing-out of the land, for which it was the instrument, and this meant the consolidation of a certain "unity" of the village in relation to the town, a "unity" which benefited the well-to-do and middle elements among the peasantry.

The Bolshevik Party's move to form poor peasants' commit-tees was thus followed by an unrepresentative minority of that class. Recognizing this, the party concluded that it would be dangerous to persist in pursuing this line, especially at a time when the offensive of the White Guards and interventionists was being intensified and it was essential to strengthen the alliance between the proletariat and the peasantry as a whole.

Toward the end of 1918, the abortive attempt to generalize the formation of poor peasants' committees was dropped (though not systematically). By the beginning of 1919, these committees had mostly merged with the peasant soviets. Thus there opened a new phase in the Bolshevik Party's peasant policy: henceforth, the emphasis was placed much more on the middle peasants, whose numbers had, moreover, in-creased as a result of the democratic revolution in the coun-tryside.

III. The years 1919–1920 and the orientation on the middle peasantry for the building of socialism

At the Eighth Congress of the Bolshevik Party (March 18–23, 1919), Lenin directed the party's attention particularly to "the problem of our attitude towards the middle peasants." This problem, he said, could not be brought to the forefront "until we had made secure the basis for the existence of the Soviet Republic," but it must now be tackled directly, in order to "lay the sound foundations of communist society."[27] Ex-plaining the attitude to be adopted, Lenin declared:

> This attitude cannot be defined simply by the answer—struggle or support. As regards the bourgeoisie our task is defined by the words "struggle," "suppression," and as regards the rural pro-letariat and semi-proletariat our task is defined by the words "our support," but this problem is undoubtedly more complicated. On this point, the socialists, the best representatives of socialism in

the old days, when they still believed in the revolution and faithfully adhered to its theory and ideals, talked about *neutralising the peasantry,* i.e., making the middle peasants a social stratum which, if it did not actively help the proletarian revolution, at least would not hinder it, that would remain neutral and not go over to the side of our enemies. This abstract, theoretical formulation of the problem is quite clear but is inadequate. We have reached the stage of socialist development when we must draw up definite and detailed rules and regulations *which have been tested by practical experience in the rural districts* [my emphasis—C. B.] to guide us in our efforts to place our relations with the middle peasants *on the basis of a firm alliance* and so preclude the possibility of a repetition of those mistakes and blunders we have repeatedly made in the past. These blunders estranged the middle peasants from us . . ."[28]

These few sentences are of fundamental importance. They pose the question of what was later called "the integration of the middle peasant into socialism." They reject the previously held belief that the middle peasants could not be an ally in the building of socialism, so that the proletariat could only aim to "neutralize" them. They declare that in the building of Communist society, the middle peasant can and must be a "firm" ally. They condemn the "mistakes and blunders" of the past, consisting in the belief that the only possible allies in the countryside, for the building of socialism, were the rural proletarians and semiproletarians. They raise the problem of what the concrete conditions are for establishing this "firm alliance" which has not yet been realized.

Lenin does not claim to be in a position to answer this question there and then. He considers it necessary to study the experience of work in the countryside. However, he warns expressly against continuing a situation in which "the blows which were intended for the kulaks very frequently fell on the middle peasants. In this respect we have sinned a great deal."[29]

The context shows that this mistake was not unconnected with the way in which the poor peasants' committees were formed and with the role that these committees played in the sphere of requisitioning and food supply.

The mistakes of orientation made in the second half of 1918 are certainly to be explained in part by the place previously given to the idea of mere "neutralization" of the middle peasant, but above all by the lack of any practical experience before that time, and by the presence in the party of a "rightist-leftist" tendency. The latter was disposed to consider any change in labor relations that gave rise to collective forms of production as a step toward socialism, even if it was imposed from above by coercion, provided that the state of the dictatorship of the proletariat was the agent of this change.

On March 13, 1919, at the First Congress of Farm Laborers of Petrograd Gubernia, Lenin spoke very firmly against the tendency of certain party officials to "compel" peasants to join collective farms. He reminded his hearers that "the Soviet government must not under any circumstances resort to coercion . . . Agricultural communes are established on a voluntary basis; the adoption of collective tillage must be voluntary; the workers' and peasants' government must refrain from exercising the slightest compulsion, and the law prohibits this."[30]

Clearly, when he recalled these principles, Lenin was not concerned with the formal aspect of legality: what mattered to him was to stress that the founding of agricultural communes by force could not give rise to communist forms of labor.

At this same congress Lenin also spoke against the compromise of forming "state farms" in which the participants retained individual holdings. He considered that if such holdings existed they would be a germ of decomposition in the state farms. Thus, for instance: "If private vegetable plots, animals, poultry and so forth were permitted again, we should revert to the small farming that had existed hitherto. If that were the case, would it be worth while to have all this bother? Would it be worth while establishing state farms?"[31]

In his report of March 23, to the Eighth Congress of the Bolshevik Party, Lenin again discussed the policy of allying with the middle peasant in order to build socialism. He emphasized once more that it was necessary to refrain from resorting to coercion, that the peasants must not be dragged by

force onto a path they were not ready to follow. He dwelt at
length on this idea, because it was not easily accepted by
certain party members. He said: "If we were to act in the same
way towards the middle peasant (as we acted to crush the
bourgeoisie) it would be such idiocy, such stupidity, it would
be so ruinous to our cause, that only provocateurs could deliberately act in such a way . . . You cannot create anything here
by coercion. Coercion applied to the middle peasants would
cause untold harm."[32] And again:

> We must particularly stress the truth that here by the very nature
> of the case coercive methods can accomplish nothing . . . *Here
> coercion would ruin the whole cause.* Prolonged educational
> work is required . . . On this question we must say that we do
> encourage communes, but they must be so organised *as to gain
> the confidence of the peasants . . . Nothing is more stupid than
> the very idea of applying coercion in economic relations with
> the middle peasant.* The aim is not to expropriate the middle
> peasant but to . . . learn from him methods of transition to a
> better system, and *not to dare to give orders![33]*

The principles are clear—no violence in dealing with the
middle peasants; work must be carried on among them to
convince them, to win their confidence, so that they themselves will change the economic relations; learn from the
peasants, do not dare to give them orders.

The Bolshevik Party formally accepted these principles, but
the administrative organs showed only partial respect for them
during 1919 and 1920, and even violated them where requisitioning was concerned. Only after the introduction of the
NEP were these principles really respected—and then they
were jettisoned again when the collectivization campaign was
launched at the end of the 1920s.

The party's rallying to the point of view voiced by Lenin
was expressed in the adoption of a resolution "On the Attitude
to the Middle Peasants."[34] It condemned "arbitrary action on
the part of the local authorities" in dealing with the middle
peasants, who "are not exploiters since they do not profit by
the labour of others," and it encouraged the formation of
agricultural communes on an exclusively voluntary basis. It

condemned the way requisitioning had been carried out among the middle peasants and declared that such requisitioning must be exercised with moderation. Finally, it dwelt at length on the help and support that the Soviet power must render to the middle peasants so that they might improve their individual holdings, through being backed up by cooperatives providing services and financing. This resolution is of all the greater importance from the standpoint of principle in that it was adopted at a time when the illusions of "war communism" about "direct" transition to communism were at their height.

In practice, the resolution was applied very unevenly. The objective process of the class struggle proceeding in Russian society as a whole, the party's weak roots in the countryside, and the acute crisis in the supply of food to the towns meant that the Bolshevik Party could only partially honor the decisions of the Eighth Congress regarding the middle peasants.

(a) The emergence of socialist relations in the countryside

It was in the matter of the transition to collective cultivation and the need for no coercion to be used in this field that the decisions of the Eighth Party Congress had most effect.

In October 1919, in *Economics and Politics in the Era of the Dictatorship of the Proletariat*,[35] Lenin observed that in the transition to collectivism in agriculture Russia had as yet taken only the "first steps."[36] Indeed, in 1919 there were only 2,100 agricultural communes with some 350,000 members, and these figures later diminished: there were only 1,520 communes in March 1920. Some of them had had to dissolve in the face of the hostility shown by other peasants: this hostility, stirred up by the kulaks, sometimes led to the murder of commune members by peasants from neighboring villages.

The agricultural communes were formed mainly by the poor and landless, not by middle peasants. Some of them were first established by workers from the industrial centers, as happened in 1918, for example, on the outskirts of Petrograd—

which shows the close connection the industrial workers still retained with agriculture.[37]

Another form of socialist production was constituted in this period by the "Soviet farms," or "state farms" *(sovkhozy)*. These were formed by the Soviet state and not directly by the toilers themselves, and those who worked in them were paid wages. Their socialist character depended on the extent to which they were actually subordinate to the state of the proletarian dictatorship.

In 1919, the number of state farms was a little larger than the number of agricultural communes—3,500—and this figure even rose to 4,400 in 1920. They were still relatively small affairs, most covering less than 200 hectares, usually poor land of which not even half was under cultivation.

Finally, alongside these two forms there were *artels*, that is, producers' cooperatives of a lower type which carried on collective cultivation of fields that remained privately owned. These *artels* were a little more numerous than the communes: 1,900 in 1919 and 3,800 in 1920.[38]

Altogether, these forms of production represented almost nothing in the immense ocean of individual production. Nevertheless, their *importance from the standpoint of principle* was considerable.

The poor development of collective production in its various forms showed that socialist ideas had barely penetrated the countryside, and was also due to the fact that the Bolshevik Party thereafter refrained from imposing these forms, especially as it did not view this as the main task at a time when the principal contradiction was still that which confronted the workers and peasants with the White Guards who were defending the landlords and capitalists, and with imperialism.

(b) Helping the middle peasant

The help for the middle peasant provided for in the Eighth Congress resolution did not materialize. In view of the condition of Russia's economy at the time, it was not possible to supply the peasants with improved seeds, artificial fertilizers, or pedigree stock, or to set up centers for repairing machinery or clearing land for tillage. All these intentions remained at that time so many aspirations.

The chief form of help rendered to the middle peasant was political. The local authorities ceased (more or less) to treat him as a kulak as far as his holdings were concerned. He was promised, in a decree adopted in the summer of 1920, that his land would not be taken from him—this was current practice in a number of *mirs*—as long as he cultivated it with his own hands, even if its area was larger than allowed by the regional norms of distribution.[39] This decree was aimed at supporting the middle peasant even against the demands of the poor peasants. The official commentary noted that the decree "creates stability in rural farming. It is necessary that every peasant should be convinced that his share will remain his own, that it will not be taken away from him because the majority wish to make another redistribution."[40]

To sum up, the middle peasant, one of the chief beneficiaries of the agrarian revolution, did not receive, between 1919 and 1921, any material aid from the Soviet power, but the attitude officially adopted offered him reassurance as to his future, whereas previously he had felt threatened by the one-sided emphasis laid on alliance with the poor peasants and by the activities of the committees formed by a section of the latter.

(c) The problem of requisitioning

The decisions of the Eighth Congress on requisitioning were not respected. The middle peasants—who were defending the Soviet power by force of arms: without them victory over the White Guards and the imperialist forces could not have been won—handed over to the Soviet state hardly any of that part of their produce which they did not consume themselves. They sold a big proportion of it on the black market, thus giving priority to their own immediate material interests

over the needs of the front and of the workers and peasants
who were fighting there.

In his speech of November 19, 1919, to the First All-Russia
Conference on Party Work in the Countryside, Lenin pointed
out the dual character of the middle peasant. On the one hand,
he said, the peasant is a toiler, a man who lives by the sweat of
his brow, and who therefore sides with the worker, but on the
other hand "the peasant as a proprietor with a surplus of grain
is accustomed to regarding it as his property which he can sell
freely"—and, Lenin added, "anyone who sells grain surpluses
in a hunger-ridden country becomes a profiteer, an exploiter,
because the starving man will give everything he has for
bread." [41]

Basing himself on this formulation, Lenin said that the middle peasant must be given dual treatment, depending on
whether he was acting as a toiler or as an exploiter. He reminded his hearers that renunciation of coercion in dealings
with the middle peasant referred not to freedom for him to
exploit the proletariat, but to the principle that "there can be
no question of forcibly imposing socialism on anyone." [42]

In December 1919 the Seventh Congress of Soviets adopted
a resolution which called explicitly for a strengthening of
measures of requisitioning and their extension to all agricultural products. In practice, these measures affected almost all
holdings capable of producing a "surplus" over subsistence
needs.

Such measures were essential in order to ensure the survival of the soldiers at the front and the workers in the factories
(whose rations were already minimal). At that moment and in
this field, recourse to coercion was dictated by the economic
and military situation and by the nature of the relations between the mass of the peasants and the Soviet power, which
were not such as to cause the majority of the peasants to hand
over their produce of their own free will to organs of the state
with nothing to give them "in exchange."

The general requisitioning measures adopted at the end of
1919 nevertheless helped to worsen the political relations
between the peasantry and the Soviet power, that is, the al-

liance of the working class with the middle peasants, most of whom found themselves being treated as speculators and "exploiters." Moreover, on the economic plane, these requisitioning measures discouraged agricultural production, which declined considerably.

The Soviet power tried to resist this decline by imposing sowing plans upon the peasants, that is, by resorting, in this sphere as well, to coercion.[43] Actually, it was almost impossible to ensure the carrying out of these plans on the basis of individual production. The situation therefore worsened, since, by affecting an ever-larger number of peasants, the requisitioning measures provoked increasing discontent on the part of the peasantry toward the Soviet power.

At a conference of chairmen of *uyezd* (district), *volost* (county), and village executive committees of Moscow gubernia, on October 15, 1920, Lenin took note of this discontent. It had been manifested during the conference in such a way that the spokesmen of the government had often found difficulty in expounding their opinions. In one of his speeches Lenin said: "If extreme dissatisfaction and impatience have been expressed here so often, we all know that freedom of speech is the primary rule of procedure at meetings. At this meeting you have broken this rule—it is because the majority of the peasants are experiencing all too severely the effects of the very grave situation that has arisen in the localities. Most of the peasants are feeling all too severely the effects of famine, cold and excessive taxation."[44]

Thus, contrary to what the Bolshevik Party had wished, the year 1920 was a year in which the great majority of the peasants were subjected to severe requisitioning in order to provide for the needs of the front and of the towns. This entailed serious political consequences. At the end of the autumn of 1920 and during the winter of 1920–1921, when the White and interventionist armies had practically been defeated, peasant revolts broke out in various regions, particularly in the south and southeast of Russia, and compelled the Ministry of Food Supplies to suspend all collecting and requisitioning of grain in thirteen provinces.[45]

The crisis in the grain collections at the end of 1920 was obviously not merely due to the peasants' refusal to sell part of their produce. It was connected also with the failure of the harvest, which was due to the war, to economic disorganization, and to the discontent felt by the peasants, many of whom restricted production to what was needed for their own consumption. Consequently, according to generally accepted estimates, annual grain production fell from 72.5 million metric tons in the period 1909–1913 to under 35 million in 1920, and the peasants' own consumption was less than 17 million metric tons, a catastrophic reduction of about 40 percent as compared with prewar figures.[46]

The grave situation in agriculture, the discontent of the peasantry, which was in rebellion in some provinces, and, finally, the victory over the Whites and the imperialist armies, led the Bolshevik Party to make a rectification in its peasant policy, as it was now actually in a position to do. This rectification took place as part of a new conception of economic policy in general—what was called the New Economic Policy. The latter will be discussed in the last part of this book. Here I shall examine only some of the decisions and measures which relate more particularly to the Bolshevik Party's peasant policy and its immediate effects on the class struggle in the countryside.

IV. The rectification of the Bolshevik Party's peasant policy and class relations in the countryside at the end of "war communism" and the beginning of the NEP

At the end of 1920 and at the beginning of 1921, Lenin emphasized the need for a thorough rectification of the party's peasant policy. This did not take effect in practice, however, until March 1921, after the peasant discontent fanned by the SRs and Mensheviks had given rise to rural insurrections and contributed to the Kronstadt rising.

In his report to the Tenth Party Congress, on March 8, 1921, Lenin mentioned, as he had already done before, that the policy of requisitioning carried on without adequate knowledge of the possibilities and needs of the peasantry in the different regions had helped "to intensify the crisis in the peasant economy considerably,"[47] so that the peasants' "dissatisfaction with the proletarian dictatorship is mounting,"[48] and this made it necessary to rectify relations between the working class and the peasantry.

(a) The peasants' demands and the reestablishment of "freedom of exchange"

On March 15, 1921, in his report on the substitution of a tax in kind for requisitioning, Lenin spoke at length and explicitly about the rectification that had become necessary in the party's policy toward the peasantry:

> Under no circumstances must we try to hide anything; we must plainly state that the peasantry is dissatisfied with the form of our relations, that it does not want relations of this type, and will not continue to live as it has hitherto. This is unquestionable. The peasantry has expressed its will in this respect definitely enough. It is the will of the vast masses of the working population. We must reckon with this, and we are sober enough politicians to say frankly: let us re-examine our policy in regard to the peasantry. The state of affairs that has prevailed so far cannot be continued any longer. We must try to satisfy the demands of the peasants who are dissatisfied and disgruntled, and legitimately so, and who cannot be otherwise. We must say to them: "Yes, this cannot go on any longer." How is the peasant to be satisfied, and what does satisfying him mean? Where is the answer? Naturally, it lies in the demands of the peasantry.[49]

These last formulations again show that, in Lenin's case, besides the theory that serves as guide to revolutionary action, there was another essential factor in the working out of a correct political line: the lessons of experience and the demands of the masses themselves.

In order to meet the peasants' demands, Lenin and the Bolshevik Party acknowledged that, in the situation of the moment, the peasants must be given freedom to dispose of their produce once they had paid their taxes, and a certain degree of freedom must be allowed to small-scale trade and small-scale industry. At the same time, "concessions"[50] of a limited kind were offered to foreign capital. Under the conditions then existing, it seemed to the Bolshevik Party that it was only by taking this path that the country could be saved from famine and economic breakdown, and the dictatorship of the proletariat consolidated, for the latter was seriously threatened by the discontent of the peasantry, with the prospect it opened up of an end to the alliance between workers and peasants.

The concrete forms that were subsequently to be assured by the reestablished "freedom of exchange" varied from time to time. The initial formula of still "regulated" exchange gave way to "free" commercial exchange and to the restoration of commodity circulation on a substantial scale. These variations were extensions of the original rectification, of the abandonment of "war communism," and of the adoption of the NEP.

The principal decrees inaugurating the NEP were published in the days immediately following the Tenth Congress. On March 21 came the decree putting an end to the requisitioning of foodstuffs, and on March 28 Lenin signed the decree "freeing" trade, the buying and selling of foodstuffs, and abolishing restrictions on the transport of these goods.

(b) The agrarian legislation of 1922

We shall see later how, on the basis of practical experience, the original conception of the NEP became transformed. Here, in discussing class relations in the countryside, it is essential to say a few words about the decree of May 22, 1922, on land associations, or land societies.

This decree gave practical recognition to the *mir*, while trying to transform it so as to make its functions more compatible with those of the various organs of the Soviet power. This attempt did not enjoy much success: under the new name of "land association" (*zemelnoye obshchestvo*), it was more or less the same old *mir* that continued to exist. Like the *mir*, the "land association" functioned at village level.

The land code of November 15, 1922, embodied the provisions of the decree of May 22. It sought to provide satisfactory conditions for the development of individual cultivation, since this was what, to an overwhelming extent, prevailed within the transformed *mir*. At the same time, the land code of 1922 established more precise foundations for the constitution of agricultural communes, which could be formed either within a given land association or by several villages acting together.

The land association—that is, the transformed *mir*—was administered by a general assembly *(skhod)* of all who had the right to vote and by elected organs. In principle, this change was important since participation in the *skhod* was previously confined to peasants who were heads of households, whereas henceforth, in theory, all who were aged 18 or over and possessed some land were to participate and to join in electing the governing bodies. The *skhod* decided who had the right to belong to the *mir* and who was allowed to leave it, and it could decide on the type of cultivation and on the mode of distributing the land. The renovated *mir* was juridically a person, with power to buy and sell.

The reality of the new *mir* was considerably different from this, however. After the promulgation of the land code, just as before, actual political power in the localities was usually wielded by the rich and well-to-do peasants through the *skhod* and its elected head, or "plenipotentiary," who was, as a rule, himself a rich peasant.

The *skhod,* largely dominated by the rich and well-to-do peasants, took precedence over the rural soviets. It was in practice the sole judge of how the land was to be shared out. Sometimes it went so far as to deprive the poorest peasants of the little land they had,[51] on the grounds that they were not able to cope with a holding. This situation continued until collectivization, as was acknowledged, for example, in an analysis of the situation in the countryside made at the end of 1928: "The village Skhod continues to occupy the predominant position in the life of the village."[52]

Some Soviet writers[53] consequently consider that the consolidation of the *mir* favored the rich peasants, and that they were even its chief advocates since, given the lack of a real presence of Bolshevik Party members in the villages, they were able to profit by their dominant position in the *skhod*. This claim is probably correct. The rich peasants were not, generally speaking, the best cultivators, but they skillfully combined farming with commercial activities and even with usury, and they also rented out draft animals and agricultural tools or machines.

The 1922 code sought to combat the tendency to "miniparcelization," and to promote the concentration of land within each holding, so as to remedy a situation that involved considerable loss of cultivable land used as paths and as balks separating plots, and obliged the peasants to travel great distances (sometimes the different plots making up a single holding were located fifteen or twenty kilometers from the farmhouse,[54] which meant increased transportation costs). These efforts conflicted, however, with the redistributions of land carried out from time to time by the *mir,* and which the law also strove to restrict—with only relative success.

Finally, the code authorized the leasing of land for a period not exceeding three years, on condition that it be cultivated without the employment of wage labor. At the beginning of 1923 the employment of wage labor was permitted, subject to certain limitations.

In this way some of "the peasants' demands" were satisfied. Given the relation of forces in the countryside, however, these demands broadly corresponded to the demands of the rich peasants who were able to influence the mass of the countryfolk.

(c) The economic position of the peasantry
immediately following the civil war,
and class differentiation in the countryside at
the beginning of the NEP

The peasantry was the social group whose economic position underwent the greatest fundamental improvement as a result of the revolution. The land at its disposal was increased by 50 percent. The dues it formerly had to pay to the state were abolished, and it was no longer obliged to pay rent for land leased from the landlords, since the latter had been expropriated. Accordingly, the peasantry actively supported the revolution and enabled the Red Army to beat the White and imperialist forces. Without the support of a mass which constituted more than two-thirds of the population, victory would have been impossible. The victory of the Red Army, which was extremely poorly equipped and supplied, was and could only be a *political* victory—that of the worker-peasant alliance.

The enlargement of the area of land available to the peasants and the elimination of the landlords basically improved the position of the peasantry, but its immediate economic situation nevertheless suffered substantial deterioration. This happened, first, because the prices of industrial goods (which could practically be found only on the black market) rose much more quickly than those of agricultural products, and, secondly, because agricultural production itself collapsed,[55] and the requisitions carried out until the end of 1920 took such quantities of produce from the peasants that they were reduced to hunger

The strengthening of the economic position of the poor and middle peasants. The revolution changed a section of the former poor peasants into middle peasants and improved their relative position.

It is extremely difficult to arrive at a numerical estimate of the changes that occurred inside the peasantry between 1917 and 1922. To be serious, it would need to be based on detailed studies which have not been undertaken. It is necessary therefore to confine oneself to broad figures whose significance must not be overestimated, especially as they relate essentially to the *division* of land among "peasant holdings," and not to the division of the peasants into *classes.*

Among the various estimates that have been made, the one that gives the most likely seeming figures is due to N. D. Kondrat'ev and N. P. Oganovsky.[56]

	Percent	
Cultivable area per holding	*1905*	*1922*
Between 0 and 2.7 desyatins	15.8	15.1
Between 2.7 and 5.4 desyatins	34.7	35.2
Between 5.4 and 13.1 desyatins	40.0	45.8
Over 13.1 desyatins	10.5	3.9

The classification of holdings in terms of size cannot, of course, be interpreted as the direct equivalent of a division of the peasantry into poor, middle, well-to-do, and rich peasants. Actually, peasants owning the same area of land might belong to different categories, depending on the quality of their respective pieces of land, the means of production other than land at their disposal, etc. From the standpoint of the changes which took place among the peasantry, the conclusions to be drawn from the above table, as from other sources, must therefore be formulated with great caution.

Allowing for this reservation, it will be seen that the group of peasants who were poorest in terms of land diminished slightly. The middle peasants who were poorer than others in terms of land saw their proportion increase slightly, while that of the rest of the middle peasants increased markedly, and the proportion of peasants rich in terms of land fell by two-thirds.

One must, however, be careful not to draw hasty conclusions from the above table, as the totality of concrete conditions in which many poor and middle peasants found themselves in 1920–1922 meant that they did not cultivate all the land at their disposal. One reason for this was that it was mainly the land that was shared out, and only rarely the other means of production. This was indeed the traditional practice in the *mir,* and it was usually maintained by the better-off peasants who dominated the *mir* and accepted by the poorest peasants. The latter, as a rule, considered the principal reason for their poverty to be lack of land, and that it was this deficiency that had to be put right. In the period when the poor peasants' committees flourished, they showed little interest in agricultural equipment.[57]

As a result of the lack of correspondence between the division of land and the division of other means of production (but also for other reasons connected with the marketability of part of agricultural production), uncultivated land in 1922–1923 amounted to about 30 percent of the area under cultivation in 1913. Therefore, if what is taken into account is actually cultivated land, we see that the proportion of smaller holdings (those roughly corresponding to the poor and middle peasants) increased from 43.8 percent to 49.6 percent between 1917 and 1922, whereas the proportion represented by the in-between group diminished (from 42.7 percent to 39.2 percent), as did that representing the well-to-do and rich peasants[58] (from 13.5 percent to 11.2 percent).

In short, the Russian Revolution enabled the poor peasants and the less well-off middle peasants—categorized in terms of land—to improve their economic position (increasing by 30 percent and more the average amount of land in their possession). Nevertheless, by 1922 it had not improved the immediate economic situation of these peasants. Such an improvement was not to be experienced until the NEP got under way (between 1923 and 1926).

All the same, since possession of land seemed the most important thing in the eyes of most peasants, the increase in the amount held by the poor and middle peasants constituted a decisive victory for them. Hence, the undoubted political support given to the Soviet power by the peasant masses during the civil war. As we know, this did not prevent a section of the peasantry from starting to revolt, when the civil war was nearing its end, against this same power, which had gone too far with its requisitioning and its banning of free trade. The peasantry then formulated the demands to which the NEP gave satisfaction, thus consolidating afresh the bonds between the broad masses of the peasantry and the Soviet power.

The Russian peasantry and the village petty bourgeoisie. In the main—that is, with the obvious exceptions of the rural proletariat and poor peasants at one extreme, and the rich peasants at the other—the Russian peasantry of this period belonged to the petty bourgeoisie. It was involved in com-

modity relations, and occupied in the Russian social formation (in which capitalist relations, scarcely transformed,
continued to be dominant) the intermediate position characteristic of the petty bourgeoisie.

True, part of what was produced by the middle section of
the peasantry was intended for its own consumption, but
another part was intended for sale in order to obtain in exchange the sums of money which the peasants needed for
their consumption, both productive and unproductive. The
peasants' production was therefore dominated by the requirements of the reproduction of conditions of production
that were realized through circulation.

As far as that part of the peasantry was concerned which
formed the village petty bourgeoisie, and also as regards the
rural bourgeoisie, the domination of production by market
conditions was very thorough. Thus, the decline in production
that took place in 1917–1922 was partly due to the depreciation of the rouble and to the lack of industrial goods obtainable
in exchange for agricultural produce: this situation blocked
the social conditions for agricultural production and contributed to its decline. The first years of the NEP showed to what
an extent Russian agriculture could be affected by price and
market conditions.

That the middle section of the peasantry belonged to the
petty bourgeoisie was due to its place in the relations of
production. In the absence of ideological and political activity
by the Bolshevik Party which could have made it possible to
transform the social practices of this part of the petty
bourgeoisie, its practices also remained petty bourgeois, at
both the economic and the political levels.

Thus, at the economic level, the sharp fall in the amount of
produce provided by agriculture was due only in part to a
worsening of the material conditions of production. In fact, the
material means for maintaining a relatively high level of production existed almost everywhere. If the amount produced
fell dramatically between 1917 and 1921, this was because the
mass of the peasants who could have been producing to supply the towns, the factories, and the front had reduced their

production to more or less the level required for their own subsistence, and had done this because they could get nothing, or almost nothing, in exchange for what they might have supplied. In this matter, what was decisive was the petty bourgeois practice of "giving nothing for nothing." For the moment, the towns could give nothing, and so they were (voluntarily) given nothing, or almost nothing. The petty bourgeois practice of exchange thus took precedence over solidarity with the soldiers (the workers and peasants at the front), with the town workers (the brothers and cousins of the peasants in the villages), or even with the peasants in those regions where the harvest had failed.

In noting this fact, we are not, of course, drawing up some sort of "indictment" of the Russian peasants of that time, but noting a class practice, and the Bolshevik Party's inability at that time to transform it (whereas the subsequent experience of the Chinese Revolution has shown that it can be done).

At the political level, the peasant revolts of the winter of 1920–1921, and the Kronstadt rising which was a continuation of this movement, testify to the petty bourgeois class nature of the support given by the peasantry to the state of the proletarian dictatorship. This support was unstable insofar as it emanated from the middle peasants, who formed the bulk of the peasantry and influenced a section of the poor peasants. The middle peasants supported the Soviet power as long as it was helping them get rid of the landlords and seize a certain amount of land, but their support faltered once the war was over and the Soviet power did not allow them then to develop their commercial activities as they wished. This was the vacillating support of a petty bourgeoisie that wanted to dispose "freely" of "its own" products and carry on trade in them—a type of support symbolized in the formula used by the Russian peasants: "Up with the Bolsheviks (who helped to overthrow tsardom and get rid of the landlords); down with the Communists." In order to understand what the NEP meant for the Russian peasantry at the beginning of the 1920s, one needs to recognize the class character of the peasantry's practice, both economic and political, and to appreciate that the Bolshevik Party was not in a position to transform this practice.

This incapacity of the party was due to many reasons. Some were connected with its own history: its weak roots in the countryside, its too rigid conception of the relations between class situation and class practice (as a result of which the leading role of the Bolshevik Party was predominantly political rather than ideological), etc. The other reasons were connected with the actual situation in Russia—the types of social differentiation existing in the Russian countryside, the influence of the petty bourgeois ideas of the SR party, and the effects of the functioning of the *mir*, even in its renovated form.

The rural bourgeoisie. If we confine our attention to changes in the division of cultivable land, we arrive at false conclusions regarding the changes undergone by class relations in the countryside. These conclusions would be especially misleading as regards the rich peasants, whose share of the cultivable land was reduced between 1917 and 1922. To form a judgment of the economic position of the rural bourgeoisie, we need above all to take into account the division of the means of production other than land. Unfortunately, overall figures on this subject are not available. The fragmentary information we have suggests that the inequality in the division of these means of production was reduced a little, but that it persisted and continued to be one of the vital material foundations for the relations of exploitation that were reproduced at village level, that is, for the differentiation of the peasantry into poor, middle, and rich peasants, with the rich peasants constituting the nucleus of a rural bourgeoisie.

It is first of all necessary to dispose of the idea that only the division of the land mattered, as the peasants "could produce for themselves" the other means of production, since these were "so simple." That is a plainly unrealistic notion. While a swing-plow could sometimes be made by an individual for personal use, this was not the case with a wheeled plow or a scythe, and even less so with a cart; as for draft animals, these had to be bought, since they were not redistributed, and that called for large sums of money—for most poor and middle peasant households, the death of their one draft animal was an economic catastrophe which plunged them into the lowest social category.

The means of production owned by the poor peasants were, in fact, very inadequate. Thus, in Northwest Russia, a region for which some usable figures exist, 29 percent of the holdings belonging to the *mir* had no tools at all, and there were only 35 draft animals for 100 holdings. For the RSFSR as a whole, the number of swing-plows per 100 desyatins sown was only 9.6 in 1920, and the number of wheeled plows only 11.2 (it was no more than 9.6 in 1923).

The unequal availability of equipment had, moreover, a decisive influence on yield per desyatin. In one and the same region, the yield from well-equipped holdings was often more than 60 percent greater than that from holdings with average equipment.[59]

However, the problem of the differentiation among the peasantry is not to be reduced to a problem of "inequality": it was a problem of class differentiation. At one of the poles of village society were the agricultural semiproletariat and the poor peasants exploited by the rich peasants (and sometimes by the better-off middle peasants) from whom they had to hire horses, plows, and other instruments of agricultural production. At the opposite pole was the rural bourgeoisie, the kulaks, who exploited the semiproletarians, the poor peasants, and some of the middle peasants.

There are no figures for this exploitation, but it is known to have been severe (thus, it was said that a poor peasant had to hand over one-third of his crop to the owner of the horse he had borrowed in order to till his land). We know, too, that under Soviet rule this exploitation often assumed concealed forms so as to avoid state intervention: but, in any case, it was real and heavy exploitation.

What was present here was capitalist parasitism combined with a slow development of capitalism in agriculture. The kulak got more income from hiring out his tools of labor and speculating in grain than he got from improving his own farming. The observations that Marx and Engels had already made in the second half of the nineteenth century were basically still valid in 1920–1922.[60]

The rural bourgeoisie had a considerable economic and political impact. Through the *mir,* it tended to dominate the village and manipulate the mass of the peasants who were, in part, economically dependent upon it. This was all the more the case in that the Soviet administration was far away, located in the chief town of the district, and was even itself, in some places, much under the influence of the kulaks.

The resulting polarization of the village turned the middle peasants into a petty bourgeoisie striving to become rich and struggling to save itself from falling into the ranks of the semiproletariat and the poor peasants. This petty bourgeoisie was thus also driven to exploit, so far as it could, the poorer strata of the peasantry.

It was on the basis of these social relations, these class relations and these class practices, that the state apparatus underwent transformations which we must now examine.

Notes

1. *CW,* vol. 26, p. 260.
2. The SRs were also in favor of nationalization of the land, which Lenin considered, before the establishment of the dictatorship of the proletariat, as being merely the "last word" of the bourgeoisie revolution.
3. *CW,* vol. 26, pp. 260–261.
4. The *zemstvo* was a local or provincial system of administration in the old Russia. Each *zemstvo* was headed by an assembly elected by the nobility and property-owning classes. The agricultural and agrarian statistics of the old Russia were compiled by the *zemstvo* officials.
5. *CW,* vol. 1, pp. 11–125.
6. It is usually estimated that at the beginning of the century the land controlled by these village communities amounted to about half of all the land under cultivation, the rest consisting of the

estates of the landlords, the land held by peasants who had left the *mir*, "settlement" lands (mainly in the regions which had been conquered by tsarist Russia in the previous hundred years), and estates belonging to the state, the crown, and religious institutions.

7. See Marx and Engels, *The Russian Menace to Europe*, p. 221.
8. Marx and Engels, *Selected Works*, vol. 1, pp. 100–101. The principal writings of Marx and Engels on Russia consist, first, of two articles by Engels in the *Volksstaat* of April 16 and 21, 1875, the content of which Marx had approved, and which, with some others, were published as a pamphlet under the title *Soziales in Russland*, preceded by a long foreword. This collection was reissued in Russian in Geneva in 1894, under the title *Friedrich Engels o Rossii*, with an afterword by Engels and a preface by Plekhanov. Then, secondly, there is Marx's correspondence with Vera Zasulich, in which the chief item is a letter of March 1881, of which three drafts have survived, the last of these being practically identical with the letter that was eventually dispatched. Not long afterward, Marx wrote some unpublished notes which are known as his "Notes on the reform of 1861 and the development connected with this in Russia."

    Engels's writings of 1875 are in Marx and Engels, *Werke*, vol. 18, pp. 556–567 and 584–586, and vol. 22, pp. 421–435. Marx's writings mentioned are in ibid., vol. 19, pp. 384–406 and 407–424. (For English versions of some of these, see Marx and Engels, *The Russian Menace to Europe*, Chapters 17–21.)
9. Marx and Engels, *The Russian Menace to Europe*, p. 226.
10. Marx and Engels, *Selected Works*, vol. 2, p. 407.
11. *CW*, vol. 8, p. 86.
12. Shanin, *The Awkward Class*, p. 64.
13. Chayanov, *The Theory of Peasant Economy*, p. 67. These figures were compiled for one *uyezd* (county). A desyatin is 2.7 acres.
14. Another part of the land was kept back as a "state land fund," to serve as the basis for "Soviet" or "state" farms.
15. Anfimov, *Rossiiskaya derevnya*, p. 91.
16. It has been estimated that, on the eve of October, in 47 provinces of European Russia, 10 percent of peasant households had left the *mir*, though in some regions this percentage was as much as 20–30 percent. See Narkiewicz, *The Making of the Soviet State Apparatus*, p. 118.
17. Averages mean little in this context, as the amount of land recov-

ered varied enormously from one region to another. These variations were due to the relative size of the holdings that were detached from the *mir* before the revolution, and also—though to a rather slight degree, since the party's influence in the rural areas was itself slight—to the role that the Bolshevik Party was able to play. It seems that in the regions where "separated" holdings (*otruby* or *khutora*) were comparatively numerous they were less affected than elsewhere, since the section of the peasantry which had broken away from the *mir* constituted a real social force in those regions. Thus, in Petrograd province, where such holdings, a good many of which were actual capitalist farms, made up 28.7 percent of all holdings in 1916, they were still 22.7 percent in 1922. See Sharapov, *Razreshenie.*

18. For European Russia as a whole, the land at the disposal of the peasants increased by about 50 percent. See Volin, *A Century of Russian Agriculture,* p. 133.

19. See Narkiewicz, *The Making of the Soviet State Apparatus,* p. 27.

20. On this point see Dobb, *Soviet Economic Development,* pp. 104–105, and Carr, *The Bolshevik Revolution,* vol. 2, pp. 59–60.

21. *CW,* vol. 28, pp. 174–175.

22. Ibid., pp. 227 ff.; quotation on pp. 303–304.

23. Ibid., pp. 338 ff.; quotation on p. 341.

24. Ibid., pp. 343, 344.

25. He touches on this subject in his speech to the Sixth Congress of Soviets (ibid., p. 142), and in his speech to the poor peasants' committee delegates (see ibid., p. 175).

26. See his speech to the First Congress of Land Departments, in *CW,* vol. 28, p. 340.

27. Opening speech at the Eighth Congress, in *CW,* vol. 29, pp. 143–145.

28. Ibid., pp. 144–145.

29. Ibid., p. 159.

30. Ibid., p. 44.

31. Ibid., pp. 43–44.

32. Ibid., p. 210.

33. Ibid., pp. 210–211. The "communes" mentioned here were not the traditional village community (*mir*) but agricultural communes in which the peasants came together to carry out *collective labor.*

34. Ibid., pp. 217–220.

35. *CW,* vol. 30, pp. 107 ff.
36. Ibid., p. 108.
37. On these agricultural communes formed by town workers, see Sharapov.
38. The figures given here are taken from Carr, *The Bolshevik Revolution,* vol. 2, p. 160, and Narkiewicz, *The Making of the Soviet State Apparatus,* pp. 42–43.
39. *Izvestiya,* June 10, 1920.
40. Quoted in Narkiewicz, *The Making of the Soviet State Apparatus,* p. 43.
41. *CW,* vol. 30, pp. 143 ff.; quotation on p. 146.
42. Ibid., p. 146.
43. I shall show later on how, during the summer of 1920, the illusion arose that it would be possible to increase agricultural production by forcible means and that such means would even enable socialism to be built.
44. *CW,* vol. 31, p. 335.
45. Statement made to the Tenth Party Congress, quoted in Carr, *The Bolshevik Revolution,* vol. 2, p. 173, n. 2.
46. The figure for grain production in the period 1909–1913 is taken from *Narodnoye Kh.SSSR v 1958,* p. 70, and that for 1920 is calculated from Krzhyzhanovsky, *Desyat',* pp. 124–125. The total for prewar consumption by the peasants is given according to current estimates, while that of 1920–1921 is quoted in Grosskopf, *Le Problème des Céréales,* p. 122. Though not strictly comparable, being based on unreliable statistical foundations and tending to *overestimate the decline in production and consumption,* these figures give some idea of the magnitude of the fall in both.
47. *CW,* vol. 32, p. 175.
48. Ibid., p. 178.
49. Ibid., pp. 215 and 217.
50. By "concessions" was meant opportunities accorded to foreign capital, under very strict controls, to invest in certain industries, especially factory production, to bring into Russia the equipment the country lacked, and to transfer abroad the profits made.
51. Carr and Davies, *Foundations of a Planned Economy,* vol. 1, p. 121, n. 2.
52. Quoted in Carr, *Foundations of a Planned Economy,* vol. 2, p. 248, n. 7.

53. See Ustinov, "K voprosu o formakh zemlepolzovaniya," pp. 143–149.

54. Figure given by Grosskopf, *Le Problème des céréales*, p. 55.

55. The decline in overall agricultural production has been officially estimated at 40 percent, as compared with the figure for 1913 (see *Narodnoye Kh.SSSR v 1958*, p. 52) and even more so far as grain was concerned. The view is often expressed that a quarter of what was actually produced was concealed, so that the real decline in production was only 20 percent; but this seems an optimistic estimate.

56. Quoted in Grosskopf, "Appropriation," p. 515. (Percentages given to the nearest decimal.)

57. See Grosskopf, *Le Problème des céréales*, p. 87.

58. Cf. the estimates of Kondrat'ev and Oganovsky, quoted in Grosskopf, *Cahiers*, p. 516.

59. On these points, see Kondrat'ev and Oganovsky, especially pp. 60–61 and 123.

60. It was with reference to Russia's rich peasants, the kulaks, that Engels used the expression "capitalist parasitism" in his 1875 article on social conditions in Russia (Marx and Engels, *Selected Works*, vol. 2, p. 390).

Part 3
The transformation of the principal instruments of the proletarian dictatorship

Analysis of the transformations undergone between 1917 and 1922 in the principal instruments of power enables us to grasp some of the political changes that began at that time (changes which were often emphasized by Lenin), and which later on gave rise to increasingly negative consequences for the proletariat. It also enables us to see that these transformations were the result of an objective social process, the outcome of a class struggle, and not the "product" of the theoretical or organizational conceptions of the Bolshevik Party. Although some of these conceptions, through their partial "inadequacy," did fail to enable the effects of the transformations that were going on to be foreseen, or their consequences to be prevented, one should not confuse a partial failure to control an objective social process with its driving force.

To get to the root of the matter, let it be recalled that political relations are never "decreed": in the last analysis they are always the form assumed by fundamental social relations at the level of production. As Marx wrote in the introduction to his *Contribution to the Critique of Political Economy*, "each mode of production produces its specific legal relations, political forms, etc."[1] This determination of political forms by modes of production enables us to understand how it was that the limited extent to which changes were effected at the level of production relations (particularly in the division of labor in the factories, the division of labor between town and country, and class divisions in the rural areas), tended *in the final analysis* to offset the achievements of the October Revolution. Viewed over a period of several decades, this determining relation also explains why, in the absence of a renewed revo-

251

lutionary offensive attacking production relations in depth, and of a political line permitting such an offensive to develop successfully, the dictatorship of the proletariat itself has ended by being annihilated, and why we are seeing in the Russia of today, under new conditions, a resurgence of internal political relations and of political relations with the rest of the world which look like a "reproduction" of bourgeois political relations, and even of those of the tsarist period.

The determination of the political level by the economic level—the relation which Lenin summed up admirably in his well-known formula: "Politics is concentrated economics"—is obviously a relation of determination in the final analysis, and not a "relation of expression," such as would make political relations a mere "expression," "another face" of economic relations. The political level is *relatively independent* of the economic level.

This relative independence explains how the revolutionary struggle could bring down the political power of the bourgeoisie and establish the dictatorship of the proletariat, as happened in October 1917, without production relations and property relations having been previously or simultaneously revolutionized—this revolutionization becoming possible only after the bourgeoisie had been deprived of power and the proletariat had become the ruling class.

The need for uninterrupted revolution, for the revolutionary struggle to be continued under the dictatorship of the proletariat, is due precisely to the fact that without such a struggle the fundamental economic relations cannot be transformed in depth. And as long as they have not been radically transformed—destroyed and rebuilt—and insofar as they contain elements of capitalist relations, the prevailing social relations provide an objective basis for bourgeois social practices which tend to ensure the reproduction of the former political relations, to weaken the dictatorship of the proletariat and, eventually, by consolidating the positions from which the bourgeoisie can carry on its class struggle, to reestablish all the conditions for the dictatorship of the bourgeoisie, as well as this dictatorship itself.

One of the issues in the class struggle under the dictatorship of the proletariat is the development of proletarian social practices. It is this development alone that makes it possible to transform social relations as a whole in a revolutionary way. Without it, bourgeois social practices are reproduced, and ensure, at every level of the social formation, conditions favorable to the bourgeois class struggle, to the consolidation and reestablishment of bourgeois social relations.

Historical experience shows that one of the vital and irreplaceable tasks of a revolutionary party is to assist the advance of proletarian practices. To this end the party must constantly pay attention to the ripening of class contradictions, taking account of all aspects of these contradictions. The Bolshevik Party coped very unevenly with this task, and thereby allowed bourgeois social practices to be reproduced, and consolidation to proceed in the capitalist social relations to which the October Revolution had administered no more than an initial shakeup, mainly at the political and juridical levels. The process of consolidation of these relations showed itself first in a process of transformation of the principal instruments of the proletarian dictatorship. I shall now analyze the main aspects of this process, the significance and effects of which were, and could not but be, appreciated only partially by the Bolshevik Party, the first revolutionary party to have to cope with the unprecedented historical task of guiding the construction of socialist social relations.

Note

1. Marx, *Contribution to the Critique of Political Economy*, p. 193. Marx expresses the same idea in *Capital*, vol. III, p. 772.

1. The transformation of the central organs of power and the administrative machinery of state

The Soviet power evolved very quickly toward a system of political relations profoundly different from that which Lenin had outlined in *The State and Revolution*. According to Engels's expression, taken over by Lenin, the characteristics of this system should have made the Soviet power something that was "no longer a state in the proper sense of the word."[1] This power should have been based fundamentally upon the local soviets, with the central organs of state serving mainly the purpose of centralization. In practice, relations of this sort, partly "non-state" in nature, which did appear in embryonic form in the Soviet system, failed to become consolidated. Concentration of power in the central organs of state occurred instead of mere centralization. The role of the local soviets either failed to materialize or else tended to diminish, as did that of the congress of soviets. This tendency continued and was accelerated under "war communism." It gave rise to an ever more pronounced trend toward the administrative machinery of state acquiring independence. This machinery was not really subjected to control by the masses and it even tended to escape from the effective authority of the Bolshevik Party.

I. The transformation of relations between the central governmental organs

According to the Bolshevik Party's original plans, central state power was to be held by a congress of soviets, which would meet every three months. In the intervals, central state power was to be exercised by the All-Russia Executive Committee of the Soviets, or CEC (VTsIK, in the Russian abbreviation), elected by the congress. Actually, after 1918, although no formal change was at first made in the rules, the congress of soviets met only once a year. In 1921 the Ninth Congress of Soviets formally resolved that subsequent congresses should be annual only, and this not merely in the case of the All-Russia Congress but also where the district congresses of soviets were concerned.

Not only did the congresses of soviets meet less frequently, but their authority was reduced. After July 1918 the chairmen of the VTsIK and the Sovnarkom no longer presented reports to the congress on the activities of the organs over which they presided: previously, these reports had to be discussed and ratified by the congress.

The VTsIK itself, derived directly from the All-Russia Congress of Soviets, became less active, even while the number of its members increased, reaching 300 in 1920.[2] Originally the VTsIK was to have remained in permanent session, but in practice its meetings were held at long intervals and became more and more infrequent. In 1921 it met only three times.

In December 1919 such power as the VTsIK retained was virtually transferred to its chairman, whose role was soon reduced to that of a formal and honorific "head of state."[3]

During "war communism," the state organ which actually played the dominant role was not the one that emanated from the All-Russia Congress of Soviets, but the Council of People's Commissars, which Lenin headed until his death. From the formal standpoint, important decisions were taken, indifferently, in the name of the Sovnarkom, of the Central Committee of the party, or jointly by one of these organs and the VTsIK. As will be seen, there was also a considerable gap between the formal concentration of power in certain central organs and the actual exercise of this power, which tended to shift toward the administrative organs, though these were in theory subordinate. On more than one occasion Lenin noted that this was the real state of affairs, which he tried to alter.

II. *The process of eliminating the bourgeois and petty bourgeois parties and their press*

The Bolshevik Party had no preconceived "program" regarding the place to be occupied in the system of the proletarian dictatorship by the democratic and bourgeois parties and press. Before the October Revolution, however, a clear distinction was made between the parties and publications which directly expressed the interests of the bourgeoisie (such as the Constitutional Democratic Party, or Cadets), against which repressive measures would have to be taken, and the democratic parties and press which voiced the aspirations of the petty bourgeoisie. With regard to the latter, the Bolshevik Party considered that the principal aspect of the struggle to wrest the masses from their influence was constituted by ideological class struggle, which implied confronting these parties in the soviets and allowing them to have their own newspapers. This attitude, of course, did not mean that these parties or publications would be allowed to carry on counter-revolutionary activity with impunity.

In fact, in the period immediately following October, the Bolshevik Party in power allowed the democratic parties to pursue their activities: the party even negotiated with a view to their possible participation in the government, and it exercised only limited repression against the bourgeois press and parties.

(a) The Cadet party and its press

The Cadet party was not at once suppressed after the October Revolution. Only at the end of November 1917, when this party was openly supporting Kaledin's preparations for a counter-revolutionary revolt, was it declared a "party of enemies of the people" and banned by a decree of the Sovnarkom.[4] Cadet deputies, together with deputies belonging to other bourgeois parties, were nevertheless elected to the Constituent Assembly and took part in its brief meeting.

As regards the bourgeois press, the Soviet government showed itself at first more tolerant in its practice than in its declarations. In principle, the bourgeois press was to have been closed down. As Lenin recalled in his speech on the press on November 4, 1917: "Earlier on we said that if we took power, we intended to close down the bourgeois newspapers. To tolerate the existence of these papers is to cease being a socialist . . . We cannot provide the bourgeoisie with an opportunity for slandering us." However, he went on, "we are not bureaucrats and do not want to insist on the letter of the law everywhere . . ."[5] Its application would depend on local conditions, which meant that the Soviet power was not at that stage disposed to follow a policy of crude suppression.

In practice, during the winter of 1917–1918 and the spring of 1918, the Soviet power refrained from banning all the bourgeois papers. Thus, when the Cadet party had been dissolved, its newspaper, *Svoboda Rossii*, continued to appear, and was circulating even during the summer of 1918, in the midst of the civil war.[6] It disappeared only later, when the military conflict became so acute that publication of a paper which represented the views of the enemy could no longer be tolerated.

The Cadets were to reappear officially for the last time when an All-Russia Committee for Aid to Famine Victims was set up by a decree of July 21, 1921; this committee was to take part in obtaining international relief for the famine-stricken regions of Russia. The Soviet government then nominated several well-known Cadets to serve on this committee, where they sat alongside Mensheviks, SRs, and, of course, Bolsheviks (one of whom acted as chairman). It soon became obvious that the bourgeois members of this organization were trying to negotiate directly with foreign representatives, in an endeavor to establish themselves as a "countergovernment." The committee was thereupon dissolved by a decree of August 27, 1921, and its principal bourgeois members were arrested.[7] The Cadets then vanished from the political scene. In 1922, that is, early in the NEP period, the last bourgeois publications, including the "liberal" economic periodical, *Ekonomist*, ceased to appear.[8] These facts show that it was essentially in response to changing political situations, to the critical conjuncture of the war years and the grave difficulties that followed them, that the Bolshevik Party in power gradually suppressed all the activities of the bourgeois organizations and publications, since these activities were not confined to ideological struggle but constantly tended toward open counter-revolution. A parallel process went on with regard to the "democratic" parties and press, but this process was more complex and developed more slowly.

(b) The initial negotiations with the "democratic" parties

Although the October insurrection was directed not only against the bourgeoisie but also against the policy of support to Kerensky's Provisional Government, which was being followed by the "democratic" parties, the Bolshevik Party did not at first treat the latter as counter-revolutionary parties. Not only did it not ban them, but it tried to get them to participate in the new government. When the Mensheviks and SRs decided to leave the Congress of Soviets, Lenin said on October 29, 1917, at a meeting of regimental delegates of the Petrograd garrison: "It is not our fault that the Socialist Revolutionaries and the Mensheviks have gone. They were invited to share political power, but they want to sit on the fence until the fight against Kerensky is over." And he added: "Here everyone knows that the S.R.s and the Mensheviks went because they were left in a minority. The men of the Petrograd garrison are aware of this. They know that we wanted a coalition Soviet government."[9]

In fact, during the night of October 25–26, the Mensheviks and SRs had refused to recognize that power was now held by the soviets and had decided to leave the congress thus siding with the counter-revolution. Nevertheless, on October 29 the central committee, in the absence of Lenin, Stalin, and Trotsky, agreed to discuss with these parties[10] the forming of a coalition government.[11] But the "democratic" parties showed open hostility to the Soviet power. They demanded that the VTsIK include a large number of bourgeois representatives (members of the municipal councils of Petrograd and Moscow), and that Lenin and Trotsky be excluded from any coalition government. On November 1 Lenin, while agreeing that these negotiations could "serve as diplomatic cover for military preparations," said that the time had now come to break them off: it was henceforth a question of standing "either with the agents of Kaledin or with the rank-and-file." [12] He moved a resolution to this effect, but the Central Committee rejected it by ten to four.[13] The next day Lenin declared that those in favor of continued negotiation with parties refusing to recognize the power that had emerged from the October Revolution and the congress of soviets had "departed completely from all the fundamental positions of Bolshevism and of the proletarian class struggle in general."

The resolution he put before the Central Committee declared: "To yield to the ultimatums and threats of the minority of the Soviets would be tantamount to complete renunciation not only of Soviet power but of democracy, for such yielding would be tantamount to the majority's fear to make use of its majority, it would be tantamount to submitting to anarchy and inviting the repetition of ultimatums on the part of any minority." [14]

This resolution was adopted by only eight to seven, after three votes had been taken. As a result of the final vote, the minority withdrew from the Central Committee[15] and several people's commissars resigned from the government. But the minority's attempt to continue talks with the Mensheviks and SRs came to grief on the anti-Sovietism of these parties, which, after having demanded that the Bolshevik Party practically renounce leadership of the government, ended by deciding to put an end to the negotiations.[16] The breakaway minority then returned to the Central Committee.

It must be emphasized that in its resolution of November 2, the Central Committee did not rule that the parties which had withdrawn from the congress of soviets must be excluded from it. Indeed, the resolution, moved by Lenin, said: "The Central Committee affirms that, not having excluded anybody from the Second All-Russia Congress of Soviets, it is even now fully prepared to permit the return of those who walked out and to agree to a coalition within the Soviets with those who walked out, and that, consequently, all talk about the Bolsheviks refusing to share power with anybody else is absolutely false."[17]

After the breakdown of the talks with the Menshevik and SR parties, the Bolsheviks, Lenin included, still continued to try and negotiate with the Left SRs, who had not walked out of the congress. When the Soviet government was formed they had been asked to participate, but had refused.[18] After the resignation of the people's commissars who supported the line of the minority in the CC, fresh approaches were made to the Left SRs. Following protracted negotiations, agreement was reached on December 12, 1917 and a coalition government formed, made up of eleven Bolsheviks and seven Left SRs. A Left SR became deputy-chairman of the Cheka. This coalition government lasted until the end of February 1918, when the agreement between the two parties failed owing to the opposition of the Left SRs to the peace negotiations with Germany. Nevertheless, for a time even after the resignation of the Left SR people's commissars, relations continued to be quite good with this party, which was still represented in the commissions of the VTsIK, in some departments of the people's commissariats, and even in the Cheka. When the peace treaty of Brest-Litovsk was actually signed, however, and the civil war began, relations with the Left SRs definitely deteriorated.

The Bolshevik Party thus decided how to act toward the "democratic" parties in response to the policy actually being followed by the latter—their hostility to, or acceptance of, the Soviet power. Provided the activity of these parties was not dangerously counter-revolutionary, it was not hindered. Depending on the intensity of the contradictions, and in particular on the military situation during the civil war, broader or narrower opportunities for activity were allowed to these parties: they were not treated in a uniform way, since what mattered was their actual attitude to the Soviet power.

(c) The policy of the Socialist Revolutionary Party

The "democratic" party most immediately and openly hostile to the Soviet power was the Socialist Revolutionary Party (from which the Left SRs had broken away, as will be seen). At the time of the October Revolution, the social base of this party was constituted by the rural intelligentsia—the staffs of the *zemstvos* and cooperative societies, the schoolteachers, and the officials of the villages and country districts. Between February and October 1917, this party drew closer and closer to the Cadets, and it opposed the Soviet power and the dividing up of the land by the peasants. Before they were nationalized, the Russian banks helped the party financially, and it also received funds from American businessmen. As early as October 26, 1917, it decided to launch armed action against the Soviet power, and for this purpose entered into negotiation with Cossack regiments and army cadets. After the dissolution of the Constituent Assembly, it resorted to individual terror and committed several assassinations. During the civil war, the SR party openly supported the counter-revolution, participating in several anti-Bolshevik "governments."[19]

Despite these counter-revolutionary activities, the SR party was not dissolved by the Soviet government. Until the civil war began, it took part in the work of the soviets (for it had withdrawn only from the congress of soviets) and its papers continued to appear, although these were increasingly subjected to censorship (which had been established in March 1918). When the civil war got under way, however, the SRs were expelled from the soviets on grounds of their "association with notorious counter-revolutionaries,"[20] but their party was not formally dissolved, and at certain periods its activity was more or less tolerated.

This tolerance was not fruitless. Thus, in February 1919 the SRs of Petrograd denounced the counter-revolutionary movement and foreign intervention. By a decision of the VTsIK dated February 25, 1919,[21] SRs who took this position were readmitted to the Soviet organs. Thereafter, it was possible for some SR meetings to be held, and at the end of 1920 SR delegates even participated, though without the right to vote, in the Thirteenth Congress of Soviets.

(d) The Left SRs

The Left SRs were during a certain period dealt with rather differently. They had broken away from the SR party during the war, and had a different social base, with considerable influence among the middle peasants. In October 1917 they continued to take part in the congress of soviets, and soon afterward formed a distinct party, their constituent congress being held in November.[22] Although this party then entered the Soviet government and the VTsIK, a break between it and the Bolsheviks became inevitable early in 1918, first of all because of the signing of the peace treaty of Brest-Litovsk, to which the Left SRs were totally opposed. In the summer of 1918 they denounced the decision to set up the poor peasants' committees and send workers' detachments into the countryside, and in July they broke with the Soviet power in startling fashion.

This open break took place at the Fifth Congress of Soviets, where the 1,132 delegates included 754 Bolsheviks and 352 Left SRs. The Left SR representatives used the congress platform to call for revolt. One of them congratulated some military units which had mutinied. A Left SR leader, Maria Spiridonova, declared: "Some of the differences between us are only accidental, but on the peasant question we are ready for battle." She announced that the Left SRs would go over to terrorist action and that she herself would confront the Bolsheviks with revolver or bomb in hand. The chairman then stopped her from continuing her speech. The next day, men inspired by the Left SR movement murdered the German ambassador, hoping to cause a resumption of hostilities, and the party launched an armed insurrection in Moscow. Thereafter, the Left SRs were regarded as being in the camp of counter-revolution. Actually, their party split. Those who associated themselves with counter-revolutionary activities were expelled from the soviets and arrested when they took part in uprisings. The activity of those Left SRs who held aloof from terrorism was not prohibited, and repression was directed against them only in a limited way. If they decided to continue working in the soviets, they were not expelled from them.[23] Clearly, the Bolshevik Party was taking account of the Left SRs' social base, and wished to avoid a definitive break with them. This hope was not realized, though, for an increasing number of Left SRs engaged in counter-revolutionary activity, while others fell victim to the sectarianism of some of the Bolsheviks.

(e) The anarchists

The relations of the Soviet power and the Bolshevik Party with the anarchists also testified to the former's willingness to cooperate with those who were not engaged in counter-revolutionary activity. These relations were, however, rendered confused by the extreme variety of tendencies that existed among the anarchists, some of whom gave occasional support to the Soviet regime while others were violently hostile to it. Cooperation with the anarchists was also made difficult by the presence among them of declassed and adventuristic elements. In any case, until April 1918 the anarchists functioned without restraint, especially in the two capitals. In that month, a police operation was carried out against one of the anarchist offices in Moscow, as counter-revolutionary officers had infiltrated among them. In July 1918 some anarchists took part in the attempted revolt by the Left SRs, and in September 1919 an anarchist group attacked the Bolshevik Party offices in Moscow, killing twelve people and wounding more than fifty.[24]

Between 1918 and 1920 Lenin strove to maintain good relations, in spite of everything, with the anarchist tendencies which were linked with certain sections of the proletariat. In August 1919, in a letter to Sylvia Pankhurst, he stated that "very many anarchist workers are now becoming sincere supporters of Soviet power," adding that these were "our best comrades and friends, the best of revolutionaries, who have been enemies of Marxism only through misunderstanding, or, more correctly . . . because the official socialism prevailing in the epoch of the Second International (1889–1914) betrayed Marxism . . ."[25] In July 1920, in his theses on the tasks of the Second Congress of the Communist International, Lenin wrote that it was "the duty of all Communists to do everything to help all proletarian mass elements to abandon anarchism and come over to the side of the Third International."[26] The policy followed by the Bolshevik Party toward the anarchist elements in the proletariat was aimed at making it possible to carry on the ideological struggle against anarchism in good conditions, avoiding measures of repression and helping the workers who were under the influence of anarchist theories to realize that these theories were mistaken and could not lead to the victory of the revolution.[27]

One of the "peasant" tendencies in the anarchist movement, headed by Nestor Makhno, was particularly strong in the Ukraine. For a time Makhno led an army of peasants, and the Bolshevik Party negotiated with him in order to organize joint action against the White armies. This cooperation could not last very long, though, for the Makhnovists were violently anti-Bolshevik: they did not tolerate Communist propaganda in the villages under their control, and exterminated party members who showed up there.[28] In November 1920 the agreements between the Soviet power and Makhno's forces broke down, and the latter were quickly defeated and scattered by the Red Army.

After the end of the civil war the Kronstadt rising caused new clashes with the anarchists, but later they recovered a certain amount of freedom of expression: their organization had an office in Moscow and printed various publications. It was toward the end of the NEP that the last remaining anarchist organizations were broken up.

(f) The Mensheviks

Relations with the Mensheviks were also largely governed by their attitude to the Soviet power. Immediately after the October Revolution, the Mensheviks walked out of the congress of soviets, along with the SRs. However, their party was not dissolved, either, and they took part in the work of the soviets until July 1918. After the attempted revolt of the Left SRs, the Mensheviks, too, were excluded from the Soviet organizations on grounds of counter-revolutionary activity. Those Mensheviks who engaged in specific anti-Soviet operations were arrested during the summer of 1918. The functioning of the Menshevik organizations which confined themselves to ideological struggle was not systematically hindered, however, for the Soviet power wished to confine the battle against petty bourgeois ideology to the plane of persuasion and argument and not of repression.

At the end of October 1918, the Mensheviks' central committee met for five days in Moscow and adopted a resolution of support for the Soviet government in defense of the conquests of the revolution. Although the wording of this resolution was confused and contradictory, the Bolshevik Party saw it as a sign that the Menshevik leaders were turning away from their counter-revolutionary attitude; on November 30, 1918, a decree of the VTsIK canceled the earlier decision excluding the Mensheviks from the Soviet organs. This did not apply, of course to "those groups of Mensheviks who continue to be allied with the Russian and foreign bourgeoisie against the Soviet power."[29]

Even though relations with the Mensheviks continued to be strained throughout 1919, owing to the ambiguity of their attitude, the Menshevik leaders were invited in December 1919 to attend the Seventh Congress of Soviets. Several of them, such as Dan and Martov, addressed the congress. The former called for "the single revolutionary front," while the latter demanded "a restoration of the working of the constitution, . . . freedom of the press, of association and of assembly."[30] Lenin, referring to the life-and-death struggle going on between the Soviet power and the world bourgeoisie, replied that Martov's slogan was, in fact "back to bourgeois democracy," and he added that "when we hear such declarations from people who announce their sympathy with us, we say to ourselves: 'No, both terror and the Cheka are absolutely indispensable.' "[31]

During 1920 the Menshevik Party carried on its activities in Moscow and in the provinces. It possessed offices, printed several papers and, although all its doings were closely watched, took part in elections to local soviets, winning some hundreds of seats. The Mensheviks held meetings, convened their central committee, organized in August 1920 a conference of their party (which was reported in the Soviet press), and were also very active in the trade unions, in which they worked as an organized group. When the Eighth Congress of Soviets met, Menshevik delegates were invited. These invitations enabled the ideological struggle to be carried on before a huge audience, and also helped to counteract the attitude of the lower organs of the Bolshevik Party and the soviets, which saw fit to prevent the election of Menshevik delegates to any bodies higher than the local soviets.

The Eighth Congress of Soviets was the last in which Menshevik or SR delegates took part. During the winter of 1920–1921, the anti-Bolshevik activity of both parties was an important factor in fostering the conditions for the Kronstadt rising: the Mensheviks used their position in the trade unions to promote extension of the strikes that broke out in Petrograd, while the SRs encouraged the development in certain regions of active peasant resistance to the Soviet power.

(g) The development of repression of the "democratic" parties and press

Just as their counter-revolutionary activity in the second half of 1918 had resulted in the jailing of some Mensheviks and SRs, so their subversive conduct in the winter of 1920–1921 brought repression down upon them and caused the Soviet power to place increasing restrictions on their organizations and press.

In this connection there was a considerable difference between the Bolshevik Party's practice from 1921 onward and the line Lenin had taken even during the civil war. Thus, in November 1918, speaking about the Mensheviks who had shown that they repudiated an anti-Soviet attitude, Lenin said: "We must not now turn them away, on the contrary, we must meet them halfway and give them a chance to work with us." [32] In the same period Lenin warned that "it would be . . . foolish and ridiculous . . . to insist only on tactics of suppression and terror in relation to the petty-bourgeois democrats when the course of events is compelling them to turn in our direction." [33]

He also expressed himself in favor, at one and the same time, of banning the bourgeois press (meaning the press that was bourgeois either in its source of funds or in its openly counter-revolutionary character) and of allowing freedom to the "democratic" press, that is, the publications of mass organizations or of parties willing to carry on a political struggle within the Soviet system.

Thus, soon after the October Revolution, a draft resolution composed by Lenin declared that the press which was not dependent on capital would be left free. Dated November 4, 1917, it stated that "for the workers' and peasants' government, freedom of the press means liberation of the press from capitalist oppression, and public ownership of paper mills and printing presses; equal right for public groups of a certain size (say, numbering 10,000) to a fair share of newsprint stocks and a corresponding quantity of printers' labour." [34]

The project was never put into practice, first, owing to a grave shortage of paper, and then, from 1918 onward, owing to increasingly tense political circumstances, especially as a result of the development of the civil war. In March 1918 censorship was introduced (though it did not at first apply to duplicated sheets and leaflets, as would be the case later on), and starting in July of that year, numerous Menshevik, SR, and anarchist publications were banned. Until 1921, however, it was usually enough for these publications to assume a different title for them to be able to reappear, even when their contents were violently critical of the Bolshevik Party.

It was, in fact, from 1921 on, in the disastrous situation that prevailed in that year, and after the attempt of the committee set up in July 1921 to enter into direct negotiations with the imperialist governments, that repression hardened against the "democratic" parties and press, and became more and more systematic. It does not appear, though, that Lenin at that time envisaged the banning of the "democratic" parties, which, in his view, were "inevitably engendered by petty-bourgeois economic relations,"[35] and it has even been claimed that in 1922 he was contemplating "the revival of some degree of press freedom."[36]

The actual practice of the Bolshevik Party took a different direction, partly owing to the counter-revolutionary activity of many SRs and Mensheviks. In February 1922 forty-seven SR leaders were charged with anti-Soviet conspiracy, and in June their trial began. It ended with a number of convictions,[37] and both the SR and Menshevik parties now found their activities increasingly obstructed. Nevertheless, they were not banned. The VTsIK decree of August 8, 1922, which confirmed the sentences passed on the convicted SRs (but suspended execution of these sentences), even gave implicit recognition to the legal existence of their party, since it declared: "If the party of the S.R.s in deed and in practice discontinues its underground conspiratorial terrorist and military espionage activity leading to insurrection against the power of the workers and peasants, it will by doing so release from paying the supreme penalty those of its leading members who in the past led this work . . ."[38]

All the same, the legal existence of these "democratic" parties was thereafter increasingly a fiction: though not formally dissolved, their activity became practically impossible. Their leaders were often arrested and most of them eventually emigrated. Their press could no longer be produced in Russia, though for some years it continued to be circulated there. Gradually, a certain number of Mensheviks and SRs who did not emigrate joined the Bolshevik Party. In this way Russia soon became, during the first years of the NEP, a "one-party state."

The original attempt to grant the "democratic" parties a place in the political relations that were being formed under the proletarian dictatorship had thus failed. This failure was due mainly to the illusions entertained by these parties, which thought they could overthrow the proletarian power by means of subversive agitation, and so refused, on their own initiative, to fit into the new political relations. This attitude was certainly fostered by the mistakes of the Bolshevik Party, which often preferred to apply methods of repression instead of relying mainly on ideological struggle.

The very great difficulties encountered by the Soviet power at the beginning of the 1920s—difficulties which created a situation that seemed hopeless—played a vital role in this connection. They gave rise to the illusion in the petty bourgeois organizations that the dictatorship of the proletariat could be overthrown, an illusion which led them to choose the path of subversion in preference to that of finding a place for themselves in the system of the proletarian dictatorship. These parties were the first to suffer the consequences of their mistake, for they disappeared altogether as a result of the repression that descended upon them: but their disappearance did not have a good influence on the development of the Soviet system, or on the Bolshevik Party. The party did not have to wage the same ideological struggle it would have faced had these parties remained in existence: it was not obliged to reply to their criticisms,[39] in a way that could only have proved helpful to the development of revolutionary Marxism.

III. The transformation of the role of the soviet organs

A process parallel to that which led to the transformation of the relations between the central organs of government, reducing to a formality the role of the elected assemblies—that is, the central soviet bodies—went forward at the level of the soviets of the provinces, districts, and towns, and in the local soviets.

Here, too, effective power shifted from the congresses to the executive committees, and, in fact, within the latter, on the one hand, to the Bolshevik Party (in this case, as we shall see, often only formally), and, on the other, to a permanent administrative machine.

It is important to emphasize how objective this process was, bringing transformations that were not "wished for," but happened of themselves. This process, moreover, had begun before the establishment of the dictatorship of the proletariat. Thus, already in April 1917 it was possible to observe that the Petrograd soviet "had been transformed into a well-organised administrative machine. Several hundred office-workers, mostly secretaries, were actively engaged in its service . . . The executive of the Soviet was obviously escaping from the supervision that the deputies were supposed to exercise over it."[40]

After the October Revolution this process continued, transforming at all levels, local and provincial, the relations between the administrative machinery and the deputies to the soviets, and consequently, the interest that the masses took in the activities of their representatives. This process led to the inflation of an administrative apparatus which was increasingly in the hands of the former bourgeoisie (mainly members of the old corps of officials), and which tended to become independent of the proletarian ruling authority.

In 1920 Lenin noted that this was the situation: "Any person in authority who goes to the rural districts, as delegate or representative of the Central Committee, must remember that we have a tremendous machinery of state which is still functioning poorly because we do not know how to run it properly . . . The Soviet government employs hundreds of thousands of office workers who are either bourgeois or semi-bourgeois, or else have been so downtrodden that they have absolutely no confidence in our Soviet government."[41]

The authority of the local soviets was affected even more profoundly by another development, namely, the increasing concentration of power in the hands of the various central organs of government. This concentration, due at first to the demands of the military struggle, and then, more lastingly, to the weakness of the local political cadres, aroused from time to time protests by the "lower" soviet organs, which did not always readily agree to accept subordination to the central authorities.

The process whereby the effective authority of the local

soviets passed to the central organs of government and, still more, to the central administrative machine, affected adversely the working people's interest in the functioning of the basic soviet organs. As a result, the soviets were not a system of government by the masses, as Lenin recorded when he wrote, in March 1919: "The Soviets, which by virtue of their programme are organs of government *by the working people* are in fact organs of government *for the working people* by the advanced section of the proletariat, but not by the working people as a whole."[42]

A decree of the Sovnarkom in April 1921 sought to increase participation by women workers and peasant women in the executive committees of the soviets. They were to be employed in administrative capacities, either on a temporary basis or permanently. This decree had no effect on the indifference of the masses toward the soviet organs, which no longer played more than a very much reduced role, with effective administration concentrated in the hands of a permanent bureaucratic apparatus over which the soviets exercised, in fact, no real control.

Thus, between 1918 and 1921 a process of withering of the soviet organs went forward. These organs offered less and less opportunity for the working people to express their criticism or to control the corps of officials. The state's administrative machine became more and more independent, more and more separate from the masses: and the role played by this machine also made it hard for the Bolshevik Party to control and give political guidance to the state machine.

IV. The state administrative machine becomes independent of the party and the government

At the center, the leading role of the party in relation to the government was shown as early as October 16, 1917, by the conditions in which the Sovnarkom, headed by Lenin, was formed, and by the role assumed on that occasion by the Central Committee of the RSDLP (B). This leading role was a matter of principle, but it was not enough for the Bolshevik Party to proclaim it for the party to exercise *in reality* concrete leadership of the country's affairs. Actually, during the first period of Soviet power a considerable part of the administrative machine was not guided by the party and the government. This was so not only in remote country areas but even in the towns, including the capitals, Petrograd and Moscow.

Jacques Sadoul notes that in early 1918 the Bolshevik cadres, themselves dedicated militants, were surrounded by administrators of bourgeois origin, "careerists and corruptionists who seem to have no other defined ideal than to fill their pockets fast." He added that these people had "developed with brilliance the regime of bribe-taking which was already notorious in tsarist Russia," and that, as a result, corruption was tending to infect certain party circles. Sadoul mentions, in particular, commissions of between 10 and 15 percent, payment of which enabled members of the former bourgeoisie, whose funds were theoretically frozen, to draw from their safe deposits all the valuables or money they wanted.[43]

Relations between the central organs of government and the state administrative machine changed during "war communism," but remained nevertheless such that a divergence was often to be observed between the orders issuing from the highest level and the actual doings of the administration.

As early as March 1918 an attempt was made to increase the central government's control over the administrative machine. It took the form of establishing the People's Commissariat for Control of the State. This measure had no serious results, and so the Eighth Party Congress decided in March 1919 that "control in the Soviet republic should be radically reorganised in order to create a genuine, practical control of a socialist character." The leading role in exercising this control should be entrusted to party organizations and trade unions.[44]

As a consequence of this decision a new People's Commissariat for Control of the State was formed on April 9, 1919, with Stalin as commissar: he held at the same time leading positions in two other organs that had been recently formed— the Politburo and the Orgburo.

In fact, however, the People's Commissariat for Control of the State did not succeed in changing the situation very much. A decree of February 7, 1920, aimed afresh at improving the control exercised over the administration by transforming the commissariat into a "Workers' and Peasants' Inspection" (RKI, or Rabkrin), also headed by Stalin. This organ was intended to develop a new type of relationship with the masses. The decree provided that "the fight against bureaucratism and corruption in soviet institutions" must henceforth be carried on by workers and peasants elected by the same assemblies which elected deputies to the soviets. The idea was thus, in principle, one of organizing mass control over the state administrative machine. In April 1920 the trade unions were also associated with the work of Rabkrin. Under conditions in which the soviet organs were declining in activity, however, Rabkrin was doomed to remain a bureaucratic organ of which Lenin would say, a few years after its creation: "The People's Commissariat of the Workers' and Peasants' Inspection does not at present enjoy the slightest authority. Everybody knows that no other institutions are worse organised than those of our Workers' and Peasants' Inspection, and that under present conditions nothing can be expected from this People's Commissariat."[45]

V. *The development of the Red Army*

The October Revolution was accompanied by the collapse of the old feudal-bourgeois military machine of tsardom, which literally disintegrated. The order for demobilizing the entire old army, which was officially promulgated on March 2, 1918, ratified a de facto situation, a tremendous victory of the masses: the breakup of one of the instruments of repression used by the exploiting classes.

However, largely for the same reasons that governed the general process already analyzed (but also for other reasons to be examined later), the October Revolution did not succeed in building an army that was definitely proletarian in character, characterized by new ideological and political relations which could have been an instrument in the struggle for socialist transformation of social relations and against the subsequent rise of bourgeois forces.

(a) The creation of the Red Army

The Red Army did not result from the merging of squads or detachments of workers and peasants. Armed forces of that character did exist, having emerged directly from the struggles preceding October, and their nucleus was the Red Guards. These forces were too meager, however, for the Soviet power to be able to rely on them alone in facing up to the enormous military effort it had to undertake. The Red Guards and other revolutionary detachments formed only a minority element in the Soviet army. The latter had to be built up quickly, "from above."

The old machinery of the Ministry of War, transformed into the People's Commissariat for War and the Red Army, played a substantial part in this process. Purged of its overtly counter-revolutionary elements and brought under control by the Bolshevik Party, it was entrusted with the task, as Trotsky put it, of "unifying and organising the huge military apparatus inherited from the past, which though disorganised and disordered, is mighty owing to the quantity of values it includes, and adapting this to the army that we now wish to form." [46]

This quotation shows clearly that the Red Army was largely continuous with "the military apparatus inherited from the past." The "values" that the Red Army conserved were thus, in part, *the rules of discipline, the hierarchical relations*, etc., of the old tsarist army.

The commanders of this army were to some extent revolutionary officers risen from the ranks, but there were also many former tsarist officers. Some of these had "rallied" to the

Soviet power, for a variety of reasons, while others were incorporated by order of the Soviet state:[47] all of them were appointed, not elected. The role accorded to the former tsarist officers was due in part to "technical requirements" and, still more, to the decisive importance accorded to the "military skills" which were supposed to be mainly concentrated in the old officer corps. The idea of the "neutrality" of technique was at work here—an idea frequently expounded by Trotsky.

For example, in his report of March 28, 1918, to the conference of the Bolshevik Party of the City of Moscow, Trotsky said that the "technicians, engineers, doctors, teachers, ex-officers constitute, just like the inanimate machines, national capital[48] belonging to the people which it is our duty to take stock of, organise and adopt if we are to solve the vital problems facing us."[49]

This conception was bound up with the idea that there is no strictly proletarian way of fighting and making war. In Trotsky's view, military tactics are determined not by the class nature of the power organizing the military operations, but by the level of development of the productive forces. He therefore declared that it was wrong to suppose "that now, on the basis of our low technical and cultural level, we are already able to create tactics, new in principle and more perfected, than those which the most civilised beasts of prey of the West have attained."[50]

At the same time, Trotsky had a mechanistic notion of the relations between the nature of the ruling class and the army placed under the domination of that class, a notion expressed in the same article: "The composition of the army and the personnel of its command is conditioned by the social structure of society. The administrative supply apparatus depends on the general apparatus [i.e., the machinery of state—Trans.], which is determined by the nature of the ruling class."[51]

This undialectical way of presenting the problem rules out a priori the possibility of any contradiction developing between the class in power and its own machinery of state—administrative, military, etc.

The new military apparatus was markedly affected by the

place given in it to the former tsarist officers, and more especially to the younger generation of the old officer corps, by the role of the old military academies in the training of the new cadres, and by the retention of many principles characteristic of the army that had just been dissolved. Here we see at work a "technicist" conception according to which there is an "institutional form" for an army, dictated by the prevailing techniques. Trotsky gave clear expression to this notion when he said: "We must have an effective armed force, constructed on the basis of military science. The active and systematic participation of military specialists in all our work is, therefore, a vital necessity. We must ensure that the military specialists are able conscientiously and honestly to make their contribution to the work of building the army."[52]

In the absence of real practical military experience before the establishment of the Soviet power, the "technicist" conception of the army and of military tactics, which prevailed widely in the Bolshevik Party, stood in the way of the building of an army of a new type. It favored, on the contrary, the formation and consolidation in the Red Army of hierarchical relations of the feudal-bourgeois type, and this all the more rapidly because, from the spring of 1918 onward, a general process began whereby the machinery of state became increasingly independent.

In Trotsky's case this conception was combined with great distrust of the masses. Speaking of their recent past, he said, for instance, that they were "merely a compact mass that lived and died just as a cloud of grasshoppers lives and dies,"[53] and, speaking of their present, he said that they were possessed by "the most elementary instincts," so that "the mass-man . . . tries to grab for himself all that he can, he thinks only of himself and is not disposed to consider the people's class point of view."[54]

The old hierarchical relations retained by the Red Army (in a more or less modified form) were imposed upon the revolutionary cadres in the army and upon the newly qualified officers emerging from the Soviet military academies. As soon as they were promoted, the young officers found themselves placed at a certain level in these hierarchical relations, they enjoyed material privileges, and they learnt to trust their technical knowledge more than the working masses in arms.

Control of this army by a proletarian state dictatorship obviously presented grave problems. Control of the officers by the soldiers was ruled out by the facts of the situation, especially since recruitment was based on conscription, which resulted in the mass-scale incorporation of peasants who were as yet little influenced by the Bolshevik Party. In these circumstances, the tasks of political control were entrusted to political commissars appointed by the Soviet power. While these commissars were chosen on the basis of their proven devotion to the dictatorship of the proletariat, the officers were appointed above all on the basis of their "technical ability." One of the principal tasks of the political commissars was thus to check that the army was not used by the officers for counter-revolutionary operations: on the other hand, in principle, they refrained from interfering in the way military operations were conceived. The latter—except on the highest plane of strategy—were regarded as being essentially "technical." It was for the officers to conduct them as they saw fit. Trotsky said on this point: "Where purely military, operational questions are concerned, and even more so as regards questions relating to the battle itself, the military specialists in all branches of the administration have the last word." [55]

(b) The problem of the local militias

During the summer of 1918 the Soviet power decided to form a "militia of the rear" (decree of July 20, 1918). Actually, the conceptions that prevailed in the formation of the Red Army, together with concern not to risk putting military means in the hands of the SR and Menshevik enemies of the Soviet power who were still active, got in the way of any serious development of these militias. The price paid for this failure was a heavy one. In 1919 the rear was not prepared to withstand the enemy's increasingly numerous cavalry raids, and a system of local militias had to be improvised. These were set up, in certain regions at any rate, with a success that tended to prove that it was possible to develop forms of armed struggle other than those that the Red Army could conduct, and that such a development might have been of great service to the defense of the Soviet power. Trotsky was obliged to recognize this: "The deep breakthrough by Mamontov's cavalry made it urgent to create local forces from scratch. We can say that, this time, our Soviet apparatus showed sufficient flexibility and aptitude in concentrating all its efforts upon an unexpected task: in many places . . . groups and detachments, not only of infantry but of cavalry as well, were created literally 'out of nothing.' "[56]

On this occasion were displayed the remarkable qualities, the capacity for initative, and the "military skills" of the worker and peasant masses solving for themselves, "out of nothing," by their own powers, the problems involved in an "unexpected task."

However, the ruling notions regarding "military science" and the structure to be given to the armed forces, together with the resistance opposed by the new officer corps to military initiatives that were not under their control, meant that the system of local militias was not developed extensively. It was, instead, looked upon with suspicion. The same happened with the partisan detachments the necessity of which, in view of enemy incursions, Trotsky had also to recognize, while endeavoring to restrict their role in conformity with the demands voiced by the "military authorities."[57]

(c) The Red Army's victories and its nature as a people's army

The Red Army, formed in the conditions just recalled, won victories the historical significance of which was immense. Backed by absurdly inadequate material resources, with industry disorganized and operating in slow motion, and with very little to eat, it defeated the White Guards who were backed by the interventionist forces of the imperialist powers. The Russian soldiers who, not long before, had revolted against continuance of the imperialist war waged by the Provisional Government, displayed extraordinary heroism, an indomitable will to defend the Soviet power. Without that will, victory would not have been possible.

The victories which the Red Army wrested from armies that were infinitely better equipped testify to the profoundly popular character of the October Revolution. They show, too, that, owing to its dual character, at once proletarian and democratic, the revolution could be defended by an army that was not constructed on proletarian principles, provided that this army was actually subject to political guidance by the proletariat and that the general political line followed by the leading party was basically correct. The mistakes of "war communism," since they did not deeply shake the will of the Red Army's soldiers to struggle and conquer, must be regarded as being of secondary importance.

As Lenin said in his speech of May 13, 1920, at an enlarged conference of workers and Red Army men:

> In the final analysis, victory in any war depends on the spirit animating the masses that spill their own blood on the field of battle. The conviction that the war is in a just cause and the realisation that their lives must be laid down for the welfare of their brothers strengthen the morale of the fighting men and enable them to endure incredible hardships. Tsarist generals say that our Red Army men are capable of enduring hardships that the Tsar's army could never have stood up to. The reason is that every mobilised worker or peasant knows what he is fighting for, and is ready to shed his own blood for the triumph of justice and socialism.[58]

Although, in the conjuncture of the civil war and the fight against imperialist intervention, the revolutionary will of the soldiers and the masses was the deciding factor in the victories of the Red Army, it is nevertheless true that this army, as an instrument of state, did not possess the fundamental features of a proletarian army.

Indeed, the internal political relations of the Red Army corresponded at bottom to the demands of a democratic revolution (a revolution made by the peasants fighting for the land

and against the landlords) led by the proletariat. These relations enabled the Russian revolution to cope with the principal tasks facing it at the stage at which it then stood. However, constituted as the Red Army was, this army could not be an instrument suitable for making the transition to the next stage of the revolution. It was not a proletarian army but a people's army subordinated to the dictatorship of the proletariat. It was thus very different from what the People's Liberation Army (PLA) in China was to be from the outset. This army was formed directly by the Chinese Communist Party, from the ground up, by merging into army corps the most combative elements of the proletariat and the peasantry who had already committed themselves to struggle under the leadership of the party. Accordingly, from the beginning, the PLA was under the ideological and political guidance of the Chinese Communist Party, with its officers under the control of the soldiers helped by political commissars.

As regards the Soviet Red Army, the following two points need especially to be stressed.

(1) It was a centralized army (as is the PLA) and not a collection of people's militias. An army of this type seems necessary if military forces are to be formed that possess the mobility and unity over a vast area which are required for fighting the armies of centralized, imperialist states. These were the exigencies that dictated, in Russia as in China, the formation of a real army.[59]

(2) The Red Army's subordination to the dictatorship of the proletariat was at the outset (for a number of reasons, and particularly owing to the conditions under which the officer corps was recruited) more a matter of political than of ideological leadership by the Bolshevik Party. The political leadership was ensured, in the main, by the presence of political commissars alongside the officers of the Soviet army.

The weakness of the ideological leadership exercised by the proletariat over the Soviet Red Army resulted from an historical process, from the concrete conditions in which this army had had to be built. This weakness had as its counterpart the still mainly bourgeois character of the dominant ideological and political relations within the Red Army—whence the importance of "external signs of respect," the markedly different living conditions (quarters, food, etc.) of officers and soldiers, etc.

Since the internal political relations of the Red Army were not predominantly proletarian, the same was true of its relations with the masses. One of the most significant indications that this was the case was Trotsky's move to form "labor armies," made up principally of soldiers who, though demobilized, could be recalled to the colors at any moment. This move shows that participation in productive labor was not one of the normal tasks of the Soviet Red Army. It shows also the fear that existed of allowing the former soldiers to "disperse," of letting them "wander off" and of not being able to reincorporate them easily in the event that they should be needed again for military tasks—which confirms that the Red Army's discipline was founded more on bourgeois forms of maintaining discipline than on the predominance of proletarian ideology.

While its formation took place in basically the same way as that of the state's civil administrative system, the Red Army nevertheless had some distinctive features that made it an instrument much more closely subject to the political ruling power. The institution of political commissars was one of the means of ensuring a political subordination which was absolutely necessary in view of the vital importance of the Red Army's task of waging armed struggle against the bourgeoisie and imperialism in order to ensure the very survival of the Soviet power. This task obliged the Bolshevik Party to focus upon the Red Army attention and efforts that were beyond all comparison with those that were devoted, in the same period, to the civil administration.

During the "war communism" period, and even long afterward, the Bolshevik Party watched with quite special vigilance over everything that went on in the army. It sent into the army a large proportion of its best political forces. However, this exceptional vigilance and attention could not by themselves alter the political relations, in particular the relations between soldiers and officers, prevailing in the Soviet army. This army did not become a proletarian army; on the contrary, getting caught up in a general process, the army's bourgeois features were gradually reinforced.

On the morrow of "war communism," one of the principal contributions made by the Red Army was to release for service in the civil administration and the state's economic apparatus a number of energetic and experienced administrators. They strengthened in their new settings those forms of "efficiency" that could be achieved by means of strict discipline of the traditional type, which is quite different from proletarian discipline.

VI. *The establishment and development of the Cheka*

The proletarian character of the October revolution was shown in its ability to smash the apparatus of repression of the tsarist and bourgeois rulers. Like the old army, the old police apparatus was shattered during the October days. The same thing happened with the old judicial system (which was formally abolished by a decree of November 24, 1918);[60] the functions of that organization were taken over by revolutionary tribunals directly representing the masses.

In the concrete circumstances in which the revolutionary process developed, the Soviet power quickly equipped itself with an apparatus for security and for the repression of counter-revolution. This apparatus grew out of the Military Revolutionary Committee, of which it was a commission, the "extraordinary commission," or Cheka (from the initials of the Russian name). When a decree of the Sovnarkom, dated December 7, 1917, dissolved the Military Revolutionary Committee, the Cheka was kept in being, and when the seat of government was moved in March 1918 from Petrograd to Moscow, the Cheka went with it and took up residence in Lubyanka Square. Its importance grew as the civil war progressed.

The dictatorship of the proletariat was then fighting for its life, and the Cheka was one of the instruments that it employed in its fight against the bourgeoisie and imperialism. During the second half of 1918, when the activities of the SRs and Mensheviks were increasingly serving the interests of the counter-revolution, it was decided to use the Cheka to keep an eye on their organizations.

In the extremely tense situation of autumn 1918, an official decision, dated September 19, authorized the Cheka to make arrests and carry out executions without reference to the revolutionary tribunals, thus giving official approval to a practice which had already become established. As Peters, one of the heads of the Cheka wrote: "In its activity the Cheka is completely independent, carrying out searches, arrests, shootings, afterwards making a report to the Council of People's Commissars and the Soviet Central Executive Committee."[61]

At the end of 1918 and during 1919 the struggle for survival waged by the dictatorship of the proletariat consciously assumed the form of "revolutionary terror," in imitation of the "Terror" imposed in 1793 by France's Committee of Public Safety.[62] The Cheka was the agency charged with implementing this revolutionary terror. Its power to destroy its opponents, and the secrecy surrounding it made the Cheka especially susceptible to playing a relatively independent role. Already in 1919, indeed, it sometimes went beyond the limits that were in principle laid down for its activity, and struck not only at counter-revolutionary acts but also at mere expressions of discontent—as when repression was extended to middle peasants protesting against excessive requisitioning. Some of the actions of the Cheka—whose powers of intervention increased with the passage of time, especially when it acquired its own armed forces—thus conflicted with the political line laid down by the top leadership of the Bolshevik Party.

At the Eighth Party Congress, in March 1919, Lenin warned the party and the repressive organs against coercion of the middle peasants. The resolution adopted on this question stated:

To confuse the middle peasants with the kulaks and to extend to them in one or another degree measures directed against the kulaks is to violate most flagrantly not only all the decrees of the Soviet government and its entire policy, but also all the basic principles of communism, according to which agreement between the proletariat and the middle peasants is one of the conditions for a painless transition to the abolition of all exploitation in the period of decisive struggle waged by the proletariat to overthrow the bourgeoisie.[63]

However, this resolution did not succeed, any more than did the earlier decisions of the Sixth Congress of Soviets (late 1918) or the subsequent resolutions of the Ninth Party Congress, in keeping the Cheka's activity within the limits that the Soviet power wished to lay down for it.

The Cheka thus very soon acquired a relative degree of independence, as was shown by the fact that it was necessary to repeat the resolution of the Sixth Congress of Soviets ordering the release, within a fortnight of their arrest, of all persons detained by the Cheka, unless definite charges of counter-revolutionary activity could be brought against them.[64] Similarly, it seems that not much respect was shown in practice to the resolution of the Sixth Congress of Soviets, according to which the VTsIK and the local soviets' executive committees had the right to supervise the Cheka's activities: this resolution included also a reminder that "all functionaries of the Soviet power" were obliged to observe strict obedience to the law, and it gave citizens the right to appeal against violation of their rights by these functionaries.

The year 1919 was marked, however, by large-scale counter-revolutionary offensives, and in this situation the Bolshevik Party granted new powers to the Cheka, cutting across previous decisions to subject its work to closer control.

On April 15, 1919, the powers of the Cheka were strengthened in order to deal with acts of banditry and breaches of Soviet discipline. For this purpose "corrective labor camps" were established, to which could be sent those persons who were convicted by the revolutionary tribunals,

the local soviets, or the Cheka. The provincial departments of
the Cheka were given the responsibility of setting up these
camps, where detainees were to be employed on work of
benefit to Soviet institutions. Separate camps were set up for
children and minors.[65]

On October 21, 1919, another decree established a "special
revolutionary tribunal" under the immediate authority of the
Cheka, with the task of "waging merciless struggle" against
thieves and speculators. At that time the crime of speculation
included the unauthorized conveyance of any quantity of
foodstuffs, however small, from country to town.

At the beginning of 1920 this "special tribunal" was
abolished, but in November of that year the local organs of the
Cheka were endowed with the same powers as those possessed by the military revolutionary tribunals, including the
right to carry out sentences on the spot, merely reporting the
executions to the People's Commissariat of Justice.[66]

Generally speaking, the work of the Cheka between 1917
and 1921 came gradually to have two aspects. On the one
hand, it was an instrument for "maintaining law and order,"
intervening in certain cases to prevent theft and speculation,
enforce various requisitioning measures in the countryside, or
ensure respect for labor discipline. On the other, it was an
instrument of political struggle, both against open agents of
counter-revolution and against members of those parties
which were associated with counter-revolutionary activities.

During those years, cases of interference by the Cheka in
the internal life of the Bolshevik Party were exceptional. In
some cases, though (in particular toward the end of this
period, and especially during the preparations for the Tenth
Party Congress and immediately after it), this interference was
sufficiently serious to provoke reactions from party members,
causing a Bolshevik speaker at the Ninth Congress of Soviets
(December 23–28, 1921) to call for a complete reorganization
of the Cheka organs with the aim "of restricting their competence and of strengthening the principles of revolutionary
legality." A resolution including this phrase was passed by the
congress.[67]

Subsequently, on February 8, 1922, the VTsIK issued a decree abolishing the Cheka and its local commissions. This decree transferred the responsibilities of the Cheka to the People's Commissariat of Internal Affairs, creating within the latter a "state political administration" (GPU) entrusted with fulfillment of the functions of the former Cheka, under the supervision of the people's commissariat in question. In principle, the political sections of the GPU in the provinces, autonomous republics, and autonomous regions were to be responsible to the executive committees of the local soviets. This measure was intended to ensure better control by the Soviet authorities over the activities of the security organs. At the same time, the GPU was allotted "special army detachments," one of the functions of which was to "combat crime in the Army and on the railways."

In theory, the GPU enjoyed much more limited freedom of action than the Cheka had enjoyed de facto. In particular, preventive detention was to last no more than two months, after which any person arrested by the GPU must either be released or handed over to the judicial authorities, unless the VTsIK should decide otherwise. These restrictions were ignored, however, and "political offenses" continued to be dealt with quite outside the judicial system, with the GPU, in this connection, even assuming powers that were still more extensive and arbitrary than those wielded by the former Cheka—though the subordination of the GPU to the Commissariat of Internal Affairs had been decided with a view to limiting its powers. In 1923, after the establishment of the Union of Soviet Socialist Republics, the GPU shook off even formal control by the Commissariat of Internal Affairs.[68]

One other point that needs to be mentioned is that, after the Tenth Party Congress (1921), first the Cheka and then the GPU participated directly and officially in the work of the party's Control Commission. This meant increasing interference in the life of the Bolshevik Party by a repressive organ which had its own apparatus and its own files and card-indexes (based on sources of information that could not be checked). Increasingly, one of the activities of the GPU was to consist in probing within the Bolshevik Party in order to identify and track down "dissident" members.[69]

The widening of the GPU's activities and the arbitrary character of its decisions contributed to creating an atmosphere unfavorable to free expression of opinion and free development of initiative. At the Eleventh Party Congress (March 27-April 2, 1922), the last he was able to attend, Lenin himself denounced the irregular extension of the GPU's scope, but this did not prevent the process from continuing whereby that institution was strengthened, and its activities merged more and more closely with those of the party's Central Control Commission and of the People's Commissariat of Workers' and Peasants' Inspection—of which commissariat Lenin was to say, not long before his death, that it "does not at present enjoy the slightest authority."

Finally, in 1921, and even more markedly in the years that followed, the position acquired by the organs of repression and the scope of their activities created a situation utterly different from what Lenin had envisaged in 1917 and at the beginning of 1918.

Notes

1. Engels to Bebel, March 18–28, 1875, in Marx and Engels, *Selected Correspondence*, p. 357, and Marx and Engels, *Selected Works*, vol. 3, p. 34. Lenin discusses this passage in chapter IV, section 2, of *The State and Revolution* (*CW*, vol. 25, pp. 439 ff.).
2. The Fifth Congress of Soviets (1918) had fixed the membership of the VTsIK at 200.
3. See Carr, *The Bolshevik Revolution*, vol. 1, pp. 220–230.
4. Ibid., vol. 1, p. 122.
5. *CW*, vol. 26, p. 285.
6. Carr, *The Bolshevik Revolution*, vol. 1, p. 177.
7. Ibid., vol. 1, p. 186.
8. Carr, *Socialism in One Country*, vol. 1, p. 65.
9. *CW*, vol. 26, pp. 269–270.
10. Broué, *Le Parti bolchévique*, p. 99.

11. As we have just seen on that same day Lenin, addressing the
    regimental delegates of the Petrograd garrison, said that "we
    wanted [my emphasis—C.B.] a coalition Soviet government,"
    implying that he *no longer* wanted this.
12. Lenin's remarks at the CC meeting of November 1, 1917, in *CW*,
    vol. 26, pp. 275–276.
13. Liebman, *Leninism under Lenin*, p. 240.
14. *CW*, vol. 26, pp. 277–278.
15. Among the members of this minority were Kamenev, Zinoviev,
    Rykov, Nogin, and Milyutin (*CW*, vol. 26, pp. 557–558).
16. Liebman, *Leninism under Lenin*, p. 242.
17. *CW*, vol. 26, p. 278.
18. Ibid.
19. Liebman, *Leninism under Lenin*, pp. 243–246.
20. Carr, *The Bolshevik Revolution*, vol. 1, pp. 170–171.
21. Ibid., p. 180.
22. *CW*, vol. 26, p. 555.
23. Liebman, *Leninism under Lenin*, pp. 256–257 and 313.
24. Ibid., pp. 252–253.
25. *CW*, vol. 29, pp. 561–562.
26. *CW*, vol. 31, p. 201.
27. Ibid., pp. 32–33.
28. Liebman, *Leninism under Lenin*, p. 253.
29. Carr, *The Bolshevik Revolution*, vol. 1, p. 180.
30. Report of the Seventh Congress (in Russian), pp. 60–63, quoted
    in Carr, ibid., p. 182.
31. Quoted in ibid., p. 182
32. *CW*, vol. 28, p. 198.
33. Ibid., p. 191.
34. *CW*, vol. 26, p. 283.
35. *CW*, vol. 32, p. 230.
36. Serge, *Memoirs of a Revolutionary*, p. 163.
37. Carr, *The Bolshevik Revolution*, vol. 1, p. 189.
38. Trial proceedings, quoted in ibid., p. 190.
39. It is pertinent here to quote Mao Tse-tung's remarks in an article
    of April 25, 1956, reissued on December 27, 1965, by the Central
    Committee of the Chinese Communist Party. In this article,
    entitled *On the Ten Great Relationships*, Mao Tse-tung dis-
    cussed the Chinese CP's relations with the democratic parties
    and the non-party democrats. After asking: "Is it really better to
    have one party or several parties?" he replied: "As things are

now, it would seem to be better to have several parties. Not only was this so in the past, it may very well be so in the future too, right up to the time when all parties wither away. Long-term co-existence and mutual supervision between the Communist Party and the various democratic parties has advantages" (Schram, *Mao Tse-tung Unrehearsed*, pp. 74–75).

40. Anweiler, *Die Rätebewegung*, p. 133.
41. Lenin's speech of June 12, 1920, to the Second All-Russia Conference of Organizers Responsible for Rural Work, in *CW*, vol. 31, pp. 168 ff.; quotation on pp. 177–178.
42. Lenin, report to the Eighth Party Congress, March 19, 1919, in *CW*, vol. 29, p. 183.
43. Sadoul, *Notes sur la révolution bolchévique*, p. 217.
44. Quoted in Carr, *The Bolshevik Revolution*, vol. 1, p. 231; *K.P.S.S. v Rezolyutsiyakh*, p. 445.
45. Lenin, "Better Fewer but Better" (1922), in *CW*, vol. 33, p. 490.
46. Trotsky, *Kak vooruzhalas' revolyutsiya*, p. 101.
47. Ibid., p. 145.
48. Note the use of the term "capital," used in the empirical sense of an accumulation (in this case, an accumulation of knowledge), which conceals the fundamental reality: the *social relations* (and the social practices) of which all these "specialists" were the carriers and agents.
49. Trotsky, *Kak vooruzhalas' revolyutsiya*, p. 37.
50. Trotsky, *Military Writings*, p. 145.
51. Ibid., p. 136.
52. Trotsky, *Kak vooruzhalas' revolyutsiya*, p. 135.
53. Ibid., p. 38.
54. Ibid., p. 39.
55. Ibid., p. 102.
56. Ibid., p. 289.
57. Ibid., pp. 283–284.
58. *CW*, vol. 31, p. 137.
59. In China, the need to form an army was recognized as soon as the question of Red political power arose. Thus, Mao Tse-tung wrote in "Why is it that Red political power can exist in China?" (October 5, 1928): "The existence of a regular Red Army of adequate strength is a necessary condition for the existence of Red political power. If we have local Red Guards only [these were armed units whose members carried on with their ordinary productive work—C.B.], but no regular Red Army, then we can-

not cope with the regular White forces, but only with the land-lords' levies" (Mao Tse-tung, *Selected Works*, vol. 1, p. 66).

60. For details, see Begaux-Francotte, "La *prokuratura* soviétique," pp. 52–53.
61. Quoted in Fainsod, *How Russia Is Ruled*, p. 360.
62. The Soviet power's resort to terror is often "explained" by the constant reference by the Bolshevik leaders to the experience of the French Revolution of 1789–1793. But this reference was relevant only because of the actual nature of the Russian Revolution, the *particular form* in which the proletarian revolutionary process and that of the democratic revolution were *combined*, and the considerable place occupied by the latter as compared with the former, owing to the weakness of the Bolshevik Party's ideological role in relation to the democratic revolutionary process. The place assumed in the Russian Revolution by state centralization and by coercion exercised by specialized organs is to be explained in the same way. This *particular form* of combination of the two revolutionary processes was not present in the Chinese Revolution, in which the proletarian ideology guiding the Chinese Communist Party played a leading role in the rural areas as well.
63. *CW*, vol. 29, p. 217.
64. Carr, *The Bolshevik Revolution*, vol. 1, p. 178.
65. Ibid., vol. 2, pp. 212–213.
66. See *Sobranie*, 1919, p. 504; 1920, pp. 22–23, 115, and 454.
67. Quoted in Carr, *The Bolshevik Revolution*, vol. 1, pp. 187–188.
68. Ibid., vol. 1, p. 189.
69. Ibid., p. 218.

2. *The changes in the Bolshevik Party, the guiding instrument of the proletarian dictatorship*

Before October 1917 the Bolshevik Party was essentially a party of revolutionary activists who took upon themselves political and ideological tasks among the masses. They propagated the revolutionary ideas of Marxism, organized the workers, analyzed the political situation, the class contradictions, and guided the class struggle along the path of revolution, taking account of the state of mind of the masses and drawing lessons from their experience. It was a small party mainly composed of tried and tested militants who were ready for the greatest sacrifices.

After October the party still had to carry out these same tasks, but it had also to cope with new ones. As the principal instrument of the proletarian dictatorship, it had to take part in the management of public affairs, be present in the organs of power at all levels, both the elected organs and the administrative ones, determine the economic, military, and administrative aims to be attained, and contribute to their attainment. The party's new functions and the place it held in the power structures called for an increase in membership.

The Bolshevik Party underwent a massive influx of new members. (As we have seen, in March 1920 it had nearly 612,000 members, compared with 24,000 in 1917.) Some of the newcomers were undoubtedly motivated by a desire to serve the revolution, but others looked on a party card as an aid to the furtherance of their ambitions. The danger of such members flooding in became very real by the end of 1920. In 1922, despite the purges, the party's numbers were regarded by Lenin as too big, and its recruitment insufficiently selective. He considered that, in the then existing conditions, with the

Soviet proletariat decimated by the imperialist and civil wars and undermined by unemployment, a party membership of between 300,000 and 400,000 was still "excessive."[1] However, the transformations undergone by the Bolshevik Party during those years were not merely quantitative, nor mainly determined by the influx of careerist and ambitious elements. They were connected with the ever-closer relations being formed between the party apparatus and a state administrative machine whose proletarian character proved especially weak. The types of practice that developed in the machinery of state, including the Red Army and the Cheka, thus produced effects on the functioning of the party, on the relations between its different levels, and on its relations with the masses.

I. The Bolshevik Party's relations with the state machine

The party's role as "the ruling party," the party in power, meant, as Lenin rightly observed, that "we had inevitably to merge the party and Government leadership."[2] However, the forms assumed by such a merger may vary. The merging of the "leaderships" can be the result of mass work carried out by the party, which brings forward activists capable of shouldering responsibilities in the various branches of government and strengthening the party's leading ideological and political role. But this "merging" can also result from the appointment to posts of responsibility of militants who, though active, are not closely linked with the masses locally. After October the conditions were such, in many areas, that it was often the second type of "merging" that took place.

The Bolshevik Party had hardly any footholds in the rural districts, in the small and middle-sized towns, and in vast regions of Russia. In countless localities it possessed no basic organization, nor even activists who were already connected with the masses in these localities and capable of playing a leading role among them. The party had to send all across the country organizers and cadres drawn from the big industrial centers. Lacking a sufficient number of members, it had to entrust the activists it dispatched hither and thither with a great number of functions, to be performed simultaneously, including administrative responsibilities. Soviet organs often did not exist at all in a certain place, or else were so composed that it was impossible to find among their members reliable persons who could be entrusted with the indispensable tasks of administration.

A report by Podbelsky, a people's commissar who was sent to make a tour of the countryside, describes the situation he found in July 1919 in Tambov province: "Strictly speaking, there is no Soviet government in the majority of the *uyezdy*. At present the soviets exist in most places only on paper; in reality, representatives of kulaks and speculators, or self-interested people, or cowards, who carry out the work without any definite direction, work under the name of Soviets."[3]

These pseudosoviets—like, for that matter, most of the normally elected soviets—were "served" by a bureaucratic apparatus made up of officials inherited from the old regime, persons who were corrupt, formalistic, or indifferent to their work. It was under such conditions that the few party activists who could be spared from the central organs and the army had to assume a multitude of responsibilities. They had to do this without being able to rely locally on a collective of communists linked with the masses, for in many places such a collective was either nonexistent or only embryonic. Given the urgency of their tasks, they had to get on with them before the embryonic party organizations had been transformed into proper ones, and before genuine soviets had been created.

A situation like this inevitably entailed a series of effects on the way the party itself operated. It led locally, in a great number of towns and districts, to activists taking on a plurality of functions, to a lack of control by basic party organs (since these hardly existed) over activists who were loaded with many responsibilities, and, often, to the absorption of these activists in tasks that were essentially administrative in character, to the detriment of political and ideological tasks, that is, of work among the masses.

Some of the delegates to the Eighth Party Congress (1919) described in detail the sort of thing that was happening at that time. They mentioned, for instance, that very often, in the provinces, the chairman of the party committee was also the chairman of the soviet, of the Cheka, of the revolutionary tribunal, and of yet other institutions. They showed that this confusion of functions strengthened the tendency for the executive committees to take over the role of the soviets (where these existed), and for the party committees to substitute themselves for the party organizations.[4]

In other words, the party apparatus tended to merge with the administrative apparatus (the characteristics of which we have already seen) and at the same time tended to substitute itself for the party organizations, that is, to act in their place and not to submit to control by the rank and file of the party— the basic organizations of the party being, in many places, barely existent.

Under these conditions, the party came to be dominated by an increasingly weighty administrative machine, instead of really running its own affairs. This was the situation that Lenin described in his report of March 27, 1922, to the Eleventh Party Congress, when he used the metaphor of "the man at the steering wheel," meaning the ruling party in charge of the state. The state machine, he said, "did not operate in the way we wanted. How did it operate? The machine refused to obey the hand that guided it. It was like a car that was going not in the direction the driver desired, but in the direction someone else desired . . ."[5]

As Lenin made clear, this "someone else" was the capitalists, the speculators, and the administrative apparatus which was under the influence of the bourgeoisie and tending to become "independent" of the proletarian dictatorship.

The continuation of this passage shows that Lenin clearly recognized the possible outcome of the evolution that had begun in the preceding years. Shortly after evoking this image of "the man at the steering wheel," Lenin raised the question of the direction that the Soviet power might take, and, analyzing the new tactic of certain Russian émigrés grouped around Ustryalov,[6] did not hesitate to declare that one of the dangers to which the Soviet power was exposed was indeed that of eventually evolving into "the ordinary bourgeois state."[7]

Lenin then described the type of relationship which had become established (this was in 1922) between the party and the state machine: "If we take Moscow with its 4,700 Communists in responsible positions, and if we take that huge bureaucratic machine, that gigantic heap, we must ask: who is directing whom? I doubt very much whether it can truthfully be said that the Communists are directing that heap. To tell the truth, they are not directing, they are being directed."[8] He went on: "Communists who are put at the head of departments—and sometimes artful saboteurs deliberately put them in these positions in order to use them as a shield—are often fooled . . . Will the responsible Communists of the R.S.F.S.R. and of the Russian Communist Party realise that they cannot administer: that they only imagine they are directing, but are, actually, being directed?"[9]

Lenin then sketched an analogy between the situation of the Bolshevik Party, which occupied the leading positions in the state but could not really govern, and that of a conquering people which had apparently subjugated another people but, in the long run, though still occupying the latter's territory, became subject to it, because "the vanquished nation," being "more civilised," "imposes its culture upon the conqueror."[10]

The "subjection" of which Lenin spoke here meant the domination of the party by the bourgeoisie, especially the bourgeois elements present in the state machine with which the party was tending to "merge" under the conditions already outlined. This subjection could be nothing but the transformation of the Bolshevik Party into its opposite, from a proletarian party into a bourgeois party.

In 1922 this was still a distant danger, but it is not without importance that Lenin was able to recognize it, just as it is of interest to note that, about a year after the Eleventh Congress,

Lenin's point was repeated and developed by Bukharin in terms that deserve attention, since they describe in a striking way what actually came about later on.

The work in which Bukharin gave this description was entitled *The Proletarian Revolution and Culture*.[11] He started from Lenin's comment that "the real and main danger"[12] was not a direct attack, but the overthrow of proletarian class domination within the machinery of the state and the party, which would lead to full restoration of bourgeois power. Like Lenin, Bukharin referred to Ustryalov and his supporters, the *Smenovekhovtsy*.[13] Their advice to the bourgeois intelligentsia to rally to the Russian Revolution was one of the leading themes of the journal they were then publishing in Paris (under the title *Smena Vekh*). They hoped that the revolution had taken "the road to Thermidor," and their journal praised those intellectuals who had remained in Soviet Russia and joined the party or entered government service.

Bukharin outlined with remarkable precision the possibility of a restoration of bourgeois power in Soviet Russia under cover of the "monopoly of knowledge" that the bourgeoisie and its intelligentsia were supposed to possess. He showed that the *Smenovekhovtsy* were "friends" of a very special kind, who considered that the October Revolution had carried through an indispensable historical task from which a new bourgeoisie would be able to profit to the full. For the *Smenovekhovtsy* the October Revolution possessed the immense merit of having roused and mobilized "the bravest and most ruthless enemies of the rotten old regime of tsardom": it had "utterly smashed the corrupt intellectual strata who could only talk of God and the Devil," and had "set the masses in motion," thereby "opening the way to the creation of a new bourgeoisie"—a bourgeoisie which, having passed through many trials, "has fortified its will and character and is now entering history's scene . . . fresher, younger, more vigorous, more 'American.' "

This "freshness," this "vigor" of the new bourgeoisie existed, of course, only in the imagination of the *Smenovekhovtsy*. But the vision they had of the possibility that the new bourgeoisie might subvert the Soviet power and the Bolshevik Party from within corresponded to what we know today is indeed one aspect of the struggle between the bourgeoisie and the proletariat, of the struggle between two lines and two paths of development.

Denouncing the path indicated by the *Smenovekhovtsy,* Bukharin showed how the bourgeoisie was "supporting" the Soviet power in a quite special way, "gradually penetrating into the pores of the apparatus," introducing its own people, slowly but persistently changing the characteristics of the Soviet power. After thus describing the process that was going on—the very process which had worried Lenin a year earlier, when he showed that it was often not the Communists but the bourgeoisie who were really determining direction, Bukharin said that, if this process was not halted,

> we shall arrive at a situation in which all our declarations, our flags, the "Internationale," the Soviet form of government would remain outwardly in being, while their inner content would already have been transformed: this content . . . would correspond to the expectations, wishes, hopes, and interests of the new bourgeois stratum which is constantly growing, constantly getting stronger, and which, through slow, organic changes, could succeed in transforming all the features of the Soviet state, setting it gradually on the rails of a purely capitalist policy . . . The old, rotten bourgeoisie, which lived on alms from the tsarist Government . . . would then have been replaced, thanks to the Russian Revolution, by a new bourgeoisie . . . which would stop at nothing, making its way forward in the spirit of nationalism but hiding itself behind the phraseology and the banners of internationalism, so as to advance toward a new capitalist and bourgeois Russia, great and powerful.[14]

Bukharin drew from his analysis this general conclusion: "Every workers' revolution, in whatever country it takes place, inevitably runs, in the course of its development, very great dangers of the internal degeneration of the revolution, the proletarian state, and the party."[15] He said that one of the vital tasks of the period of the proletarian dictatorship was to initiate a "cultural revolution."[16] In this connection he took up the example given by Lenin of the conquest of a "civilized" people by a "barbarian" one. Lenin gave this example in order to show how the working class risked losing power by gradually adopting the forms of social organization of the class it had overthrown. Bukharin added:

> The working class can mechanically subjugate its opponent . . . it can take physical possession of all that exists, and yet it can at the same time be absorbed by the enemy's cultural forces . . . This danger inevitably threatens every working class which seizes state power. If it were to happen, we should be transformed into a new class made up of the new technical intelligentsia, a part of the new bourgeoisie . . . because we should have become cut off, without noticing it but absolutely, from our general proletarian base, and in this way we should be transformed into a new social formation.[17]

Bukharin rejected the illusion that the proletarian class origin of the cadres would constitute an adequate safeguard against their transformation into a new bourgeois class, for, he said, it was perfectly possible to imagine a situation in which a part of the working class became separated from the working masses, acquiring a monopolistic position and transforming itself into a new class.[18]

This observation regarding the general character of the process of recovery of power by the bourgeoisie—that is, the universal character of the struggle between two roads—is particularly interesting, as is the idea developed by Bukharin (following up earlier suggestions by N. Krupskaya) that only a "cultural revolution" can halt the trend toward capitalism, even though he puts forward only very vague formulations as to the conditions and forms of such a cultural revolution.

While the process of internal bourgeois subversion of the Soviet power, begun during the civil war and continuing after it, bears a universal character and therefore provides general lessons, it is nevertheless true that the specific form assumed by this process at the beginning of the NEP was destined— contrary to Bukharin's forecast—to be completely overturned a few years later, when the NEP was abandoned and the Bolshevik Party took the path of collectivization and the five year plans.

II. The transformation of internal relations in the Bolshevik Party

During the civil war, internal relations in the Bolshevik Party gradually changed. This change was bound up, to some extent at least, with the new and urgent tasks which had to be fulfilled by the ruling party. But it was also due, and to a greater extent, to the specific conditions under which the Bolshevik Party was obliged to fulfill its tasks: it had suddenly to cope with extensive and complex economic and military problems at a time when the administrative state apparatus through which it operated was essentially nonproletarian and when its relations with the peasant masses were far from being close and trusting.

In order to appreciate the scale of the changes that took place after the October Revolution, one must remember that the Bolshevik faction, and then the Bolshevik Party, had experienced for many years an intense political life which included ample discussion even at the most difficult moments. When faced with complex or new problems, the party leadership did not, as a rule, take decisions until after holding discussions that were thorough, detailed, and as open as possible, given the nature of the problem at issue.[19] Not only were these discussions largely open in character, but members who held a point of view differing from that of the majority of the Central Committee could address themselves directly to the party as a whole. They could do this either through the party's official organs or through publications of their own, periodical or otherwise.[20]

As for the principles governing the discussions and the ideological and political disputes, these were, in practice, the same that the Chinese Communist Party was later to proclaim explicitly: unity—struggle—unity. By virtue of these principles, party members who came to conclusions differing from those of the majority of the Central Committee were not made objects of a "ruthless struggle" or of "merciless blows."[21] The party expected participants in discussions to put forward concrete analyses and undertake theoretical investigations that would help real progress to be made toward a serious solution of the problems at issue.

Even when, on certain questions, the number of active participants in a discussion was limited, this limitation was in no way imposed by administrative methods or regulations, and the rank and file were frequently called upon to give their views, which meant that the discussion affected the mass of the membership. After the middle of 1918, however, a gradual change set in.

(a) Modifications in relations between the rank and file of the party and the higher party bodies

The first changes appeared during the struggle against the White insurrection and imperialist intervention. These changes were favored by the dispersal of a great many of the leading figures, whose time was increasingly taken up with tasks that were precise, urgent, and of absolutely decisive immediate importance, especially on the civil war front.

In the last few months of 1918 the party leadership was obliged to take, on its own, a number of highly important decisions, often without consulting the basic organizations. The party's capacity to function as a body was all the more limited at that time because the political leadership possessed practically no central apparatus by means of which it could maintain regular contact with the basic organizations. At the beginning of 1919, the Central Committee staff consisted of fifteen people, grouped around Sverdlov, the secretary of the CC.

Between June 1918 and the beginning of 1919 the leading bodies met only rarely. Nearly all decisions were taken by direct contact between Lenin, chairman of the Sovnarkom, Sverdlov, and the party members in charge of the various sectors.

In this period, the tendency for the party to merge with the state machine was such that Preobrazhensky went so far as to suggest—without provoking a storm of protest—that the party should be dissolved, on the grounds that it had become completely merged with the state machine. Osinsky put forward some practical proposals tending in the same direction—e.g., that the Central Committee, the VTsIK, and the Sovnarkom be merged. These suggestions were not followed.[22]

The Eighth Party Congress (March 1919) marked an important turning point. It began to reconstruct the party, to give it a structure more suitable for enabling it to carry out its task as a ruling party. Henceforth, the CC was to meet at least twice a month, and in the intervals between its meetings, decisions would be taken by a new organ, the Political Bureau, or Politburo. A similar organ had existed previously on a quite temporary basis, in connection with the preparation of the October insurrection.

The first nontemporary Politburo was formed in March 1919, at the Eighth Congress. It was made up of five permanent members (Lenin, Kamenev, Trotsky, Stalin, Krestinsky) and three "substitute" members (Zinoviev, Bukharin, Kalinin). This Politburo soon became the real leadership of the party, taking all the important decisions, which became operative at once.

The Eighth Congress also declared in favor of the forming of a People's Commissariat for Control of the State, which was placed under Stalin's direction. As mentioned earlier, this became in 1920, still under Stalin, the Workers' and Peasants' Inspection—the Rabkrin, or RKI.

Another decision of importance for the subsequent life of the party was taken by the Eighth Congress, namely, the establishment of the Orgburo, the Organization Bureau. It had also five members, including Stalin. It was to meet three times a week and "direct all the party's organizational work." In addition a Secretariat of the Central Committee was formed, responsible, in principle, for executive tasks. Stalin was present here, too, having been appointed secretary of the Central Committee after Sverdlov's death on the eve of the Eighth Congress.

In 1919 the secretariat of the CC was, in theory, a "mere technical organ." Gradually, however, the secretariat and the Orgburo were to become a sort of administrative leadership, paralleling the party's political leadership, an evolution confirmed three years later when, on April 4, 1922, the post of General Secretary was created. Stalin became General Secretary by decision of the Central Committee elected by the Eleventh Party Congress.

The Eighth Congress was thus the starting point in a rapid change in the conditions in which the Bolshevik Party functioned, and in its internal relations. Increasingly, the party became a structured body, subject to a discipline of a type quite different from what it had previously known—a discipline in which there was a certain element of administrative centralism, though this was as yet only nascent.

In the circumstances that prevailed in 1919, with acute class struggle and difficulty in controlling a state machine in which bourgeois practices were predominant, the effects of the tendency to administrative centralism began to make themselves strongly felt. A process can be seen to have started by which the party's administrative organs became independent of its leading political organs—a process closely linked with that in which the state machine was becoming independent of the proletarian dictatorship. This process grew more pronounced as the years went by. To the increasing role played by the party's central administrative organs corresponded an inflation of the administrative staff attached to the Central Committee. This staff increased from 15 members at the beginning of 1919 to 150 in March 1920, and 602 a year later.[23] Highly structured departments were formed. The two departments of the party administration that played the most important roles were the Orgotdel (in charge of organization and regulation) and the Uchraspred (in charge of keeping records of proceedings, maintaining registers and card-indexes, and assigning party members to particular tasks). There were also other departments, groups, and bureaus which gradually came to supervise, ever more closely, the activities of the party cadres.

In practice, the party secretariat and the Uchraspred made most assignments, with only some of these coming before the Orgburo, the *elected* body. Thus, between April and November 1919, the Uchraspred made 2,182 assignments, as against 544 made by the Orgburo.[24] Between April 1920 and mid-February 1921 the Uchraspred made 40,000 assignments.

For some time these assignments were made without much of a selection procedure, but increasingly they came to be decided on the basis of central card-indexes that were maintained with ever-greater efficiency. In November 1921 the Uchraspred possessed reports on about 23,500 party cadres, who were divided into groups in accordance with their specialty. A few months later, the Uchraspred had an index covering about 26,000 cadres. These records enabled it to follow a party member's "career"—and, to a large extent, to determine its course. In June 1922, through a merger with the Orgotdel, the Uchraspred became even more powerful. It was then put under the direction of L. M. Kaganovich. The Orgotdel now had its own staff of "instructors," charged with inspecting the party's local organizations and having access to all documents and all meetings, including secret ones. These instructors could make any recommendations they liked with a view to amending the decisions of provincial party committees, though the latter retained the right of appeal to the Central Committee.

In this way a process developed which increasingly stripped political power from the party conferences that were held at province, town, and district level. The gradually diminishing role of provincial party conferences was reflected in the lengthening intervals between their meetings; and also, especially, in the fact that, although these conferences still elected their committees, the latter were dominated by the holders of a few key posts whose appointment had been decided on by the central administrative organs. Fairly soon, the committee elected by the conference played only a consultative role, whereas the real decisions were taken by the "bureau" (at first called the "presidium") of this committee.

Gradually, then, a structure was formed in which rank-and-file decisions assumed secondary significance, the vital ones being taken at the top, by an administrative apparatus. In this way it came about that the secretaries of provincial party committees were more and more frequently appointed from the center, and the powers of these political officials increased rapidly. The provincial party secretary ceased to be dependent on the party conference and the party committee. On the contrary, it was the members of these bodies who increasingly became dependent on the provincial party secretary and, through him, on the central administrative apparatus. This apparatus was structured in the image of the state machine: its members were divided into five categories corresponding to the five salary grades of government officials.[25]

In principle, the increasing role accorded to the central administrative apparatus was intended to ensure "better management" of the party cadres and a rational selection of leading personnel. In practice, it led quickly to an increasing degree of political control by the party's internal administration (itself controlled only with difficulty by the elected leading bodies) over the organization as a whole, and especially over its cadres. This control was exercised especially through the system of "assignments" and "transfers," which made it possible to alter the balance of political forces in a particular party organization. By means of "transfers," party members whose notions differed from those of the party's administrative heads could be isolated. These transfers corresponded at first to the requirements of a good system of assignment, or to justifiable administrative sanctions. In 1921, however, at the time of the struggle against the Workers' Opposition, such measures began to be used as a means of uprooting oppositionists from local party organizations in which they had a certain influence, and of reducing the freedom of expression enjoyed by the party cadres.

The provincial, municipal and district party organizations protested many times against this development. It was in response to these protests that in September 1920 a Central Control Commission was set up, with a pyramid of local control commissions to which party members could appeal against arbitrary decisions by the party's administrative apparatus. This method of recourse to an organ independent of the party's administrative apparatus functioned, more or less, until 1922, when a change was made. In order to avoid conflicts between the control commissions and the party's administrative apparatus, a resolution of the Eleventh Congress[26] decided to "unify" the work of the local control commissions. These became practically a new branch of the central administrative apparatus: instead of helping to supervise it, they became an additional instrument at its disposal.

The transformation of relations between the administrative directorate of the party and the rank and file also altered the relations between the political leadership (CC and Politburo) and the party as a whole. The administrative apparatus (especially its central nucleus) became a second center of party leadership: a center which, though formally only "administrative," was in reality, of course, also a political center that could exercise an influence over the party's political leadership, even determining the line its decisions would take, and the way these decisions would be applied.

In 1921, at the Tenth Party Congress, Lenin explicitly warned against the growth of the "bureaucratic" apparatus, which was tending to raise a screen between the party leadership and what was really going on in the country. Later, Lenin was to emphasize—but without his idea being followed up in practice—the need to cut down the bureaucratic apparatus and to ensure that the party was supervised not only by its rank and file but even by non-party people. Thus, in his article "Purging the Party"[27] Lenin said that the party should rid itself of bureaucratized elements and that, in order to do this, the suggestions of the masses should be sought:

> In appraising persons, in the negative attitude to those who have "attached" themselves to us for selfish motives, to those who have become "puffed-up commissars" and "bureaucrats," the

suggestions of the non-Party proletarian masses and, in many cases, of the non-Party peasant masses, are extremely valuable. The working masses have a fine intuition, which enables them to distinguish honest and devoted Communists from those who arouse the disgust of people earning their bread by the sweat of their brow, enjoying no privileges and having no "pull."[28]

(b) The conception of the party becoming "overgrown" by its administrative apparatus

Until the Tenth Congress the changes in internal relationships within the Bolshevik Party seemed to many of its members to be a consequence of the exceptional circumstances connected with the civil war and the imperialist intervention, and this was why the manifestations of these changes provoked only a few protests (mainly from old party members).

The resolution of the Tenth Congress (1921) still reflected the idea that these changes in the party's internal life were only transitory and conjunctural. This congress adopted, at one and the same time, resolutions intended to promote more democratic relations, enabling the rank and file to express themselves better, and resolutions restricting opportunities for criticism, largely under the influence of the fears aroused by a political situation marked by the peasants' growing discontent and culminating in the Kronstadt rising.

Actually, the Tenth Congress resolutions calling for the development of more democratic relations within the party remained inoperative, so that in 1922, at the Eleventh Congress, fresh protests arose against the predominance of administrative and hierarchical relations. A resolution passed by this congress declared: "The Party organizations have begun to be systematically overgrown by a large apparatus which serves these organizations. This apparatus which is gradually spreading, has itself begun to acquire a bureaucratic coating and to absorb an excessive share of the Party's forces."[29]

The Eleventh Congress's protest against the "overgrowing" of the party by a "large apparatus" had no effect. The party's administrative apparatus—that is, the secretariat of the Central Committee, and the central departments and bureaus—were to take practically no notice of this resolution: the administrative apparatus only broadened and expanded the sphere of its interventions.

The conception of the party being "overgrown" by its apparatus defined in an ambiguous way the result of a twofold process: a process which led to the one-sided domination of the party's rank and file by the party's central organs, and a gradual process of shifting of authority within the central organs themselves, that strengthened the position of the administrative organs in relation to the political leadership elected by the congresses. Later, the effects of this second process would seem to disappear—when the very composition of the congresses, and of the political leadership elected by them, would be very largely determined by the central administrative organs! In 1922–1923, things had not gone that far, and the distinction between the authority of the administrative apparatus and that of the party's political leadership was still real.

The first aspect of the process of "overgrowing" against which the Eleventh Congress protested, corresponded to a large extent to the desire to preserve the proletarian character of party policy. It was a matter of concentrating vital decisions in the hands of an experienced revolutionary "old guard," since this was a period when the party was receiving a massive influx of new members, some of whom, though devoted to the revolution, were as yet inexperienced, while others were joining the party in order to get important positions or to facilitate their career in state service.

At the beginning of 1922 Lenin drew attention to the changes that had taken place in the composition of the Bolshevik Party, when he said that "taken as a whole (if we take the level of the overwhelming majority of Party members), our Party is less politically trained than is necessary for real proletarian leadership in the present difficult situation."[30] Lenin considered that this state of affairs was bound to get worse in the absence of rigorous measures, which were not taken, and in that event he expected to see "a big increase in the efforts of petty-bourgeois elements, and of elements positively hostile to all that is proletarian, to penetrate into the Party."[31]

In the historical conditions of 1918–1923, preserving the proletarian character of party policy meant concentrating authority in the hands of those who embodied the historical experience and theory of the revolutionary movement, Russian and international—in other words, in practice, at the start of this period, in the hands of the Political Bureau and the Central Committee.

The other aspect of this process of "overgrowing"—and the more dangerous aspect as regards preservation of the proletarian character of the Bolshevik Party—was the concentration of an increasing number of decisions (those that shaped the internal life of the party and its very composition) in the hands not merely of the heads of the central administrative bodies but in those of a corps of party officials. This concentration of power had the result of removing many vital decisions both from control by the rank and file and from control by the Central Committee and the Political Bureau. By its growth in numbers, its complex structure, the conditions under which it was recruited (increasingly similar to those applying to an unrevolutionized state administrative service), the corps of party officials and the administrative organization came to acquire a larger and larger measure of independence.

The transformation of the Bolshevik Party between 1918 and 1923 thus presented a twofold aspect: on the one hand, it tended to preserve the proletarian character of party policy; on the other, it tended to bestow independence upon the party's administrative apparatus and thereby increase the freedom of action of a body of officials who, in the conditions then existing, were increasingly bourgeois and petty bourgeois.

This second aspect became increasingly important in the period following the Tenth Congress. There developed within the Bolshevik Party political relationships of a bourgeois kind, marked by increasing independence of the party officialdom in relation to the rank and file and to the masses, and gradually ousting the former proletarian political relationships.

On the eve of Lenin's death, the concentration of power in the hands of the party's administrative apparatus and its corps of officials had already gone far. At the time of the Twelfth Congress, held during April 17–25, 1923, when Lenin was very seriously ill and unable to attend, many old Bolsheviks called for a change in internal relations, and for a return to relations such as would enable the party as a whole to lead a more active and genuine political life. At this congress, the old Bolshevik V. Kosior condemned the way the General Secretary was influencing the party's orientation by making changes in members' assignments so as to get out of the way those who dared to voice criticism, and by giving preference to docility over ability and a firm proletarian attitude. Others, such as Bukharin and Rakovsky, used Lenin's own words,[32] in denouncing Great-Russian chauvinism and the policy of Russifying the minorities being carried out by the party's General Secretariat. But these protests were ineffectual.

In the months that followed, when Lenin was no longer able to direct public affairs, arrests of party members who expressed critical views became frequent. In September 1923 Dzerzhinsky, an old Bolshevik and first head of the Cheka, told a subcommission of the Central Committee: "The decline of our Party, the extinguishing of our internal life, the replacement of election by appointment are becoming a political danger."[33] This did not prevent Dzerzhinsky himself, shortly afterward, from intensifying repression of groups of oppositionists among the workers and demanding of the Political Bureau that every party member be called upon to denounce to the GPU anything that might be considered "oppositional activity."[34]

In practice, the change in internal relationships within the party had already reached such a point that a genuine reactivation of its internal political life would have required open intervention by the rank and file and also, doubtless, large-scale intervention by all those workers who were inspired by a proletarian conception of how the party should function and relate to the state machine and the masses. The conditions for a development of this sort were not present; and so the crisis of leadership that opened after Lenin's death led to a new concentration of power in the hands of the party's administrative apparatus, thus confirming the forecast made by Lenin in his letter to Molotov of March 26, 1922.[35]

Thereafter, the political power wielded by the party's administrative apparatus was to increase rapidly. This did not mean, however, that the political leadership of the party passed completely into the hands of its administrative apparatus, slipping away from the influence of the Central Committee and the Political Bureau, but that the influence of these bodies tended to diminish, while there was an increase in that of the administrative apparatus which, through the very circumstance of its growing independence from the rank and file and the masses, was open to influence and penetration by the bourgeoisie.

III. The effects of the changes in the Bolshevik Party on the way the party functioned

The tendency for the party to become merged with a state administrative machine which was itself becoming independent of the masses, and to be "overgrown" by its own administrative apparatus, were not without consequences where the class character of the political practices in the party was concerned. These consequences made themselves felt first and foremost in the "everyday life" of the party, that is, in its style of leadership and in its underlying ideology.

(a) The style of leadership

The strengthening of the two tendencies mentioned above created favorable conditions for the development of bourgeois political practices. Thus, instead of a democratic and proletarian leadership such as Lenin endeavored to maintain, emphasizing the centralization of correct ideas, persuasion, and broad discussion, there was gradually substituted a style of leadership of quite a different order, in which the giving of orders and insistence on unquestioning discipline were the main features.

This different style of leadership, and the ideological relations underlying it (such as "respect" by the "lower" bodies for the will of the "higher" ones), tended to transform a section of the party membership—in the first place, the political cadres—from militants into officeholders who were principally concerned to know what their superiors expected of them, rather than to analyze a situation and point out to the party leadership the mistakes that had been made, so as to help in rectifying them, to assess for themselves the state of mind of the masses so as to warn the leadership in good time against ill-considered measures, and so on. In this way a set of new political practices appeared which the Bolshevik Party had in previous times hardly known.

These practices were those of party members who were turning into "functionaries," "members of the apparatus," or, as they were already starting to be called, *apparatchiki*. At the time, Sosnovsky, an old Bolshevik, described in these terms the way such *apparatchiki* behaved:

> They are neither hot nor cold. They take note, "for information and execution," of all the circulars they receive from the CC or the Guberniya committees. Unhurriedly, they do their duty in carrying out "campaigns": they keep precise statistical accounts of these campaigns, set down on square-ruled forms all the party's revolutionary activity, and are pleased with themselves when all the squares have been filled and they can report to the center the "thorough" fulfillment of all directives received. From party workers of this sort, plans, programs, instructions, theses, questionnaires, and reports pour out as though from a cornucopia . . . They are happy when outward calm prevails in their organization, when there are no "squabbles" and nobody is fighting anybody else.[36]

Early in 1921 the Tenth Congress had sought to put an end

to this style of leadership and to the lack of workers' democracy which characterized it—a style which was thought to be connected with the "militarization" of the party, itself a consequence of the civil war. Thus, Bukharin, speaking on behalf of the Central Committee, said:

> We must strive towards workers' democracy, and put this into effect with the same vigour we showed in the previous period in militarising the Party . . . By workers' democracy within the Party must be understood a form of organisation which ensures that all members can participate actively in Party life, in discussion of all questions that arise and in deciding how to answer them, and also in the building of the Party . . . Workers' democracy makes impossible the system of appointment, and is characterised by the election of all organs, from top to bottom, by the responsibility of these organs, and by their subjection to control.

The report stressed the need for "broad discussion of all important questions, absolute freedom of criticism within the Party and collective working out of Party decisions." [37]

It is well-known that the resolutions adopted by the congress, following the line proposed by Bukharin in the name of the Central Committee, did nothing to alter the existing style of leadership, which instead became more prominent in the years that followed.

In September 1921, in a letter to Stalin, Lenin vigorously denounced another aspect of the repressive style of leadership which was tending to become established in the party. He stigmatized one of the practices of the administrative apparatus, which consisted in "exposing" rather than "improving." In a later piece of writing he also denounced the toadyism of the members of the apparatus and what he ironically called "Communist conceit." [38] In one of his last works, *Better Fewer but Better*,[39] he did not hesitate to write: "We have bureaucrats in our Party institutions as well as in the Soviet institutions."

In denouncing "bureaucracy" in the party and the state, Lenin was continuing a campaign he had been waging for several years.

The term "bureaucracy," in itself purely descriptive, has had a remarkable history. At first it was used to reprove the behavior of certain cadres—their authoritarianism, their "personal" style of leadership, their careerism, and so on, which seemed to be due to "features of character" rather than to a particular form of organization. Very soon, however, it acquired a second meaning, describing both a form of organization (which obstructed proletarian democracy) and the resulting style of work. Subsequently the term "bureaucracy" was used to describe a social stratum: it was in this sense that Trotsky used it, in accordance with a well-established tradition.[40] Finally, some have even seen in the bureaucracy a new social class and the basis of a new mode of production.[41]

Since this is not the place to discuss these various conceptions, I will confine myself to noting that what is usually referred to, when the descriptive term "bureaucracy" is used, is the situation conferred on the agents of certain social apparatuses by a set of relationships which make of these agents a group placed in a position of relative independence both in relation to the dominant class (some of whose powers the group concentrates in its hands) and to the dominated classes. When, from 1921 onward, Lenin and other Bolsheviks denounced the rise of "bureaucracy," they were referring to a set of practices and relationships which put the leading officials of the state and the party in a position of relative independence. That time saw only the beginning of practices that were later to become consolidated and deprive the proletariat of power, placing it instead in the hands of this leading group, which then became a state bourgeoisie insofar as it had at its disposal all or most of the means of production and activated them on the basis of *capitalist production relations* (in particular, the capitalist division of labor). While in 1921 that situation was still a long way off, what was truly and ultimately at stake in the struggle against "bureaucracy" was the position of the proletariat as the dominant class, with "the bureaucracy" representing the embryo of a new bourgeoisie in the apparatus of the state and of the ruling party.

(b) The membership and social composition of the Bolshevik Party

I have already mentioned that the speed with which party membership increased, and the extent of the changes undergone by its social composition between 1917 and 1923, contributed to the transformation of internal relationships in the party. The process actually worked both ways: while the sudden and poorly supervised increase in the number of members and the alteration in their social make-up had the effects mentioned, it was also true that the transformation of the party's style of work and leadership, and the close ties binding it to a state administrative machine which was not really proletarian, helped to attract bourgeois or petty bourgeois elements, and even to bourgeoisify the world view of party members who were of proletarian origin.

The changes affecting the party had two main aspects. First, there was the influx into the party of bourgeois and petty bourgeois elements, which had been denounced by Lenin in 1919, at the Eighth Congress, when he mentioned that "old bureaucrats" who had been driven out of the administration had had to be recalled, and that some of them, disguising themselves as Communists, had slipped into the party.[42]

Between 1921 and 1923, Lenin frequently returned to this problem. He referred to the ever-growing danger of "a big increase in the efforts of petty-bourgeois elements, and of elements positively hostile to all that is proletarian, to penetrate into the Party."[43] He emphasized the need to turn to the non-party masses in order to get rid of the "lordly ones" and the "bureaucratized" elements in the party, and he urged that the only persons to be regarded as workers, and so to be entitled to the short probationary period of six months before being admitted to party membership, should be those "who have actually been employed in large industrial enterprises for not less than ten years."[44]

The other aspect of the changes affecting the party was perhaps even more serious because it was less directly controllable, namely, the changes in the world view of many party members and in particular of the cadres.

These changes were closely bound up with changes in the party's role and place in political relationships as a whole and, more especially, with the intimacy of its ties with the state administrative machine, and with the growth of its own administrative functions.

These changes helped attract bourgeois and petty bourgeois elements, and even, to a certain extent, to make their entry "necessary." At the same time, these changes, and their effects as a whole, helped to alienate from the party those revolutionary militants who refused to bow to the demands of strict administrative rules and to the routine and type of discipline required in a centralized administrative organization tending to cut itself off from the masses. Rejection of this form of organization, of its rules and methods of discipline, contributed to some of the struggles that went on in the party between 1918 and 1923. This rejection was also expressed in the sporadic attempts by some rank-and-file members to oppose the party's "bureaucratization." The defeat of these attempts led to disappointed militants leaving the party, or even being expelled from it for having criticized the administrative apparatus. Such expulsions took place especially during the party purges about which something will be said later.

The multiplication of administrative tasks of a certain type helped also to change profoundly the conditions of existence of the party cadres responsible for these tasks, and so to transform their world outlook, since, in the last analysis, it is conditions of existence that determine consciousness.

What was involved here was, in the first place, "specialization" of administrative functions. As a result of this "specialization," those who held such responsibilities were increasingly absorbed into activities which severed them from production and from the conditions in which the great majority of the population lived and worked. They thus tended to become separated from the masses and to look down on them "from the height of their responsibilities."

This tendency was accentuated by the fact that most administrative tasks were carried on outside the organs of self-administration by the masses and without any supervision by the latter, through an administrative apparatus that was centralized, hierarchical, and becoming more and more formalistic. At the beginning of 1923 Lenin criticized this development, saying: "As regards precedence, the observation of the forms and rites of office management, our 'revolutionariness' often gives way to the mustiest routine."[45]

It is in the light of these considerations that the figures regarding the increase in party membership, its social make-up, and the assignment of party members to different types of activity assume their true significance.

As regards the increase in membership, we have already seen that this rose from 24,000 in 1917 to 612,000 in March 1920. It reached 732,000 in March 1921 and exceeded 860,000 three years later.[46]

This rapid growth in party membership might be seen as a symptom of "health," if one were to ignore the concrete conditions in which it took place, and the effects it had. As regards the circumstances of this growth, there are several points that deserve attention.

In the period closed by the Eighth Congress (March 1919), the Bolshevik Party followed, more or less, an "open-door" policy, which led to a rapid increase in membership, which reached the figure of 350,000, or thereabouts, at the time of the congress. The congress decided to undertake a registration of the membership with a view to expelling any who were found unworthy. So began a period in which a mass purge was carried out. By autumn 1919, the party had no more than about 150,000 members. In October–December 1919, a particularly difficult moment in the civil war, when the risk of careerist elements trying to get into the party seemed diminished, a third period opened. Recruitment was again carried out on a mass scale, so that party membership rose to nearly 612,000 by the time of the Ninth Congress. This policy continued until the eve of the Tenth Congress.

The Tenth Congress (1921) was the starting point for a fresh purge. The aim of the decisions adopted by the congress was to "proletarianize" the party to a greater extent by expelling "non-Communist elements," reducing the number of party members occupying administrative posts, and increasing the recruitment of workers. All the tendencies in the party agreed on the need to realize this aim.[47]

Application of the decisions of the Tenth Congress contributed to reducing party membership to less than 500,000 in January 1923. After Lenin's death—and against his wish that party membership be reduced to under 400,000—a new recruitment campaign was launched, which sharply increased the number of party members by about 70 percent in a little over a year.

However, the change effected in the proportion of workers in total party membership was not very great. But the abrupt reversals in recruitment policy and the conditions in which the purges took place entailed a certain number of negative consequences.

An important aspect of the purge campaigns, which partly accounts for their negative effects, was their essentially "administrative" character. In practice the purges were not carried through with the help of the masses, and especially not with the help of the non-party masses. In 1921 the purge was effected by a central control commission with subordinate local commissions. In the prevailing circumstances, this procedure considerably strengthened the powers of the party's administrative apparatus. The latter succeeded in eliminating those, whether among the rank and file or among the cadres, who were critical of its "bureaucratic" style of work, or else in reducing them to silence through fear of getting purged. The protests raised at the time suggest that numerous members or supporters of the former "left" oppositions were got rid of in this way. There are, of course, no statistics enabling us to judge the relative importance of this kind of "purge" as compared with those expulsions that were justified on political or moral grounds. It is known, however, from the statements issued by the former Workers' Opposition, that the latter was affected in this way, and that many who held opinions similar to those of this opposition, especially among the working-class members of the party, preferred to leave the party of their own accord rather than risk being expelled from it on false pretexts.[48]

The sharp reversals in recruitment policy also played a role of some significance (though they were not, of course, the only factor) in the transformation of the party's composition—which, moreover, did not always evolve in the way desired by the party congresses and the party's leading bodies.

One of the inevitable consequences of the expansion of the party's total membership was the reduction in the proportion of its members who had belonged to it before the revolution. Already by March 1919 only 8 percent of the members had been Bolsheviks before February 1917, and only 20 percent had joined before October.[49] These figures show that after 1919 the great majority of party members had no experience of the party's earlier life and the political relations that then prevailed in it. This facilitated acceptance of the establishment of new relations, especially the lack of control by the rank and file over the selection of cadres, and also contributed to nonparticipation by the rank and file in critical analysis of the party line, of mistakes that the party might have made, and of the behavior of cadres. Furthermore, given the fundamentally new composition of the party (made up to the extent of about 80 percent of fresh, inexperienced members), those, whether among the rank and file or among the middle-ranking cadres, who might have wished to maintain the old relationship in the face of the rise of new ones, found themselves isolated. In fact, from 1921 onward, in the course of the struggle waged against the former Workers' Opposition, a high proportion of old party members of proletarian origin, who had been active during the underground period of the party's history, were excluded from all positions of responsibility, if not expelled altogether.

The changes in the party's social composition are not always revealed very clearly in the available statistics. This unclarity is due in the main to the way that members were classified socially. Classification was based, as a rule, on the occupation followed by each person just before or at the moment of joining the party. It was therefore sufficient to have been a worker for a very short time, often merely in order to enter the party with greater ease: as Lenin noted, this was quite a widespread way of getting oneself regarded as a "proletarian," and forever afterward being classified in the party's statistics as one of its "worker" members.

This point needs to be kept in mind when interpreting statistics relating to the composition of the party. These show that in October 1919, just after the first "purge" period, when a certain number of bourgeois and petty bourgeois elements were eliminated, 52 percent were "workers"—which means that this had been their social position at a certain moment. The same figures show 15 percent of the membership as "peasants," though we know that this term often merely meant party members living in the country, and included members of the rural intelligentsia. Nevertheless, the statistics enable us to see that the actual distribution of jobs was such that over 53 percent of party members were government officials, 8 percent were party and trade-union officials, and that, among the 11 percent employed in industry, many held managerial and administrative positions.[50] Less than three years later it was estimated that two-thirds of the party members held positions of "responsibility" which gave them a certain degree of authority and some material advantages.

In order to obtain an overall view of the changes effected in the party's social composition (while not forgetting the limited significance of these figures), one can refer to a statistical table given in the *Bolshaya Sovyetskaya Entsiklopediya*, which gives the following percentages:

Social Composition of the Bolshevik Party[51]

	Workers	Peasants	Office workers and others
1917	60.2	7.6	32.2
1918	56.9	14.5	28.6
1919	47.8	21.8	30.4
1920	43.8	25.1	31.1
1921	41.0	28.2	30.8
1922	44.4	26.7	28.9
1923	44.9	25.7	29.4

If we take the years 1921–1923, when the decision to "proletarianize" the party was being put into effect, it will be seen that this did indeed result in an increase in the percentage of members who were of proletarian origin, together with a decrease in the percentage of those whose origin was other than "worker" or "peasant."

It must be added, though, that it is not by increasing the percentage of worker-members that one "automatically" brings about a genuine proletarianization of the party, that is, the predominance within it of members having a proletarian world outlook. A certain *ouvriérisme* may even result in the recruiting of workers who lack a high level of political consciousness. Lenin warned against this danger, but recruitment campaigns among the working class did not always avoid it.

Altogether, despite the fact that the Bolshevik Party had been able successfully to lead the October revolution and the fight against the landlords, the Russian capitalists, and imperialism, and despite its having attracted a high proportion of the most combative elements of the working class, the rapid inflation of its membership, the form taken by the purges, the nature of the tasks to which many of its members were assigned, and the conditions under which they were called upon to accomplish these tasks, gradually had the effect, during the years 1917–1923, of rendering the proletarian character of the party more fragile.

(c) The fragility of the proletarian character of the party and of its leadership

In 1922 Lenin did not regard as remote the dangers threatening the party's stability and its proletarian character as a result of the changes in its internal relations, its style of leadership, and its social composition, and he therefore sought for means of preserving the party from these dangers.

In March 1922 he sent two letters to Molotov, the second within a few days of the first, in which he dealt mainly with the problems connected with maintaining the proletarian character of the party. In the first of these letters, dated March

24, Lenin referred to the fact that, as things were, many petty bourgeois appeared as "workers" and even managed to pass as such. On this theme he wrote: "There is no doubt that we constantly regard as workers people who have not had the slightest real experience of large-scale industry. There has been case after case of petty-bourgeois, who have become workers by chance and only for a very short time, being classed as workers. All shrewd White-Guards are very definitely banking on the fact that the alleged proletarian character of our party does not in the least safeguard it against the small-proprietor elements gaining predominance in it, and very rapidly too."[52]

In order to cope with this situation and ward off the danger that the Bolshevik Party might become a bourgeois and petty bourgeois party, Lenin suggested a whole series of measures that he considered would enable this danger to be fought or removed. As we know, these suggestions were not carried out. The statutes adopted by the Twelfth Party Congress, held on April 17–25, 1923, when Lenin was ill and remained at Gorki, did not include, otherwise than in a formal way, some of his proposals, and departed from them in their actual content.[53]

On March 26, 1922, in his second letter, Lenin returned to the same subject: "If we do not close our eyes to reality we must admit that at the present time the proletarian policy of the Party is not determined by the character of its membership but by the enormous undivided prestige enjoyed by the small group which might be called the Old Guard of the Party. A slight conflict within this group will be enough, if not to destroy this prestige, at all events to weaken the group to such a degree as to rob it of its power to determine policy."[54]

These lines are of very great importance. They bring out in a striking way one of the essential features of the revolutionary movement of the proletariat, namely, that it cannot conquer and advance toward socialism unless it is guided by a party which is headed by revolutionaries who are well-equipped theoretically and who enjoy the full confidence of the working people. The leading role played within the party by such revolutionaries (who form what was later to be called, in

China, the "proletarian headquarters") constitutes the ultimate safeguard of the party's proletarian character and of the possibility of preserving it.

By asserting as he did that the party's proletarian policy depended on the unity of the "old guard," Lenin had in mind several dangers.

(1) The danger of an open split that would make it impossible to maintain the dictatorship of the proletariat in a country where most of the population were peasants. In the conditions prevailing at that time, a split would inevitably have engendered two parties: one which would have continued to try to base itself on the working class, but by following an *ouvriériste* policy which would have cut it off from the other popular strata, and a party which would have tried to base itself mainly on the peasantry, increasing the "concessions" made to the latter. We shall see later that many elements in the platform of the "left" oppositions involved especially the first of these dangerous possibilities, because of their *ouvriériste* character. This was the danger that Lenin had in mind in his "Letter to the Congress."[55]

In this memorandum Lenin mentioned the danger that an open split could be caused by the development of growing contradictions between the working class and the peasantry. He wrote: "Our Party relies on two classes and therefore its instability would be possible and its downfall inevitable if there were no agreement between those two classes. In that event this or that measure, and generally all talk about the stability of our C.C., would be futile. No measures of any kind could prevent a split in such a case."[56]

(2) The danger of a hidden split which could occur as a result of the expulsion of some of the members of the party leadership at that time. This type of split is referred to in the succeeding part of this same "Letter to the Congress." Lenin does not link this danger directly with divergences regarding the political line, but rather with the style of work of two of the principal party leaders, Stalin and Trotsky. Of the former Lenin says that he "has unlimited authority concentrated in his hands, and I am not sure whether he will always be

capable of using that authority with sufficient caution." Of the
latter he says: "He is personally perhaps the most capable
man in the present C.C., but he has displayed excessive self-
assurance and shown excessive preoccupation with the purely
administrative side of the work." [57]

These observations have often been interpreted as referring
to certain features of the "psychology" of the two leaders, and
that is not wrong; but they relate above all to a certain style of
leadership which, in Lenin's view, was dangerous for the
unity of the party. Accordingly, after having made these comments, Lenin goes on: "These two qualities of the two outstanding leaders of the present C.C. can inadvertently lead to
a split, and if our Party does not take steps to avert this, the
split may come unexpectedly." [58]

Ten days after dictating this letter, Lenin added a postscript
in which he recorded an even more severe judgment on Stalin's type of leadership and his character:

> Stalin is too rude and this defect, although quite tolerable in our
> midst and in dealings among us Communists, becomes intolera-
> ble in a Secretary-General. That is why I suggest that the com-
> rades think about a way of removing Stalin from that post and
> appointing another man in his stead who in all other respects
> differs from Comrade Stalin in having only one advantage,
> namely, that of being more tolerant, more loyal, more polite and
> more considerate to the comrades, less capricious, etc. This cir-
> cumstance may appear to be a negligible detail. But I think that
> from the standpoint of safeguards against a split and from the
> standpoint of what I wrote above about the relationship between
> Stalin and Trotsky it is not a detail, or it is a detail which can
> assume decisive importance. [59]

(3) The danger that the party line might no longer be determined by the "old guard," that is by a proletarian leading
nucleus which had proved itself during many hard years of
struggle and enjoyed a high degree of prestige. If this danger
materialized, it would mean that the party's political line
would no longer be decided by a truly "proletarian headquarters" but by the party's administrative apparatus, and this
would open the way to loss of power by the proletariat and to

the restoration of a bourgeois dictatorship operating through a state machinery which had lost its proletarian character.

(4) Finally, Lenin saw emerging, even if there were no open or hidden split, the threat of worsening relations of trust between the party and the masses, such as would make it ever more difficult to elaborate a proletarian political line and rectify mistakes. The danger of such a development was all the more serious in that the party had seen, in the early months of 1921, at the time of the Kronstadt rising, the beginning of a deterioration of this kind, and in 1923 its effects had not been completely overcome. We shall see later the fundamentally important political consequences which Lenin deduced from this situation when he drew up his balance sheet of five years of revolution.

In order, however, to appreciate fully the implications and significance of the changes experienced by the Bolshevik Party, it is essential to see these changes in the setting of the overall social process which developed in the period 1917-1923, and then to analyze the way in which the class struggle produced effects inside the Bolshevik Party, in the form of clashes between different tendencies or different political lines, or elements of such lines. This will be examined in Part Four, after I have explained what I have meant up to now in referring to the process whereby the state machinery became "independent."

Notes

1. *CW*, vol. 33, p. 255.
2. Lenin's report, March 8, 1921, to the Tenth Party Congress, in *CW*, vol. 32, p. 177.
3. See Narkiewicz, *The Making of the Soviet State Apparatus*, pp. 64–65.
4. See the report of the proceedings of the Eighth Party Congress for details.
5. *CW*, vol. 33, p. 279.

6. Ustryalov was a former Cadet who had emigrated. Together with other émigrés, including former "ministers" of the White Guard "government" formed by Kolchak, Ustryalov published in Prague a symposium entitled *Smena Vekh* ("A change of landmarks"), in which he advocated penetration of the Soviet machinery by his cothinkers. He considered that, with the NEP, which was beginning at the time when he formed his group, evolution toward capitalism was inevitable. He claimed that "the Bolsheviks . . . will arrive at the ordinary bourgeois state, and we must support them. History proceeds in devious ways" (quoted by Lenin in ibid., p. 286).

7. *CW*, vol. 33, p. 286.

8. Lenin's political report of the Central Committee, presented to the Eleventh Party Congress, March 27, 1922, in ibid., p. 288.

9. Ibid., pp. 288–289.

10. Ibid., p. 288.

11. This was a talk given in Petrograd on February 5, 1923, and published as a pamphlet, *Proletarskaya revolyutsuja i kultura*.

12. *CW*, vol. 33, p. 287.

13. The name was derived from *Smena Vekh* (see note 6). See also Carr, *Socialism in One Country*, vol. 1, pp. 56 ff.

14. Quotations from Bukharin, *Proletarian Revolution and Culture*, pp. 6–8.

15. Ibid., p. 33.

16. Ibid., pp. 33–35.

17. Ibid., p. 43.

18. Ibid., p. 44.

19. The content of these discussions and disputes are discussed in Part Four.

20. In the early months of 1918 the "left Communists" issued a publication of their own, entitled *Kommunist*.

21. These expressions were used by Mao Tse-tung to describe the forms of "ideological struggle" of which invective and intimidation are features. See on this point his writings "Rectify the Party's Style of Work" and "Oppose Stereotyped Party Writing," in *Selected Works*, vol. 3, pp. 35–68.

22. Except in the special case of Soviet Latvia, on which see Broué, *Le Parti bolchévique*, p. 129.

23. See the *Izvestiya* of the CC of the RCP(B), a bulletin which appeared regularly from May 1919 to October 1929, especially the issues of December 2, 1919, March 5, 1921, and March 1923: quoted in Schapiro, *The Communist Party of the Soviet Union*, p. 250.

24. See Schapiro, *The Communist Party*, p. 253.
25. Ibid., p. 258.
26. *K.P.S.S. v Rezolyutsiyakh*, vol. 1, p. 636.
27. *CW*, vol. 33, pp. 39 ff.
28. Ibid., pp. 39–40.
29. *K.P.S.S. v Rezolyutsiyakh*, vol. 1, p. 621.
30. *CW*, vol. 33, p. 256.
31. Ibid., p. 257.
32. For instance, in a letter he sent to Kamenev on October 6, 1922, in which he wrote: "I declare war to the death on dominant-nation chauvinism." (This was published for the first time in *Pravda* of January 21, 1937. See *CW*, vol. 33, p. 372, and vol. 42, p. 605.) He expressed the same attitude in his memorandum on "The Question of Nationalities or 'Autonomisation,' " in *CW*, vol. 36, pp. 605 ff.
33. Quoted by Kamenev in *Pravda*, December 13, 1923.
34. Broué, *Le Parti bolchévique*, p. 182.
35. *CW*, vol. 33, pp. 256–258. The contents of part of this letter will be discussed later.
36. Sosnovsky, *Dyela i lyudi* [a series of articles reprinted from *Pravda*], pp. 173–174. The article quoted appeared in 1921.
37. Reports and resolutions of the Tenth Party Congress; see Broué, *Le Parti bolchévique*, p. 159.
38. *CW*, vol. 33, pp. 42, 275.
39. Ibid., pp. 487 ff.
40. As Christian Rakovsky has pointed out, "There is no Communist brochure which, in relating the treason of the German Social-Democratic Party on 4 August 1914, does not at the same time point out the fatal role which the bureaucratic upper circles both of the Party and the trade unions played in the history of the backsliding of this Party" (see "The Occupational Hazards of Power," written by Rakovsky in August 1928. The passage quoted will be found on page 126 of the book *De la bureaucratie*, by Preobrazhensky, Rakovsky, and Trotsky, in which the early meanings of the term "bureaucracy" are to be observed). An English translation of Rakovsky's work was published, under the title "Power and the Russian Workers" (the quoted passage is on p. 108).
41. This is, for example, the conception of Claude Lefort, in *Eléments d'une critique de la bureaucratie*.
42. *CW*, vol. 29, pp. 182–183.
43. *CW*, vol. 33, p. 257.
44. Ibid., p. 254. Lenin's recommendation was not followed.

45. *CW*, vol. 33, p. 497.
46. Broué, *Le Parti bolchévique*, p. 131, and *Problèmes politiques et sociaux*, p. 33.
47. See Report of Tenth Party Congress (1921), especially pp. 230–231 and 330–331: see also Rigby, *Communist Party Membership*, pp. 93–94.
48. See Schapiro, *The Communist Party*, p. 237.
49. Ibid., p. 237.
50. Ibid., p. 238.
51. *Bolshaya Sovyetskaya Entsiklopediya*, vol. 11, article "V.K.P.(b)," column 533. The figures were usually compiled on the eve of the party congress, about March or April of each year.
52. *CW*, vol. 33, p. 254.
53. *K.P.S.S. v Rezolyutsiyakh*, pp. 655 and 656.
54. *CW*, vol. 33, p. 257.
55. The letter was to have been read to the party congress which met after Lenin's death, but this did not happen. Only a partial "communication" of its contents was made to an enlarged session of the Central Committee. The complete contents of the letter remained an official secret until 1956.
56. *CW*, vol. 36, p. 594.
57. Ibid., pp. 594–595.
58. Ibid., p. 595.
59. Ibid., p. 596.

3. The objective character of the process whereby the state machinery of the proletarian dictatorship acquired independence

The tendency for the state administrative apparatus to acquire independence, the development of bourgeois practices and relations within the coercive apparatus of the proletarian dictatorship, and the transformations that took place inside the Bolshevik Party itself constituted, at bottom, different aspects of one and the same objective process which, for convenience, I shall call the process whereby the state machinery of the proletarian dictatorship acquired independence.

Lenin commented on many occasions that the Soviet organs were not being run by the working people themselves. He denounced the usurpation, by an anonymous and elusive apparatus, of power that should have been exercised by the soviets. He stressed the need to "give power back to the soviets." However, the process whereby the state machinery was acquiring independence triumphed over the resolutions of the party congresses, over the decisions of the party's leading bodies, and over Lenin's appeals. Before examining the social foundations of this process we must show what its class effects were.

I. The class effects of the process of acquiring independence and the call for a new destruction of the state machine

The class effects of this process consisted in a weakening of the conditions for the exercise of proletarian dictatorship, through the penetration of the apparatus of this dictatorship by bourgeois elements and the reinforcement of bourgeois practices.

Lenin acknowledged this situation when, addressing the Eighth Party Congress in 1919, he said that the Soviet power had been obliged, after it had "dispersed these old bureaucrats," to "place them in new posts." He added: "The Tsarist bureaucrats began to join the Soviet institutions and practise their bureaucratic methods, they began to assume the colouring of Communists, and, to succeed better in their careers, to procure membership cards of the Russian Communist Party. And so, they have been thrown out of the door but they creep back in through the window."[1]

The "bureaucratic distortion" of which Lenin spoke in December 1920 gave a particular character to the dictatorship of the proletariat in the USSR, which was also connected with the place occupied by the bourgeoisie and bourgeois practices in the machinery of the dictatorship.

A little over a year later, in January 1922, in his theses on the role of the trade unions and the NEP, which were adopted by the Eleventh Party Congress, Lenin drew precise conclusions from what he had said in December 1920, for he now spoke of the existing state as being a *"transitional type* of proletarian state," so that a proletarian class struggle needed to be waged against its shortcomings and mistakes, against the capitalist appetites which eluded its control, and against "all sorts of survivals of the old capitalist system in the government offices," which were such as to justify having recourse to *"the strike struggle."*[2]

At the end of 1922, addressing the Fourth Congress of the Communist International, Lenin went further in his characterization of the state administrative apparatus, which he identified with the tsarist apparatus:

> We took over the old machinery of state, and that was our misfortune . . . We now have a vast army of government employees, but lack sufficiently educated forces to exercise real control over them. In practice it often happens that here at the top, where we exercise political power, the machine functions somehow, but, down below, government employees have arbitrary control and they often exercise it in such a way as to counteract our measures

. . . Down below . . . there are hundreds of thousands of old officials whom we got from the Tsar and from bourgeois society and who, partly deliberately and partly unwittingly, work against us.[3]

Finally, not long before he was definitely condemned to silence by illness, Lenin delivered his most severe judgment on the "Soviet" state machine. It was nothing, he said, but the machine "which . . . we took over from Tsarism and slightly anointed with Soviet oil." And he added that "the apparatus we call ours is, in fact, still quite alien to us; it is a bourgeois and Tsarist hotch-potch . . . "[4] Thus, right down to his last writings, Lenin denounced the process whereby the state machinery was acquiring independence, and the resurgence of an apparatus "taken over from Tsarism." Toward the end of 1920 Lenin went so far as to say: "It is the task of the Soviet government to completely destroy the old machinery of state as it was destroyed in October, and to transfer power to the Soviets."[5]

As we know, the reconstituted old machinery of state was never destroyed as Lenin demanded—on the contrary, it developed and became consolidated. After the end of the NEP, that is, after the disappearance of the private bourgeoisie, it became one of the centers in which the bourgeois forces became concentrated.

The class effects of the process whereby the state machinery acquired independence were a weakening of the proletariat's leading role in its own state machinery and, correlatively, a strengthening of the bourgeoisie. It was therefore a process of class struggle. We must examine the objective basis for this process, and the conditions that enabled it to develop as it did.

II. The objective basis of the process

The objective basis for the process of class struggle which led to the machinery of the proletarian dictatorship acquiring independence cannot be reduced merely to the existence of classes in general. This basis must be sought in the totality of relations and practices which existed concretely at that moment and gave specific features to the classes confronting each other. It was, in fact, these relations, and the practices that developed on the basis of these relations, which determined both the forms of existence of the classes and the forms assumed by the struggle between them.

To realize what the objective basis was for the process whereby the state machinery acquired independence, it is necessary to start from the stage at which the Russian Revolution found itself in the years 1917–1923. It was the characteristics of this stage that determined the changes which occurred in social practice and relations, and therefore in the forms in which the bourgeoisie and the proletariat clashed in this period.

What was characteristic of the stage at which the Russian Revolution then stood was that its principal task was still democratic. It was still, above all, a matter of the proletariat in power helping the peasant masses in the struggle against the White Guards, that is, against the landlords, and thereby strengthening the alliance between the proletariat and peasantry under the leadership of the proletariat. This was the main task, both during "war communism" and at the beginning of the NEP.

Indeed, the fact that the Bolshevik Party believed for a time (beginning in the second half of 1918) that the "building of communism" was already on the agenda did not make this come true. This illusion—subsequently acknowledged to be such by Lenin[6]—merely made more difficult the accomplishment of the revolution's principal task, it did not cause it to "go away."

The nature of the stage of the Russian Revolution at that time, and the concrete conditions of the revolution's previous development, limited the transformations that could take place in social relations and relations between classes. The transformations realized within these "limits" were of fundamental historical importance: they corresponded to the transfer of power into the hands of the proletariat, and the expropriation of the landlords and of a large part of the private bourgeoisie. On the other hand, the socialist transformation of

the economic relations could only begin to appear: the socialization of the means of production had been barely started. A
transformation of that kind can be effected only in the course
of a relatively long historical period and can be effected on a
large scale only when it is the principal task before the proletariat and its party. This can be the case only after contradictions such as those that were still dominant in 1917–1923 have
already been dealt with—that is, after the tasks of the democratic revolution have been accomplished, in the main, and
the worker-peasant alliance has been consolidated.

Between 1917 and 1923, the Russian Revolution did not and
could not attain the strictly socialist stage of the development
of the revolutionary process. Consequently, bourgeois or prebourgeois economic relations, unaltered or hardly altered,
were still dominant. The capitalist division of labor was almost intact, individual or patriarchal production predominated in the countryside, and the division of labor between
town and country was unaltered. On the basis of these
bourgeois or prebourgeois relations, bourgeois or prebourgeois ideological and political relations developed. To
use Marx's own expression,[7] these economic relations were
the "secret" of the political forms that came into being at that
time—in other words, of the process whereby the machinery
of state acquired independence.

What has been said enables us to grasp the basis of the
process, but does not reveal the conditions that made it possible, or that would have permitted a struggle to have been
waged against it. These conditions must now be analyzed.

III. The conditions for the development of the process whereby the state machine acquired independence, and for struggle against this process.

The fundamental condition for the process to occur
whereby the state machinery of the proletarian dictatorship
acquired independence, was the predominance of bourgeois

or prebourgeois social relations and the development, on that basis, of bourgeois social practices. These practices made possible the reproduction of capitalist relations, or the transformation into capitalist relations of "precapitalist" relations.

When the bourgeoisie is in power, it is the dominant agent of the expanded reproduction of capitalist relations, but it is also—under the constraint of the contradictions of the capitalist mode of production—the agent of a contradictory practice of transformation of capitalist relations. Thus, elements that prefigure socialist relations are introduced. They are placed in a wholly subordinate position, subjected to the requirements of overall reproduction of capitalist relations, and they cannot but remain so, in the absence of a proletarian revolution which can make them dominant. As Marx points out more than once when he deals with joint-stock companies, the stock exchange, trusts, capitalist nationalization, and so on, the process of conserving capitalist relations proceeds by way of the formal transformation of these relations.

Historical materialism enabled Marx to show the contradictory character of the capitalist process of reproduction, which, though it reproduces the dominant relations, also transforms them. Marx thus founded, in contrast to the various "utopian socialisms" which were unable to change the world, scientific socialism which reveals, in the very womb of present-day society, the conditions for the socialism which the proletariat will have to compel this society to give birth to. This is the significance of what Marx says in the *Grundrisse*, when he writes: "But with bourgeois society . . . there arise relations of circulation as well as of production which are so many mines to explode it. (A mass of antithetical forms of the social unity, whose antithetical character can never be abolished through quiet metamorphosis. On the other hand, if we did not find concealed in society as it is the material conditions of production and the corresponding relations of exchange prerequisite for a classless society, then all attempts to explode it would be quixotic.)"[8]

This analysis gives its full meaning to the metaphor of the *bringing to birth* of a new world with which present-day society is "pregnant"—this bringing to birth for which the proletariat acts as midwife, provided that it develops revolutionary practice.

The social practices of the proletariat, inserted in the antagonistic social relations of capitalism, also bear a dual character: they are practices of conservation and of transformation of the existing social relations. To the extent that the proletariat remains fundamentally dominated by bourgeois ideology, its practices, including its practice of class struggle, remain subordinate to the requirements of capitalist reproduction (and this is still so under the dictatorship of the proletariat): this dictates the limits to trade-union action which has not been transformed by a revolutionary orientation with a scientific basis (utopian aspirations are not enough to change the world). It is only insofar as the proletariat is guided by revolutionary theory (itself the product of analysis of its own struggles, the struggles of all the oppressed classes, and the conditions of reproduction and transformation of the existing relations), that it can cause to predominate practices which transform social relations, and which, instead of ensuring the conservation of existing relations and the continued dominance of capitalism, smash these relations and this dominance, open the way to socialism, and so constitute not merely proletarian practices but proletarian revolutionary practices.

To return to the process whereby the state machinery of the proletarian dictatorship acquires independence (which is the beginning of a process of domination by the bourgeoisie concealed in this machinery), we see that the fundamental condition for an effective struggle against this process is the predominance of proletarian revolutionary practices in the sphere of the relations to be transformed. These practices, and these alone, make possible a revolutionary transformation of social relations, dominance for the socialist elements in these relations—provided that they intervene at the appropriate moment in history, when united and coordinated action by the revolutionary forces is possible.

At the level of generalization corresponding to the above propositions, it can therefore be said that the condition for the process to be possible whereby the state machinery of the proletarian dictatorship acquired independence in the period 1917–1923, was the predominance of bourgeois practices and the weakness of revolutionary practices in the sphere of the relations to be transformed. This predominance was closely linked with the historical moment at which the Russian Revolution then stood, and this is the reason why the process developed with the speed and in the forms we have seen.

For a fuller understanding of the process, however, without which no lesson can be drawn from the way it actually developed, we need to advance beyond the foregoing generalities and return to the historical moment in which the process was situated, and so to the concrete characteristics of the period in which it took place. These characteristics were such as to compel the concentration of revolutionary efforts upon a first-priority aim, namely, the defense of the proletarian dictatorship. They did not permit the socialist transformation of social relations as a whole to be put on the immediate agenda.

(a) The urgent immediate tasks

Here the decisive pressure of urgent immediate tasks made itself felt. During "war communism," the Soviet power, which had only just come into being, had to cope with the combined military onslaught of the White Guards and the interventionist forces of most of the imperialist powers. It was necessary, at any price, to feed the towns and the armies at the front without delay, or otherwise the Soviet power would simply have been swept away.

In the conditions in which the proletarian power had been established, and given the predominance of commodity relations and petty bourgeois practices among the peasantry (the practice of "giving nothing for nothing"), when industry had almost nothing to offer to the villages and the urgent needs of war made it impossible to wait, the Soviet power had in practice no other course open to it but the one that it followed.

It had to resort to requisitioning, and to discipline imposed either by "vanguard" workers or by the state machine. This had to be done, even if it was bound to mean a momentary worsening of relations between the proletariat and part of the peasantry, and so to a development of the contradictions between the apparatus of Soviet power and the section of the masses upon which this apparatus exerted constraint.

Repeating in June 1920 the slogan he had issued earlier, "Everything for the war!" Lenin emphasized the nature of the emergency:

> This is a question of saving the lives of tens of thousands of our finest comrades, who are perishing at the front, in the foremost ranks. It is a matter of saving ourselves from the famine which is imminent just because we are not fighting the war to a finish, when we can and must do that, and quickly too. For this, discipline and subordination must be enforced at all costs and with the utmost severity. The least condonement, the least slackness displayed here, in the rear, in any peaceful pursuit, will mean the loss of thousands of lives, and starvation in the rear.[9]

(b) The historical relations between the Bolshevik Party and the rural population

The emergency situation gave all the less opportunity for the Bolshevik Party to develop other methods, and thereby help the peasantry to transform its own practices, in that it was itself almost entirely unrepresented, as an organization in the countryside. We have seen how the attempt to set up genuine poor peasants' committees failed. With few exceptions, these committees were neither developed nor consolidated, while the rural soviets remained largely under the control of the village bourgeois, themselves influenced by the SRs, who were often engaged in counter-revolutionary activity. The proletarian political cadres were still too few in number, and their presence at the front too essential, for it to be possible for them to be sent en masse into the countryside, or to help the poor and middle peasants to escape from the ideological influence of the rural bourgeoisie, and help them develop a revolutionary practice of thoroughgoing and systematic solidarity with the front and with the towns.

The slightness of the Bolshevik Party's direct influence in the countryside was reflected in the slight degree of participation by the peasants in elections to the rural soviets. Between 1919 and 1922 this participation was of the order of 22 percent, falling sometimes even as low as 9 percent,[10] and the percentage of party members in the rural soviets of the Russian provinces varied between 0.3 percent and 1.8 percent.[11] Their influence was thus extremely limited. At the level of the rural district *(volost)*, the party's position was a little better: 11.7 percent of the deputies to the soviets at this level were party members. Only at the level of the county soviets was the situation very different, especially if one looks at the executive committees, which in 1922 consisted to the extent of 81 percent of party members, or candidates for party membership—but 76 percent of these deputies had joined the party only after the revolution, and many of them were administrators who had belonged to the old state machine. As for the administration serving the soviets and their executive committees, it was composed mainly of the remains of the former administration, which had been first smashed and then put together again,[12] as Lenin pointed out on several occasions.

The extreme weakness of the party's roots in the countryside was thus one reason why bourgeois and petty bourgeois practices predominated over vast areas of Russia. In most villages, and even in many small and middle-sized towns, the party members were only "a drop in the ocean," as Lenin put it. Their numerical weakness prevented them from undertaking broad campaigns of explanation and from systematically gathering from the masses opinions and suggestions that would have made it possible to develop new practices. Consequently, the weight of the reconstituted former apparatus (or that of the new apparatus which was no less separated from the masses) was all the heavier, and bourgeois practices developed within it.

In its turn, the reconstitution of a state machine similar to that of tsardom, and the development of authoritarian relations between this machine and the masses, produced ideological effects which included distrust on the part of some of the workers and peasants toward the "established authorities" and even fear of repression. These ideological effects contributed to more or less isolate from the masses those party members who found themselves far from the centers and the Soviet organizations in which the party effectively exercised its leading role. The fact that these centers and organizations existed played a decisive role in the defense of the proletarian power; but it could not suffice to bring about a proletarian transformation of social practices on a countrywide scale.

(c) The lack of adequate previous experience of the requirements for socialist transformation of social relations and social practices

Between 1917 and 1923, there thus prevailed in Russia objective conditions which favored the process whereby the state machinery acquired independence, with the reconstitution of an apparatus of the bourgeois or prebourgeois type— or, in Lenin's striking phrase, "a Tsarist apparatus slightly anointed with Soviet oil." There were other factors, too, which set limits to the Bolshevik Party's action, connected with the party's lack of experience regarding the conditions for transforming social practices and relations, and also determined by certain theoretical conceptions which were held by the party.

Without claiming that the Bolshevik Party's line of action could have been really very different from what it was, given the stage at which the Russian Revolution found itself, the urgency and magnitude of the tasks facing the party, and the latter's size and distribution, it is nevertheless possible to conceive that the process whereby the machinery of the proletarian state acquired independence could have been combated more effectively, and so slowed down, if the party had possessed previous experience of the requirements for struggle against a process of this sort. It is a historical fact that this experience was lacking and that the very general pointers to correct action which were suggested by a limited amount of practice proved inadequate.

What might or ought to have been done to combat the process whereby the state machine acquired independence, and the positions of the bourgeoisie in Russian society became strengthened (in new forms), was not something that could be "invented." It was necessary to learn from actual practice, drawing lessons from the mistakes made and compiling a balance sheet of these mistakes. Ideas do not fall from heaven, they arise from practice. Not necessarily from successful practice; they can also arise from setbacks, provided that those who have suffered these setbacks (or others placed in more or less similar conditions) draw the lesson to be learned from them. It was only in and after 1921 and 1922, that the Bolshevik Party, and Lenin in particular, were able to start drawing lessons from their own experience. I shall come back to this point in Part Five.

(d) The party's theoretical conceptions and the balance sheet of the years 1917–1922

We are justified in thinking today, when we compare the practices and the theoretical formulations which were dominant in the Bolshevik Party in 1917–1922 with the formulations and practices which dominate the thought and action of the Chinese Communist Party, that some of the conceptions prevalent in the Bolshevik Party constituted an obstacle to the path that might have led to an effectual struggle against the process whereby the state machinery of Soviet power acquired independence. It is, of course, ridiculous to "write history with ifs" and to try and imagine "what would have happened if conditions had been different": all the same, it is possible to affirm, for it is a fact, that some of the Bolshevik Party's theoretical conceptions prevented the party, for a time, from understanding and foreseeing the real nature and implication of a process some of the effects of which it condemned.

Among the conceptions which had the effect of concealing what was happening may be mentioned (I shall come back to the point at the end of the book) the party's notions regarding the role that could be played by certain forms of centralization and state capitalism. Up to a certain point, and within the narrow limits imposed by the objective conditions, these notions had the effect of preventing the Bolshevik Party from marking out a path that would have enabled the masses to develop, on the basis of their own experience, practices differing from those which then predominated on many occasions—revolutionary practices which (within these limits) would have given more life to the soviets and the mass organizations.

Some additional observations are certainly pertinent here.

It must be stressed, first and foremost, that mistaken conceptions are never the determining factor in a social process. What determines the development of such a process is the existing state of social relations and social practices. It is not ideas (even those ideas of which the party is the bearer), that make history, but the masses.

The role played by correct conceptions is nevertheless a vital one. Such conceptions can help the masses to develop in a systematic way their own revolutionary practices and give up practices which enslave them. Correct conceptions open up a path, but they "create" nothing, except possibilities: possibilities for the masses to strengthen their revolutionary practices, to unify and coordinate them. Correct conceptions do no more than this, but also no less.

This is what Lenin rightly asserted in *What Is to Be Done?*: "Without revolutionary theory, no revolutionary movement." This proposition obviously does not mean that it is theory that "creates" the revolutionary movement, but that theory guides this movement, showing it the path that enables it to continue to advance. It does not do this by "inventing" anything, but by drawing lessons of theoretical importance, of universal bearing, from the movement itself in all its historical magnitude.

To return to the problem with which we are concerned

here, that of the process whereby the state machinery of the proletarian dictatorship acquired independence, we must conclude from the foregoing that it was not the weak points in the theoretical conceptions of Bolshevism that lay "at the origin" of this process, as is claimed by an idealist conception of history, but that these conceptions and their inadequate subsequent rectification contributed to the fact that the Russian masses were not guided along the path that would have enabled them to develop, unify, and coordinate their revolutionary practices to the degree necessary to "destroy afresh" the reconstituted tsarist apparatus.

The theoretical conceptions of Bolshevism included a certain number of weak points because they were in part inherited from a labor movement which had departed from revolutionary Marxism. The Bolshevik Party, emerging as it did from the Second International, was not able to rid itself at one blow, in the absence of practical experience, of everything that had been wrong in the Second International's conceptions. This elimination process could take place only gradually, through a class struggle in theory itself.

Here, too, we must look at the historical circumstances, for it is not at just any moment at all that the weaknesses in revolutionary theory—those features in which the influence of bourgeois ideology is still felt—can be eliminated. This elimination, and the rectifications it makes possible, are themselves part of an objective process. They become possible only on the basis of a maturing of contradictions, a maturing that the application of an inadequate theory brings about within the revolutionary movement: they take place at the moment when these contradictions can be effectively dealt with.

When we speak of the "theoretical heritage" of the Second International which the Bolshevik Party did not manage to shake off, we must include in this a certain conception of centralism which was not democratic centralism, and a certain conception of the role of the centralized machinery of state. Also, when we consider the reasons why the Bolshevik Party did not succeed in ridding itself of these conceptions in 1917–1922, we must remember that these reasons were partly bound up with the nature of the stage at which the Russian Revolution then found itself—the principally democratic task the revolution was then fulfilling. The predominance of this task tended to cause methods and notions to prevail which were similar to those that characterized the French Revolution, namely, Jacobin notions and methods, which were, indeed, included in the heritage of the Second International.

Rosa Luxemburg, who supported the October Revolution, noted the points of similarity between the French and Russian revolutions when, toward the end of 1918, she wrote of "a dictatorship in the bourgeois sense, in the sense of the rule of the Jacobins."[13] She observed that, with political relations of this kind prevailing, "life in the soviets must . . . become more and more crippled," with a fading-out of vitality from the public institutions, so that "only the bureaucracy remains as the active element."[14]

At the same time she acknowledged that "it would be demanding something superhuman from Lenin and his comrades if we should expect of them that under such circumstances they should conjure forth the finest democracy, the most exemplary dictatorship of the proletariat . . . "[15] By recognizing the part played by concrete historical conditions, Rosa Luxemburg took her stand on the ground of historical materialism and not of idealism.

The tendency for Jacobin methods to predominate in this period was indeed the result of the conjunction of the effects of particular historical conditions with Jacobin conceptions which were not at all alien to Bolshevism,[16] though Marx and Engels had warned against nostalgia for Jacobinism.[17]

At all events, during the years 1917–1922 the process whereby the principal state machinery of the proletarian dictatorship acquired independence was already a reality, and this fact did not fail to affect to a considerable degree the ideological and political struggles that went on inside the Bolshevik Party.

Notes

1. *CW*, vol. 29, pp. 182–183.
2. *CW*, vol. 33, p. 187 (my emphases—C.B.)
3. Ibid., pp. 428–429.
4. *CW*, vol. 36, pp. 605, 606.
5. *CW*, vol. 31, pp. 408 ff.; quotation on p. 421.
6. See Part Five.
7. Marx, *Capital*, vol. III, p. 772.
8. Marx, *Grundrisse*, p. 159. What Marx means by *Verkehrs-verhältnisse*, here rendered as "relations of circulation," is what he elsewhere refers to as "generalised interdependence."
9. *CW*, vol. 31, p. 175.
10. See Narkiewicz, *The Making of the Soviet State Apparatus*, p. 60.
11. In the non-Russian provinces, where a special effort seems to have been made to ensure that the party's influence in the soviets was greater, the corresponding percentage ranged from 11 to 25 percent; ibid.
12. Ibid., p. 61.
13. Luxemburg, *The Russian Revolution*, p. 48.
14. Ibid., p. 47.
15. Ibid., pp. 54–55.
16. For example, in 1904, in *One Step Forward, Two Steps Back*, Lenin defined a "revolutionary Social-Democrat" as "a Jacobin who wholly identifies himself with the *organisation* of the proletariat—a proletariat *conscious* of its class interests." (*CW*, vol. 7, p. 383).
17. See *The Holy Family*, pp. 163–165, and Engels's letter to Marx, September 4, 1870, in *Selected Correspondence*, pp. 302–303.

Part 4
The ideological and political struggles inside the Bolshevik Party

Analysis of the ideological and political struggles which took place in the Bolshevik Party enables us to appreciate the ideological foundations of the party's line and activity, and the nature of the help that the party was able to give to the struggles of the masses—the latter being the determining factor in all historical transformations.

This analysis is not merely of "retrospective" interest. It helps us not only to understand the ideological trends which clashed in Lenin's time and had an influence on all the revolutionary struggles of this period, but also to understand better the significance and implications of the ideological struggles which took place subsequently in the Bolshevik Party, in the Communist International, and in the international labor movement, immediately after Lenin's death and much later, and which are still going on today. With such an analysis one can see the conflict between the ideas of revolutionary Marxism—ideas which are always open to enrichment by practical experience and theoretical reflection—and bourgeois or petty bourgeois conceptions "presented" in "Marxist" language, that are one of the "sources" of modern revisionism.

Analysis of the ideological and political struggles that went on in the Bolshevik Party in Lenin's time also enables us to see more distinctly the exceptional position occupied in the party by Lenin, his vital role in the adoption of a revolutionary line. The term "exceptional" is appropriate for emphasizing the fact that, on certain crucial questions, Lenin took up positions that proved to be correct, but was often the only one, or almost the only one, to defend these positions. There was indeed a considerable gap between Lenin's living Marxism

345

and the tendency of most of the other Bolshevik leaders to be content with repeating formulas which had already been overtaken by the course of history. To quote only one example, it is well known that Lenin, while still in exile, denounced all policies of "support," even "conditional support," for the Provisional Government formed after the February 1917 revolution. He put forward the slogan of direct struggle for the dictatorship of the proletariat at a time when nearly all the Bolshevik leaders were taking up a much more "cautious" attitude. Only gradually did they rally to the position which had been Lenin's from the outset. It is not easy to explain the special place held by Lenin in the party, even though this place—which put him not merely at the head of the party but ahead of it—was confirmed every time that life called for an important reformulation of strategy and tactics or a rectification of the line that had been followed down to that moment. It can be said, however, that the two essential factors which account for it are his distinctive capacity for listening to the masses and the solidity of his theoretical training. These two elements, combined with his political courage, which enabled him to dare to go against the tide, not to be afraid of being momentarily isolated, explain why Lenin was generally in advance of his party—including in his acknowledgment of mistakes made by the party and by himself.

Analysis of the ideological and political struggles that developed inside the Bolshevik Party also enables us to appreciate the magnitude of the rectifications which Lenin began to undertake from late 1920 onward, continuing right down to 1923, and which opened up new vistas which the other party leaders accepted only to a very partial extent (this point will be given special consideration in Part Five).

Before analyzing the most significant aspects of these ideological and political struggles, we must recall some of the changes that took place in the party's relations with the masses. This will be done very briefly, as the fundamental aspects of the matter have already been examined.

1. The changes in the Bolshevik Party's relations with the masses

The transformations that took place in the relations between the masses and the Bolshevik Party had their roots in the transformation of social relations and relations between classes. Directly, however, they resulted from the political line followed by the party, the correct or incorrect orientation it gave to its activity, and so from its analysis of the contradictions and its ability to deal correctly with the principal contradiction at each stage of the revolution. A study of the changes in relations between the party and the masses must therefore be linked with a study of the principal tasks facing the party at different moments.

When we look at the Bolshevik Party's relations with the masses, what is most difficult is to define the principal aspect of these relations. The latter were necessarily very complex. Indeed, these relations were always strongly differentiated. They were not the same with the working class as with the peasantry. And where each of these classes was concerned, relations were different depending on whether advanced elements were involved, or backward elements (more or less dominated by bourgeois and petty bourgeois ideology), or intermediate elements. As a general rule, during the years following the October Revolution, the advanced and intermediate elements of the masses supported the Bolshevik Party: if this had not been so, the Soviet power could not have resisted the military offensives of the Whites and the imperialists, and the huge economic difficulties due to the different forms of resistance and sabotage practiced by the bourgeoisie and to the economic chaos caused by six years of war.

What was at stake, however, in the relations between the party and the masses, was the consolidation of the dictatorship of the proletariat, the party's ability to expand the ranks of the advanced elements by gradually winning support from those who at the outset had been intermediate or backward elements. This was a continuous struggle, a struggle aimed at wresting from bourgeois influence the fraction of the masses still subject to this influence. It was also a struggle which had its ups and downs, for the mistakes made by the party or by some of its members were reflected in a decline in the backing given to it by part of the masses. Studying the relations between the party and the masses means, therefore, above all, throwing light not upon the support given to the Bolsheviks by the advanced and combative elements, a support without which the Soviet power would have collapsed, but upon the attitude of the intermediate elements; their hesitations and fluctuations (themselves connected with changes in living conditions and with the decisions taken by the Bolshevik Party) determined the greater or lesser degree of solidity of the dictatorship of the proletariat, and its aptitude for developing from its initial transitory form to a higher form. It is therefore from this angle that we must study the changes in the party's relations with the masses.

I shall not go over again the period between February 1917 and May 1918, except to recall that during those months the Bolshevik Party's influence over the masses was developing rapidly. Between February and October of 1917, an increasing number of working people, especially in the towns, came to support the Bolshevik Party, participating in the activity of the revolutionary organizations and backing up the initiatives taken by the Bolsheviks. In October, the relation of class forces became such that the power of the bourgeoisie collapsed and gave way to the dictatorship of the proletariat.

In the months that followed, the deeds of the Bolshevik Party in power (especially its help to the democratic revolution of the peasantry and the signing of the treaty of Brest-Litovsk) brought it an increased basis of support among the masses, especially among the peasantry, even though the difficulties of everyday life—difficulties connected with the consequences of the war and the maneuvers of the capitalists—were, of course, exploited by the bourgeois and petty bourgeois parties, that is, in the main, by the Mensheviks and SRs. These parties had been so badly discredited by their conduct in the period of the Provisional Government that their influence was not then such as seriously to embarrass the Soviet power—though this did not apply in certain sectors which, although restricted, were important from the economic standpoint: thus, the Menshevik leaders of the railroad workers' union helped aggravate the disorganized state of transportation.

After the civil war began, relations between the party and the masses entered a more difficult phase, owing, first of all, to the party's overestimation of the extent to which socialist ideas had penetrated the peasantry, and also to mistakes made in assessing the conditions under which socialist transformation of production relations was possible in the rural areas at that time.

I. From the attempted "proletarian offensive" in the countryside to the orientation on the middle peasant

In connection with the mass mobilization undertaken by the Bolshevik Party, in and after the second half of 1919, to cope with the White rebellions and foreign intervention, the illusion arose that the situation had become favorable for the launching of a "proletarian offensive" among the peasantry. This was the period when the party thought that the time had already arrived to begin "the real work of building socialism," because it believed that "the majority of the working peasants are striving towards collective farming."[1]

At that time the party thought it could stir up a revolutionary movement among the poor peasants, and organize them in separate committees, distinct from the soviets. As we know, these attempts at a "proletarian offensive" failed. The situation was not ripe for it. The revolution in the countryside could not then proceed beyond the democratic stage.

The first attempt, to be abandoned later, involved the formation of the poor peasants' committees. Launched in June 1918, at the time of the split between the Bolsheviks and the Left SRs (who controlled many village soviets), this attempt did not result in a movement with firm foundations among the mass of poor peasants. Only a minority of the latter took part in the movement, and these peasants often pursued narrowly personal aims and attacked the middle peasants. Where the poor peasants' committees became active, they set themselves in opposition to the peasant soviets and sought to form a "second ruling authority," dividing the peasantry at a moment when, in the face of the onslaught of the White and imperialist armies, it was necessary to unite the working class and the peasantry in the same fight.

Already in November 1918, hesitation and anxiety regarding the consequences of the development of the poor peasants' committees arose in the Bolshevik Party and in the VTsIK. When a congress of the poor peasants' committees of the Petrograd region was held, at which the representatives of these committees asked for all the political powers of the soviets to be transferred to their own committees, Zinoviev (apparently with the agreement of the party leadership) tabled a resolution declaring that, though the committees had fought against the kulaks, in carrying out their task, they "were inevitably obliged to go beyond the limits of the decree of 11 June," with the result that "a dual power was created in the countryside leading to fruitless dispersal of energy and confusion in relations."[2]

A week later, the Sixth Extraordinary All-Russia Congress of Soviets unanimously adopted a similar resolution.

On December 2, 1918, the VTsIK decided to dissolve the poor peasants' committees, because of the situation of "dual power" which had developed in the countryside.[3] Actually, the uneven development of the class struggle as between regions meant that at the moment when the poor peasants' committees were being suppressed in Russia, they were developing in the Ukraine, which had then been reconquered by the Soviet power after the collapse of German imperialism.

The decision to dissolve the poor peasants' committees was not a "concession" to the kulaks. It was dictated by a desire to avoid a split between the proletarian power and the middle peasants. The weakness of the Bolshevik Party in the rural areas prevented it from being able to give proper guidance to the poor peasants' committee movement, and safeguard it from becoming isolated from the middle peasants. In principle, the latter should have been included in the poor peasants' committees (instructions to this effect were sent out several times by the party leadership) but, in practice, the middle peasants were often treated as though they were kulaks.

After December 1918, the Bolshevik Party increasingly sought to widen its influence among the middle peasants and, more generally, among the petty bourgeoisie. At the end of November, Lenin had published his article "Valuable Admissions of Pitirim Sorokin," in which, writing of the least proletarian and most petty bourgeois strata of the working people who were turning toward the Soviet power, and of the hesitating and neutral elements, he said: "The slogan of the moment is to make use of the change of attitude towards us which is taking place among them." In this connection he emphasized the need for "agreement with the middle peasant, with the worker who was a Menshevik yesterday and with the office-worker or specialist who was a saboteur yesterday."

While declaring that there was no question of departing from the line of building socialism, or forgetting the past vacillations of the petty bourgeois democrats, Lenin concluded: "When profound world-historic changes bring about an inevitable turn in our direction among the mass of non-Party, Menshevik and Socialist-Revolutionary democrats, we must learn and shall learn to make use of this change of front, to encourage it, to induce it among the various groups and sections of the population, to do everything possible to reach agreement with them . . ."[4]

The decisions made between December 1918 and March

1919 were the preconditions for a new attempt at direct alliance with the middle peasants which was launched in March 1919.

We know that at the Eighth Party Congress, held in that month, Lenin tried to define a new attitude toward the middle peasants, "a numerous and strong section of the population." On this occasion, he said that it was not enough, at the stage then reached by the Soviet revolution, to "neutralise the peasantry," but that it was necessary to "place our relations with the middle peasants *on the basis of a firm alliance* and so preclude the possibility of a repetition of those mistakes and blunders we have repeatedly made in the past. Those blunders estranged the middle peasants from us, although we of the Communist Party, the leading party, were the first who helped the Russian peasants to throw off the yoke of the landlords and establish real democracy, which gave us every ground for counting on their complete confidence."[5]

The new party program adopted by the Eighth Congress was clearly oriented toward an alliance with the middle peasants. It expressly recalled that the middle peasants were not part of the exploiting classes, and that therefore no coercion must be used toward them. It called for measures to be taken to help the middle peasants to increase the productivity of their holdings, and said that they should be taxed only to a moderate extent.

II. Requisitioning and the development of the contradictions between the Soviet power and the peasantry

During 1919, and still more during 1920, it proved impossible to put into effective practice the principles laid down at the beginning of 1919 and ratified by the Eighth Party Congress, owing to the increasing disparity between production, agricultural deliveries, and the needs of the front and the towns for agricultural products. In order to cope with this disparity, the Soviet power was led, as we have seen, to increase requisitioning, which meant striking, often in an indiscriminate way, at the middle peasants (who were the most numerous body of producers).

During the civil war, the mass of the peasantry felt the objective necessity of this requisitioning and endured it as a necessary evil. Matters changed markedly after the middle of 1920, when victory became certain. At that moment, the continuation of requisitioning, and even its aggravation in the face of declining agricultural production, provoked serious discontent among many of the peasants, and serious tension developed between them and the Bolshevik Party.

From June 1920 onward, this tension increased all the more rapidly because the party thought it could pursue the policy of requisitioning indefinitely, seeing in it even a necessary instrument for the "building of socialism," which seemed an immediate task.

Some of Lenin's writings testify to the illusions that prevailed in those days. Thus, during the Second All-Russia Conference of Organizers Responsible for Work in the Rural Areas, on June 12, 1920, he said that "the proletarian dictatorship should display itself primarily in the advanced, the most class-conscious and most disciplined of the urban and industrial workers . . . educating, training and disciplining all the other proletarians, who are often not class-conscious, and all working people and the peasantry." Discipline must be imposed upon them from outside, without any "sentimentality," for "the working man, as we have inherited him from capitalism, is in a state of utter benightedness and ignorance, and does not realise that work can be done not only under the lash of capital but also under the guidance of the organised worker."[6]

At that time Lenin looked upon the requisitioning measures as not merely temporary, having to be applied because of war conditions, but as measures that were inherent in the dictatorship of the proletariat, in the nature of the relations existing between the proletariat in power and the peasant masses.

It was characteristic of the illusions associated with "war

communism" that the Bolshevik Party viewed the requisitioning measures as an integral part of the "frontal attack" on
capitalism which it thought it was then conducting. And so,
after having been adopted provisionally as measures dictated
by circumstances, the requisitioning measures came to be
looked upon as normal "socialist measures," and not only by
Bukharin—who then advocated the use of coercion with regard to the peasants, as can be seen in his book *The Economics
of the Transformation Period*[7]—but also by Lenin.

When, during the summer of 1920, Lenin read Varga's analysis of the experience of the Hungarian revolution, which
stated that "requisitions do not lead to the goal since they
bring in their train a decrease of production," he put two
question marks in the margin.[8] Soon after reading Varga's
work, Lenin expressed approval of what Bukharin said in *The
Economics of the Transformation Period,* where he asserted
that the constraint exercised by the proletarian dictatorship
with regard to the peasantry could not be considered as "pure
constraint," since it "lies on the path of general economic
development." Lenin noted in the margin: "Very good."[9]

In November 1920 Lenin even thought that, as a result of
the big increase in the amount of grain that the state had been
able to obtain through requisitioning, "We have convinced
the peasants that the proletariat provides them with better
conditions of existence than the bourgeoisie did; we have
convinced them of this by practice." He added: "His [the
peasant's] is a wait-and-see attitude. From being neutrally
hostile he has become neutrally sympathetic."[10]

Actually, at that moment the peasants' discontent had been
manifesting itself openly for two months already.[11] In September 1920, with the demobilization of the army and the
ending of the White Guard menace, there began to appear
what was called "peasant banditry," which was simply the
expression of profound discontent in the countryside. This
"banditry" developed above all in the central and southeast-
ern regions. The province of Tambov was especially affected
by a movement of this kind.

During the winter of 1920-1921, the People's Commissariat

for Food Supplies was finally obliged to suspend the requisitioning in thirteen provinces, as a result of the troubles that were developing in them.[12] Thereafter, expressions of peasant discontent continued to occur until the official abandonment of requisitioning measures in March 1921.

Despite this situation, Lenin was still saying, in December 1920, that the constraint applied to the peasants was necessary, and a means of increasing agricultural production. At the Eighth Congress of Soviets, while emphasizing the need for efforts to convince the peasants, especially the working peasants, the poor and the middle sections, he nevertheless said that "in a country of small peasants, our chief and basic task is to be able to resort to state compulsion in order to raise the level of peasant farming," and he urged that "the apparatus of compulsion" be "activated and reinforced."[13]

These statements were his last of the kind. Departing further and further from this favorable attitude toward the use of compulsion in dealing with the peasants, Lenin carried out an increasingly thorough rectification of his conception of the relations between the proletarian power and the peasantry. We shall see in Part Five how Lenin went about this rectification, its place in the balance sheet he drew up for the five years of the revolution, and the extent to which what he then said influenced the conceptions that prevailed in the Bolshevik Party. For the moment I shall give only a few indications of the beginning of a reevaluation of peasant policy which Lenin undertook in early 1921.

III. The peasants' discontent and the beginning of a reevaluation of the Bolshevik Party's peasant policy

In January 1921 Lenin met many peasant delegations. He became more and more aware of the mistakes that had been made in the countryside. In February he drafted some theses "concerning the peasants." He proposed to "satisfy the wish

of the non-Party peasants for the substitution of a tax in kind
for the surplus appropriation system (the confiscation of
surplus grain stocks)," and to "reduce the size of this tax as
compared with last year's appropriation rate." He also proposed to "give the farmer more leeway in using his after-tax
surpluses in local trade, provided his tax is promptly paid up
in full."[14] On February 17 and 26, *Pravda* published two
articles explaining the need for the measures proposed by
Lenin, and the Central Committee appointed a special commission to work out a scheme along these lines. Thus, in the
weeks leading up to the Kronstadt rising, Lenin had drawn the
party on to a new path, which was to be that of the New
Economic Policy.

On March 7, 1921, the Central Committee examined and
approved the scheme worked out by the special commission.
On March 8 and 15, Lenin spoke in support of the scheme at
the Tenth Party Congress.[15] These two speeches were presented in the form of reports in which Lenin gave a first
reevaluation of the policy followed down to that time by the
Bolshevik Party. They are of great importance. In them we
find explicit admission of the mistakes made, and an explanation of their immediate source, namely, the party's earlier
misunderstanding of the state of mind of the peasant masses.

In his report of March 8, Lenin spoke of the mistakes made
not only in the party's "calculations" and "plans," but also "in
determining the balance of forces between our class and those
classes in collaboration with which, and frequently in struggle
against which, it had to decide the fate of the Republic." He
went on: "With this as a starting point, let us return to the
results of the past."[16]

The frankness and sharpness of the self-criticism which
Lenin made at this time, and which he called on the whole
party to take part in, were in accordance with the proletarian
revolutionary character of Lenin's style of leadership. The
way he oriented himself toward a new political line was typical of this style of leadership. Confronted with a difficult
situation due to past errors (not only to these errors, moreover,
but also to the exigencies of a military struggle which he had
had to conduct under extremely complex conditions), Lenin

sought and found the elements of a new political line (of a line adjusted to the requirements of a situation that was also new) in the demands of the peasants themselves, in their aspirations.

It was on that basis, and on that of an analysis, free from whitewashing, of a setback that was admitted to be such, and treated like a scientific experiment, as an objective process the outcome of which was being assessed, that Lenin took a decisive step in the rectification of the Bolshevik Party's relations with the peasantry. As we shall see, it was by carrying further his rigorous analysis of the mistakes made during "war communism" that, between 1921 and 1923, Lenin opened up radically new vistas for the peasant policy of the proletarian dictatorship. In doing this, Lenin effected, in a series of stages, a major rectification of part of his conceptions regarding relations between the proletariat and the peasantry. The thoroughness of this rectification was so great that it forbids us to consider Lenin's earlier writings on peasant problems as still expressing the conclusions at which Lenin had arrived when he drew up the balance sheet of five years of revolution.

The beginning of this rectification, in the first months of 1921, and its subsequent deepening, did not of course fall from heaven: they resulted from both a concrete and a theoretical analysis of the most serious crisis the proletarian dictatorship had experienced until that time.

Before discussing this crisis, which had repercussions inside the Bolshevik Party in the form of an ideological and political crisis of unprecedented seriousness, we must briefly recall the way relations had evolved between the Bolshevik Party, the vanguard of the proletariat, and the mass of the workers.

IV. The relations of the Bolshevik Party with the mass of the workers

The Bolshevik Party's relations with the mass of the workers were very different, and developed very differently, from its relations with the peasant masses. Not only was the Bolshevik Party organically present in the working class, at least in the cities and big industrial centers, where the most militant elements of the working-class masses were to be found, but its ideology, its theoretical conceptions, and its political practice were always closely linked to the proletariat, and especially to its most advanced elements.

The closeness of these links—which, obviously, did not rule out the existence of contradictions between the party and more or less extensive sections of the working class, especially in a country like Russia where mistakes in policy toward the peasants inevitably produced negative effects among the proletariat—corresponded to the Leninist principles regarding the party's style of leadership and its leading role in relation to the working class.

(a) The relations between the party and the proletariat

I have considered earlier the Leninist conception of the party, which insists on respect for certain principles where the party's relations with the working-class masses are concerned—attention to the workers' initiative as a source of instruction for the party; confidence in the revolutionary energy of the proletariat; presence of the party amidst the proletariat and close links (going as far, in Lenin's words, as "merging") with its advanced elements; and the need to allow the working people to convince themselves by their own experience.

Lenin's revolutionary Marxism included other principles, connected with the party's role as the instrument for working out a political line and as the bearer of revolutionary theory. In this respect, what is essential is the party's role as political guide and theoretical educator. For Lenin, a party which does not fulfill this role is not a revolutionary party: it does not rise above the level of "economism" and "spontaneism," according to which absolutely any initiative or aspiration of the masses is revolutionary. This emphasis on the role of the party as educator and guide is found in the very first of Lenin's major political interventions, especially in *What Is to Be*

Done? Bolshevism thereby radically distinguished itself from German Social Democracy, including the latter's revolutionary tendency, one of whose most outstanding representatives was Rosa Luxemburg.

Thus, in his article "On the Junius Pamphlet," Lenin wrote: "A very great defect in revolutionary Marxism in Germany as a whole is its lack of a compact illegal organisation that would systematically pursue its own line and educate the masses in the spirit of the new tasks . . . "[17]

The party's appropriate role as educator and guide of the proletariat corresponds to the place which Leninism ascribes to revolutionary theory, and to the acknowledged need to struggle against bourgeois ideology as the dominant ideology. This role implies rejection of the "naive" conception according to which the proletariat is ready at any moment and on a mass scale to engage in revolutionary action. Leninism here links up with Marx's analyses which distinguish between the theory of the proletariat (a theory which draws scientific conclusions from the existence of the proletariat, from the *relations* in which the proletariat is involved, and from the *struggles* it wages) and what the proletarians *imagine* their role and their interest to be in any given situation. We recall what Marx wrote on this point: "The question is not what this or that proletarian, or even the whole of the proletariat *considers* as its aim. The question is *what the proletariat is,* and what, consequent on that *being,* it will be compelled to do."[18]

These Leninist principles, put into practice by the Bolshevik Party, enabled it to take the lead in the revolutionary movement of the masses, and help the masses to overthrow the dictatorship of the bourgeoisie and establish the dictatorship of the proletariat in October 1917.

(b) The leadership practice of the Bolshevik Party after the establishment of the proletarian dictatorship

After the dictatorship of the proletariat was established, the actual practice of the Bolshevik Party was far from always in strict conformity with the Leninist principles according to which the party should persuade the mass of workers, trust them, and allow them to become convinced of what is correct through their own experience.

The internal changes in the party, the necessity for rapid action, the disintegration of the proletariat (whose ranks were emptied of the most combative elements, while being penetrated by many bourgeois and petty bourgeois elements), the military emergencies, the disastrous economic situation, the hunger and cold that drove the less advanced section of the working-class mass to despair, did not allow these principles to be fully and constantly applied. They are, moreover, not "fetishes" but guides to action. It is essential that they be respected as fully as possible, but absurd to try to "apply" them in any and every situation. The Bolshevik Party rightly considered that the fact that it had driven the bourgeoisie from power in Russia was an event of world importance, and that, consequently, everything must be done to prevent the bourgeoisie and imperialism (then waging armed struggle) from restoring their dictatorship. This was the meaning of Lenin's slogan: "Everything for the Front!"

The advanced elements of the proletariat and of the broad proletarian masses were conscious of the objective necessities of the situation. They participated with extraordinary vigor in the struggles being waged on the military and production fronts, showing trust in the Bolshevik Party, and eventually winning victory in spite of extreme material difficulties. This political victory par excellence proves concretely that the most active elements of the proletariat and the popular masses (whose resistance to the imperialist war had, a few years earlier, brought about the downfall of tsardom) gave active support to the Bolshevik Party, and also that the political line and practice of the party were fundamentally correct.

This fundamental correctness does not mean that no mistakes were made. Once victory had been won over the White and imperialist armies, the mistakes which had been made— and which were admitted by Lenin when he drew up his critical balance sheet of "war communism"—entailed not only a worsening of the party's relations with the peasant masses, as has already been explained, but also a falling-off in its relations with part of the working class. This unfavorable evolution in relations between the party and the masses led to the political crisis of the winter of 1920–1921.

V. The political crisis of the winter of 1920–1921

The gravity of the political crisis of the winter of 1920–1921 resulted from the conjunction of discontent among a section of the peasantry, who were subjected to requisitioning, with a dramatic worsening of living conditions in the towns. Since the beginning of 1920, inflation had assumed enormous proportions. In April the food rations officially issued to the urban workers (representing that part of the requisitioned produce which did not go to the soldiers of the Red Army) accounted for only 30 to 50 percent of what was needed for survival, which explains the immense role played at that time by the black market.[19]

On the black market the prices of many products were, as early as April 1920, forty or fifty times as high as the official prices. Subsequently, the currency was devalued still further, and workers more and more frequently received their pay in kind.[20] This collapse of the currency was one of the factors which contributed to the development of the illusions of "war communism." One aspect of these illusions was, indeed, the identification of the "disappearance of money" with the building of entirely new economic relations leading to the abolition of wage labor.

The extreme shortage of goods condemned the townspeople, and also many peasants, to hunger and cold, while the factories were paralyzed by the lack of fuel. This situation gave rise to serious discontent on the part of the petty bourgeoisie and the less advanced elements of the working class, who blamed the Bolshevik Party for their difficulties and refused to accept that these were the result of several years of imperialist war, civil war, and foreign intervention.

The worsening of the economic situation lay behind the

peasant revolts that developed from the end of 1920 onward and the strikes that broke out in February 1921, in Petrograd, Moscow, and other industrial centers. These strikes were not directed against the Soviet power, but were essentially elementary expressions of the discontent of the workers who were suffering from very inadequate feeding. However, the workers' demands also included some anarchist, SR, or Menshevik slogans. Some of the leaders of these political movements thought, indeed, that the moment had come to launch once more an anti-Bolshevik operation. Their hopes actually collapsed very soon. Thus, in Petrograd, the stoppages of work began on February 24, and continued for two days. On February 26, the Petrograd Soviet and the defense committee headed by Zinoviev started a campaign of explanation. At the same time, measures were taken to improve the food supplies available to the factory workers (this was done, apparently, by "raiding" the Red Army's stocks), and suppress the activities of the SRs and Mensheviks who were trying to subvert the Soviet power (a leaflet issued by the SRs called for the Constituent Assembly to be convened, while a Menshevik appeal demanded a "fundamental policy change"). The campaign of explanation undertaken by the Bolshevik Party and the Petrograd soviet clarified the situation: on February 28, the strikes in Petrograd ended, the signal for return to work having being given by the Putilov works, that "workers' stronghold."[21] In the other towns affected, the course of events was similar—which confirms that the discontent of the striking workers was not general and profound in character, but due essentially to the difficulties of everyday life.

In the countryside, however, a real political crisis developed early in 1921. It affected part of the armed forces, and had serious repercussions a few days after the Petrograd strikes had ended. The discontent which prevailed at that time in the Kronstadt naval base then took concrete form in the holding of a number of general meetings of the sailors and workers of the naval base, which elected a conference of about 300 delegates. On March 2, 1921, this conference elected in its turn a bureau of five members, presided over by Petrichenko, senior clerk on the battleship *Petropavlovsk*. Soon afterward, this bureau, having been enlarged to fifteen members, proclaimed itself a Provisional Revolutionary Committee and came out in opposition to the Kronstadt soviet.

Events then followed swiftly. By order of the committee, three Bolshevik leaders were arrested, including the deputy Vasilyev, a genuine revolutionary who had nothing about him of the "bureaucrat" type the committee claimed to be attacking. Pressure was brought to bear on the members of the Bolshevik Party to leave the party, and, in the confused atmosphere that prevailed in Kronstadt, at least one-third of them did this. Some days later, when tension was mounting between the Soviet power and the Revolutionary Committee, several hundred Communists were arrested.[22]

The program of the leaders of the insurrection was a mixture of various slogans intended to mobilize as wide a degree of support as possible, with the aim of developing a movement that would dislodge the Bolsheviks from power throughout Russia. Certain features of this program were especially significant. It was demanded that the soviets be opened to the SRs and the Mensheviks—many of whom had entered into arrangements with the counter-revolutionaries, or, where they had come to power locally and temporarily as a result of the retreats which the Red Army had been forced to make during the civil war, had served as "bridges" for the White Guards, whom they were unable to resist even if they had wanted to. The Kronstadt leaders also called for the establishment of "non-party soviets," which was a way of excluding Bolshevik candidates in the event elections should be held in conformity with this demand.

Among the significant features of the Kronstadt program was the demand for abolition of political commissars in the Red Army, though it was this institution which enabled control to be maintained over the ex-tsarist officers in the army. Not surprisingly, some high-ranking officers of the tsarist army served the Kronstadt rebels faithfully, even though they did not, of course, push themselves to the forefront: this was the case with General A. N. Kozlovsky and the officers under his command.[23]

On the economic plane, the Kronstadt program called, essentially, for freedom of trade and respect for peasant property.

Actually, the content of this program, though significant, was of secondary importance. What was decisive were the social and political forces that backed the Kronstadt movement.

In order to grasp the nature of these forces, we must distinguish between the leaders of the movement and the masses who were behind them. Relatively little is known about the former. We do know, however, that one of them, A. Lamonov, was a former SR Maximalist and, especially, that the chairman of the Revolutionary Committee, S. R. Petrichenko, had belonged to the Bolshevik Party for a few months. He had then left the party and engaged in counter-revolutionary activity, for which he was several times arrested. Later he had tried to join the Whites, but they had rejected his services because he had been a member of the Bolshevik Party.[24]

As regards the social basis of the movement, it must be said that at the beginning of 1921 the sailors of former times who had been among the strongest supporters of the Bolsheviks during the October days were no longer more than a minority in Kronstadt. The bulk of the forces that supported the Revolutionary Committee consisted of young recruits from the Ukraine, without any political training, who responded readily to the "antiauthoritarian" slogans of the leaders of the Revolutionary Committee. The dominant ideological current among the Kronstadters was, in fact, anarcho-populist, anti-state, and strongly marked by Slavonic nationalism, anti-Semitism, and Orthodox religious feeling. More than once we find among them the "amalgam" propagated by the Whites: "Communist means Jew."[25]

On the international plane, the Kronstadt movement was fully supported by all the counter-revolutionary tendencies. The actual relations between the Kronstadt leaders and the National Center formed in Paris, mainly by former Cadets, have never been clarified. Some things are certain, however. A few weeks before the revolt, the National Center had drawn up a plan, known as the Secret Memorandum, which assumed that Kronstadt could be used as the base for a new counter-revolutionary onslaught on Petrograd. During the revolt, all the forces of this Center, together with the SRs in exile, were mobilized to help it, millions of francs being collected for the purpose in a few days. Finally, when the revolt had been suppressed, eleven of the fifteen members of the Revolutionary Committee (whom the Bolsheviks suspected of being in contact with the National Center and its representatives in Finland) took refuge with counter-revolutionary elements.[26]

In fact, contrary to the hopes entertained by the leaders of the revolt, it produced hardly any echo in Russia.[27] In the eyes of the masses at large, the Bolshevik Party, regardless of the mistakes it might have made, was still the only bulwark against restoration of the bourgeois order.

The Bolshevik Party naturally did all it could to stop the revolt from spreading or even from continuing. The location of Kronstadt close to Petrograd, on the one hand, and to the counter-revolutionary forces in Finland, on the other—did not permit protracted "negotiations." It was necessary to crush the revolt before the ice melted. Once the water was free of ice, Kronstadt could be reached by sea by the White and imperialist forces, and this would have meant a direct military threat to Russia's chief city.

After sending an ultimatum calling upon the rebels to surrender, and receiving a negative reply from the Revolutionary Committee, the Red Army took the offensive. On March 17, the main attack was launched, and by early morning of March 18 all resistance had ceased in the allegedly impregnable fortress of Kronstadt. So ended an especially sad episode of the crisis of the winter of 1920–1921—an episode which deserves attention from two standpoints.

First, the very fact that the revolt could occur confirms that discontent among a section of the masses, especially the peasants (or those who were of peasant origin, like the young recruits in Kronstadt), had then reached the pitch of explosion in some places, so that some of the peasantry were wide open to the petty bourgeois propaganda of the SRs, Mensheviks, and anarchists, or even of men who were supported de facto by the Cadet party, though they employed ultrarevolutionary language.

Secondly, the absence of any extension of the Kronstadt

revolt despite the appeals that were issued, shows that in the eyes of the broadest masses, whatever tension there might have been where particular problems were concerned, such as requisitioning, the Bolshevik Party was still the party that had led the revolution and whose capacity for organization had ensured victory in the struggle against the landlords, the capitalists, and imperialism.

The Kronstadt episode led the Bolsheviks to harden their attitude more than ever against the former "Soviet parties," which now seemed to be conniving with the most reactionary political émigrés and with the Anglo-French imperialists (who backed the National Center). It was now more than ever out of the question to allow these parties to take part again in the work of the soviets. Inside the Bolshevik Party itself there was no hesitation regarding the line to be followed, in the given circumstances, toward the revolt. On this point the party showed remarkable unity. In other forms, however, the discontent that had arisen among the masses produced splits in the party and conflicts between different tendencies. Ideological and political struggle had always been part of the life of the Bolshevik Party, but the gravity of the crisis of the winter of 1920–1921 caused the party leadership to alter the conditions governing the conduct of this struggle. In order to understand the implications of the decisions taken on this point by the Tenth Party Congress, and to appreciate the Bolshevik Party's ideological vitality, it is necessary briefly to recall some aspects of the internal struggles that had taken place in the party; and it will be useful to carry our study of these struggles a little beyond the period of the Tenth Congress.

Notes

1. Lenin, *CW*, vol. 28, pp. 341–344.
2. A report of this meeting in Petrograd was given by Zinoviev to the Sixth Extraordinary All-Russia Congress of Soviets, the proceedings of which are quoted in Carr, *The Bolshevik Revolution*, vol. 2, p. 162.

3. Ibid., p. 163.
4. *CW*, vol. 28, pp. 192, 193–194.
5. Lenin's speech opening the Eighth Party Congress, March 18, 1919, in *CW*, vol. 29, pp. 143 ff.; quotation on pp. 144–145.
6. *CW*, vol. 31, pp. 176–177.
7. Bukharin, *The Economics of the Transformation Period*, p. 159.
8. Quoted in Carr, *The Bolshevik Revolution*, vol. 2, p. 173.
9. *Leninsky Sbornik*, vol. 11, p. 369. See also Bukharin, *The Economics of the Transformation Period*, pp. 93 and 216.
10. *CW*, vol. 31, p. 418.
11. Lenin had noted this discontent in October 1920, but he ascribed it not to the system of requisitioning itself but only to the *excesses* committed in the way requisitioning was carried out.
12. See the report of the Tenth Party Congress, p. 231, quoted in Carr, *The Bolshevik Revolution*, vol. 2, p. 173.
13. *CW*, vol. 31, p. 505.
14. *CW*, vol. 32, p. 133.
15. See Lenin, *CW* (3rd ed.), vol. 26, for details regarding these main stages in the transition to the NEP.
16. *CW*, vol. 32, p. 173.
17. *CW*, vol. 22, pp. 305–319; quotation on p. 307.
18. Marx and Engels, *The Holy Family*, p. 53.
19. The inadequacy of wages and rations was often admitted: for example, by the Fourth Trade Union Congress, held in April 1920, and by the Tenth Party Congress (1921). See the reports of these congresses, pp. 119 and 237 respectively; quoted in Carr, *The Bolshevik Revolution*, vol. 2, p. 243, n. 2 and 3.
20. Ibid., pp. 260–261.
21. *Pravda o Kronshtadte*, quoted in Anweiler, *Die Rätebewegung*, p. 311.
22. Paul Avrich, *Kronstadt 1921*, p. 186.
23. Ibid., pp. 98–99. On March 2, 1921, Kozlovsky said to the Bolshevik commissar: "Your time is past. Now I shall do what has to be done" (ibid., p. 100).
24. Ibid., pp. 94–95. Avrich mentions some facts about other members of this committee.
25. Ibid., pp. 172–180.
26. Ibid., pp. 106–125 and 208–209.
27. Only a few anarchist clubs in Moscow and Petrograd distributed leaflets calling for support of the revolt (Anweiler, *Die Rätebewegung*, p. 318).

2. The ideological and political struggles in the Bolshevik Party before the civil war

The tradition of Bolshevism is a tradition of ideological and political struggle. In 1903, when Bolshevism came into being as a distinct political trend, and one year after the publication of *What Is to Be Done?* Lenin said that it was essential to "hospitably throw open the columns of the Party organ for exchanges of opinion," and that the party must have at its disposal all, absolutely all, the material needed to form an independent judgment. He condemned those who had an exaggeratedly stern and stiff attitude toward so-called "anarchistic individualism," for he considered it preferable for the party's life to be tolerant, "even if it involves a certain departure from tidy patterns of centralism and from absolute obedience to discipline."[1]

In 1904 Lenin reaffirmed his conviction that a broad exchange of views, and even battles between tendencies, were essential to party life.[2] The existence of divergent views within the party was inevitable, being an effect of the class struggle, since the party was not an "isolated islet of socialism." It was inevitable that party members should at certain moments fall under the influence of bourgeois ideology: by discussion in the party one could fight to prevent ideological representatives of the bourgeoisie from taking over leadership of the proletarian movement; but in order to do this, one must remain on the terrain of Marxist analysis and not compromise on principles. Once decisions had been adopted, of course, these were obligatory upon everyone, since the party was not a discussion group but an organ of struggle which must be disciplined and obedient to its leading bodies.

Lenin's line on ideological struggle was considered by the party as a whole as necessary to the functioning of democratic centralism and to respect for discipline in the application of decisions. This line prevailed not only until 1917 but also in the first years following the October Revolution. Discussions within the party were even exceptionally lively in that period, reflecting the magnitude of the class struggle that was going on in the country.

The conflicts that took place on the very eve of October and in 1917–1918 found expression in a number of documents, analysis of which enables us to bring out the chief conceptions that existed in the party at that time and to grasp their essential class content.

I. The ideological and political struggles in the party between February and October 1917

Between February and October, two lines became defined inside the Bolshevik Party. First, before Lenin's return from exile, there was the line of support for the Provisional Government. Whereas Lenin put forward the slogan of revolutionary struggle against the bourgeoisie and refusal to fight under its orders, a section of the Bolshevik leaders gave conditional support to the Provisional Government.

This "defensist" line was maintained, from March 14, 1917 onward, by *Pravda,* which had just been taken over by Kamenev and Stalin. In the first issue of *Pravda* published under the new editorship, Stalin said that "the rights won must be upheld so as to destroy completely the old forces and, in conjunction with the provinces, further advance the Russian revolution."[3] In the next day's issue, Kamenev expressed an even more clear-cut "defensist" attitude, and on March 16 Stalin said that it was necessary to "bring pressure on the Provisional Government to make it declare its consent to start peace negotiations immediately,"[4] which amounted to adopting the Menshevik standpoint of "pushing the bourgeoisie from behind," instead of a consistent Bolshevik line of standing at the head of the masses and ahead of them.

Seven years later, in a speech to a plenum of the Communist group in the All-Union Central Council of Trade Unions, Stalin referred to this period and admitted his mistake, but tried to justify it by showing that he had not been alone in the attitude he had taken up. "The Party (its majority)," he said, "adopted the policy of pressure on the Provisional Government through the Soviets on the question of peace and did not venture to step forward at once from the old slogan of the dictatorship of the proletariat and peasantry to the new slogan of power to the Soviets."[5]

Lenin's arrival on April 3, 1917, enabled the revolutionary line he advocated gradually to become victorious, but this did not happen without resistance. Kamenev still declared, the day after the publication of Lenin's "April Theses," which looked toward proletarian revolution: "In so far as concerns Lenin's general scheme, it appears to us inacceptable, since it starts from the assumption that the bourgeois revolution is *finished* and counts on the immediate transformation of this revolution into a socialist revolution."[6]

Kamenev soon found himself isolated, with Stalin and Zinoviev rallying to Lenin's theses. Even so, the triumph of the revolutionary line was not yet complete. Thus, in September 1917, there was a majority in the Central Committee in favor of Bolshevik participation in a "democratic conference" formed independently of the soviets, whereas Lenin had put forward the slogan: "All Power to the Soviets." Only Lenin's threat to resign from the Central Committee induced the latter to revoke its decision.

Soon afterward, Lenin called on the Central Committee to prepare for insurrection. He was supported by a majority of 10 to 2—the minority consisting of Zinoviev and Kamenev. These two waged a public campaign against Lenin's revolutionary line. At the time, Stalin—who was, seven years later, to present these divergences as a mere matter of "different shades of opinion"—pronounced the following judgment:

"There are two policies: one is heading towards the victory of the revolution and looks to Europe; the other has no faith in the revolution and counts on being only an opposition."[7]

Zinoviev and Kamenev were not expelled from the party, as Lenin had demanded. By a majority of 5 to 3 the Central Committee simply decided (on October 20) to accept their resignation. In practice, even this resignation did not take effect: immediately after the insurrection, Zinoviev and Kamenev were again participating in the work of the Central Committee and entrusted with important political responsibilities.

After October, the struggle between the two lines continued, of course, but the concrete problems it involved were different.

II. The struggles over the problem of a "coalition government"

Among the questions that gave rise to serious divergences was, as we have seen, that of forming a "coalition government." It arose in this way. After the formation, in the evening of the day of the insurrection, of a homogeneous Bolshevik government, the latter came under heavy pressure from the SRs and Mensheviks, who demanded that a "coalition government" be formed, to be made up of all the parties represented in the soviets. The Central Committee agreed to enter into negotiations with the SRs and Mensheviks, but, whereas for Lenin these negotiations were merely a tactical operation (as he put it: "a diplomatic move to distract attention from operations of war"[8]), for Kamenev and Zinoviev they were really intended to lead to the formation of a coalition government.

A fresh crisis broke out in the party leadership when Lenin proposed on November 1, 1917, to call off these talks. Zinoviev, Kamenev, and Rykov opposed this move, which was nevertheless approved by the Central Committee. Kamenev and Rykov, who had been the Bolshevik Party's delegates for the negotiations, went so far as to violate the decision by failing to act in accordance with it.

During the winter of 1917–1918 and the spring of 1918, an extremely profound crisis occurred. Not only did it cause divergences in the Central Committee and in some of the party organizations, it developed on a much wider scale. The period saw the formation of the group of "left Communists." The ideological struggle that broke out at this time was concerned principally with the question of the peace of Brest-Litovsk and with the conception of "state capitalism."

III. *The struggles in the Bolshevik Party and the peace of Brest-Litovsk*

The crisis provoked by the peace negotiations held at Brest-Litovsk, and then by the treaty itself, opened on January 5, 1918, when, by decision of the Central Committee, peace negotiations were begun with German imperialism. It became apparent that the latter would sign a peace treaty with the Soviet power only if immense territories were ceded to it: Poland, Lithuania, Byelorussia, and the half of Latvia occupied by the German army.

Lenin declared for acceptance of these conditions and for the immediate conclusion of a treaty. He was aware of the country's desire for peace. He knew, too, that the disorganized state of the armed forces was such that they could not resist a renewed German offensive. Trotsky was for trying a delaying tactic ("neither peace nor war"). Bukharin favored "revolutionary war" (at a time when no force existed to wage such a war), but finding himself isolated, he supported Trotsky's line, so that Lenin was placed in a minority in the Central Committee (9 votes were cast for Trotsky's line and only 7 for Lenin's).

Following this decision by the Central Committee, the German army resumed its offensive on all fronts and penetrated deeply into Soviet territory. On January 17, Lenin put forward his proposal once more and was again defeated (Trotsky and Bukharin claimed that the German offensive would have the effect on the international labor movement of arousing a revolutionary wave of support for the Soviet power), this time by 6 votes to 5.

The German army advanced so rapidly that on January 18 the Central Committee held another meeting, and now Trotsky came round to Lenin's view, which was approved by the central committee—though only by 7 to 5.

The position maintained for several days by the majority of the members of the CC—a position which, while outwardly "left," was really nationalist and petty bourgeois—and the defeats suffered during that period meant that Soviet Russia had now to accept additional demands from German imperialism. To the territories already listed for annexation were added the Ukraine, Livonia, and Estonia. As a result, in the area it controlled, the Soviet power would lose 26 percent of its population, 27 percent of the cultivated land, and 75 percent of the capacity for producing iron and steel.

Lenin called for the peace treaty to be signed without further discussion. The Central Committee hesitated. Stalin proposed that the German demands be not accepted purely and simply, but that negotiations be reopened. However, Lenin's proposal was adopted by 7 votes to 4.[9]

On March 3, 1918, the Treaty of Brest-Litovsk was formally signed—but the weeks which had passed since the negotiations began showed how deeply the party was divided. Basically, this division counterposed those who agreed with Lenin that maintenance of a proletarian power in Russia was vital for the future of the world revolutionary movement to those who thought it would be better for this power to disappear rather than survive at the price of concessions they considered inacceptable. The signing of the treaty did not put an end to the crisis which had begun in the party, as was shown by the declarations issued by various regional party organizations (which at that time still expressed their disagreements publicly).

After the Central Committee's decision to sign the treaty,

the party bureau of the Moscow region voted a resolution declaring that it would no longer recognize the authority of the CC until an extraordinary party congress had been held and a new CC elected.

The existing Central Committee formally acknowledged the right of those who did not agree with the decision it had taken to express their view. Commenting on the resolution of the Moscow regional bureau, Lenin wrote: "It is quite natural that comrades who sharply disagree with the Central Committee over the question of a separate peace should sharply condemn the Central Committee and express their conviction that a split is inevitable. All that is the most legitimate right of Party members, which is quite understandable."[10]

The day after the actual signing of the treaty, on March 4, 1918, the Petrograd party committee brought out the first issue of a daily paper entitled *Kommunist*—the organ of the "left Communists," who formed an opposition moving openly toward a split and the formation of a new party.

IV. The "left Communists" and state capitalism

After Brest-Litovsk, the "left Communists" directed their attacks increasingly not so much against the line on foreign policy and military problems, as against the concessions which the party leadership thought it necessary to make to that part of the bourgeoisie which agreed to collaborate with the Soviet power. These attacks reflected the pressure brought to bear on the party by a part of the working class wishing to retain the existing forms of organization of the factory committees and of "workers' control," and unwilling to let posts of responsibility or leadership be given to capitalists and bourgeois technicians, engineers, and administrators, in the factories and in the various organs of the VSNKh.

At this time, as we have seen, the majority of the Central

Committee decided to change the Soviet power's relations with a section of the bourgeoisie whose skill was considered indispensable for the management and administration of the state-owned factories and for coordinating economic activities. The former capitalist administration of the enterprises was thus partly maintained or reestablished, and concessions were granted in the matter of salaries to the bourgeois specialists and technicians, so as to ensure their collaboration. The principle of one-man management of enterprises was adopted, and it was decided to introduce a system of bonuses, under trade-union control, in order to bring about an increase in the productivity of labor.

The "left Communists" denounced these measures. In the first issue of *Kommunist* they attacked "a labour policy designed to implant discipline among the workers under the flag of 'self-discipline,' the introduction of labour service for workers, piece rates, and the lengthening of the working day." According to *Kommunist*, "the introduction of labour discipline in connection with the restoration of capitalist management of industry cannot really increase the productivity of labour." It would only "diminish the class initiative, activity and organisation of the proletariat. It threatens to enslave the working class. It will arouse discontent among the backward elements as well as among the vanguard of the proletariat. In order to introduce this system in the face of the hatred prevailing at present among the proletariat against the 'capitalist saboteurs,' the Communist Party would have to rely on the petty-bourgeoisie as against the workers." Consequently, it would "ruin itself as the party of the proletariat."

The same issue of *Kommunist* denounced "bureaucratic centralisation, the rule of various commissars, the loss of independence for local soviets, and in practice the rejection of the type of state-commune administered from below." Bukharin recalled that Lenin had written in *The State and Revolution* that "each cook should learn to manage the State," and added: "But what happened when each cook had a commissar appointed to order him about?"

The second issue of *Kommunist* carried an article by another member of the "left Communist" group, Osinsky, who wrote:

> We stand for the construction of the proletarian society by the class creativity of the workers themselves, not by the ukases of the captains of industry . . . If the proletariat itself does not know how to create the necessary prerequisites for the socialist organisation of labour, no one can do this for it and no one can compel it to do this. The stick, if raised against the workers, will find itself in the hands of a social force which is either under the influence of another social class or is in the hands of the soviet power; but the soviet power will then be forced to seek support against the proletariat from another class (e.g., the peasantry) and by this it will destroy itself as the dictatorship of the proletariat. Socialism and socialist organisation will be set up by the proletariat itself, or they will not be set up at all: something else will be set up—state capitalism.[11]

Lenin answered these statements by showing that, at the actual stage of the Russian Revolution at that time, it was not a question of "building socialism," nor, therefore, of undertaking to change in depth the relations of production, but of coping as expeditiously as possible with the growing disorganization of the economy. It was in order to explain this immediate task that Lenin put forward the notion of "state capitalism under the dictatorship of the proletariat."

The Seventh Party Congress, held at the beginning of March 1918, condemned the line of the "left Communists" and declared in favor of the measures proposed by Lenin. After this congress, the organizational forces which until then had been at the disposal of the "left Communists" in the party collapsed very quickly—partly as a result of administrative measures, transfers of cadres, and so on. *Kommunist* ceased to appear every day. Its production was shifted to Moscow, where a few more numbers appeared; but the "left Communists" lost the majority they had held in that city, and also in the Ural region. They gave up the idea of founding a new Communist party, and decided to remain in the Bolshevik Party.

A year later Lenin drew a positive conclusion from this crisis, saying: "The struggle that flared up in our Party during the past year was extremely useful. It gave rise to numerous sharp collisions, but there are no struggles without sharp collisions." [12] By then the former "left Communists" had resumed their place in the party, and some were again holding leading positions.

The crisis experienced by the Bolshevik Party in early 1918 showed the capacity it then possessed for allowing an open ideological struggle to develop within it. The crisis also showed the coming together of ultra-left and petty bourgeois attitudes, in particular where problems of peace and war were concerned, with attitudes which undoubtedly reflected the aspirations of part of the party's working-class base. It was certainly no accident that it was in Moscow, Petrograd, and the Ural region—that is, in the major industrial centers—that the "left Communists" found their main support.

By the end of the spring of 1918, the group of "left Communists" had disappeared as such, but many elements of its political line—for example, its opposition to administrative centralism, which it sought to replace by greater initiative on the part of the working people, both in the soviets and in the workplaces—were to reappear again and again, giving rise to new oppositions. I shall return to this point.

In any case, the problems raised by the "platform" of the "left Communists" sank into the background when the principal contradiction shifted; the outbreak of the White revolt, backed by imperialist intervention, brought to the forefront the problems of armed struggle.

Before proceeding to analyze the period that opened then, I must emphasize once more the scale of the struggles that Lenin had to carry on, before and after October 1917, in order to win victory for his ideas. This needs emphasis because the extensiveness of the discussions and disputes, and the frequency with which Lenin was put in a minority, show that, contrary to what is alleged in the "official history" of Bolshevism, open ideological and political conflicts were particularly intense at this time. Emphasis is also called for because these conflicts show the pressure to which the Bolshevik Party was subjected by the class contradictions developing in Russian society as a whole.

The foregoing also shows—and this is important for understanding what was to happen after Lenin's death—that during the decisive period between February 1917 and June 1918 no group of leaders appeared in the Central Committee who firmly and constantly upheld the same views as Lenin—at best, some of them rallied more easily or more quickly than others to his views.

While there was no group of leaders of whom it can be said that they took up more or less regularly the same attitude as Lenin, it is, however, possible to identify two successive tendencies which had serious divergences with Lenin.

One of these was a "rightist" trend which manifested itself especially between February and December 1917. It included not only Kamenev and Zinoviev, but also, sometimes, Stalin—that is, the men who were to form the leading nucleus of the party immediately after Lenin's death, what has been called the *troika*, the "triumvirate," that succeeded him.

The other tendency developed mainly from January 1918 onward. It included Trotsky, Bukharin, and also Stalin (who supported Lenin on the need to conclude the treaty of Brest-Litovsk only at the last moment). This was, above all, the trend of the "left Communists." It commanded larger forces than the previous one, and lasted longer. Positions close to those of this tendency were to be advocated subsequently by various other oppositions.

With Soviet Russia's entry into a period of armed struggle against White revolt and foreign intervention, however, many problems presented themselves in new forms. We must now consider the principal aspects of the ideological struggles which developed in the Bolshevik Party during the civil war period.

Notes

1. *CW*, vol. 7, pp. 115–116.
2. See, e.g., *One Step Forward, Two Steps Back*, in *CW*, vol. 7, pp. 203 ff.
3. Stalin's article in *Pravda* of March 14, 1917: "The Soviets of Workers' and Soldiers' Deputies" (Stalin, *Works*, English edition, vol. 3, p. 1). See also Carr, *The Bolshevik Revolution*, vol. 1, pp. 85–86.
4. Stalin, *Works*, vol. 3, p. 8.
5. Ibid., vol. 6, p. 348. The idea that it would have been correct to "go against the tide" was not even mentioned.
6. Quoted in Carr, *The Bolshevik Revolution*, vol. 1, p. 91.
7. Stalin, *Works*, vol. 3, p. 407.
8. Central Committee minutes, published in 1929, quoted in Carr, *The Bolshevik Revolution*, vol. 1, p. 118.
9. It was characteristic of the petty bourgeois lack of realism of the "left Communists," whose chief representative at that time was Bukharin, that they refused, in the event of hostilities being resumed, to accept help from Russia's former "allies," France and Britain, whereas Lenin was ready to accept "potatoes and munitions from the hands of the imperialist bandits."
10. *CW*, vol. 27, p. 68.
11. Quoted in Brinton, *The Bolsheviks and Workers' Control*, pp. 38–39.
12. *CW*, vol. 29, p. 74.

3. The ideological and political struggles during "war communism"

During most of the "war communism" period, ideological and political struggles were less acute than in previous years, the party's attention and efforts being mainly concentrated on problems of defense. The Bolshevik Party was, on the whole, relatively united in its views on these problems, so that they did not give rise to major disputes, especially since those members who differed from the majority usually came into line quickly. There were, however, some acts of indiscipline amounting to a sort of "undeclared opposition" to the policy decided on by the congresses and the Central Committee, and some of the questions raised by the "left Communists" reappeared during this period. Most important, new divisions appeared from 1920 onward, when victory drew near and "postwar" problems had to be faced. These new divisions became noticeable at the Ninth Party Congress, and more plainly still toward the end of 1920. Let us first, though, consider the period preceding that year.

I. The oppositions of 1918 and 1919

Even before the White revolt broke out, opposition to Lenin's policy on nationalities made itself apparent. It was not an open opposition, but it became manifest in the party's practical activity. Although this opposition had no immediate effects, it is important to recall it for it reasserted itself, with serious consequences, as soon as the civil war was over.

One of the first expressions of this trend occurred in April 1918, when a Soviet government for the Ukraine was formed under the leadership of the Bolshevik N. A. Skrypnik. Although, on April 3, 1918, Lenin sent a message of support to the Ukrainian Soviet government, expressing his "enthusiastic solidarity with the heroic struggle being waged by the working and exploited people of the Ukraine, who now constitute one of the vanguard detachments of the world social revolution," Stalin, who was at that time People's Commissar for Nationalities, opposed the formation of this Soviet government of a Ukraine independent of Russia. Stalin's attitude produced the following reaction from Skrypnik: "We must protest in the strongest possible way against the statement of Commissar Stalin. We must declare that the Central Executive Committee of the Ukrainian Soviet base their actions, not on the attitude of any Commissar of the Russian Federation, but on the will of the toiling masses of the Ukraine, as expressed in the decree of the Second All-Ukraine Congress of Soviets. Declarations like that of Commissar Stalin would destroy the Soviet regime in the Ukraine . . . They are direct assistance to the enemies of the Ukrainian toiling masses."[1]

Stalin's hostility to the formation of a Soviet republic which was not included within the Russian Soviet Republic did not remain an isolated episode. This was a manifestation of a political conception that was to be reaffirmed on numerous occasions, and subsequently to be supported by the Russian bourgeoisie in emigration and by elements of this class in the Soviet state and the Bolshevik Party. It surfaced again in May 1918, for example, when Stalin sent to Stepan Shaumyan, the Soviet representative in Daghestan, where counter-revolutionary armed bands were then operating, instructions which made no distinction between the counter-revolutionary leaders and the peasant masses whom they had misled. These instructions were to act without hesitation and "make examples by reducing to ashes a certain number of villages."[2]

(a) The "military opposition"

After the summer of 1918, another opposition developed which had a "left-wing" look about it, and was known as the "military opposition." Not many documents have been published regarding this tendency, although it existed relatively openly and included among its avowed supporters such men as Voroshilov, E. N. Yaroslavsky, A. Z. Kamensky and S. Milin, some of whom were at that time—and in many cases remained—very close to Stalin.[3]

One of the points of the program of the "military opposition" was refusal to accept the recruitment of military specialists to the Red Army. Stalin, though he made no public declaration favorable to the "military opposition," took decisions in 1918 on the Tsaritsyn front, where he was in charge politically, which corresponded to the line of this group, removing a number of officers from their posts in violation of the instructions of the Revolutionary War Council of the Republic and those of the CEC and the CC. As a result of these measures, Stalin was eventually himself removed from his position on the Revolutionary War Council of the Southern Front, while S. N. Sytin, whom Stalin had wanted to deprive of his command, was confirmed in his appointment. It is known, too, that Lenin spoke out severely at the Eighth Party Congress (in an unpublished speech) against decisions of the Revolutionary War Council of the Tenth Army, taken at the instigation of the "military opposition," which had resulted in serious losses by the Red forces.[4]

By and large, however, this opposition played only a comparatively minor role. Its importance was mainly symptomatic. The way it functioned shows that at that time there were, within the party apparatus, elements which were sufficiently well-organized to be able to oppose, for a certain period at least, the decisions of the CC and the Soviet government.

(b) The Eighth Congress and the new party program

During the preparations for the Eighth Congress some parts of the earlier "platform" of the "left Communists" continued to be defended by a small number of members who had belonged to that group. Among them was V. Smirnov.[5]

Other well-known Bolsheviks, such as Osinsky and Sapronov, defended similar positions.

At the Eighth Party Congress (March 18–23, 1919), Osinsky demanded that workers be brought on to the Central Committee in sufficient numbers to "proletarianize" it: four years later, Lenin was to make a similar proposal. At the same congress, Sapronov and Osinsky called for the soviets to function more democratically, instead of being reduced to the role of mere organs of ratification ("rubber stamps"). These views were rejected by the congress which declared, on the contrary, for a high degree of administrative centralization. This was the congress which set up the Politburo, the Orgburo, and the Central Committee secretariat.

The Eighth Congress adopted a new party program, in which Point 5 of the economic section read:

The organised apparatus of social production must primarily depend upon the trade unions . . . Inasmuch as the trade unions are already (as specified in the laws of the Soviet Republic and as realised in practice) participants in all the local and central organs administering industry, they must proceed to the practical concentration into their own hands of the work of administration in the whole economic life of the country, making this their unified economic aim . . . The participation of the trade unions in the conduct of economic life, and the involvement by them of the broad masses of the people in this work, would appear at the same time to be our chief aid in the campaign against the bureaucratisation of the economic apparatus of the Soviet Power.[6]

Actually, this Point 5 had no concrete effect: managers of enterprises were unwilling to allow the trade unions to interfere in management at the very moment when the party was insisting on these managers taking personal responsibility. The adoption of Point 5 seems to have been mainly an echo of the discontent which existed at that time in part of the working class regarding the increasing role played by the bourgeois technicians, engineers, and administrators. The principle set forth in Point 5 was later, moreover, to be viewed as reflecting a "syndicalist distortion": it was to be the point of departure in a conflict between the majority of the Central Committee and one of the new oppositions, which demanded that this section of the party program be honored.

II. The year 1920 and the party crisis

It was in 1920, mainly from the time of the Ninth Party Congress (March 29–April 5), that an important political crisis broke out, a crisis that continued, growing more serious and assuming new aspects, until the Tenth Congress. March 1920 saw the appearance of a new "left" opposition in the group calling itself "Democratic Centralism." The composition of this group had little in common with that of the "left Communists," though Osinsky, Smirnov, and Sapronov were included. The "Democratic Centralism" group denounced what they saw as excessive centralization and abuse of authoritarian methods. In 1920–1921 they intervened actively in the discussion in which Trotsky and Bukharin maintained positions differing from those of Lenin, who opposed Trotsky's plan for complete subjection of the trade unions to the state machine.

(a) The position of Trotsky and Bukharin in 1920–1921

At the moment of the Ninth Congress, the majority of party members were still under the influence of the conceptions of "war communism"; they favored the adoption of measures for the "militarization of labor" and strict subordination of the trade unions to the administrative apparatus of the state. The measures in question did not, however, have the same significance or implications for all the different tendencies which existed in the Bolshevik Party and which were generally represented even in the party leadership. For some, the measures taken at this time were essentially conjunctural, whereas others saw in them decisions of "principle" which should be adhered to even after the war. These divergences gave rise to conflicts which lasted until the Tenth Congress.

In 1920 Trotsky was one of the "theoreticians" most resolutely in favor of "militarizing" labor and the trade unions. He
denied that the measures discussed by the Ninth Congress
were only circumstantial and provisional in character. He saw
in them, on the contrary, the expression of lasting needs which
pointed in the direction of transforming the trade unions into
state organs strictly subordinate to the government, with their
leaders appointed by the government and the party. Addressing the Ninth Congress, Trotsky said that "the mass of the
workers must be bound to their jobs, made liable to transfer,
told what to do, ordered about." "Before it disappears," he
declared, "state compulsion will, in the period of transition,
reach its highest degree of intensity in the organisation of
labour." In a pamphlet written for the congress, he urged that
"planned, systematic, persistent and stern struggle be waged
against desertion from labour, in particular by the publication
of black lists of labour-deserters, the formation of penal battal-
ions made up of these deserters, and, finally, their confine-
ment in concentration camps."[7] At the same congress, Trotsky
insisted that the "militarisation [of labor] is unthinkable without the militarisation of the trade unions as such, without the
establishment of a regime in which every worker feels himself
a soldier of labour who cannot dispose of himself freely; if the
order is given to transfer him, he must carry it out; if he does
not carry it out he will be a deserter who is punished. Who
looks after this? The trade union. It creates the new regime.
This is the militarisation of the working class."[8] Radek concluded a speech to the congress with an appeal to organized
labor "to overcome the bourgeois prejudice of 'freedom of
labour' so dear to the hearts of Mensheviks and compromisers
of every kind."[9] He was, however, the only speaker to use
such expressions.

The Ninth Congress did not adopt the line advocated by
Trotsky and Radek. It refused to see in coercion and militarization of the workers the supreme form of socialist organization of labor, and declared that militarization of labor could be
justified only by war conditions. Point 14 of the resolution on
"The present tasks of economic construction" said that "the

employment of entire labour armies, retaining their military organisation, can be justified only in so far as this is necessary in order to keep the army as a whole in being for military purposes."[10]

The congress thus declined to follow Trotsky in his idea of the militarization of labor and of the trade unions as measures required for the transition from capitalism to socialism. It even adopted one of the proposals of the "Democratic Centralism" group, for the setting up of a control commission charged with publicizing abuses in the use of coercion, "without regard to the position or function of the persons so incriminated." This was actually a mere sop to the demands of the group: the commission seems never to have functioned.

Throughout 1920 and early 1921, Trotsky continued to advocate the same ideas, coming increasingly into conflict with the different ideas held by Lenin. Addressing the Third All-Russia Congress of Trade Unions, Trotsky even offered a sort of apologia for forced labor, asking, for example: "Is it true that compulsory labour is always unproductive? . . . This is the most wretched and miserable liberal prejudice: chattel slavery too was productive . . . Compulsory slave labour . . . was in its time a progressive phenomenon."[11]

By this retrospective apologia for slavery, Trotsky claimed to show that resort to militarization of labor could be justified throughout an entire historical period—provided it was decided upon by the Bolshevik Party, the instrument of the proletarian dictatorship. As an advocate of state compulsion, Trotsky opposed those who wanted to allow greater independence to the trade unions, in which they saw one of the forms of expression of proletarian democracy. It is not unjustified to anticipate events at this point by quoting a passage from one of Trotsky's speeches at the Tenth Party Congress (in which, rather than attack Lenin's line, he took the Workers' Opposition as his target):

> They have come out with dangerous slogans. They have made a fetish of democratic principles. They have placed the workers' right to elect representatives above the Party. As if the Party were not entitled to assert its dictatorship even if that dictator-

ship temporarily clashed with the passing moods of the workers' democracy . . . The Party is obliged to maintain its dictatorship . . . regardless of temporary vacillations even in the working class . . . The dictatorship does not base itself at every given moment on the formal principle of a workers' democracy.[12]

The idea of an "infallible" party, situated outside the class struggle and by its mere existence guaranteeing the perpetuation of the dictatorship of the proletariat, was at that time common to Trotsky and Bukharin—hence the latter's idea of "compulsory self-discipline."[13]

According to Bukharin, the proletariat imposes discipline "on itself" through the party and the state. He represented the party as both "identical" with the proletariat and at the same time "superior" to it, which in his view justified the coercion exercised by the party upon the mass of the workers, this coercion being identified with "self-discipline." Bukharin argued along the same lines regarding state power, its various organs, and the authority of the technicians appointed by the state.

To a large extent, it will be seen, the theses of Trotsky and Bukharin were rooted in the idea of the infallibility of the party, of its superiority, "by its very nature," in relation to the masses, of the "guaranteed permanence" of its proletarian character and that of the state which it leads, whatever the party's ideological and political practices may be.

The theses of Trotsky and Bukharin implied also that the party had been assigned a new role: no longer was it a vanguard with the task of guiding the masses, while remaining alert to their initiatives and their criticisms—it now had the role of controlling and coercing the masses.

It was in his book *The Economics of the Transformation Period* that Bukharin developed in a systematic way the nondialectical conceptions on which he claimed to base his political views. Now the Bukharin who in 1918 had opposed the appointment in each enterprise of a single manager, personally responsible for the way it was run, saw in the establishment of one-man management "a *form* of proletarian administration of industry, compressed and consolidated"; and for him "the militarisation of the population . . . constitutes a method of self-organisation of the working class and organisation of the peasantry by the working class"—so that, in certain circumstances, the dictatorship of the proletariat can take the form of "a military-proletarian dictatorship."[14]

Furthermore, Bukharin saw in the distribution of rations in kind, instead of wages in money form, the disappearance of wage labor, and this, for him, justified the conscription of labor. He considered that during the period of transition the monetary system would collapse, and, with it, the commodity system in general, this being made manifest through devaluation of the currency.[15]

(b) The theses of the Workers' Opposition[16]

Whereas Trotsky was expressing support for extremely accentuated centralization and militarization, a different tendency was developing in the party. This tendency extended the ideas of the former "Democratic Centralism" group which, enlarging its membership through the entry of party members like Shlyapnikov and Alexandra Kollontai, who had not belonged to "Democratic Centralism," now took its stand on Point 5 of the economic section of the program adopted in 1919 by the Eighth Party Congress. It denounced the development of authoritarian practices in the party and in the state machine, and also the ascendancy of many bourgeois elements.

Workers' Opposition advocated a radical alteration in the party line—handing over the management of industry to the trade unions. (The expression "trade unionization of the state" was used to describe this policy.) The Workers' Opposition wanted the factory committees to play a big role, and it also called for a much more egalitarian policy on wages.[17]

As Lenin saw it, the theses of the Workers' Opposition reflected a "trade-unionist" (that is, a "syndicalist-economist") outlook alien to Marxism, which ignored the leading role of the party of the proletariat.

The theses of the Workers' Opposition were widely dis-

cussed in January and February 1921. They were published in
Pravda on January 25, and circulated in pamphlet form by
their supporters. On the eve of the Tenth Congress (March
8–16, 1921), the Workers' Opposition possessed seemingly firm footholds in the party organizations in a number of
industrial areas—Moscow, the Donets Basin, etc.—but it was a
minority in the party as a whole, and poorly represented at the
congress.

(c) Lenin's fight against the ideas of Trotsky and Bukharin

During the months leading up to the Tenth Party Congress,
a huge political battle was waged. One of the first episodes in
this battle took place on November 8–9, 1920, at meetings of
the Bolshevik faction at the Fifth Trade Union Conference
and in the Central Committee. Trotsky said that it was necessary to continue applying the measures that had been taken
during the civil war, and even to extend them, regardless of the
fact that they had been emergency measures. He defended the
view that the Soviet state should be able to remove from their
posts, by a simple decision from "above," those trade-union
leaders whose ideas on problems of discipline and wages
differed from the ideas of the majority in the Central Committee. He thus declared in favor of "statization of the trade-
unions," aimed at turning the latter into instruments for increasing production and the productivity of labor. He wished
to see reasserted, even in the new conditions that were emerging at the end of 1920, the right to replace any trade-union
leaders who did not agree that the task of the trade unions was
to serve production.

On November 8, 1920, Trotsky clashed with Lenin, who
recalled that the measures adopted by the Ninth Congress had
been exceptional in character and that the new features of the
situation, which was no longer dominated by war emergencies, must be taken into account. Lenin's view carried the day
by a narrow margin. By eight votes to six, Trotsky's view was
defeated and Lenin's resolution adopted. This resolution de-

clared that "a gradual but steady transition must be effected
from urgency procedures to a more even distribution of
forces," and that it was necessary to "extend to the entire trade
union movement those methods of the broader application of
democracy, the promotion of initative, participation in the
management of industry, the development of emulation, and
so forth . . . "[18]

The Central Committee adopted a resolution directed
against the positions supported by Trotsky. This condemned
"the degeneration of centralisation and the militarising of
labour into bureaucracy, arrogance, petty functionarism and
pestering interference in the trade unions." A commission was
set up to study relations between the party and the trade
unions, with Zinoviev as rapporteur.[19]

The divergences in the Central Committee reached such a
pitch that it was decided, at the beginning of December 1920,
to open a broad public discussion. The entire party leadership—Lenin, Trotsky, Bukharin, Zinoviev, Stalin, Shlyapnikov, and many others—took part in the discussion.

Important episodes in the political battle included two
meetings held in December 1920. On December 24, Trotsky
spoke to a gigantic gathering of trade unionists and delegates
to the Eighth All-Russia Congress of Soviets. Six days later, a
meeting took place at which several party leaders spoke, including Lenin, Zinoviev, Trotsky, Bukharin, and Shlyapnikov: the speeches were published in 1921 under the title
The Role of the Trade Unions in Production. A week after this
second great meeting, Zinoviev addressed another gathering
in Petrograd.[20] Throughout January 1921, *Pravda* published
nearly every day an article about the problems of militarizing
labor and "statizing" the trade unions.

Gradually, Lenin's arguments (which were supported in
this discussion by Zinoviev and Stalin), together with the
evolution of the objective situation itself, weakened the position of the group represented by eight members of the Central
Committee (Trotsky, Bukharin, Andreyev, Dzerzhinsky, Krestinsky, Preobrazhensky, Rakovsky, and Serebryakov). They
found themselves no longer supported by more than a dwin-
dling minority, while the Workers' Opposition took up attitudes

which were radically opposed to Trotsky's—but which were not in accordance with Lenin's views, either.

The battle of the winter of 1920–1921 provided the occasion for Lenin to denounce the dogmatic stereotypes which Trotsky and Bukharin were employing to "justify" their positions. Lenin thus broke openly with a problematic which was not merely that of Trotsky and Bukharin, but which had implicitly also been that of nearly the entire party, namely, the problematic which identified the Soviet state with a "workers' state."

In December 1920, without as yet carrying through this break to completion, and without using the formulations he was to produce later, Lenin set forth a certain number of basic propositions. The most important of these criticized the one-sided character of the theses of Trotsky and Bukharin, which "reduced" the Soviet state to a "workers' state", whereas the real nature of the Soviet state was extremely complex.[21]

The nature of this state was such as to oblige the workers to have organizations of their own which were sufficiently independent of the party in power to be able to "protect the workers from their state."[22] About a year later, Lenin returned to this problem, when, on January 12, 1922, he put before the Central Committee a resolution (which was adopted unanimously) on "The role and functions of the trade unions under the New Economic Policy."[23] The resolution pointed out that there could be an "antagonism of interest" between the working class and the management of Soviet state enterprises, and that "strike struggle" might be justified by the necessity facing the workers of combating bureaucratic distortions and survivals from the capitalist past.[24]

Lenin's fight against the line of Trotsky and Bukharin (and of some other leaders of the Bolshevik Party) is of substantial importance. It shows that the divergences between Lenin and those two members of the Political Bureau were based on what he called "our different *approach* to the mass, the different way of winning it over and *keeping in touch* with it."[25]

The discussion brought to light divergences that went even deeper, affecting, at bottom, the whole question of what was meant by the dictatorship of the proletariat. Trotsky and

Bukharin conceived the Soviet state in a mistakenly abstract way, as being, so to speak, the "pure expression" of proletarian dictatorship, whereas Lenin sought to elucidate the *dual nature* of the Soviet state, a "workers' state" insofar as it was led by a proletarian party (and insofar as this party remained proletarian), yet also a "bourgeois or petty-bourgeois state" by virtue of a number of its features—its dependence on bourgeois administrators, technicians, and specialists, and the political relations that largely prevailed in the work of its administrative organs. Lenin did not shrink from adding that the "workers' state," in the true sense, was "an ideal we shall achieve in 15 or 20 years' time, and I am not sure that we shall have achieved it by then" [26]—the prospect of achieving it being dependent, of course, on the disappearance of those features which made it impossible to call the Soviet state of 1921 a workers' state.

This discussion gave Lenin the opportunity to recall that the fundamental problem of the dictatorship of the proletariat is that of the struggle to consolidate proletarian power—and, therefore, the struggle to win the masses—and not, as Trotsky maintained, the struggle for production. In his pamphlet *Once Again on the Trade Unions,* Lenin made this observation, the significance of which transcends by far the limits of the particular polemic of that period: "Trotsky and Bukharin make as though they are concerned for the growth of production, whereas we have nothing but formal democracy in mind. This picture is wrong, because the *only* formulation of the issue (which the Marxist standpoint *allows*) is: without a correct political approach to the matter the given class will be unable to stay on top, *and, consequently,* will be incapable of solving its *production problem* either." [27]

Notes

1. This telegram was sent to the Soviet government by N. A. Skryp-nik, head of the Soviet government of the Ukraine, on April 6, 1918. It was mentioned by the old Bolshevik A. V. Snegov during

a discussion organized by the Institute of Marxism-Leninism on June 26–28, 1966, and is quoted in Roy Medvedev, *Let History Judge*, p. 16.

2. Reproduced in *Pravda*, September 20, 1963.
3. D. Yu. Zorina wrote, a few years ago, an article which has remained unpublished, "On the Problem of the Military Opposition." See Medvedev, *Let History Judge*, p. 15.
4. See Medvedev, *Let History Judge*, pp. 14–16, n. 26–28.
5. Smirnov and other former "left Communists" were among the accused in the trials of 1936–1937—alongside others who in 1918–1920 were among the chief opponents of the views advocated by that group.
6. *K.P.S.S. v Rezolyutsiyakh*, vol. I, p. 422 (translated in appendix to Bukharin and Preobrazhensky, *The ABC of Communism*, p. 447).
7. Trotsky, *Sochineniya*, vol. 15, pp. 126, 132, 138.
8. Report of the Ninth Party Congress, 1934 ed., p. 101; quoted in Carr, *The Bolshevik Revolution*, vol. 2, pp. 214–215.
9. This part of Radek's speech was published in *Izvestiya* of April 2, 1920. It is not without interest to note (as does Carr, *The Bolshevik Revolution*, vol. 2, p. 215) that Radek's speech was not included in the official report of the congress, on the pretext that it would be published as a separate pamphlet (see congress report, p. 277). Actually, no such pamphlet ever saw the light.
10. *K.P.S.S. v Rezolyutsiyakh*, vol. I, pp. 487–488.
11. Congress report, published in Moscow in 1920, pp. 84–97; quoted in Brinton, *The Bolsheviks & Workers' Control*, p. 64.
12. Quoted in the footnotes of Kollontai, *The Workers' Opposition*.
13. Bukharin, *Economics of the Transformation Period*, p. 156.
14. Ibid., pp. 128–129.
15. Ibid., p. 146.
16. Some of Lenin's criticisms of these theses are considered later.
17. Report of the Tenth Party Congress, appendix 2, pp. 789–793 (Shlyapnikov, speech of December 30, 1920, on the organization of the economy and the tasks of the trade unions), quoted in Brinton, *The Bolsheviks and Workers' Control*, pp. 72–73.
18. *CW*, vol. 31, pp. 374–375.
19. Broué, *Le Parti bolchévique*, p. 141.
20. Carr, *The Bolshevik Revolution*, vol. 2, pp. 224 ff.
21. On this point see "The Trade Unions, the Present Situation, and Trotsky's Mistakes," in *CW*, vol. 32, pp. 19 ff., especially pp. 24–25.
22. Ibid., p. 25.

23. *CW*, vol. 33, pp. 184 ff.
24. Ibid., pp. 185, 187.
25. *CW*, vol. 32, p. 22.
26. Ibid., p. 24.
27. Ibid., p. 84.

4. The ideological and political struggles at the end of "war communism" and the beginning of the NEP

The struggles that developed in the Bolshevik Party during the winter of 1920–1921 mark a turning point in the party's history, on two accounts. On the one hand, a certain way of seeing the problem of relations between the party and the trade unions, reflecting the practice of "war communism," which the groups headed by Trotsky and Bukharin wanted to treat as a "principle," ceased to be officially approved after the Tenth Congress. This did not mean that the practices underlying this conception disappeared altogether: nevertheless, they were now on the downgrade, and were no longer defended in the name of the alleged "demands" of the proletarian dictatorship. During the five year plans, however, ideas similar to Trotsky's were to reappear, especially those concerning the "productionist" and "disciplinary" tasks considered as the essential functions of the trade unions.

On the other hand, the Tenth Congress was the last to have been preceded by a broad, open discussion. At subsequent congresses, the various oppositions would not be allowed to express themselves with such freedom, which meant a break with the Bolshevik tradition. Increasingly, the means of expression were to be withdrawn from opposition tendencies, in the end disappearing altogether.

I. The Tenth Congress of the Bolshevik Party and the close of the debate with the two oppositions of 1920

The diversity of the tendencies which clashed in the period preceding the Tenth Congress testified to the magnitude of

395

the ideological struggles in the Bolshevik Party and the depth of the crisis it was undergoing. When preparations for the congress began in December 1920, there were seven distinct "platforms," and at the congress two organized tendencies were still opposing the theses maintained by Lenin.[1]

After extensive discussion, the Workers' Opposition succeeded in drawing up a document which received the support of related tendencies, while Trotsky and Bukharin, on their side, had also worked out a joint statement which was backed by eight members of the Central Committee (so that the motion they put before the congress was called "the motion of the eight"). The majority of the Central Committee held the same views as Lenin, and the motion reflecting their views was called "the motion of the ten": among its backers were Stalin, Tomsky, Zinoviev, and Kamenev.

The Tenth Congress put an end to the debate between the Central Committee majority and the two main opposition tendencies. Eighteen delegates voted for the Workers' Opposition motion, 50 for that of "the eight," while "the motion of the ten" received 336 votes.[2] The hardest fight at the congress was waged against the Workers' Opposition, as the line of "the eight" had already been plentifully criticized in the previous months.

(a) The rejection of the Workers' Opposition theses

During the Tenth Congress, especially lively attacks were directed against the ideas of the Workers' Opposition, which up to that time had benefited to some extent from the criticism aimed at Trotsky's ideas, that is, at tendencies to authoritarianism, administrative solutions, and "productionism," and from the confusion caused by certain formulations of Bukharin's, which sought to build a bridge between Trotsky's line and that of the Workers' Opposition by calling both for "statization of the trade unions" and "trade-unionization of the state."[3]

Originally, some of the Workers' Opposition theses represented, as Lenin acknowledged, a healthy reaction against the authoritarian tendencies which had developed during "war communism," and reflected the genuine aspirations of broad sections of the working class. But the Workers' Opposition systematized these aspirations in a one-sided way, ignoring the contradictions between the working class and the peasantry, and it carried its formulations beyond the point at which they squared with what was needed to consolidate the dictatorship of the proletariat. This opposition also "forgot," no less than did Trotsky and Bukharin, the fundamental problem, that of power, which requires that maximum attention be paid to what Lenin rightly called "the revolutionary interest" to which "formal democracy must be subordinate."[4] Despite appearances, the theses of Trotsky and those of the Workers' Opposition both advocated an orientation which, if adopted, would, in the given situation, have led "to the collapse of the Soviet power" through failure to take account of the totality of concretely existing class relations.[5]

There were also other reasons for the severity of the defeat suffered at the Tenth Congress by the Workers' Opposition. The very preparations for the congress had been carried out in a highly "administrative" fashion; the weight in the party of bourgeois and "bureaucratized" elements was considerable, and was reflected in the number of votes cast for the theses of Trotsky and Bukharin; and many wavering delegates were anxious to contribute to party unity at a difficult moment by voting for the motion of the Central Committee majority.

The need to take account of "the revolutionary interest" was one of the chief arguments used by Zinoviev against that part of the program of the Workers' Opposition which called for the convening of an All-Russia Supreme Congress of Producers. Zinoviev pointed out that, at such a congress, "the majority *at this grave moment* will be non-party people, a good many of them S.R.s and Mensheviks,"[6] and the task of the hour was to win over the non-party mass organizations in support of the Soviet power.

The platform of "the ten" recognized that, in principle, some of the demands included in that of the Workers' Opposition were correct—for example, the point about the need for greater equality in wage levels—but considered that these demands corresponded to long-term objectives which could not be regarded as immediate aims. The platform of "the ten" also rejected the statization of the trade unions called for by Trotsky. It reaffirmed the necessity for the party to play a leading role in trade-union work: "The Russian Communist Party continues unconditionally to direct, through its central and local organisations, all the ideological side of trade-union work . . . Selection of the leading personnel of the trade-union movement must take place under the Party's guiding supervision. However, the Party organisation must be especially attentive to the applying of normal methods of proletarian democracy in the trade unions, where the selection of leaders must, above all, be made by the organised masses themselves."[7]

While the theses of the Workers' Opposition had been extensively discussed before the congress, this was no longer the case during its actual sessions. It was the moment when the Kronstadt crisis occurred, which revealed that the main task of the moment was to settle correctly the problem of relations with the peasantry. Lenin therefore spoke principally about this problem, confining himself, where the platform of the Workers' Opposition was concerned, to an essentially polemical attack, in which he compared it to the policies of the anarchists and syndicalists. He also seemed to threaten the Workers' Opposition in an indirect way, as when he said: "We have spent quite a lot of time in discussion, and I must say that the point is now being driven farther home with 'rifles' than with the opposition's theses. Comrades, this is no time to have an opposition. Either you're on this side or on the other, but then your weapon must be a gun, and not an opposition. This follows from the objective situation, and you mustn't blame us for it."[8]

Soon afterward, Lenin had to explain that when he spoke of "countering it with rifles," he did not at all mean carrying on a "discussion" in that way with the Workers' Opposition, but with the declared enemies of the party. Furthermore, later on in the debate Lenin several times praised what he regarded as sound in some of the proposals of the Workers' Opposition.[9]

(h) The resolution on party unity

As regards the subject of ideological conflict within the Bolshevik Party, the Tenth Congress was of major importance, for it passed a resolution laying down new rules which prohibited factions. In principle, this resolution forbade the formation within the party of groups organized on the basis of a "platform" and having their own internal discipline, that is, tending to constitute a sort of party within the party. The ban was adopted as a temporary measure justified by exceptionally difficult circumstances.[10] Any party member, including any member of the Central Committee, who acted in violation of this resolution, could be expelled by decision of the Central Committee. This was an extremely severe penalty, putting exceptional power into the hands of the majority in the CC. Application of it would enable a CC, after being elected by a party congress, to alter its own composition.

Commenting on this provision of the "unity resolution," Lenin said: "Our Party has never allowed the Central Committee to have such a right in relation to its members. This is an extreme measure that is being adopted specially, in view of the dangerous situation. A special meeting is called: the Central Committee, plus the alternate members, plus the Control Commission, all having the same right to vote. Our rules make no provision for such a body or plenum of 47 persons; and never has anything like it been practised."[11]

The circumstances in which the party was to function after Lenin's death would enable this resolution to be used as a means of preventing the expression of opinions diverging from those of the Political Bureau and the party secretariat, thereby completely altering the conditions under which ideological struggles could be carried on in the party.

This outcome contradicted a number of provisions contained in the resolution on party unity, which did not con-

demn internal party disputes and even allowed for the publishing of a periodical, *Discussion Bulletin*. Lenin's speeches
at the Tenth Congress show, too, that he recommended that in
the event of "disagreement on fundamental issues," this
should be settled by "appeal to the Party," and also that, when
a party congress proved unable to arrive at a satisfactory degree of unity, elections to the Central Committee be carried
out "according to platforms," so that the main rival tendencies
should secure representation thereon.[12]

In practice, despite what was said at the Tenth Congress,
the "unity resolution" was to become the point of departure
for increasing restrictions on open ideological struggles
within the party: the *Discussion Bulletin* was never published. Gradually, after Lenin's death, the majority in the CC
or the Politburo, or even the party secretariat, were to claim a
monopoly of correct conceptions and the right to decide what
might or might not be really discussed in the party.

In another way, too, the Tenth Congress limited the possibility of open ideological debate, for it considerably reduced
the authority of the CC, which was precisely where extensive
and thorough discussion took place. From this time onward, in
fact, the Central Committee ceased to be the party's supreme
body between congresses. The intervals between its meetings
were made longer: henceforth, it was to meet only once every
two months, and its powers were in practice delegated to the
Political Bureau, which, beginning in 1921, had only seven
members. Inside the Political Bureau itself the dominant position was increasingly held by representatives of the party's
administrative apparatus, those who headed the secretariat,
the assignments office, and so on. Thus, the Political Bureau,
which had formerly been a mere executive organ of the Central Committee, was transformed into the supreme body of the
party, closely linked with the administrative apparatus and the
secretariat of the Central Committee, whose own powers were
greatly increased.

The Tenth Congress thus marked in more than one way the
close of the debates of the last phase of "war communism": by
its condemnation of the theses of the two oppositions, and by

the de facto restrictions it imposed on open discussion inside the Bolshevik Party. It was in a deeper sense, however, that this congress constituted the end of one period and the beginning of another, for it set in motion the New Economic Policy (NEP),[13] the principal features of which were abandonment of the requisitioning of agricultural produce, a tax in kind being substituted for this, and the introduction of a certain amount of freedom of trade between agriculture and industry. Gradually, the application of the NEP altered the political atmosphere by enabling the bourgeoisie and petty bourgeoisie to develop a variety of private activities which contributed, among other things, to aggravating an economic inequality which bore especially heavily upon the working class and the poor peasants.

Under the influence of the changed political atmosphere connected with the NEP, and also, and especially, as a result of the changes made in the Bolshevik Party, open ideological struggle within the party gradually disappeared. Increasingly, these struggles took place only among the top leaders of the party, inside the Political Bureau—in some cases, perhaps, in the Central Committee, but without the participation of the party members or cadres as a whole.

Before saying something about the "undeclared" ideological and political struggles which marked the early period of the NEP, before Lenin's death, it is desirable to indicate some of the limits to the disagreements between the party majority and the Workers' Opposition, and to recall the issues which at that time underlay all the ideological and political conflicts in the party.

II. The limited nature of the disagreements between the party majority and the Workers' Opposition

Of all the ideological struggles that took place in the Bolshevik Party between 1918 and 1921, the most significant, both in its implications and in its limitations, was the one aroused by the theses of the Workers' Opposition. The implications of these theses were considerable, in that they raised a number of absolutely fundamental questions. The Workers' Opposition pointed to the grave dangers threatening Russia's socialist future as a result of the increased powers enjoyed by bourgeois specialists and administrators. It fought for the granting of broad rights of initiative to the workers and for greater trust to be shown in relation to them, with the establishment of forms of organization such as would allow the workers really to develop their own initiative. It called for an effective struggle against the tendencies for the administrative apparatuses to acquire independence and to dominate the masses. It declared for freedom of criticism in the party, and for the working people as a whole, especially for the workers and their trade unions. It demanded that all party members engage regularly in productive manual labor and that inequality in wage levels, which had been intensified during "war communism," be reduced.

These theses of the Workers' Opposition repeated to a large extent the ideas expounded by Lenin in his "April Theses" and in *The State and Revolution*. They voiced the aspirations of part of the Soviet working class and expressed some of the requirements for the revolution's progress toward socialism.

They were presented at a particularly difficult moment, during the social and political crisis of the winter of 1920–1921, the moment of Kronstadt—that is, when forces objectively hostile to the dictatorship of the proletariat and liable to be directly used by imperialism were intervening openly in the political situation, and were formulating demands which seemed to coincide, partly at least, with the theses of the Workers' Opposition. It was undoubtedly this conjuncture which caused Lenin to take up a particularly stern attitude toward the Workers' Opposition and to refrain from according a thorough critical examination to its theses.

It is enough to read what Lenin said at the Tenth Congress to see how far this congress was overshadowed by the

Kronstadt events, and the extent to which the Workers' Opposition was blamed for putting its theses forward precisely at that moment. Thus, in his speech of March 9, 1921, Lenin, addressing his remarks to the Workers' Opposition, said: "You have come to the Party Congress with Comrade Kollontai's pamphlet which is entitled *The Workers' Opposition*. When you sent in the final proofs, you knew about the Kronstadt events and the rising petty-bourgeois counter-revolution. And it is at a time like this that you come here, calling yourselves a Workers' Opposition. You don't seem to realise the responsibility you are undertaking, and the way you are disrupting our unity!"[14]

Shortly after saying this, Lenin went even further, practically identifying the Workers' Opposition with the anarchists and syndicalists, who did not accept the necessity for Communist leadership if the proletarian dictatorship was to be preserved. This certainly failed to correspond to anything actually said by the Workers' Opposition; but it did correspond to the conclusions that could be drawn from their theses, if the "logic" of these theses were pushed to its ultimate conclusion.

Independently of the conjuncture, however, other factors relative to the *content* of the theses considerably restricted their effective significance. In the first place, they lacked theoretical articulation. Even when they expressed fundamental concerns, and dealt with questions which must be answered if the revolution was to advance toward socialism, they were not argued in a well-grounded way. They were not founded upon a rigorous analysis of the relations between the economic base and the superstructure, between productive forces and production relations. Furthermore (like the theses of the majority), they practically ignored the decisive problem of the conditions for a genuine political alliance with the peasantry. In the case of the theses of the Workers' Opposition this was a particularly grave weakness, as the increased role which this opposition claimed for the workers' trade unions might easily lead, through giving priority to the satisfaction of the workers' demands, to a deep split with the peasantry. In this respect the Workers' Opposition took up an *ouvriériste* position which was incompatible with the leading role of the proletariat, especially in a country where the majority of the people were peasants.

On the whole, the theses of the Workers' Opposition voiced aspirations which were partly correct, but they did not constitute a break with the elements of economism that still remained in the Bolshevik Party's overall positions: this was their major weakness in relation to defense of the proletarian dictatorship and the leading role that the party of the proletariat must necessarily play in that defense.

Concretely, the theses of the Workers' Opposition included contradictions which considerably reduced their impact. Thus, on the one hand, they demanded that the producers' trade unions should play a directing role in the economy (which opened the way to "syndicalist" practice that gave primacy not to the proletariat's overall policy but, instead, to the interests of separate sections or trades), while, on the other, they denounced, and with reason, the "bureaucratization" which had taken place in Soviet trade unionism during the period of "war communism." This caused Lenin to comment, when speaking of the Workers' Opposition theses presented by Sapronov: "The 'Sapronovites' have gone so far as to insist in the same thesis (3) on a 'profound crisis' and a 'bureaucratic necrosis' of the trade unions, while proposing, as being 'absolutely' necessary, the 'extension of the trade unions' *rights* in production' . . . probably because of their 'bureaucratic necrosis'? Can this group be taken seriously?"[15]

The principal weakness of the theses of the Workers' Opposition lay, as has been said, in their failure to tackle the problem of the basic conditions for maintaining and strengthening the dictatorship of the proletariat—the problem of the leading role of the proletarian party and that of the specific relations between this party and the masses as a whole. This needs to be made clear by a closer examination of some of the concrete questions that were taken up during the discussion at the Tenth Congress.

(a) The problem of the "mode of appointment" of cadres and functionaries

Implicit in the dispute between the Workers' Opposition and the CC majority was the question of the relations of mutual trust that ought to exist between the Bolshevik Party and the masses as a whole, if the party was to be able to fulfill its leading role correctly. Instead of taking up this problem in an explicit way, however, the CC majority and the Workers' Opposition argued about the mode of appointment of the leading personnel in the political, administrative, and economic spheres. As the CC majority saw it, the party could not really carry out its leading role unless a substantial proportion of the leading personnel, in the trade union as elsewhere, were appointed by the party. As the Workers' Opposition saw it, only the election of such personnel was in conformity with socialist principles and would guarantee the confidence of the masses in the leaders they had chosen.

By discussing the question in this way the Workers' Opposition refused to analyze, first of all, the actual situation. Moreover, by imprisoning itself in the ideological issue of "election versus appointment from above," it remained captive to the politico-juridical ideology of the bourgeoisie, and so was prevented from raising in a clear-cut way the true problem of the concrete relations which, in a given situation, ought to prevail between the party and the masses.

In order to understand what lay behind the proposals of the Workers' Opposition, it is helpful to recall that they continued the line of the various "left" oppositions which had appeared in the Bolshevik Party since early 1918. These oppositions commonly referred to Lenin's own words in defense of the "principle" of electing all functionaries, as when he said: "All officials, without exception, elected and subject to recall *at any time,* their salaries reduced to the level of ordinary 'workmen's wages'—these simple and 'self-evident' democratic measures, while completely uniting the interests of the workers and the majority of the peasants, at the same time serve as a bridge leading from capitalism to socialism."[16]

Now, already at the Ninth Party Congress (March 29–April 5), Lenin had rejected the views of those who referred to his previous statements, as he considered the latter to be inapplicable in the existing conditions, and even incompatible with the lessons of two years in power. He said that after "two years of experience" it was impossible to discuss certain problems as if they were being encountered for the first time: "We committed follies enough in and around the Smolny period. That is nothing to be ashamed of. How were we to know, seeing that we were undertaking something absolutely new?"[17]

In that same report presented to the Ninth Congress on behalf of the Central Committee (March 29, 1920), Lenin attacked those who advocated collective management and election of cadres and leading personnel, in the trade unions or other apparatuses, saying: "All these outcries against appointees, all this old and dangerous rubbish which finds its way into various resolutions and conversations must be swept away. Otherwise we cannot succeed. If we have failed to master this lesson in these two years, we are lagging, and those who lag get beaten."[18]

In reality, what was concealed behind this pseudoproblem of "election versus appointment from above" was a real problem, namely, that of consulting the masses—not only appealing for their suggestions but also, and above all, for their criticisms. Only such consultation and such seeking for criticism can enable the party to concentrate the initiatives and indications coming from the masses, so as to arrive at conclusions conforming to the general interests of the proletarian dictatorship.

The real problem, in fact, is not that of the "mode of appointment" but that of the actual, concrete relationship between the party, the machinery of state, and the masses. And the nature of this relationship is not basically determined by the "mode of appointment" of the persons making up the staff of the state machine. It depends upon a set of social practices, and the ideological relationships developing through these practices.

At the beginning of 1921 Lenin was trying harder and harder to find a basis for considering this problem other than that defined by the contrast between appointment from above and election. He saw clearly the need to open up new opportunities of expression for the aspirations of the masses, and he knew very well that, if such expression was kept within the forms of bourgeois democracy, there was serious danger of a bourgeois political offensive developing by way of the activity of the Mensheviks, SRs, and anarchists. It was in order to change the basis on which the problem was approached, to get away from the issue of "appointment from above versus election," that Lenin envisaged numerous conferences of non-party people. These conferences were to enable the Bolsheviks to hear the criticisms of the masses, to *take account* of these criticisms, and to answer them in a practical way. Early in 1921, for example, Lenin wrote, replying to some Bolsheviks who were afraid that such conferences of non-party people might turn out to favor the Mensheviks and SRs: "Non-Party conferences are *not* an absolute political weapon of the Mensheviks and Socialist-Revolutionaries plus anarchists." [19]

Actually, as a result of the worsening of the political and economic situation, especially through the famine of 1921, the final text of Lenin's pamphlet on the tax in kind was much more reserved than his first draft had been, when the question of conferences of non-party people was concerned—precisely because of the continuing influence of the Mensheviks and SRs, especially among the peasant masses. Thus, Lenin said in this pamphlet:

> The Mensheviks and Socialist-Revolutionaries have now learned to don the "non-Party" disguise. This has been fully proved. Only fools now fail to see this and understand that we must not allow ourselves to be fooled. Non-Party conferences are not a fetish. They are valuable if they help us to come closer to the impassive masses—the millions of working people still outside politics. They are harmful if they provide a platform for the Mensheviks and Socialist-Revolutionaries masquerading as "non-party" men. [20]

In practice, then, owing to the extreme difficulties that marked the end of "war communism," and the recrudescence of the activities of the petty bourgeois parties which was facilitated by these difficulties, the Bolshevik Party in 1921 did not take the path of a broad campaign of discussion among the masses and systematic listening to their criticisms.

(b) The acquisition of independence by the machinery of state and the concepts of efficiency and inefficiency

Another ideological "pair of opposites" helped to define in the wrong way the ground on which discussion and thinking developed concerning the acquisition of independence by the machinery of state. This was "efficiency versus inefficiency." The conduct of the argument in these terms tended to reduce a problem that was fundamentally *political* to the level of a *technical* problem. In the main, the case for a certain degree of independence for the administrative apparatus of the state was based, more or less, on the concept of "technical efficiency," and most of those in the party who were opposed to this independence also put forward considerations relating to the concept of efficiency.

Outwardly, the Workers' Opposition tended to break through the circle in which discussion and thinking about these problems had been confined up to that time, when it declared that the political problem of the relations between the organs of power and the mass of the workers could not be solved either by absorbing the trade unions into the state machine (which was the proposal of Trotsky and Bukharin) or by saying that one must wait until the masses were sufficiently "educated" before it would be possible to restore life to the Soviet institutions.[21]

The Workers' Opposition rightly denounced the illusions which postponed the return to Soviet democracy to a distant future—to the day when the masses had become better "educated": educated by whom?—but they were not able to show the road to self-education of the masses, to the training of the masses through their own mistakes, under conditions that would not lead to a rapid restoration of the dictatorship of the bourgeoisie and imperialist domination. In fact, the Workers' Opposition remained on the ground of "economism," the "spontaneist" form which suggests that the proletariat's position in production "generates" spontaneously proletarian class consciousness in this class, thereby, in effect, "dodging" the whole problem of education and self-education. Contrary to certain appearances, here again the Workers' Opposition, by not abandoning a certain form of "economism," took its stand on the same ground as the CC majority, even though it came, at the given moment, to different practical conclusions.

At the end of "war communism," the Bolshevik Party hoped that the masses would be drawn back into the working of Soviet democracy in a spontaneous way, through the recovery of production and the development of exchange. This hope expressed a certain "economism" from which Lenin himself was not entirely free when, instead of explaining the acquisition of independence by the state machine and the development of bureaucracy by the totality of social relations and the bourgeois class struggle, he saw in it a result of the economic situation itself, that is, a consequence of the disorganization of exchange, of want,[22] and so forth. Such an analysis could suggest that a "withering away" of bureaucracy would ensue from a recovery of production, centralization of production, a campaign against illiteracy, etc. This was not, of course, Lenin's point of view: he explicitly associated the existence of bureaucracy with petty commodity economy and the existence of bourgeois and petty bourgeois elements, and treated as "quacks" those who claimed to attack bureaucracy without attacking its social foundations.[23] Nevertheless, some of Lenin's writings were interpreted subsequently in a narrowly "economist" sense, especially by the Trotskyists, who claimed to "explain" the existence of "bureaucracy" by the "low level of development of the productive forces."

To return to the Workers' Opposition, it can be said that its defeat resulted principally from the extreme limitedness of its proposals, its incapacity (due, no doubt, to "spontaneity-worshipping *ouvriérisme*," and to lack of sufficient experience) to open up a truly new road of political struggle that would enter into the play of the contradictions and ensure a strengthening of the proletarian dictatorship. This limitedness and this incapacity, which were shared by other Bolshevik leaders, helped block the path to the attempts made later (especially by Lenin) to improve the party's practice in the direction of a mass line, so as to draw the peasants on to the road to socialism. The "left" oppositions which appeared later on showed themselves, in this respect, still more backward than the Workers' Opposition. The door was thus opened for an offensive by right opportunism, though this did not come forward in a clearly-defined shape.

Before considering this last point, let us recall what was ultimately at stake in the ideological and political struggles going on in the Bolshevik Party.

III. The issue involved in the ideological and political struggles in the Bolshevik Party

The historical experience of proletarian parties, especially of the Bolshevik Party and the Chinese Communist Party, shows that what is involved in the disagreements that arise in such parties (even when the differences seem to be concerned only with "shades of opinion") is the working out of a correct political line that can enable the working class to conquer and then to consolidate its ideological and political hegemony. In the long run, it is the proletarian character of the party itself that is at issue. And this character can be lastingly maintained only if the ideological unity of the party is based on the principles of revolutionary Marxism, and if the party, in its functioning, respects these principles, thus constituting a revolutionary vanguard supported by the working masses. The ideological unity of a proletarian revolutionary party cannot long survive mistakes in its political line: a party which over a long period follows a nonproletarian line must eventually be forced to deny the principles it swears by, and lose the support of the advanced elements of the proletariat and the masses.

However, a wide discussion aimed at drawing the lessons of the results practically achieved through actually applying the political line is essential in order to determine (especially when no previous experience is available) the more or the less correct aspects of the line that has been followed, and the rectifications the line requires in view of the experience acquired and the changes that have occurred in the objective situation. This discussion is needed because there is no "recipe" stating a priori that a certain measure or a certain slogan does or does not serve the basic interests of the proletariat—except where obvious violations of the principles of revolutionary Marxism are concerned. Only a thorough study of reality, of practice, and of the contending theses enables the party to decide correctly how to solve the problems posed by the concrete elaboration of a correct line and by the practical application of this line. Only respect for democratic centralism—provided that democracy is its dominant aspect —can enable those who, though they uphold correct conceptions, are in the minority, to make themselves heard, if they themselves dare to "go against the tide."

A given political line is proletarian in character only if it does not violate the principles of revolutionary Marxism: but it must also correspond effectively to the needs of the actual situation, thus making it possible to deal correctly—from the standpoint of the proletariat—with the principal contradiction in the particular situation prevailing, and with the secondary contradictions which are subordinate to this one.

In a situation which is evolving quickly, a political line or slogan that was correct at a particular moment may become wrong quite soon afterward. For example, the slogan "All Power to the Soviets" was a correct slogan from February 27 until July 4, 1917, in a period when armed counter-revolution presented no threat. It ceased to be correct after July 4 when, as Lenin wrote, "the counter-revolutionary bourgeoisie, working hand in glove with the monarchists and the Black Hundreds, secured the support of the petty-bourgeois Socialist-Revolutionaries and Mensheviks, partly by intimidating them, and handed over real power to the Cavaignacs, the military gang . . . "[24] What applies to a particular slogan or measure applies also to the concrete political line of a party. This line can be revolutionary and proletarian only if it corresponds to the needs of the actual situation. Accordingly, when the situation changes—when, for example, a period of civil war gives way to a period of peaceful construction—appropriate changes have to be made in the party line, in the measures the party takes, and in the slogans it issues.

In order to cope with the demands facing it, a proletarian party must be able to recognize and rectify in good time the mistakes it has made. A revolutionary party can make mistakes, even serious ones, without losing its proletarian character, but it loses this character when it becomes lastingly incapable of *recognizing* that it has made a mistake, and of correcting its political line accordingly.

The process of recognizing and rectifying mistakes can develop fully only under conditions of sufficiently open ideological struggle: without such a struggle it becomes more and more difficult to work out and apply a proletarian line, and, in the long run, to preserve the party's proletarian character—and also, consequently, if the party is in power, the proletarian character of the state.

When, in a proletarian party, several political lines are in conflict, all of which seem to correspond to the needs of the revolution, it is only by applying theoretical analysis and concrete analysis (and so, also, by critically examining past and present practice) that it becomes possible to decide which of these lines really best serves the interests of the proletariat. Open discussion, criticism and self-criticism are thus of very great importance. They make it possible to carry out analyses which are as thorough as possible, to appreciate the significance of all the shades of difference, to draw up a detailed balance sheet, and to deduce lessons from past mistakes, and thus to rectify past errors.

As long as social classes exist, *the class struggle going on in society is reflected in the party in the form of ideological and political struggle.* The proletarian line, the one which in the given situation is best calculated to serve the interests of the proletariat, is therefore inevitably confronted by a bourgeois line. The latter is the one which, in the given conditions, serves best the interests of the bourgeoisie. In relation to the bourgeois and proletarian lines, the other lines represent right or "left" opportunist orientations. In circumstances where it corresponds better to the interests of the bourgeoisie, an opportunist line may become a bourgeois line. At a given moment, the existence of a definite bourgeois line conceals the bourgeois content of a particular opportunist tendency, which thus seems to "blend" with the proletarian line, but will at a later stage come into open conflict with the latter. A correct ideological struggle requires that at each moment the principal target must be the bourgeois line, without losing sight of the opportunist tendency. Thus, in November–December 1920, Lenin's principal target was the Trotsky-Bukharin opposition: then, when that trend had been practically beaten, he took as his principal target the Workers' Opposition. There is no "recipe" for "spotting at first glance" the bourgeois line of the moment. It is often a line which seems to be particularly "close" to the revolutionary line, for it is in this way that a great number of party members can be more easily misled. It may seem merely to take revolutionary orientations to their "logical conclusion." Only when its true class character has been exposed does the bourgeois line cease to seem "close" to the revolutionary line: but its place is then inevitably taken by another tendency which, in turn, seems to "blend" with (or be "indistinguishable from") the revolutionary line.

Those who defend a bourgeois line are, objectively, representatives of the bourgeoisie inside the proletarian party, but this does not imply that they are its "conscious agents." One has, therefore, to start from the assumption that they (and, a fortiori, those who have merely been influenced by a non-proletarian line) can be won over to the proletarian line: this is why it is important to "leave a way out" for those who oppose the proletarian line, provided that they are not splitting the party and are not playing a double game.

It is clear, and experience confirms this, that there is no "guarantee" that a proletarian party will always, at every moment, rally round the line which is correct from the standpoint of the interests of the proletariat, the revolutionary line.

The definition of the proletarian revolutionary line can therefore not be left to a mere "majority vote," whether in a popular (or workers') assembly, in a party congress, or in a meeting of the party's Central Committee. Experience shows that, faced with a profoundly new situation, it is usually only a minority that finds the correct path, even in an experienced proletarian party. This being so, to suppose that a majority vote can settle difficulties and decide the correct line would be quite illusory. Generally speaking, what is correct does not immediately appear as such: this clarification comes about only after struggle, free discussion, experience, and the test of time.

In order that what is new and true may make its way in the world without too much difficulty, there must be no claiming that what is true and what is false can be decided by the simplistic method of voting, when what is involved calls for analysis and discussion. (This does not rule out the possibility that, where immediate practical decisions are required, it may be necessary to resort to voting before a problem has been studied in all its aspects.)

It was not accidental that Lenin was more than once beaten when votes were taken in the Bolshevik party at crucial moments, so that he had to "go against the tide." Mao Tsetung has stressed that "going against the tide is a Marxist-Leninist principle."[25] It is therefore essential that new revolutionary ideas be given the possibility of being defended, and that those who are the bearers of these ideas possess the right, and the courage, to defend them.

The problem of what is true and what is false as regards the conditions for consolidating the dictatorship of the proletariat is all the more difficult to settle because the practice of proletarian rule is historically in its infancy, as compared with the thousands of years of experience of rule possessed by the exploiting classes. This is also why what might have seemed obvious fifty years ago, and which was indeed so on the basis of experience up to that time and the corresponding development of theory, may seem today only partly true. Every scientific truth is capable of developing and getting enriched, thereby becoming a new truth through the shedding of what, in the "former truth" was really false.

If the presence within a proletarian party of a majority favorable to a particular political line, or to certain measures, does not "guarantee" the proletarian character of this line or these measures, it is nonetheless necessary, when the moment comes to act and when the highest party bodies have declared for them, that the minority submit in action, even while reserving their own opinion so as to be better able subsequently to correct mistakes. It is only if there are profound divergences, and if there is no other way to correct the party orientation, that a split is to be preferred to unity[26]—and in this case, it is those who are violating party principles who bear responsibility for the split.

Naturally, the possibility of correcting mistakes of orientation becomes more restricted when these mistakes do not emerge openly but only in the form of a certain practice, that is of an undeclared opposition.[27]

IV. *The undeclared oppositions of 1921–1923*

After 1921 a trend of undeclared opposition developed— characterized by a tendency toward right opportunism— which was able to make itself felt and to intervene practically in political decisions. This opposition was rooted in the administrative machinery of the party and the state, in the bourgeois practices and political relations which reproduced themselves within it. The bourgeois forces present in the administrative machinery used their positions to try to secure ascendancy for orientations favorable to their interests, by influencing those party leaders who, by virtue of their conception of what the party line should be, were susceptible to this influence.

During Lenin's illness,[28] a political line different from his own showed itself on more than one occasion. This line can be regarded as that of an "undeclared" opposition in the sense that it did not usually clash head on with Lenin, even though it advocated measures in contradiction to those recommended by him. The term "opposition" bears, however, a special significance in this context, since it happened more than once that the measures advocated by this "opposition"—which then had Stalin as its practical leader—obtained the support of the majority of the Political Bureau or the Central Committee. This support was usually only momentary, however, for when Lenin intervened, the organs concerned more often than not went back on the decisions they had taken. Given the rightwing orientations toward which the majority of the Central Committee and the Political Bureau tended during the period of Lenin's illness, it is not surprising that these orientations deeply affected the line of the Bolshevik Party after Lenin's death.

(a) The question of the foreign-trade monopoly

It was in connection with the question of the state monopoly of foreign trade that right-wing attitudes (which, incidentally, did not reassert themselves later in the same form) found expression at the level of the Central Committee, at the time when Lenin was beginning to feel the first effects of his illness and had to withdraw from public work for a few weeks. The Riga Conference[29] was then being held (late 1921), and Milyutin, the Soviet representative at this conference, went so far as to propose abolishing the foreign-trade monopoly.

Bukharin, Sokolnikov, and others supported Milyutin. They were convinced that the Commissariat of Foreign Trade was incapable of properly organizing international economic exchanges, and consequently they recommended either that the rules of the foreign-trade monopoly be mitigated or else that it be completely abolished. Stalin approved of these ideas, but Lenin looked on them as a threat to the future of the proletarian dictatorship. He pointed out that, if they were adopted, foreign exporters would be able to enter into direct contact with Nepmen, and this would entail danger that Soviet industry might be utterly ruined, since foreign big capital was certainly ready, if need be, to practice dumping and subsidize exports in order to paralyze Soviet industry.

For some time the Central Committee failed to agree with Lenin on this point. Only in March 1922 did he secure the adoption of a number of decrees which consolidated the foreign-trade monopoly. And even then, under the influence of those members of the Central Committee who were opposed to unqualified maintenance of the monopoly, the latter continued to be subject to question, to such an extent that foreign businessmen who were negotiating with Soviet representatives postponed signing contracts they had been about to clinch, in the hope that the monopoly was on the point of being abolished. On May 15, 1922, increasingly worried about the way things were going, Lenin wrote to Stalin urging that the principle of the foreign-trade monopoly be reaffirmed, and a formal ban be put on all talk of relaxing it.[30] Under the text of Lenin's letter (which was not published until 1959), Stalin noted: "I have no objections to a 'formal ban' on measures to *mitigate* the foreign trade monopoly at the present stage. All the same, I think that *mitigation* is becoming indispensable."[31]

After Lenin had intervened in this way, his point of view was approved by the Political Bureau at its meeting of May 22. Three days later, however, Lenin fell seriously ill: his right hand and right leg were paralyzed and it became difficult for him to speak.

It was symptomatic of the presence of a right-wing tendency in the party that the adversaries of the foreign-trade monopoly now resumed their offensive. On October 6, 1922, the Central Committee agreed to proposals by Sokolnikov which introduced important modifications in the state monopoly of foreign trade. Lenin was still sick, but he was able to follow public business, and, as a result, he intervened again with a letter dated October 13, in which he wrote: "The decision of the plenary meeting of the C.C. of 6 October (Minutes no. 7, point 3) institutes what seems to be an unimportant, partial reform . . . In actual fact, however, this wrecks the foreign-trade monopoly."[32]

Following receipt of this letter, and taking account of the political authority enjoyed by Lenin, who seemed about to take charge of affairs once more, the CC revoked its decision.

These vicissitudes testify to the importance within the Central Committee of right-wing forces, or of forces susceptible to the influence of a right-wing line. The existence of a strong "economist" tendency was shown here by the weight given to the argument that the "inexperience" of those in charge of the foreign-trade monopoly might cause the Soviet power a momentary loss of some millions of roubles, and that this consideration "justified" abandoning such a vital political command post.

During this episode Stalin showed himself constantly in favor of "mitigation" of the foreign-trade monopoly: he gave in, eventually, but only on Lenin's insistence. When he passed Lenin's letter on to the CC, Stalin accompanied it with a note in which he said: "Comrade Lenin's letter has not persuaded me that the decision of the C.C. Plenary Meeting of 6 October on foreign trade was wrong. Nonetheless, in view of Comrade Lenin's insistence that fulfilment of the C.C. Plenary Meeting be delayed, I shall vote *for* a postponement, so that the question may be again raised for discussion at the next Plenary Meeting which Comrade Lenin will attend." Finally, in December 1922, at a meeting at which Trotsky spoke in support of Lenin's attitude on the matter, the CC canceled the decision it had taken on October 6.[33]

So ended "the affair of the foreign-trade monopoly." It throws much light on the relation of forces then prevailing in the Central Committee and the Political Bureau—the relation

which decided the orientation the party leadership would take
when Lenin was no longer able to intervene.

(b) The problem of the nationalities

The problem of the relations between Soviet Russia and the
independent non-Russian republics had revealed, as early as
1918, the existence within the Bolshevik Party of a tendency
favoring a centralizing conception that would ensure dominance by the Russian government. At that time this tendency
had striven to oppose the line of the CC majority and of Lenin.
The attempt might have seemed a mere passing phenomenon,
but this was not the case. In reality there were within the
Bolshevik Party supporters of a political line strongly marked
by bourgeois nationalism. After 1921 this line found ever
clearer expression, and Lenin saw in it a manifestation of
Great-Russian chauvinism.

Already in 1918, some members of the CC, including Stalin,
had cautiously spoken out against recognition of the right of
self-determination for the Baltic countries and Finland, on the
grounds that the proletariat was not in power there. In his
report on the national question presented on January 15, 1918,
to the Third All-Russia Congress of Workers', Soldiers' and
Peasants' Soviets, Stalin voiced this idea explicitly. After saying that the bourgeoisie made use of "a national cloak" in its
struggle for power, he added that "all this pointed to the
necessity of interpreting the principle of self-determination as
the right to self-determination not of the bourgeoisie but of the
labouring masses of the given nation. The principle of self-
determination should be a means in the struggle for socialism
and should be subordinated to the principles of socialism."[34]

In using this formulation, Stalin aligned himself in practice
with the conception held at the time by Bukharin and Preobrazhensky, and included by them in their book *The ABC of
Communism*.[35]

With one exception—an appeal addressed in 1920 to the
Karelian people—the idea of "self-determination of the

labouring masses" does not appear again in official Soviet documents of the following years: but this did not prevent Stalin from trying to apply it, in Byelorussia and in the Baltic states. As for Lenin and the majority of the CC, they declared for the right of self-determination *of nations*, and this right was reaffirmed at the party's Eighth Congress, during the discussion on the national question, in March 1919. At this congress Bukharin still sought to defend the idea of "self-determination for the working classes of every nationality," even quoting in this connection Stalin's report to the Third Congress of Soviets. Pyatakov spoke in the same sense, denouncing self-determination of nations as a "bourgeois slogan" which "unites all counter-revolutionary forces." In his view, "once we unite economically and build one apparatus, one Supreme Council of National Economy, one railway administration, one bank, etc., all this notorious self-determination is not worth one rotten egg."[36] This quotation shows clearly the link between Great-Russian chauvinism and the ultra-statist ideas held by Preobrazhensky, Bukharin, Pyatakov, and some other Bolshevik leaders.

At the Eighth Congress Lenin thus found himself isolated at first in defending the traditional line of the party in favor of self-determination of *nations*. He explained that the slogan of "self-determination for the worker masses" was a false slogan, for it could be applied only where a division had already appeared between the bourgeoisie and the proletariat. Lenin declared that the right to self-determination must be accorded to nations in which such a division had not yet taken place, that it must be accepted in the case of countries like Poland, where the Communists did not yet have the majority of the working class behind them. Only in this way, he said, could the Russian proletariat avoid the charge of Great-Russian chauvinism hidden under the name of Communism.[37]

In the end, Lenin won the day: the relevant points in the party program adopted by the congress conformed to his views. The resolution on the national question mentioned, especially, that, "on the part of the proletariat of those nations which are or have been oppressor nations, it is necessary that there should be extreme discretion, and that the utmost consideration should be paid to the survival of national sentiments among the working masses of nations which have been deprived of equal rights. Only by such a policy will it be possible to create conditions for the realisation of a durable and amicable union between the diverse national elements of the international proletariat."[38]

Actually, the adoption by the Eighth Congress of the resolution which expressed Lenin's views was not sufficient to solve the problem of relations with the various nationalities,[39] especially as the Bolshevik Party subsequently underwent the changes already described.

The national problem resurfaced with special acuteness during the summer of 1922, when Lenin was again out of action as far as the direction of political affairs was concerned. The existence of a powerful undeclared opposition on this question was revealed.

In August 1922 Stalin, in his capacity as chairman of a commission charged with regulating relations between the RSFSR and the other Soviet republics, drew up a draft resolution on "autonomization." This scheme provided for the inclusion of the independent republics of the Ukraine, Byelorussia, Azerbaijan, Armenia, and Georgia in the Russian Federation as "autonomous"—that is, de facto, subordinate—republics. Under Stalin's plan the government of the *Russian* republic, its CEC and its Sovnarkom, would constitute the government of all these countries. The proposal, which would have abolished the independence of the non-Russian Soviet republics, encountered opposition from the Central Committees of the Bolshevik Party in Byelorussia and Georgia. The Ukrainian CC did not discuss the matter, but its members did not view it with favor.

When, on September 26, Lenin learned of this plan, he condemned the principle of adhesion to the RSFSR by the other republics, and proposed instead that a federation of republics be formed in which all the republics would possess equal rights. In his view, this federation should take the form of a "Union of the Soviet Republics of Europe and Asia," and *the Russian government should not be the government of the union.*[40]

The advocates of integrating the other Soviet republics into the RSFSR with a subordinate status tried to ignore Lenin's criticism. Stalin communicated his plan to the members of the CC without waiting for them to learn Lenin's opinion.[41] He even declared, during a Political Bureau meeting devoted to this question, that it was necessary to "be firm with" Lenin, and in a letter of September 27 he went so far as to speak of the "national liberalism" revealed by Lenin in this affair.[42]

The Central Committee, at its meeting of October 6, 1922, eventually approved Stalin's plan with a few alterations. The final text took only formal account of some of Lenin's comments: the term "Union" was substituted for "Federation," but the concrete provisions guaranteed in practice that Great-Russian hegemony would prevail.[43]

Lenin was thus confronted with a fait accompli. Considering that the decision taken on October 6, 1922 was one of extreme gravity, he resolved to draw a sharp line of demarcation between his views and those which had been adopted by the CC in confused circumstances—that is, without their being fully informed of the state of discussion on the matter. The very same day that he learned of the CC's decision, he wrote a letter to Kamenev in which he said: "I declare war to the death on dominant-nation chauvinism."[44]

For Lenin, that sentence was the statement of a fundamental political task, namely, struggle against a "right-wing" line which was *expressed not in a program but in a practice*. All the facts, as he saw them, confirmed the urgent need for such a struggle. A rapid worsening was indeed taking place in the crisis between the Russian Central Committee and that of the other nations, especially the Georgian CC.

The opposition between Lenin's internationalist line and that of the General Secretary then became acute, though this did not emerge publicly. From the end of October 1922 onward, Lenin's notes, messages, and diary revert constantly to his analysis of the risks involved *if the Bolshevik Party were to become aligned with Great-Russian chauvinist attitudes,* that is, with the attitudes of the bourgeoisie. He denounced big-power chauvinism and emphasized the need for actual "inequality" biased *in favor of the small nations,* so as to make up for their lack of weight in relation to the big ones. On this subject he wrote: "Anybody who does not understand this has not grasped the real proletarian attitude to the national question, he is still essentially petty-bourgeois in his point of view and is, therefore, sure to descend to the bourgeois point of view."[45]

Thus, in connection with the national question, the *touchstone of proletarian internationalism,* Lenin noted the emergence within the CC of tendencies favorable to the development of an opportunist line.

Lenin now thought it necessary to denounce firmly the pressures which had been brought to bear on the CC of the Georgian Bolsheviks by the secretariat of the Russian party, and which constituted a manifestation of big-power chauvinism. He defined his view on this point, in the document just quoted, as follows:

> I think that in the present instance, as far as the Georgian nation is concerned, we have a typical case in which a genuinely proletarian attitude makes profound caution, thoughtfulness, and a readiness to compromise a matter of necessity for us. The Georgian who is neglectful of this aspect of the question, or who carelessly flings about accusations of 'nationalist-socialism' (whereas he himself is a real and true 'nationalist-socialist', and even a vulgar Great-Russian bully), violates, in substance, the interests of proletarian class solidarity . . . [46]

Lenin considered that he had been deceived when he gave his approval to what had been put before him as a formula of "unity" for the Soviet nations. He declared that, in the prevailing political circumstances, the "unification" sought by Stalin should have been renounced: "There is no doubt that measures should have been delayed somewhat until we could say that we vouched for our apparatus as our own."[47]

A later note shows that what was at stake in this affair, as Lenin saw it, was proletarian internationalism and the future of the revolution throughout the world: "The harm that can result to our state from a lack of unification between the national apparatuses and the Russian apparatus is infinitely less than that which will be done not only to us, but to the whole International, and to the hundreds of millions of the peoples of Asia, which is destined to follow us on to the stage of history in the near future."[48]

This note—in which the interests of *the Soviet state* are counterposed to those of *the Russian and international Communist movement*—ends with sentences which show that Lenin had by that time become fully aware that *the center of gravity of the world revolution had shifted from industrial Europe to peasant Asia*. He said, for example:

It would be unpardonable opportunism if, on the eve of the debut of the East, just as it is awakening, we undermined our prestige with its peoples, even if only by the slightest crudity or injustice towards our own non-Russian nationalities. The need to rally against the imperialists of the West, who are defending the capitalist world, is one thing . . . It is another thing when we ourselves lapse, even if only in trifles, *into imperialist attitudes*[49] towards oppressed nationalities, thus undermining all our principled sincerity, all our principled defence of the struggle against imperialism. But the morrow of world history will be a day when the awakening peoples oppressed by imperialism are finally aroused and the decisive long and hard struggle for their liberation begins.[50]

The importance of this dispute and of Lenin's struggle on the Georgian question is due to what was involved, namely, *the conflict between a proletarian internationalist line and a right-wing line which tended to become identified with Great-Russian bourgeois nationalism*. Moreover, this right-wing line, though not forming the axis of a declared opposition, did eventually gather around itself greater and greater forces within the party apparatus, and was destined to prove victorious soon after Lenin's death.

In the absence of a systematic ideological struggle by the Bolshevik Party against Great-Russian chauvinism, the latter was indeed tending to develop, corresponding as it did to the "spontaneous" state of mind of a large part of Russia's popular masses, especially of the Russian peasants who, being shut up within the narrow horizon of the village, were readily inclined to look down on the other nationalities: Poles, Tatars, Georgians, etc.[51] After Lenin's death, however, the Bolshevik Party practically gave up this struggle. The party's passivity in the matter was closely connected with the mass-scale penetration of the party and state apparatuses by bourgeois administrators, engineers, technicians, and intellectuals. This penetration strengthened bourgeois ideological and political tendencies, and also the "economistic" practices connected with a certain conception of the role of technicians, and with a certain conception of the New Economic Policy and of the state in the application of this policy.

The development of a right-wing opposition on the national question was, in fact, one of the effects of the new political relations which took shape within the Bolshevik Party during "war communism." The latter period had favored a highly centralistic style of leadership in the Bolshevik Party, which had undermined the quality of the relations between the different levels in the party, between the rank and file and the top leadership, and between the political and administrative leaderships. The very way in which the party's administrative leadership tried, in 1922, to settle the Georgian affair showed the extent to which nonproletarian practices and relations had become established.

In fact, faced with the refusal of the Georgian Central Committee[52] to agree to the "proposals" (which were presented to them as orders) drawn up by the commission chaired by him, Stalin decided to resort to *administrative measures.* He appointed to jobs which put an end to their political role—in some cases removing them from Georgia—those members of the Georgian CC who refused to bow to the decisions of the secretariat. Some of the Georgian leaders were unwilling to submit to decisions which aimed at "settling" a political problem by means of administrative measures.[53] Ordzhonikidze, who at the time represented the secretariat of the RCP(B) in Georgia allowed himself, during a discussion, to use violence, striking Kabanidze, one of the members of the Georgian CC.

Ordzhonikidze's conduct testified to the appearance in party life of *the use of physical coercion against a party member in order to "change his views,"* or at least to change the way he expressed them. In Lenin's eyes this was no mere "personal defect" arising from Ordzhonikidze's "psychology," but the beginning of political relations that were full of grave danger for the future, since this meant the emergence in the party of a *bourgeois political practice of repression*, with which were associated Stalin, the party's General Secretary, and Dzerzhinsky, who was head of the GPU.

When, on December 30, 1922, Lenin learned what had happened in Georgia, he considered that it was a sign that the party was falling prey to serious *degeneration*, expressed especially by the appearance of a "style of leadership" which was quite inadmissible in a proletarian party. He expressly condemned such resort to violence, and said that what Ordzhonikidze had done, together with the background to this deed, showed "what a mess we have got ourselves into."[54] Lenin perceived that the Bolshevik Party ran the risk, if it tolerated the development of such relations, of finding itself taking a road that would lead to the stifling of any expression within the party of opinions not in accordance with those of the leaders, and more particularly of the members of the highest executive organs of the party. This would seriously jeopardize the proletarian character of the party, since preservation of this character demanded that the party remain open to discussion and criticism, and that party unity result from open and clear ideological struggle.

Lenin's state of health did not allow him to carry through to the end his study of what was implicit in the Georgian events and in some other similar incidents, nor to advise on the overall measures needed to combat, by strengthening proletarian relations among party members, the degeneration that had set in. Nevertheless, he did undertake an investigation, which he was obliged to carry out by his own means, without using the administrative party apparatus which he could no longer trust, as this apparatus supported Ordzhonikidze and was dependent on the secretariat.[55] This affair also led Lenin to dictate several notes in which he came out once more against what he called "physical means of suppression ('biomechanics')."[56] He again condemned such methods in a note of February 14, 1923, saying that "one should not fight" comrades in the course of internal party discussions.[57]

Before even learning the result of his investigation of the Georgian affair, Lenin did not hesitate to declare that what had happened there called for political sanctions. In his notes of December 31, 1922 he wrote: "Exemplary punishment must be inflicted on Ordzhonikidze . . . and the investigation of all the material which Dzerzhinsky's commission has collected must be completed or started over again to correct the enormous mass of wrongs and biased judgments which it doubtless contains. The political responsibility for all this truly Great-Russian nationalist campaign must, of course, be laid on Stalin and Dzerzhinsky."[58]

The problem of relations with the non-Russian nations and that of the style of leadership and of the nature of relations between Communists remained thereafter at the center of Lenin's preoccupations. It is symptomatic that his two very last writings were a letter threatening Stalin with a rupture of relations and a letter to the Georgian leaders Mdivani, Makharadze, etc., in which he promised them his support.[59] In this last letter Lenin told the Georgians: "I am following your case with all my heart. I am indignant over Ordzhonikidze's rudeness and the connivance of Stalin and Dzerzhinsky. I am preparing for you notes and a speech."[60]

Clearly, this affair had assumed major importance in Lenin's eyes, and he was getting ready to denounce publicly the Great-Russian chauvinism (disguised under the cloak of internationalism) of a section of the leadership of the RCP(B).

Thus, to generalize, the transformations which had taken place in the Bolshevik Party and the development of an undeclared right-wing opposition which followed an authoritarian and Great-Russian chauvinist line, led Lenin to issue a number of new indications to the party, aimed at the application of a mass line. This line was to be combated in practice by the party's administrative apparatus, which wanted to consolidate its own authority.

(c) Mass line or administrative centralism

Even before the most obvious symptoms had appeared showing the existence of a strong right-wing, authoritarian, and Great-Russian chauvinist tendency, Lenin had already indicated how to fight against the bases for such a tendency. Thus, in September 1921, he spoke of the need for a *mass struggle* against the influence of bourgeois and petty bourgeois ideology on the party. Let us recall what he wrote on that occasion:

> The Party must be purged of those who have lost touch with the masses (let alone, of course, those who discredit the Party in the eyes of the masses). Naturally, we shall not submit to everything the masses say, because the masses, too, sometimes—particularly in time of exceptional weariness and exhaustion resulting from excessive hardship and suffering—yield to sentiments that are in no way advanced. But in appraising persons, in the negative attitude to those who have "attached" themselves to us for selfish motives, to those who have become "puffed-up commissars" and "bureaucrats," the suggestions of the non-Party proletarian masses and, in many cases, of the non-Party peasant masses, are extremely valuable. The working masses have a fine intuition, which enables them to distinguish honest and devoted Communists from those who arouse the disgust of people earning their bread by the sweat of their brow, enjoying no privileges and having no "pull." [61]

Lenin gave the same orientation on more than one occasion when he wrote about how the Workers' and Peasants' Inspection should work; in one of his last writings he severely condemned the way it was run, and emphasized the fact that this body, which was headed by Stalin, was cut off from the masses. He stressed that the Workers' and Peasants' Inspection should make it possible to supervise *from below* the apparatuses of the state and the party.[62]

Taking account of the need for struggle against the development of bourgeois political relations in the party and against the right-wing tendency developing in the administrative apparatuses of the state and the party—and of the influence that these apparatuses wielded where the Central Committee itself was concerned—Lenin set out a number of pointers for action in what has been called his "Testament."[63] These related particularly to the make-up of the CC and to the selection of leaders.

On the first point, Lenin wrote that the moment had come to introduce *new blood* into the party leadership, by increasing the membership of the Central Committee to 50, or even 100, and by *choosing the new members mainly from among the workers and peasants.* He offered precise suggestions on this point:

> The workers admitted to the Central Committee should come preferably not from among those who have had long service in Soviet bodies (in this part of my letter the term workers everywhere includes peasants), because those workers have already acquired the very traditions and the very prejudices which it is desirable to combat. The working-class members of the C.C. must be mainly workers of a lower stratum than those promoted in the last five years to work in Soviet bodies; they must be people closer to being rank-and-file workers and peasants, who, however, do not fall into the category of direct or indirect exploiters.[64]

To be sure, the membership of the Central Committee was increased in 1923 and 1924, but neither among the seventeen new members elected by the Twelfth Congress nor among the fifteen new members elected by the Thirteenth Congress were there "workers of a lower stratum than those promoted in the last five years to work in Soviet bodies." On the contrary, they were party secretaries of towns and regions, a secretary of the Central Trade-Union Council (A. I. Dogadov), a secretary of the Siberian Bureau of the CC (L. V. Kosior), the

People's Commissar of Foreign Trade (L. B. Krassin), the chairman of the Gosplan, some secretaries of the Central Council of the Young Communist League, some leading personnel of the Supreme Economic Council—in other words, "eminent" representatives of the higher stratum of the administrative apparatus of the party and the state.

Consequently, Lenin's recommendations aimed at altering the make-up of the CC so as to weaken the representation in it of the right-wing tendency remained without effect. Furthermore, as we know, the Central Committee, though continuing to be an important organ, tended increasingly to play only a secondary role in relation to the Political Bureau and the secretariat: it was in those two organs, closely linked with the higher administrative personnel, that effective power was tending to become concentrated.

Lenin was not unaware of this. It is therefore not surprising that, shortly before he was finally condemned to silence by sickness, and then death, he returned, on December 24, 1922, in his "Letter to the Congress," to the question of the secretariat and the personality of the General Secretary.

A few days later, on January 4, 1923, in a continuation of his letter to the Twelfth Congress, Lenin came to the conclusion, already mentioned, about the need to remove Stalin from his post as General Secretary. Over and beyond the "personality" of Stalin, Lenin was here aiming his fire at the supporters of a certain type of *political relations* which, instead of permitting ideological struggle to be combined with the struggle for party unity, led to emphasis being put on an imposed unity, sometimes achieved by expelling old Bolshevik cadres, whose criticisms, or even mere reservations, were to be tolerated less and less.

After his disappearance from the political scene, Lenin's last recommendations were not put into practice by those who took complete command of the party leadership. This applied both to his general advice—which constituted the beginning of a new strategy for leading the poor and middle peasants along the socialist road—and to his ideas on organizational matters.

It is therefore not surprising that, after Lenin's death, both the Political Bureau and the Central Committee decided to conceal from the party the existence of his last writings, those which made up what has been called his "Testament." These writings, which were intended for the party congress, were not communicated to that assembly. Krupskaya tried, nevertheless, to ensure that the Thirteenth Congress—the first to be held after Lenin's death (May 23–31, 1924)—should be informed of them. She only managed, however, to get agreement for them to be read to a CC meeting reinforced by the most senior party members. At this meeting, after speeches by Zinoviev and Kamenev, the Central Committee decided, by 30 votes to 10, to keep the "Testament" secret and read it only to the heads of delegations to the congress.[65]

These points concerning Lenin's orientations and the tendencies which he fought against during his last two years of political activity, must not be lost sight of when the balance-sheet is drawn of five years of the Russian Revolution.

Notes

1. Broué, *Le Parti bolchévique*, p. 142.
2. On the Tenth Congress and the discussions that preceded it, see the official report of the congress, and ibid., pp. 138–143 and 157 ff.
3. For Bukharin's ideas, see Appendix 16 (*O zadachakh i strukture profsoyuzov*) to the Tenth Congress report, p. 802; quoted in Brinton, *The Bolsheviks & Workers' Control*, p. 72.
4. "Once Again on the Trade Unions," in *CW*, vol. 32, p. 86.
5. Ibid., pp. 86 and 90 ff.
6. Tenth Congress report, p. 190; quoted in Carr, *The Bolshevik Revolution*, vol. 2, p. 227 (my emphasis—CB.).
7. Point 7 of the resolution on the role and tasks of the trade unions adopted by the Tenth Congress, in *K.P.S.S. v Rezolyutsiyakh*, vol. 1, p. 540.
8. *CW*, vol. 32, p. 200; see also p. 204.
9. See Lenin's "Summing-up Speech on Party Unity and the Anarcho-Syndicalist Deviation," in ibid., pp. 257 ff.

10. The resolution banning "factions" was called the "resolution on Party unity." The text is in *K.P.S.S. v Rezolyutsiyakh*, vol. 1, pp. 527 ff.
11. *CW*, vol. 32, p. 258.
12. Ibid., p. 261.
13. In Part Five we shall see how the very conception of what the NEP meant evolved during the last years of Lenin's active life.
14. *CW*, vol. 32, pp. 195–196.
15. Ibid., pp. 51–52.
16. *CW*, vol. 25, p. 421.
17. *CW*, vol. 30, p. 459.
18. Ibid., p. 459.
19. *CW*, vol. 32, p. 325. (Lenin's notes for a draft of his pamphlet *The Tax in Kind.*)
20. Ibid., pp. 361–362.
21. See Kollontai, *The Workers' Opposition.*
22. See *CW*, vol. 32, p. 351.
23. See Lenin's speech at the Second All-Russia Miners' Congress, in ibid., p. 57, and the CC's report to the Tenth Party Congress, in ibid., p. 191.
24. "On Slogans," in *CW*, vol. 25, p. 185.
25. Quoted in *Peking Review*, September 7, 1973, p. 21.
26. This question is clearly discussed by Lenin in his pamphlet *Once More on the Trade Unions*, in *CW*, vol. 32, p. 80.
27. An opposition which develops in this way does not conform to the principle of "going against the tide," as has been noted previously.
28. Illness obliged Lenin to withdraw from his leading work for the first time at the end of 1921, then for a longer period between the end of May 1922 and October of that year, and finally in December 1922. His political activity ceased altogether in March 1923. Before that date, even when he was not in a position to lead, he frequently intervened by writing letters, notes, and articles.
29. This was a conference on economic problems of the Baltic region, held at Riga on October 28–31, 1921. The conditions for developing Russia's external trade were discussed there. V. P. Milyutin headed the Soviet delegation.
30. On these divergences regarding the foreign-trade monopoly, see *CW*, vol. 42, p. 418, 599–600, and vol. 45, pp. 549–550, 739–740.
31. *CW*, vol. 45, pp. 550, 740.
32. *CW*, vol. 33, p. 375.

33. Ibid., pp. 455–459, 528–529, 535–536.
34. Stalin, *Works,* vol. 4, pp. 32–33.
35. See Bukharin and Preobrazhensky, *The ABC of Communism,* ch. 7.
36. Report of the Eighth Party Congress, published in Moscow in 1933 and reissued in 1939, pp. 49 and 80–81; quoted in Carr, *The Bolshevik Revolution,* vol. 1, p. 274.
37. Lenin's report to the Eighth Congress, March 19, 1919, on the party program, in *CW,* vol. 29, pp. 171–172.
38. *K.P.S.S. v Rezolyutsiyakh,* vol. 1, p. 417. (Translated in appendix to Bukharin and Preobrazhensky, *The ABC of Communism,* p. 440.)
39. We have seen earlier that the question of relations between Soviet *Russia* and the *non-Russian peoples* was a matter of fundamental importance, politically and theoretically. Correct handling of these relations was necessary for the application of a political line that would enable the proletariat to play an effective leading role in relation to the revolutionary movement of the peoples oppressed by imperialism and colonialism. More broadly, what was involved here was the maintenance of the proletariat's leading role in relation to the various forms of the democratic revolutionary movement: hence the decisive importance that Lenin ascribed to this problem.
40. *CW,* vol. 42, pp. 421–423. In this letter Lenin stressed that all the members of the federation must be *"equal* republics" (p. 422).
41. Ibid., p. 602.
42. Lewin, *Lenin's Last Struggle,* pp. 51–53.
43. Anna Louise Strong mentions that one of the changes introduced by Stalin into the text which Lenin had read concerned a new measure with considerable political implications, namely, *centralization of the political police,* as a result of which the latter was no longer under "local rule," but exclusively controlled from Moscow. See Strong, *The Stalin Era,* p. 16.
44. *CW,* vol. 33, p. 372. Contrary to the usual practice, the letter is not accompanied in this edition by an explanatory note: and the commentary by the Institute of Marxism-Leninism which accompanies the letter sent by Lenin to Kamenev on September 26 (see *CW,* vol. 42, pp. 421–423, 602–605) implies that the resolution passed by the CC on October 6 was in conformity with Lenin's views—which renders incomprehensible the letter written by Lenin on that same day.
45. *CW,* vol. 36, p. 608.

46. Ibid.
47. Ibid., p. 606.
48. Ibid., p. 610.
49. My emphasis—C.B. This phrase shows that, for Lenin, there could be other "imperialist" relations besides those that were rooted in the existence of private monopolies and finance capital.
50. *CW*, vol. 36, pp. 610–611.
51. The popular nicknames used in everyday Russian speech when referring to these "non-Russian elements" were denounced by Lenin as expressions of big-power nationalism (ibid., p. 608).
52. The Central Committees of the party in the Ukraine, Byelorussia, Azerbaijan, and Armenia eventually yielded to the pressure brought to bear on them, so that relations between the members of these bodies and the general secretariat of the Russian party did not deteriorate so obviously as happened in the case of Georgia.
53. On October 22, 1922, the Georgian CC protested against the attitude of the Russian party secretariat by taking an exceptional step: nine of its eleven members *resigned as a body*.
54. *CW*, vol. 36, p. 605.
55. It was on April 3, 1922, that Stalin, who until then had borne the title of "Secretary," became "General Secretary."
56. *CW*, vol. 42, p. 620. This volume includes the service diary kept by Lenin's secretaries between November 21, 1922, and March 6, 1923 (ibid., pp. 465–494), which enables us to follow the struggle carried on by Lenin, immobilized as he was by illness, against the development of right-wing and Great-Russian. nationalist tendencies and against an authoritarian and bureaucratic style of leadership.
57. Ibid., p. 621.
58. *CW*, vol. 36, p. 610.
59. These letters were dated March 5 and 6, 1923, respectively. See *CW*, vol. 45, pp. 607–608.
60. Ibid., p. 608.
61. *CW*, vol. 33, pp. 39–40.
62. Ibid., pp. 489–490.
63. What is known as "Lenin's Testament" is made up of a series of writings dictated mainly between December 23 and 26, 1922, and completed at the beginning of 1923. These writings were intended for communication to the Twelfth Party Congress, to be held between April 17 and 25, 1923.

64. *CW*, vol. 36, p. 597. This, like the rest of "Lenin's Testament" was officially published in Russia for the first time in 1956, in no. 9 of the review *Kommunist*.
65. It was this oral communication to a restricted group that was still presented, when the "Testament" was officially published in 1956, as a communication to the congress "in accordance with Lenin's wish." See *CW*, vol. 36, pp. 712–713, n. 653.

Part 5
The balance sheet of five years of revolution and the prospects on the eve of Lenin's death

During the last years of his life, between 1921 and 1923, Lenin tried to draw up a balance sheet of the Russian Revolution and, for this purpose, to define as clearly as possible the *stages* through which the revolution had passed, together with the nature of the changes that had been effected. He sought at the same time to grasp the mistakes made and the illusions suffered from, so as to determine the tasks which needed to be fulfilled, in terms of the existing class and social relations.

This balance sheet, although incomplete, is highly important. It contains lessons that are universal in their implications and valid to this day. It deals with the fundamental problems of the transition from capitalism to communism, and in particular with those which arise at the very beginning of this transition.

A clear view of the decisive contributions to be derived from this balance sheet is hard to arrive at owing to its provisional form at the moment Lenin was obliged to stop work. At that time Lenin had not yet drawn all the conclusions toward which his analyses were leading. In order to appreciate the significance of what he said at this time, we need to continue the work he began, advancing further along the road he indicated. This we can do today by taking into account the lessons to be drawn from the course followed by the Russian Revolution after Lenin's death.

An attempt to bring out clearly the decisive lessons of Lenin's balance sheet nevertheless encounters two difficulties.

On the one hand, some of the new ideas set forth by Lenin between 1921 and 1923 were still expressed in terms that corresponded, more or less, to his earlier analyses, so that this terminology, which, though it had become inadequate, had not yet been wholly abandoned, is likely to conceal what is new in Lenin's thinking, unless one is sufficiently attentive.

On the other hand, and especially, because the Bolshevik Party grasped only partially what was new in Lenin's last writings, a "traditional" interpretation of these works has become established which needs to be set aside to some extent, if one is not to overlook some points of decisive importance.

I shall endeavor first of all to present the main features of the historical and political balance sheet drawn up by Lenin on the morrow of "war communism."

1. The balance sheet drawn up by Lenin on the period of "war communism"

When he drew up his historical and political balance sheet of the revolution, Lenin tried to define as clearly as possible the nature of the changes accomplished. This attempt was all the more necessary because the dual character of the Russian Revolution entailed a particularly complex *interweaving* of two revolutions—a proletarian revolution and a (mainly peasant) democratic revolution.

To the proletarian revolution corresponded the leading role played by the proletariat and its party. This leading role was manifested in striking fashion in October 1917: it made possible the establishment of the dictatorship of the proletariat and the accomplishment of changes that are inherent in a proletarian revolution.

To the democratic revolution corresponded the determining role played by the peasantry fighting for aims that were not socialist, such as the generalization of individual peasant production through the destruction of large-scale land ownership.

Lenin distinguished therefore between the *democratic work* and the *proletarian work* of the Russian Revolution, between the tasks and possibilities of each of these two revolutions as determined by concrete conditions due chiefly to the relations between classes and to the forms assumed by the *class struggle*.

I. The democratic work of the Russian Revolution

In an article written in November 1921 for the fourth anniversary of the October Revolution, and entitled "The Importance of Gold Now and After the Complete Victory of Socialism," Lenin pointed out that, "our revolution has completed only its bourgeois-democratic work."[1] In saying this, Lenin evidently had in mind the revolutionary elimination of large-scale land-ownership and the political superstructure that accompanied it.

The expression "bourgeois-democratic" calls for comment. In using it, Lenin referred to those changes which, in the case of previous revolutions, had been brought about by revolutions that were democratic in content (because they corresponded to the "democratic" aspirations and requirements of the nonproletarian *popular masses*), but were bourgeois by virtue of the forces leading them and of the social relations which these forces developed and consolidated.

Actually, when changes *similar* to (but not identical with) those realized during bourgeois-democratic revolutions are carried out in the course of revolutions developed through the leading role of the proletariat and its party, these changes take on *a new character, a fully democratic character*. If we retain the qualification "bourgeois" to describe these changes, we must be alert to the new function fulfilled by this qualification. It means that these changes *resemble* those carried out by a bourgeois-democratic revolution, and also—this is what is most important—that *if these changes are not followed by others, socialist in character, they can in fact open the way to a capitalist form of development*.

But is it true that the "bourgeois-democratic work" of the Russian Revolution had been "completed" by 1921? Yes, if we allow for the fact that bourgeois-democratic revolutions also permit "precapitalist" forms of production to survive, leaving them to be dissolved subsequently by the expanded reproduction of capital. No, if we consider that the bourgeois-democratic work of a revolution is not completed until it has really destroyed the obstacles to the productive accumulation of capital. There are grounds for doubting whether, in 1921, this task had been completed. Indeed, the consolidation of the *mir* and the generalization of small-scale individual peasant production after 1917 threw up new obstacles to productive accumulation. These developments favored an extension of a "patriarchal economy" cut off from the market and shut in on itself, while at the same time enabling disguised relations of exploitation and domination to develop, in accordance with the forms assumed historically by the *mir*. They thus induced a capitalist development of the parasitic type, which held back production accumulation and the growth of agricultural production. A few years' experience of the NEP were to show that, in this respect, the bourgeois-democratic work of the Russian Revolution had not been completed.

What Lenin was pointing out in 1921, as he would in 1923, was the uneven development of the democratic revolution and the proletarian revolution: the former had gone very far, whereas the latter had made relatively little progress.

This unevenness of development was determined by the very nature of the two revolutionary processes and by the way they conditioned each other. It is not necessary, of course, for the democratic revolution to have been carried through "to the end" before the proletarian revolution can take off; in the age of imperialism (the bourgeoisie having ceased to be able to lead a revolution) it is, on the contrary, essential that the two revolutions be combined. However, for the proletarian revolution to be able to undertake socialist tasks on a broad front, certain stages of the class struggle need to have been got through, for the proletariat must have strengthened sufficiently its role as leader of the masses to be in a position to lead them effectively along the road toward socialism.

In a country where the majority of the people are peasants, this presupposes that the proletariat has formed a firm alliance with the peasantry, an alliance based upon relations of profound trust.

Under the conditions of the Russian Revolution these relations needed to develop on the basis of the objective role played by the proletariat in accomplishing the tasks of the democratic revolution. For this it was necessary that the proletariat play its role in a definite way, in a way which consolidated its relations with the peasantry. In particular, the proletariat must not try to impose upon the peasantry social changes for which, as a mass, the latter were not ready. On this point the Bolshevik Party did indeed make mistakes (to which I shall return) in the course of "war communism," mistakes which reduced its power to lead the peasantry, and help guide it toward socialism. Lenin recognized this in June 1921 when, in his report to the Third Congress of the Communist International, he said: "In Siberia and in the Ukraine the counter-revolution was able to gain a temporary victory because there the bourgeoisie had the peasantry on its side, because the peasants were against us. The peasants frequently said: 'We are Bolsheviks, but not Communists. We are for the Bolsheviks because they drove out the landowners; but we are not for the Communists, because they are opposed to individual farming.' "[2]

He knew that one of the factors in the complex situation which had led the Bolshevik Party to adopt the New Economic Policy was, precisely, the will of the peasants to consolidate their individual farming and to exchange their products "freely." This being so, it was necessary to put off till later the socialist transformation of social relations in the countryside.

II. *The proletarian work of the Russian Revolution*

In his article "The Importance of Gold," Lenin also analyzed what at that moment (toward the end of 1921) the "proletarian part" of the work of the Russian Revolution amounted to.[3] For him, this work could be summarized in three main points, which he listed in the following order:

(1) "The revolutionary withdrawal from the imperialist world war; the exposure and *halting* of the slaughter organized by the two world groups of capitalist predators . . .

(2) "The establishment of the Soviet system, as a form of the dictatorship of the proletariat. An epoch-making change has been made. The era of bourgeois-democrat parliamentarian-

ism has come to an end. A new chapter in world history—the era of proletarian dictatorship—has been opened.

(3) "The creation of the economic basis of the socialist system; the main features of what is most important, most fundamental, have not yet been completed."

This statement is remarkably clear-cut. It shows the importance of the tasks accomplished, but also the magnitude of the tasks that still lay before the proletarian revolution. In this connection, the two last points of Lenin's statement deserve special attention. They show, indeed, that two of the most important tasks of the proletarian revolution were only beginning to be tackled in 1921. What Lenin was to write subsequently enables us, moreover, to appreciate better the nature of the problems that the proletarian revolution had solved and also of those that now confronted it.

(a) "The creation of the economic basis of the socialist system"

The field in which Lenin considered that "the main features of what is most important, most fundamental, have not yet been completed" was that of "the creation of the economic basis of the socialist system."

This was to be interpreted later as referring above all to the low level of the productive forces in Russia, from which it was deduced that the main thing was to "build the material foundations" of socialism. There is no doubt that Lenin did have this aspect of the revolution's tasks in mind: it really is a task without which progress toward socialism is not possible. But when Lenin spoke of the "economic basis" of socialism he did not have in mind *only* the development of the productive forces, but also, and especially, the *socialist transformation of production relations*. These are two associated tasks which have to be accomplished by the socialist revolution, two tasks which the Chinese Communist Party expresses in this concise formula: "Make revolution and promote production." These two tasks are dialectically interconnected. They constitute two contradictory aspects of a single task. The fundamental aspect of this task of the proletarian revolution is the transformation of production relations, but this does not mean that this aspect is at every moment the principal one. Actually, a socialist transformation of production relations is possible only under definite political and economic conditions. In a country like Russia this transformation required the existence of a firm alliance between the workers and the peasants. In 1921 this alliance was not firm enough. The first task of the proletarian party was to strengthen this alliance, which was one of the aims of the NEP.

Carrying through the task of the socialist transformation of production relations requires, furthermore, that the living conditions of the masses be such as to enable them really to devote themselves to this as the priority task. This means that the working people must not be absorbed by the struggle against hunger and cold, and not be crushed by day-to-day-difficulties, physical exhaustion, and sickness. The experience of the Russian Revolution, and that of the Chinese Revolution too, shows that, in order that the proletarian revolution may be able to attack the tasks involved in bringing about the most fundamental historical changes, it is necessary that the elementary tasks of everday life be fulfilled first of all, and that the proletariat and its party show in practice that they are capable not only of performing heroic exploits but also of organizing everyday life: otherwise, the trust accorded them by the broadest masses fades away, and nothing can be achieved without that trust. When that trust prevails the masses go forward, whereas confusion can lead them to commit acts of desperation. Reestablishing acceptable conditions of life, ensuring the supply of food to the towns and balanced exchanges between agriculture and industry, ending unemployment as soon as possible, were therefore also among the necessary aims of the NEP. And these aims had to be attained if the revolution was to resume its upward curve.

Thus, for Lenin, the "creation of the economic basis" of socialism meant the reconstitution and development of the productive forces and the transformation of production relations. The latter of these tasks is fundamental, but it cannot be accomplished without certain preconditions.

The pamphlet written by Lenin in April 1921 on *The Tax in Kind*[4] provides a clear analysis of the economic relations, or elements of economic relations, which existed in Russia at that time. The pamphlet showed that these relations and these elements were predominantly alien to socialism, and that the long-term historical task of the dictatorship of the proletariat was to transform this situation. The elements analyzed by Lenin belonged to what he called "the various socio-economic structures that exist in Russia at the present time."[5]

In this work of 1921, Lenin quotes long passages from a pamphlet he had written in the spring of 1918,[6] in which "the present economy of Russia" was analyzed. Lenin's reference back to this earlier pamphlet is highly significant. It shows that Lenin considered in the spring of 1921, after the ending of "war communism" (when large-scale industry had been completely nationalized), that the production relations, or "the various socio-economic structures that exist in Russia at the present time," were not merely the same as in 1918 but that their respective weight had not been fundamentally altered. At the beginning of 1921, just as in 1918, Lenin declared that "the term Soviet Socialist Republic implies the determination of the Soviet power to achieve the transition to socialism, and *not that the existing economic system is recognised as a socialist order.*"[7]

Even more important, in 1921 as in 1918, Lenin specified that what predominated was petty production, which he described as a combination of "patriarchal, i.e., to a considerable extent natural, peasant farming" with "small commodity production,"[8] and that the principal "adversaries" of this petty production were "state capitalism" and "socialism." In his view, at this time, the immediate "adversary" of petty production, capable of preventing the latter from turning in on itself and vegetating, was "state capitalism," for socialist relations were as yet embryonic, and could develop only if "state capitalism" were first strengthened.[9]

On the basis of the survey he made in 1921 of the existing economic relations, Lenin was to give attention, all through the years 1921–1923, to the conditions for socialist transformation of economic relations. We shall see what analyses he carried out and what conclusions he arrived at.

(b) The dictatorship of the proletariat in Russia

At the end of 1921, when Lenin drew up his balance sheet of the proletarian work of the Russian Revolution, he stressed that the central aspect of this work was the establishment of the dictatorship of the proletariat.

The half-century that has passed since this thesis was formulated fully confirms that the Russian Revolution opened a new epoch in the history of mankind: the epoch of the dictatorship of the proletariat, of the revolutionary struggles of the oppressed peoples, the epoch in which capitalism and imperialism are suffering major defeats.

Lenin's thesis, of course, did not mean (as we have just seen) that the proletarian work of the revolution had been "completed" in Russia itself. Nor did it mean that what had been won in October 1917 had been won "definitively." On the contrary, Lenin constantly emphasized the fragility and imperfection of the form in which the dictatorship of the proletariat had been realized in Russia. He stressed that consolidation of the proletarian power necessitated close links with the masses, a correct political line, and a thorough upheaval in the existing state apparatus—even going so far as to say that it had to be smashed all over again.

Already during the "war communism" period Lenin had acknowledged that the form of proletarian power conceived before October had not in fact been realized—that the soviets were not organs animated by the working masses but organs functioning *on their behalf.*

In 1922, in the political report which he delivered on March 27 to the Eleventh Party Congress, Lenin returned to this same idea:

Our machinery of government may be faulty, but it is said that the first steam engine that was invented was also faulty. No one knows whether it worked or not, but that is not the important point; the important point is that it was invented. Even assuming that the first steam engine was of no use, the fact is that we now have steam engines. Even if our machinery of government is very faulty, the fact remains that it has been created; the greatest invention in history has been made; a proletarian type of state has been created.[10]

In 1923, in his last piece of writing intended for publication, Lenin went further. Not only did he observe that the existing state apparatus was not truly socialist, but he added: "The most harmful thing would be to rely on the assumption . . . that we have any considerable number of elements necessary for the building of a really new state apparatus, one really worthy to be called socialist, Soviet, etc."[11]

After five years of revolution it seemed, then, that the form in which the dictatorship of the proletariat had been realized in Russia was hardly "soviet," in the strict sense of the word, and that the state apparatus was hardly to be considered socialist. Consequently, the proletarian nature of the ruling power was fundamentally determined by the proletarian character of the leading party and by the relations that this party was able to develop with the advanced elements of the working class and the popular masses.

The proletarian character of the party was also fragile. As a result of the rapid growth in its membership and the entry into its ranks of elements with little political training, it was no longer the make-up of the party that determined its proletarian character. In 1922 Lenin, as we have seen, stressed this point in the letter he sent on March 26 to Molotov, for communication to the Central Committee: "Taken as a whole (if we take the level of the overwhelming majority of Party members), our Party is less politically trained than is necessary for real proletarian leadership in the present difficult situation."[12] Let us also recall that in this same letter Lenin declared that "the proletarian policy of the Party is not determined by the character of its membership, but by the enormous undivided prestige enjoyed by the small group which might be called the Old Guard of the Party."[13]

What then characterized the transitory form of the dictatorship of the proletariat in Russia was that its existence was closely bound up with the revolutionary work accomplished by Russia's masses under the leadership of the Bolshevik Party, with the relations of trust which, over a period of years, had been formed between the party's leaders and the advanced elements of the masses, and with the capacity acquired by these leaders to deal with some of the problems presented by the struggle against the bourgeoisie.

This transitory form of the dictatorship of the proletariat was fragile, however, for the party's leading group was small in numbers, it was divided, and, above all, on several occasions the majority of its members had shown how easily they could allow themselves to be influenced by opportunist ideas, either right or "left," and by nationalist tendencies.

The significance of this factor of fragility must nevertheless not be overestimated. Historical experience shows that it is inevitable that, at various moments, the elements defending a proletarian line find themselves in the minority, even among the leaders of a revolutionary Marxist party: what is essential is that the proletarian revolutionary elements eventually make their ideas prevail, and that they take, or recover, in good time the leadership of the party. This possibility existed in those days in the Bolshevik Party, as was shown by the fact that when Lenin was at first in the minority, he succeeded in the end in getting his view accepted.

III.   *The stages of the Russian Revolution*

The balance sheet of the work accomplished after five years of revolution leads us to consider what were the stages passed through by the revolution between 1917 and 1923. Lenin suggested several "periodizations."

During the second half of 1918, when the poor peasants'

committees were developing, Lenin thought, as we know, that the Russian Revolution was entering a fully proletarian stage in the countryside as well. Subsequent facts showed him that this was not the case. In 1921, therefore, he acknowledged that the proletarian work of the revolution had been essentially political, and that, even at this level, the socialist stage had been begun only to a very partial degree.

At that moment Lenin was brought to distinguish between three major periods in the revolutionary process.

The first, covering the months between October 1917 and the spring of 1918, was that in which the revolution accomplished its main political tasks: establishment of the dictatorship of the proletariat, expropriation of the landlords, withdrawal of Russia from the imperialist war, and nationalization of the principal means of production, of transport and exchange.[14]

The second period ran from the spring of 1918 to the spring of 1921: the period of "war communism." In this period, the central tasks were economic and military.

A third period began in the spring of 1921. Lenin described it as a period of "the development of state capitalism on new lines,"[15] on the lines of the New Economic Policy.

The state capitalism of which Lenin spoke at that time embraced also the state-owned sector of industry, in which, from March-April 1918 onward, the practice had become established of "remunerating specialists at rates that conformed, not to socialist, but to bourgeois relationships."[16]

It is by taking account of the nature of the predominant economic relations that we can understand the specific form toward which the dictatorship of the proletariat tended at that time, for, in the last analysis, political forms are determined by economic relations. Revolutionary class struggle may smash the bourgeois political machinery, but as long as the fundamental economic relations (those in which the immediate producers are involved) have not been transformed, the tendency for the bourgeois machinery of state to be reconstituted is always present. However, the socialist transformation of economic relations is a task much more protracted and complex than the smashing of the state machine, and so, even after the first stage of the proletarian revolution has been traversed, struggle must still be carried on for the revolutionary transformation of the superstructure and of the production relations.

We shall see that Lenin increasingly moved toward these conclusions by way of his analysis of the mistakes made during "war communism" and of the problems presented by the building of "state capitalism" under the dictatorship of the proletariat. We shall also see how the experience of the 1921–1923 period led him to rectify his original conception of the New Economic Policy.

Notes

1. Lenin, *CW*, vol. 33, p. 112.
2. *CW*, vol. 32, p. 486.
3. *CW*, vol. 33, p. 112.
4. *CW*, vol. 32, p. 329 ff.
5. Ibid., p. 330.
6. " 'Left-Wing' Childishness and the Petty-Bourgeois Mentality," in *CW*, vol. 27, pp. 323 ff.
7. *CW*, vol. 32, p. 330. (My emphasis—C.B.)
8. Ibid., p. 331.
9. I shall examine this conception in Chapter 2 of Part Five.
10. *CW*, vol. 33, p. 301.
11. In *Better Fewer, But Better,* in ibid., p. 488.
12. *CW*, vol. 33, p. 256.
13. Ibid., p. 257.
14. Lenin's report on the NEP to the Seventh Moscow Gubernia Conference of the Russian Communist Party, in *CW*, vol. 33, p. 87.
15. Ibid., p. 100.
16. Ibid., p. 88. Lenin made this clear in 1918, when he pointed out that, owing to the position accorded to the specialists in state industry, it was capitalist relations that were being established there, "for capital is not a sum of money but definite social relations" (*CW*, vol. 27, p. 249).

2. The mistakes of "war communism" analyzed

Lenin's balance sheet of the first years of the revolution did not, of course, consist merely of an enumeration of the changes effected and the stages traversed. It included also a critical evaluation of the past activity of the Bolshevik Party. Lenin undertook an analysis of past mistakes so as to prevent their repetition. His balance sheet was also a self-criticism directed at some of the measures taken during the period of "war communism," and at the significance which had been ascribed to them.

I. The mistakes of "war communism" and their consequences

The passages in which Lenin subjects "war communism" to critical analysis are numerous, but they do not all illuminate in the same way the nature of the mistakes made and the implications of these mistakes.

(a) Lenin's analysis of the mistakes made

It was especially toward the end of 1921—at a moment when the application of the NEP (which the Bolshevik Party had adopted in the spring of that year) was encountering difficulties and calling for rectification—that Lenin set himself to analyze "war communism." Thus, in the article he published in Pravda for the fourth anniversary of the October Revolution, he wrote: "We expected—or perhaps it would be

451

truer to say that we presumed without having given it adequate consideration—to be able to organise the state production and the state distribution of products on communist lines in a small peasant country directly as ordered by the proletarian state. Experience has proved we were wrong."[1]

The mistakenness of the policy followed is clearly acknowledged here, but the nature of the mistake is not clarified. On the one hand, the passage suggests that the obstacle to a communistic organization of production and distribution lay mainly in the existence of petty peasant production. On the other, it seems still to imply that organization "on communist lines" could have been established by way of orders from the state. This formulation is aimed particularly at stressing the need for stages which must be passed through before there can be any question of a communist form of organization.

A few days after publication of the passage just quoted, Lenin returned to the same problem, saying: "We made the mistake of deciding to go over directly to communist production and distribution."[2]

Here, too, it would seem that the mistake that was made did not relate to the significance of the measures taken (which Lenin regarded as "communist measures") but to the moment when they were adopted: they were apparently premature.

Actually, however, Lenin went further than that. For him, the mistakes of "war communism" did not concern merely the moment when the measures of state organization characteristic of this period were introduced, but also the view that was taken of the nature of the social relations which these measures were capable of bringing into existence. This was said, for example, in the report Lenin presented on October 29, 1921, to the Seventh Party Conference of Moscow Gubernia, where the following formulation appears: "We assumed that by introducing state production and state distribution we had established an economic system of production and distribution that differed from the previous one."[3]

This formulation clearly recognizes that the forms of state intervention characteristic of "war communism" had not altered the economic system which existed previously, but only some of the conditions of its functioning, so that it was not the case that the economic system "differed from the previous one": the previous production relations remained intact. This led Lenin to say, in the same report: "We must take our stand on the basis of existing capitalist relations."[4]

In this passage it is made clear that one aspect of the mistakes committed during "war communism" consisted in believing that it had "destroyed" the previously existing relations, whereas in fact these relations were still there. At the Tenth Party Congress, in his report on the tax in kind, presented on March 15, 1921, Lenin had already spoken of the "dream" some Communists had entertained of being able to arrive within three years at the socialist transformation of Russia, and, in particular, of the country's agriculture.[5]

However, in the formulation quoted above, the object of criticism is not so much the idea that it would be possible by means of state action to establish communist production and distribution, as the illusion that it would be possible to go over in a very short period of time (and without any previous experience) from individual to collective farming.

Even if Lenin did not in 1921 succeed in determining precisely what the mistakes of "war communism" were, whether they consisted in the *moment* at which certain measures were taken, or in the nature of these measures, or else in the *effects* as regards transformation in economic relations that were expected to result from them, he did consider it essential to emphasize the mistaken character of the strategy adopted and of the line followed during this period. He described this strategy as a whole as being one of an attempt at "direct assault" upon capitalism, an attempt which had failed, something that "had to be resolutely, definitely and clearly regarded as a mistake."[6]

This, then, was most definitely a piece of self-criticism. The latter seemed to Lenin to be indispensable, in order that the Bolshevik Party might not fall into similar errors when working out "new strategy and tactics"—those of the New Economic Policy.[7]

The mistakes which Lenin condemned when analyzing the

policy of "war communism" related essentially to the strategic conception to which this policy corresponded. His criticism therefore did not so much concern any of the principal concrete measures which were taken as the magnitude given them and, above all, the significance ascribed to them at the time—this illusory significance was what led to the field of application of the measures adopted being extended beyond the limit of what was necessary in order to cope with war needs. Lenin brought out this point very clearly at the Tenth Party Congress, when he said:

> The harmonious system that has been created was dictated by war and *not by economic requirements*, considerations or conditions. There was no other way out in the conditions of the unexampled ruin in which we found ourselves, when after a big war we were obliged to endure a number of civil wars. We must state quite definitely that in pursuing our policy, we may have made mistakes and gone to extremes in a number of cases. But *in the war-time conditions then prevailing*, the policy was in the main, a correct one. We had no alternative but to resort to wholesale and instant monopoly, including the confiscation of all surplus stocks, even without compensation.[8]

Shortly afterward, in his pamphlet on *The Tax in Kind,* he repeated this appreciation of "war communism": "It was the war and ruin that forced us into War Communism. It was not, and could not be, a policy that corresponded to the economic tasks of the proletariat. It was a makeshift."[9]

The scale of the measures of coercion introduced under "war communism" was, indeed, largely dictated by the war needs with which the Soviet power had to cope at a time when the country was in a state of grave economic chaos, and when the prevailing indiscipline, connected with petty bourgeois conceptions that were present even in the working class, made it impossible to secure overnight a voluntary form of discipline. From the end of 1917 and still more in and after 1918, many peasants tried to keep back for themselves a large proportion of their produce, though this was needed at the front, and large-scale absenteeism developed in industry. Already in the spring of 1918 the workers in a number of factories sold off machines, spare parts, or stocks of goods so as to increase their own incomes[10] which were rapidly decreasing in real value owing to the rise in prices. In the emergency situation created by the war it was not possible to count upon "self-discipline" emerging overnight. The survival of the army and of the urban population, especially the workers, had to be ensured at all costs.[11]

During "war communism" Lenin was, in fact, the Bolshevik leader who continued to see most clearly (although he was sometimes overcome by the illusions of the time) that the measures which were then being taken were exceptional in character, dictated by war needs. Others, such as Trotsky, Bukharin, and Preobrazhensky—followed, apparently, by many party members—saw in these measures the "direct transition to communism."

(b) The effects of the mistakes of "war communism"

The policy of "war communism" did indeed enable Soviet Russia to emerge victorious, despite the physical exhaustion suffered by the workers and the breakdown of the economy. Events proved that by following this policy, the ruling power set up by the October Revolution was able to mobilize sufficient strength and to concentrate upon the essential tasks of the moment the energy and heroism of the masses fighting for the revolution.

Nevertheless, the way in which the "war communism" measures were applied, especially on account of the mistakes resulting from the illusion of "direct" transition to communism, eventually produced negative effects which became particularly serious as soon as the policy of "war communism" ceased to be justified by war needs. This became the situation in the autumn of 1920. At that time, through not deciding quickly enough to abandon the measures for requisitioning agricultural produce, militarizing labor, and "governmentalizing" the trade unions, the Bolshevik Party allowed serious discontent to develop among wide sections of the peasantry and the working class. This discontent, which increased during the winter of 1920–1921, found local expression in peasant revolts and strikes, and matured the conditions for the Kronstadt rebellion. These were the facts Lenin had in mind when he said that the mistakes made had caused the Bolshevik Party to suffer a defeat graver than any which had been suffered on the war front,[12] for the relations between the Soviet power and many sections of the popular masses took a serious turn for the worse at that time. The introduction of the NEP only gradually enabled this situation to be improved.

"War communism" had other, more lasting consequences. The withering of the activity of the soviets, which had begun already in the spring of 1918, was hastened by the extreme centralization to which this form of the militarization of economic and political relations tended. During the second half of 1918, the authority of the local soviet organs was subordinated to that of the central organs—the Revolutionary Military Council of the Russian Soviets and the local revolutionary committees derived from this body, the "Council for Workers' and Peasants' Defense," and the Cheka. The weakness of the party's local organizations favored this development, as we have seen, for "localist" or "regionalist" tendencies were not sufficiently countered by the unifying activity of the party, so that the various localities or regions tried to keep as much of their production as possible for themselves—which was incompatible with war needs. The tendency for the activity of the local soviet organs to become paralyzed was thus rooted in a real situation, but this paralysis was aggravated by the false conception held by the Bolshevik Party at that time regarding the significance of "war communism." The question must therefore be asked: what were the sources of this false conception?

II. The sources of the mistakes of "war communism"

It follows from what has been said that the mistakes made during "war communism" were not all of the same nature. Some seem to have been essentially "practical," due to the way in which the political line was carried out. Thus, the measures of coercion dictated by the emergency needs of the war and the Bolshevik Party's inability to mobilize rapidly, and on a voluntary basis, the material and human resources required by the army and for the defense and survival of the towns, were applied on too large a scale and in an arbitrary fashion. Other mistakes seem to have been essentially political and ideological, inherent in the political line itself, in the illusory attempt at "direct transition to communism."

The distinction between these two types of mistake may seem to be connected with the difference between two types of apparatus. The "practical" mistakes might appear to have been committed by state organs which were not proletarian in character and had been penetrated by bourgeois elements, while the ideological and political mistakes were due to the Bolshevik Party itself. Actually, however, this distinction is not satisfactory. On the one hand, it is not true that the "practical" mistakes were committed only by state organs that were nonproletarian in character. The workers' detachments and Bolshevik political commissars sent into the countryside usually acted in the same way as the strictly state organs. Furthermore, the carrying out of the mistaken measures of "war communism" was governed by political directives adopted by the Bolshevik Party and not by the administrative machinery of state.

On the other hand, and above all, even if we accept the distinction between the two types of mistake, it has to be recognized that since the Bolshevik Party yielded power, what played the dominant role was the political line that it, the party, decided upon.

It must therefore be acknowledged that the dominant aspect of the mistakes of "war communism" was ideological and political. These mistakes arose from the party line and from the analysis made by the Bolshevik Party of the problems it had to solve, an analysis in which certain theoretical conceptions played their part.

(a) Lenin's explanation of the mistakes made

For Lenin there could be no doubt that the mistakes of "war communism" were political mistakes, and he tried to find the explanation of them accordingly. In order to give his answer he made use of a metaphor. He compared capitalism to a fortress which the party had tried to take by storm instead of laying siege to it, which would have been the only way to capture this fortress. He added that until the storming of the fortress had been attempted, it was not possible to know that this was impossible and that only a siege would enable the fortress to be taken. In conclusion, Lenin laid down this general principle: "In solving a problem in which there are very many unknown factors, it is difficult *without the necessary practical experience* to determine with absolute certainty the mode of operation to be adopted against the enemy fortress, or even to make a fair approximation of it."[13]

Lenin's reply to the question is correct in principle, for it is true that, when one is faced with a new situation, only practical experience enables one to learn how to solve correctly the problems presented. This reply thus clearly states that, in conditions where no practical experience is available, mistakes are inevitable, and that one must make mistakes in order to make progress. This means, too, that theory cannot run ahead of practice (although it can guide practice by drawing systematic conclusions from past practice). Nevertheless, Lenin's answer is inadequate.

In giving this explanation, Lenin seems to accept—in contrast to what he writes on other occasions—that the measures of "war communism" could be regarded as appropriate not only to ensuring the urgent defense of the Soviet power, but also to smashing capitalist relations and causing communist ones to arise. The metaphor employed suggests, indeed, that the forces available to the proletariat in order to carry through the "assault" were inadequate, and that this necessitated a resort to the method of "siege"—from which it could be concluded that when the proletariat's forces had grown (through increase in the membership of the Bolshevik Party, better ideological training, improved relations with the masses, more effective subordination of the state administrative apparatus, etc.), it would be correct to engage in the same sort of "direct assault" as had failed previously. This was, in a way, the conclusion arrived at by the Bolshevik Party at the end of the 1920s. In reality, however, what was mistaken was to consider that measures of state coercion could be substituted for action by the masses and for the revolutionary transformation of ideological relations in the struggle for a radical transformation of production relations.

Lenin's explanation that it was impossible to foresee that an attempt to transform production relations by the methods of "war communism" would fail, is unsatisfactory also from another point of view. What Marx had written on the nature of production relations and on the conditions for their transformation—for example, when he analyzed the experience of the Paris Commune—ought, it would seem, to have shown that the methods of "war communism" were not such as to bring about a transformation in production relations. The Bolshevik Party, and Lenin in particular, were not unaware of Marx's analysis, and they regarded it as correct. Consequently, one cannot be satisfied with Lenin's explanation of the mistakes of "war communism," but must approach in another way the question of the origin of the illusions that made them possible.

(b) The origin of the illusions about "war communism"

Several factors seem to explain how these illusions were able to appear, to last for several years, and even to be revived at the end of the twenties.

One of these factors, the significance of which can only be briefly referred to here, is the tendency to identify the activity of the party with that of the masses, and in particular with that of the mass of the workers. To be sure, there was only a tendency toward such an identification. On more than one occasion, indeed, Lenin mentioned that some measure or other adopted by the party was not understood or accepted by the working class, and that a risk therefore existed that the class might not follow the party. The distinction between party and class was thus certainly present in Lenin's thinking.

It is true, all the same, that where most of the measures taken during "war communism" were concerned and the way in which these measures were conceived, *everything proceeded as though action by the party and of the state machine was identical with action by the masses themselves*—which reminds us of the metaphor of "merging" which Lenin used[14]—a metaphor which, if taken literally, tends to hide the contradictions that can develop between the party and the working class.

Later on, the tendency to identify the party with the class was to reemerge very strongly and, because not corrected in time, to produce most serious effects.

This, though, is only one factor in the explanation. We need to ask why practice itself did not reveal sooner that the measures taken by the party and the Soviet state during "war communism" were not leading to the destruction of the former capitalist relations and to the building of new relations. In other words, we need to consider why the economic relations that existed during "war communism" were taken to be communist relations in the process of construction.

If the question is put like this, the elements of an answer seem to be available.

First, as we have seen in connection with the role ascribed to the state economic apparatus, the Bolshevik Party had not completely broken with some of the conceptions which had taken shape in the German Social Democratic Party, identifying state ownership and state centralization with the destruction of capitalist relations—though Marx, Engels, and Lenin himself had often pointed out that development in the direction of socialism, far from implying reinforcement of the state, necessarily implies that the latter withers away, this being an effect of the consolidation of the dictatorship of the proletariat. In *The State and Revolution* Lenin clearly stresses that socialism presupposes disappearance of the state in the strict sense of the word. Lenin takes over this expression quite explicitly in the notes he made while reading the *Critique of the Gotha Programme* and other passages in Marx and Engels dealing with the problem of the state, in particular the passage in a letter from Engels to Bebel in March 1875, in which, drawing the lesson of the Paris Commune, Engels wrote: "The whole talk about the state should be dropped, especially since the Commune, which was no longer a state in the proper sense of the word . . . We would therefore propose to replace *state* everywhere with *Gemeinwesen,* a good old German word which can very well convey the meaning of the French word 'commune.' "[15]

If, despite the antistatism of *The State and Revolution,* and despite the warning given by Lenin when he used the expression "state capitalism under the dictatorship of the proletariat" precisely in order to prevent any confusion being made between state organization of production and distribution and the building of socialism, the governmental measures taken in the "war communism" period were interpreted as equivalent to "the immediate building of socialism," this was because the very magnitude of the state's action destroyed at that time the old forms of existence of capitalist relations and of the bourgeoisie, and so created the illusion that this activity led by the Bolshevik Party could be such as to smash the old economic relations.

This illusion was reinforced by the fact that the massive intervention of the state in the sphere of distribution had resulted in largely eliminating *commodity and money circulation.* They were replaced by measures of requisitioning and state-controlled distribution of products. In this situation, it was enough to identify commodity and money relations with capitalist relations (as is done in a frequent, though mistaken, interpretation of some passages in Marx) to proceed from recognition that commodity and money circulation had virtually disappeared to the conclusion that capitalist relations themselves had disappeared. This was how the illusion came to prevail that "war communism" had established socialist production and distribution.

That it was indeed an illusion was confirmed by the open resurgence of commodity exchange when "war communism" ended, when extensive application of the state measures which had removed commodity relations from the economic foreground was given up. The rapidity of this open resurgence, and the large scale on which it occurred, were due precisely to the fact that capitalist production relations had never been "destroyed," that is, replaced by new social relations. It was therefore enough for repression to be relaxed and a larger quantity of goods to become available for the commodity and money relations which had been repressed until then to come to the surface once more.

It is necessary, indeed, to emphasize that even during "war communism" the disappearance of commodity exchanges was more formal than real. In every town there were in fact places where illegal traffic was carried on almost openly, since it was tolerated by the police. An example was Sukharevka Square in Moscow, a name which even became the word commonly used in Russian to mean "black market." The scale of this illegal traffic was such that in 1919–1920 the official distribution of foodstuffs in the towns covered, generally speaking, no more than 25–40 percent of the calories needed by the inhabitants.[16]

In any case, whatever may have been the scale of the illusions which the very conditions of "war communism" caused to arise, certain facts are clear: these illusions were not analyzed at the time, and even afterward this analysis was not developed—instead, it was merely recognized that "war communism" had failed as a policy for transforming social relations. This inadequate understanding affected the formulation of the new line adopted after the abandonment of "war communism." This line was first presented as a return to the conception of "state capitalism" in the form which it had taken in the spring of 1918; then, as a really new policy, corresponding to the conception of the NEP which was formulated by Lenin in and after the autumn of 1921. Later, in Chapter 4, I shall come back to these different conceptions of the NEP, but before examining them it is necessary to consider the role played by the notion of state capitalism.

Notes

1. Lenin, *CW*, vol. 33, p. 58.
2. Ibid., p. 62.
3. Ibid., p. 88.
4. Ibid., p. 98.
5. *CW*, vol. 32, p. 216.
6. *CW*, vol. 33, p. 86.
7. Ibid.
8. *CW*, vol. 32, pp. 233–234. (My emphasis—C.B.)
9. Ibid., p. 343.
10. Liebman, *Leninism under Lenin*, p. 334.
11. Between 1918 and the end of 1920, epidemics, famine, and cold killed 7.5 million people in Russia, the First World War having already claimed 4 million victims. See Sorlin, *The Soviet People*, p. 78.
12. *CW*, vol. 33, p. 63.
13. Ibid., p. 85. (My emphasis—C.B.)
14. In August 1919, in an article entitled "Letter to the Workers and Peasants a propos the Victory over Kolchak," Lenin wrote: "The dictatorship of the working class is being implemented by the Bolshevik Party, the party which as far back as 1905 and even earlier merged with the entire revolutionary proletariat" (*CW*, vol. 29, p. 559).
15. Marx and Engels, *Selected Works*, vol. 3, pp. 34–35.
16. Carr, *The Bolshevik Revolution*, vol. 2, pp. 242–243.

3. "State capitalism"

In the period immediately after the abandonment of "war communism," between the spring and autumn of 1921, the prevailing conception of the NEP was, as we have seen, that it meant *a return to the policy of state capitalism,* the policy that the Bolshevik Party had proposed to follow on the morrow of the October Revolution. This "return" testifies to the central position occupied for a long period, in the thinking of Lenin and the Bolshevik Party, by the idea of state capitalism under the dictatorship of the proletariat.

I. The place occupied in the policy of the Bolshevik Party by the conception of state capitalism under the dictatorship of the proletariat

When we read Lenin's writings of 1917 and early 1918, we see clearly that the expression "state capitalism under the dictatorship of the proletariat" is being used in order to draw a strict line of demarcation between the legal and political changes which it was then possible to carry out, and the destruction of capitalist production relations. What had to be emphasized was that, even under the dictatorship of the proletariat, the nationalization and statization of the means of production shake capitalist economic relations only to a limited extent: they do not "abolish" these relations, any more than they cause the bourgeoisie to "disappear."

However, this expression does not serve merely a

"pedagogic" purpose, warning people not to confuse forms of state ownership with socialist economic relations. It corresponds also to a certain conception of the "stages" through which it is necessary to pass in order to reach socialism. Thus, in *The Impending Catastrophe and How to Combat It*,[1] Lenin writes: "For socialism is merely the next step forward from state-capitalist monopoly. Or, in other words, socialism is merely state-capitalist monopoly *which is made to serve the interests of the whole people* and has to that extent *ceased* to be capitalist monopoly."[2]

These propositions are themselves based on a certain number of premises. They suggest that the forms of organization of capitalism in its "most advanced" phase are necessarily those upon which the proletariat must and can base itself in building socialism. The problem of the relation between these forms and their class content (the fact that they correspond to certain class relationships) is not clearly presented, so that the only important question that seems to arise is that of who controls the use of these forms. This is what Lenin says: "In point of fact, the whole question of control boils down to who controls whom, i.e., which class is in control and which is being controlled."[3]

This is fundamentally correct, for the question of power is of primary importance, but to put the matter like this does not render pointless a number of other questions. Can the mode of control and the forms of organization required by this mode of control be the same for both of two antagonistic classes, an exploited class and an exploiting class?

If not, what changes does the exercise of power by the proletariat dictate in the concrete ways of control? Must not these ways of control themselves be modified, depending on whether the principal task of the hour is to consolidate proletarian power or to bring about socialist transformation of economic relations?

In October 1917 the question was settled—at least as far as the stage at which the revolution then stood was concerned—in favor of the possible, and even necessary, identity of the forms of organization of state capitalism under the dictatorship of the bourgeoisie and under the dictatorship of the proletariat, with one decisive reservation, namely, that control over the apparatus of state capitalism must be exercised by the popular masses themselves (and not, "in their name," by some other branch of the state apparatus). But this reservation begs exactly that very question, namely, whether the popular masses can really exercise control over the highly centralized apparatus of state capitalism. In 1917 the Bolshevik Party answered this question affirmatively.

In fact, given the concrete conditions of the time, which we have discussed earlier, it must be acknowledged that there were at that moment no other possible ways of avoiding total disorganization and "fragmentation" of the economy[4] than the measures which were then taken, and which in fact involved only a very slight degree of control by the popular masses who were, generally speaking, not interested in this sort of activity.

In any case, the problems of the general necessity of a stage of state capitalism, of its eventual role in the advance toward socialism, of the contradictions of such a stage, and of the way to deal with these contradictions, were not really discussed. At the time, the "stage" of state capitalism seemed to the Bolshevik Party to be an obvious necessity, and the "model" offered by the German war economy seemed to be one that should be emulated.

In practice, the class struggle led the Bolshevik Party in 1918 to apply, or to try to apply, two variants of the same fundamental conception of "state capitalism under the dictatorship of the proletariat."

(a) The variant applied between October 1917 and March 1918

The first of these aimed at encroaching as little as possible on the legal ownership of enterprises. It prevailed, broadly speaking, until March 1918. In the course of this period, the organization and regulation of industry by the state was seen as the main thing, and enterprises were not usually confiscated unless the workers in them demanded that this be done, or else as a "punitive" measure. At the Third Congress of Soviets, in January 1918, Lenin confirmed this orientation of policy, stating that the enterprises of some capitalists had been nationalized and confiscated in order "to compel them to submit."[5]

At the beginning of 1918, one of the immediate reasons most often put forward by Lenin in support of the policy of state capitalism, and more particularly of the policy then being followed, which involved only a limited number of expropriations and nationalizations, was the catastrophic situation in which the Russian economy then found itself. In this situation Lenin considered that it was necessary to halt momentarily the offensive against capital, the struggle to destroy capitalist economic relations and build new, socialist ones. Replying to those who wanted, on the contrary, to continue this offensive, Lenin wrote, for example, in *The Immediate Tasks of the Soviet Government:* "The present task could not be defined by the simple formula: continue the offensive against capital. Although we have certainly not finished off capital and although it is certainly necessary to continue the offensive against this enemy of the working people, such a formula would be inexact, would not be concrete, would not take into account the *peculiarity* of the present situation in which in order to go on advancing successfully *in the future,* we must 'suspend' our offensive now."[6]

Here, state capitalism appears less as a stage than as a policy of halting the revolutionary offensive. For Lenin, however, it was not a question of a real halt. As far as he was concerned, "what we are discussing is the shifting of the *centre of gravity* of our economic and political work. Up to now, measures for the direct expropriation of the expropriators were *in the forefront.* Now the organisation of accounting and control in these enterprises in which the capitalists have already been expropriated and in all other enterprises, advances *to the forefront.*"[7]

(b) The second variant

The second variant of "state capitalism under the dictatorship of the proletariat" was one that was oriented toward the large-scale expropriation of the old bourgeoisie, while retaining the bourgeois forms of state organization and regulation, in state-owned industrial enterprises as elsewhere. This second variant came into operation after the signing of the Treaty of Brest-Litovsk.

To Bukharin and the "left Communists," who protested against this conception, Lenin counterposed the attitude of the workers who, he said, "having grown out of the infancy when they could have been misled by 'Left' phrases or petty-bourgeois loose thinking, are advancing towards socialism precisely through the capitalist management of trusts, through gigantic machine industry, through enterprises which have a turnover of several millions per year—only through such a system of production and such enterprises. The workers . . . are not afraid of large-scale 'state capitalism' . . ."[8]

In this same article on " 'Left-Wing' Childishness and the Petty-Bourgeois Mentality" Lenin also put forward other arguments which presented state capitalism not as a "stage," but as a policy justified by the isolation of the Russian Revolution and the need to mark time, while holding on to power, until the proletarian revolution should triumph in Germany too.

At the beginning of 1921, when the first conception of the NEP was outlined, Lenin again stressed the need, under the conditions then existing, to have recourse to state capitalism under the dictatorship of the proletariat.

(c) The "return" to state capitalism in 1921

In Lenin's pamphlet on *The Tax in Kind*,[9] the NEP is seen essentially as a "return" to state capitalism clothed in the form that the Bolshevik Party had wanted in 1918. It will be seen later that this conception of the NEP was very temporary; it was abandoned in the autumn of 1921. Theoretically, however, it is important, testifying as it does to the considerable place still occupied by the conception of state capitalism under the dictatorship of the proletariat in the policy and ideology of the Bolshevik Party.

Concretely, state capitalism presented itself at that time in many different aspects. In his pamphlet, Lenin mentioned those that seemed to him the most important: the granting of concessions to foreign capitalists; cooperatives of small producers and petty capitalists (which Lenin distinguished, of course, from workers' cooperatives); the leasing to capitalist entrepreneurs of industrial, commercial, and mining enterprises belonging to the state, etc.[10] These aspects of state capitalism were then those most recently introduced. They must not lead us to forget the earlier aspects already established and still in force—the recruiting of capitalists and bourgeois technicians to run state enterprises, and the capitalist relations maintained in these enterprises (the capitalist hierarchy of authority and of wage levels in the state enterprises), the capitalist forms of organization of the overall management of the state enterprises, and the participation of capitalists and bourgeois technicians in these forms of organization (especially the role played by the VSNKh, to which workers' control was in practice subordinate).

These last-mentioned aspects of state capitalism deserve all the more attention because they were to persist when Soviet Russia entered what Lenin called a new phase of "retreat," one which seemed to him to signify the abandonment of state capitalism in favor of a new conception of the NEP. Actually, the break effected when the transition was made from the first to the second conception of the NEP, called into question much more than the abandonment of state capitalism, as we shall see when we analyze these two conceptions. Before doing so, however, we must examine the origins of the notion of "state capitalism under the dictatorship of the proletariat" and its place in the development of Lenin's thought.[11]

II. The origins of the conception "state capitalism" and its place in Leninism

The notion of "state capitalism" first appeared before the First World War, in the Social Democratic parties of Germany and Austria. It was in these parties that certain leaders and theoreticians, such as Kautsky and, especially, Hilferding, drew attention to the decisive role being played by the central apparatuses of state monopoly capitalism, and saw in this a prefiguring of the economic machinery which the proletariat would need in order to build socialism.

The German Social Democratic Party thus reproduced bourgeois and petty bourgeois conceptions of "socialism" against which Marx and Engels had waged ceaseless struggle. For years Engels strove, for example, to make known to the masses and the party members the antistatist theses expounded by Marx in his *Critique of the Gotha Programme.* Only belatedly did he succeed in getting the agreement of the German party leaders to the publication of this work. Soon afterward he managed to have eliminated from the Erfurt Program of the German Social Democratic Party the fresh resurgences of statism that had been contained in the original draft. The program as finally adopted declared that the party could have nothing in common with what was called "state socialism," in which the state takes the place of the private entrepreneur, "and thereby concentrates in the same hands the power of economic exploitation and political oppression."[12]

We know how sharply Lenin broke with Kautsky's ideas regarding the political apparatus of the bourgeois state and the possibility of the proletariat's making use of it. In *The State and Revolution,* for example, he wrote: "In his very controversy with the opportunists, in his formulation of the question and his manner of treating it we can now see, as we study the *history* of Kautsky's latest betrayal of Marxism, his systematic deviation towards opportunism precisely on the question of the state."[13]

Lenin showed in rigorous fashion the incompatibility of Kautsky's ideas on the question of the state with the teachings of Marx, and in doing so reminded his readers that, in order to exercise its dictatorship, the proletariat must smash the state machine of the bourgeoisie and build a political apparatus of its own, a state which is destined to wither away.

Having effected this break, however, Lenin nevertheless declared that the state economic apparatus which had been formed in the monopoly stage of capitalism must be retained. Thus, he wrote:

> In addition to the chiefly "oppressive" apparatus—the standing army, the police and the bureaucracy—the modern state possesses an apparatus which has extremely close connexions with the banks and syndicates, an apparatus which performs an enormous amount of accounting and registration work, if it may be expressed this way. This apparatus must not, and should not, be smashed. It must be wrested from the control of the capitalists; the capitalists and the wires they pull must be *cut off, lopped off, chopped away* from the apparatus; it must be *subordinated* to the proletarian Soviets; it must be expanded, made more comprehensive, and nation-wide. And this *can* be done by utilising the achievements already made by large-scale capitalism (in the same way as the proletarian revolution can, in general, reach its goal only by utilising these achievements).[14]

In Lenin's writings of this period there is still a contradiction between the class analysis of the bourgeoisie's political apparatus, which Lenin says emphatically must be smashed, and the role he assigns to the economic apparatus of state capitalism, which he presents as needing to be preserved, in order that it may be subordinated to the organs of proletarian power. The position maintained by Lenin thus fixes a limit to the work of destruction-and-reconstruction to be accomplished by the proletarian revolution. This position raises a number of questions.

The first set of questions concerns the stages to be traversed by the revolution under proletarian leadership. Lenin agrees that the revolution is not a once-and-for-all "act" but a *process that passes through stages*, and he indicates that each of these stages is marked off by the *limits* to the work of destruction-and-reconstruction of social relations which can actually be realized. However, there are some ambiguities regarding the nature of these stages, their content, and the conditions governing transition from one stage to another. For instance, state capitalism appears sometimes as a *stage* which has to be gone through for apparently "technical" reasons (it is by traversing this stage that the proletariat "learns" to manage the economy: it cannot advance until it has passed through the stage of a state capitalism which it brings increasingly under its own control); but elsewhere, state capitalism appears as a *policy* which the proletariat applies during a certain *stage in the class struggle*. This conception of state capitalism as a *policy* is one that tends to become predominant from 1921 onward.[15]

Another ambiguity is to be observed in Lenin's writings of 1918, which do not make clear whether, upon transition to the next stage of the revolution, the apparatuses of state capitalism are destined to be destroyed, or whether, on the contrary, they are destined to play a role also in the building of socialism (the latter not being, in Lenin's view, the task that confronted the Russian Revolution in 1918).

Obviously, one should not expect Lenin to answer in advance a question which the class struggle had not yet raised concretely. Nevertheless, some of his formulations in that period might suggest that the same apparatuses are destined, without being revolutionized, to play a part in socialist construction.

A second set of questions relates to the *conditions for transformation of the social relations* established in the apparatuses of state capitalism. Whereas Lenin usually "puts politics in command," and stresses that the transformation of social relations necessitated by the transition to socialism results from *class struggle* and action by the masses, he did nevertheless use formulations from which it could be concluded that, under the dictatorship of the proletariat, once private ownership of the means of production has been abolished, the transformation of social relations results from the development of the productive forces and not from the class struggle—notably, in the case of the disappearance of the division between physical and mental work. For example, he writes:

> When we see how incredibly capitalism is already *retarding* this development [of the productive forces], when we see how much progress could be achieved on the basis of the level of technique already attained, we are entitled to say with the fullest con-

fidence that the expropriation of the capitalists will inevitably result in an enormous development of the productive forces of human society. But how rapidly this development will proceed, *how soon it will reach the point of breaking away from the division of labour, of doing away with the antithesis between mental and physical labour,* of transforming labour into "life's prime want"—we do not and cannot know.[16]

This formulation, despite its cautious phrasing, shows that at the very moment when he was writing *The State and Revolution*—that is, when he was breaking with those theoretical positions of Social Democracy which he had never attacked so resolutely before—Lenin had not yet entirely abandoned the idea of a transformation of social relations (what he calls "breaking away from the division of labor") resulting, given certain political conditions, from the development of the productive forces, nor (for the two ideas are linked together) that of a relatively long-lasting role to be played by the apparatuses of state capitalism.

Actually, where these questions are concerned (the place and role of state capitalism, the conditions for the socialist transformation of social relations), two different views conflict—and coexist—in Lenin's thought. One of them, the "dominant" view, puts in the forefront the class struggle waged by the masses as a factor in the destruction-and-reconstruction of social relations and, in the first place, of social production relations; the other, the "dominated" view (in the sense that it usually plays a secondary role), sees the emergence of new production relations as being dependent on the development of the productive forces.

The presence in Lenin's thought of this second conception—which, when it is dominant, is that of economism—is not at all surprising. Certain passages in Marx (in particular, the 1859 Preface to the *Contribution to the Critique of Political Economy*) seem not to rule it out completely, and these passages, interpreted in an economistic way, played a big part in the ideology of the Second International, with which Lenin made a break that was still incomplete in 1918.

At the level of theory, the difficulty in breaking with the

economistic interpretation of certain passages in Marx lies in the fact that it is true that, in general—that is, as long as the prevailing production relations do not hinder their development—it is the productive forces that play the principal and decisive role: however, when the productive forces can no longer develop within the limitations of the prevailing production relations, the principal and decisive role is played by the transformation of the production relations. It is here that an ideological "slip" may occur, leading one to suppose that under certain conditions, namely, given the dictatorship of the proletariat, a radical transformation in production relations may be effected "peacefully," under the "pressure" of the productive forces—whereas the "necessity" of a transformation of the production-relations does not render this transformation "inevitable," but merely makes possible the opening of a period of social revolution.[17]

To return to Lenin's passage in which he refers to "breaking away from the division of labor": it suffers from the defect of suggesting (though not actually saying) that, once "the expropriation of the capitalists" has been effected, "breaking away" from the old economic relationships can thenceforth take place as a direct consequence of the development of the productive forces. An interpretation on similar lines might lead one to affirm that the transformation of the apparatuses of state capitalism and of the social relations embodied in them can likewise result from mere development of the productive forces. *This interpretation, which makes the productive forces, rather than the class struggle, the driving force of history,* and which therefore contradicts the fundamental ideas of Marx and Lenin, has been adopted by modern revisionism. It is an interpretation which *rules out the continuation of the revolution under the dictatorship of the proletariat.* It thus leads to consolidation of the elements of capitalist relationships, more or less transformed (in particular, the *capitalist division of labor*), which continue to exist after the political power of the bourgeoisie has been destroyed and a state-owned economic sector established. It thus disarms the proletariat and enables the bourgeoisie to strengthen its position—in particular as a *state bourgeoisie*. Finally, this interpretation results in hindering the further development of the productive forces.

Despite the brevity of the period of the dictatorship of the proletariat for which he was able to draw up a balance sheet (and of the very special character of this period, which was largely dominated by military tasks), Lenin's last writings show with increasing clearness that he was in the process of breaking with what he had retained of the economist interpretations of Marx's analyses. He was jettisoning more and more of what remained of "Kautskyism" in the role that, in 1918, he still assigned to state capitalism considered not as a policy, but as a form of organization which could serve directly (that is, without being revolutionized) for building socialism and for dealing with the contradictions between the proletariat and the petty bourgeoisie. Analysis of the successive formulations that Lenin gave to the New Economic Policy enables us to perceive clearly how he was moving, in 1922–1923, toward a break with his conceptions of 1918. The fact that this transformation of Lenin's ideas had not been completed, and the contradictions which, consequently, are to be found in some of his formulations, made it possible later, by interpreting his writings in a one-sided way and ignoring the movement of thought which is expressed in them, falsely to identify state capitalism with socialism, and this in the name of a "Leninism" which betrays precisely that which is new in Lenin.

Notes

1. Written in September 1917 and published as a pamphlet in late October (*CW*, vol. 25, pp. 319–365).
2. Ibid., p. 358.
3. Ibid., p. 342.
4. It needs to be recalled that the winter of 1917–1918 saw a tendency to economic disintegration: each locality, each region tried to keep for itself whatever it produced, and even seized

goods in transit across its "territory," so as to ensure priority satisfaction of its own consumer needs.

5. *CW*, vol. 26, p. 461; see also Carr, *The Bolshevik Revolution,* vol. 2, pp. 79 ff. It will be observed that the nationalization decrees adopted in those days were practically always accompanied by a "statement of reasons" which did not refer to a policy of expropriation as a matter of principle but to specific reasons which justified each separate measure.

6. *CW*, vol. 27, p. 245.

7. Ibid., p. 246.

8. "'Left-Wing' Childishness," in *CW*, vol. 27, p. 349.

9. *CW*, vol. 32, pp. 329 ff.

10. Ibid., pp. 346, 347, 349.

11. This place seems to have been even bigger in the first variant of the NEP.

12. Engels, *Critique of the Erfurt Programme,* in Marx and Engels, *Selected Works,* vol. 3, p. 432.

13. *CW*, vol. 25, p. 477.

14. *CW*, vol. 26, pp. 105–106.

15. It was in this sense of the expression that the Chinese Communist Party practiced a policy of "state capitalism" during the transition from "new democracy" to socialism. The concrete content of the policy of state capitalism was in China inevitably different to some degree from what it had been in Russia. For example, it included investment by the state in private capitalist enterprises (which became "mixed" enterprises), contracts associating private enterprises with state enterprises, and the transformation of private capitalist enterprises into state enterprises in which the former capitalists retained for a certain period their managerial function and high salaries, and were paid interest on the capital of the enterprises they had formerly owned. This policy was applied mainly in the early 1950s. Some of the economic relationships to which it gave rise continued to be reproduced until the Great Proletarian Cultural Revolution (and not all of them were destroyed by the latter).

16. *CW*, vol. 25, pp. 468–469. (My emphasis—C.B.)

17. As we know, Lenin emphasized that this period covers an "entire historical epoch," that of the transition to communism, during which a bourgeois restoration still remains possible (*CW*, vol. 28, p. 254).

4. The changes in Lenin's conception of the NEP[1]

The passages in which Lenin tackles the problems of the New Economic Policy are extremely important. He increasingly raises to the level of theory the experience, both positive and negative, of the first years of the revolution. He starts from a recognition of the failure of "war communism" and, while apparently "returning" to the conceptions of 1917–1918, actually formulates, to an increasing degree, a new strategy—a strategy enriched by experience and taking more and more into account the fact that the proletarian revolution in industrial Europe no longer seems so imminent, so that it is necessary to consider with ever-greater acuteness *the problems of building socialism in a country with a peasant majority*, and accordingly to define a new class strategy and a new economic strategy, differing from those which had been followed up to that time. To be sure, many elements of this new strategy can be found in Lenin's earlier writings, but organized in a different way.

The body of writing in which Lenin deals with these problems was continually being added to between 1921 and 1923. We see in these works literally the birth of new ideas, a broader view of the contradictions, and an ever more precise formulation of the requirements for a correct treatment of these contradictions.

It is essential to grasp the forward movement of Lenin's thinking, for the latter was a veritable "laboratory." Analyzing the progress of his thought enables us to perceive what is meant by a living application of Marxism: it is also very instructive because it illustrates the obstacles to the birth of new formulations, constituted by the existence of earlier, inadequate formulations.

477

I.   *Lenin's conception of the NEP in the*
   spring of 1921

The first conception of the NEP, formulated in the spring of 1921, presents it as aimed above all at coping with an emergency situation in which it is impossible to continue with the policy of requisitioning, and necessary to reckon with the demands of the peasantry.

Basing himself upon his analyses of 1917 and early 1918, taking account of the failure of "war communism," and paying maximum attention to the actual demands put forward by the peasants, Lenin assembled the elements of a first conception of the NEP.

This first conception was one of temporary compromises which had to be accepted so as "to hold out until the victory of the international revolution."[2] It did not aim (as Lenin was to try to do in subsequent writings) to open up a new road to socialism, but merely laid the foundations for measures that were indispensable in order to strengthen Soviet power.

On the plane of economic policy, this initial conception of the NEP (which prevailed, broadly speaking, from March to October 1921) was paralleled by two types of measures. On the one hand, as we know, requisitioning of the peasants' produce was abandoned and replaced by a tax in kind, with reestablishment of a certain degree of freedom of exchange for the peasants, as well as for small traders and small-scale industry. On the other, "concessions" were granted to foreign big capital, with the twofold purpose of setting one section of international finance capital against another and reactivating Russian industry, which was then in a practically paralyzed condition. This second component of the New Economic Policy was at that time regarded as the chief one, following as it did the line of "state capitalism," of which the NEP then seemed merely a variant. The NEP, conceived as a variant of state capitalism, was justified in Lenin's eyes by the analysis he made at that time of the relations which the proletariat was in a position to maintain with the peasant masses. In the spring of 1921, a political alliance between the proletariat and the peasantry seemed to him possible only insofar as the proletariat was fighting to uphold the democratic revolution, and not taking as its task the socialist transformation of social relations on a large scale. A policy of economic agreement with the peasantry was necessary, however, in order to consolidate the dictatorship of the proletariat—in order to "save the socialist revolution in Russia," as Lenin put it in his report of March 15, 1921, to the Tenth Congress of the Bolshevik Party. He explained his line of thought thus: "The interests of these two classes [the peasantry and the proletariat—C.B.] differ, the small farmer does not want the same thing as the worker."[3]

At the Tenth All-Russia Conference of the RCP(B), held May 26–28, 1921, Lenin returned to the same idea, pointing out that alliance between the peasantry and the proletariat had been possible under the conditions of the civil war because the White offensive also threatened the peasants with restoration of the power of the big landlords: "It is the Civil War that was the principal reason, the principal motive force, and the principal determinant of our agreement [with the peasantry] . . . It was the principal factor that determined the form of the alliance between the proletariat and the peasantry." Making the point even more clearly, he added: "As soon as we had finally done away with the external enemy . . . another task confronted us, the task of establishing an *economic* alliance between the working class and the peasantry."[4]

The "economic" (and therefore not principally political) character of the alliance between the workers and the peasants was here emphasized, it will be seen, by Lenin himself.

In this same report, Lenin still ascribed an essential position to large scale industry: "Large-scale industry is the one and only real basis upon which we can . . . build a socialist society. Without large factories, such as capitalism has created, without highly-developed large-scale industry, socialism is impossible anywhere; still less is it possible in a peasant country."[5] Furthermore, he linked the existence of proletarian class consciousness with the presence or absence of large-scale industry: "The principal material basis for the development of proletarian class-consciousness is large-scale industry."[6]

At that time, one of the aims in view was consolidating the "economic alliance" between the proletariat and the peasantry through the development of "socialist exchange" (on a nonmonetary basis) between town and country. In practice, this amounted to a rather unfavorable attitude toward the revival of rural industry, the basis of the peasants' day-to-day existence. Some of the purposes envisaged by the conception of the NEP which prevailed in the spring of 1921 were not really such as to consolidate de facto the economic alliance between the proletariat and the peasantry.

Lenin considered, however, that, taken as a whole, the concessions made to the peasantry would ensure that the contradictions between this class and the proletariat would not develop into antagonistic contradictions, though a relationship of antagonism would threaten as soon as the proletariat tried to undertake tasks other than those of the democratic revolution. In the same address to the Tenth Party Conference, Lenin expressed himself in these terms: "Either the peasantry comes to an agreement with us and we make economic concessions to it—or we fight."[7]

In this period, as Lenin saw it, the latent, constantly threatening antagonism between the proletariat and the peasantry was bound up with the petty bourgeois character of the latter: the main enemy of the proletariat was the petty bourgeois element[8]—from which followed the conclusion that "we need a bloc, or alliance, between the proletarian state and state capitalism against the petty-bourgeois element."[9]

In his report in July 1921 to the Third Congress of the Comintern, Lenin defined again, with precision, what his conception then was of the relations between the proletariat and the peasantry. As he saw it, there existed in all the capitalist countries (except, perhaps, Britain), besides the exploiting classes, also "a class of small producers and small farmers. The main problem of the revolution now is how to fight these two classes."[10]

The fight against the small producers and small farmers could not, of course, be waged in the same way as the fight against the big landowners and capitalists, for the simple reason that these social classes made up more than half of the population. Consequently, they

> cannot be expropriated or expelled; other methods of struggle must be adopted in their case. From the international standpoint, if we regard the international revolution as one process, the significance of the period into which we are now entering in Russia is, in essence, that we must now find a practical solution for the problem of the relations the proletariat should establish with this last capitalist class in Russia . . . This problem now confronts us in a practical way. I think we shall solve it. At all events, the experiment we are making will be useful for future proletarian revolutions, and they will be able to make better technical preparations for solving it.[11]

This conception, in which the petty bourgeoisie (and therefore the peasantry) were defined as the "chief enemy,"[12] was the counterpart of the conception which aimed at promoting state capitalism. We see repeated here one of the themes developed by Lenin in 1918 in his pamphlet on " 'Left-wing' Childishness," in which he stressed that in the combination of elements which "actually constitute the various socio-economic structures that exist in Russia at the present time," it was not socialism that was at grips with state capitalism, but "the petty-bourgeoisie plus private capitalism fighting together against both state capitalism and socialism."[13]

In this passage, as in others, Lenin proposes, therefore, an alliance between socialism and state capitalism against small production, state capitalism being defined not just as a policy, but as an "economic and social form" characterized by "planned state organisation," and making possible "the material realisation of the economic, the productive and the socio-economic conditions for socialism"—conditions which, in Lenin's view, seemed to be such as existed in Germany, whereas in Russia there were only the political conditions for socialism, namely, the dictatorship of the proletariat. Hence his conclusion that "our task is to *study* the state capitalism of the Germans, to *spare no effort* in copying it and not shrink from adopting dictatorial methods to hasten the copying of Western culture by barbarian Russia, without hesitating to use barbarous methods in fighting barbarism."[14]

One of the significant themes developed in the pamphlet on *The Tax in Kind* is that of bureaucracy, in which Lenin sees, not without reason, a product of the "pre-capitalist" character of Russia, the "patriarchalism" of the country's "peasant backwoods," with villages isolated one from another, over which a bureaucracy can easily impose its yoke,[15] though remaining incapable of helping the peasants to emerge from their condition—whereas the combination of the dictatorship of the proletariat with state capitalism, in the form of the NEP, seemed to him to be capable of doing this. Thus, in this conception of the NEP, state capitalism was at that time the sole means of struggling—given the restricted forces of the Bolshevik Party, especially in the countryside—against bureaucracy (that other form of development of the petty bourgeoisie), corruption, and the regime of bribe-taking. It would enable regular relations to be strengthened between town and country and help destroy the economic conditions upon which arose a superstructure that the proletarian revolution had not really been able to destroy.

Lenin added that, despite the capitalist nature of the development of exchange that was being stimulated in this way, its effects were less to be feared than those that would result from maintaining the existing conditions, since this would lead to the collapse of the dictatorship of the proletariat, whereas the development of capitalism allowed by the New Economic Policy could be kept within limits, owing to the existence of the workers' and peasants' government and the expropriation of the big landowners and the bourgeoisie.[16]

Lenin did not, of course, say that the political and economic conditions then existing were sufficient to set a limit to the development of capitalism. He wrote, for example: "The whole problem—in theoretical and practical terms—is to find the correct methods of directing the development of capitalism (which is to some extent and for some time inevitable) into the channels of state capitalism, and to determine how we are to hedge it about with conditions to ensure its transformation into socialism *in the near future.*"[17]

This formulation is interesting from a number of angles. It brings out the very provisional character of this conception of the NEP. It emphasizes the need to find "the correct methods" for restricting the development of capitalism. And it raises the problem of transforming state capitalism into socialism—thus clearly counterposing the one to the other and excluding the possibility that, since the dictatorship of the proletariat has been established, the development of large-scale industry within the framework of state capitalism can result in socialism without any need for a process of transformation which would be dependent on a correct political line. As for the correct political line, Lenin points out that it cannot be arrived at in abstract fashion: its concrete content depends on the specific handling required by the existing contradictions, and in particular, the class contradictions. In order to be correct, the concrete content of the political line must therefore be determined by practical experience, which may necessitate both bold advances (real or apparent) and temporary "retreats" connected with the implementation of new methods. The road leading to the consolidation of the dictatorship of the proletariat and eventually to the building of socialism, cannot be found in any book: it is not "straight as the Nevsky Prospekt" (to use one of Lenin's old expressions), and the methods that seem to "approach" most directly the demands of socialism, are not necessarily always those most appropriate to the situation—that is, to the demands of the class struggle. Accordingly, the variant of the NEP put forward in the spring of 1921, like its successor, was not advanced as a readymade solution of the problems but as an attempt at a solution, to be scrapped or modified if, in practice, it were to prove impracticable.

II.   *Lenin's conception of the NEP after the autumn of 1921*

A few months' experience showed that the NEP, if conceived as a new form of state capitalism and as an alliance between the latter and socialism against the petty bourgeoisie, was not viable. This was due to a number of reasons: the development of "concessions" and of exchange did not proceed easily; the weight of the machinery of state, invaded as it had been by the old tsarist bureaucracy, continued to be a crushing burden; and in these conditions the initiative from below to which the first conception of the NEP had also sought to appeal[18] did not get under way. The year 1921 was a year of famine. Industrial production made no progress. The supply of food to the towns and to those rural areas which did not produce enough to feed themselves remained gravely inadequate. Lenin drew fresh conclusions from this state of affairs, and proposed a profound transformation of the NEP.

In October 1921, in a report presented to the Seventh Party Conference of the Moscow Gubernia,[19] Lenin redefined the NEP and economic relations with the peasantry.

In the spring we said that we would not be afraid to revert to state capitalism, and that our task was to organise commodity exchange . . . What was implied by that term? . . . It implied a more or less socialist exchange throughout the country of the products of industry for the products of agriculture, and by means of that commodity exchange the restoration of large-scale industry as the sole basis of socialist organisation. But what happened? . . . This system of commodity exchange has broken down, it has broken down in the sense that it has assumed the form of buying and selling . . . We must admit that we have not retreated far enough, that we must make a further retreat, a further retreat from state capitalism to the creation of state-regulated buying and selling, to the money system.[20]

Economically, this new definition of the NEP meant a comparatively extensive reestablishment of overt commodity and money relations. The Bolshevik Party agreed thereafter to the development of these relations on a scale much greater than had been foreseen initially, when it had hoped to establish "direct" (non-monetary) relations between units of production, between agriculture and industry, town and country, the state sector and the peasants. Reestablishment of commodity and money relations was now considered essential for a real restoration of the economy. Generally speaking, it was this change in the "economic" conception of the NEP that attracted attention and appeared significant.

Actually, however, what was most important was the political implications of this second variant of the NEP. It was, in fact, the beginning of a new type of relationship between the proletariat and the peasantry, since what had been previously described as an "alliance" between state capitalism and socialism, was no longer what was aimed at. What this really meant was a new "renunciation" of the attempts to subject the peasants to state economic apparatuses, the function of which was to impose various constraints upon them and thereby to exact from them produce and conditions of exchange to which they would not otherwise have agreed. The road was thus open for seeking an alliance with the peasantry that should be not merely economic but also political. In other words, the Bolshevik Party's adoption of this second version of the NEP implied the possibility of a new realignment of class forces, a reconstruction on new foundations (not yet clearly defined at the end of 1921) of the alliance between workers and peasants—the only firm basis, in a country like the Russia of that time, for strengthening the dictatorship of the proletariat.

The concrete conditions for an advance along this newly opened road were not, however, immediately favorable. On the one hand—and I shall come back to this when dealing with the image of a "retreat" used to describe the NEP—at the ideological level it was not yet clear whether the redefinition of the relations between the proletariat and the peasantry was tactical in character (and so temporary, being dictated by circumstances) or strategic (allowing a fundamental political line to be defined). On the other hand, the feeble representation of the Bolshevik Party in the villages, a heritage from its past, was not such as to enable it to grasp overnight the profound aspirations of the peasant masses and form close ties with the poor peasants and the less-well-off middle peasants, so as to help them fight against that strengthening of the richer elements among the peasantry which the "second" NEP might favor.

As long as the concrete conditions had not been created for a political alliance between the proletariat and the decisive masses of the peasantry (who were still under the ideological and political influence of the well-to-do strata of the countryside), the worker-peasant alliance tended to assume a mainly economic character. Since, however, such an economic alliance was not a component of an effective political alliance, it was very fragile, owing to the contradictions that might deepen between the peasants in their capacity as commodity producers (trying to sell their goods at the highest prices possible) and the workers and the Soviet state.

But, though real, such economic contradictions can remain secondary, provided they are properly handled, for the fundamental interest of the broad masses of the peasantry is to find a way by which to transform radically the economic relations to which they are subject, a way that frees them from exploitation by the rich peasants, merchants, and usurers (whose forces grew during the first years of the NEP), and ensures a radical improvement in their conditions of life; the peasant masses, however, cannot find this way without the help and guidance of the proletariat, its *organization* and *ideology*, which give priority to the collective interest over the interest of the individual and over petty bourgeois egoism. When the initial conception of the NEP was changed at the end of 1921, the question arose: under what conditions, by applying what measures, can the proletariat in power achieve a political alliance of a new type with the peasants, an alliance the aim of which is not merely fulfillment of the democratic tasks of the revolution but also consolidation of the dictatorship of the proletariat in order to build socialism? This question arose moreover, ever more concretely as time went by and the prospect (once regarded as imminent) of the Russian Revolution merging with a proletarian revolution in the industrialized countries of Europe, especially Germany, became fainter and fainter.

In his last works—written at the beginning of 1923, and thus the fruit of over a year's further experience—we can see that Lenin took a decisive step toward the formulation of an answer to this question. He sets out his conclusions in concise fashion in *On Co-operation, Our Revolution;* and *Better Fewer, But Better.*[21]

(a) "On Co-operation"

In the first of these works, Lenin refers to the polemical character of some of his earlier formulations on state capitalism—which forbids us to regard everything he said previously on this subject as still representing his views in 1923.[22] But the decisive importance of *On Co-operation* lies above all in the fact that it accords a big place to co-operative production as a socialist form of production accessible to the peasantry.

He thus criticizes the attitude formerly taken up by the Bolshevik Party, which, he says, was "already beginning to forget the vast importance of the co-operatives," had given them "not enough attention," and had treated them with "contempt." He stresses that the cooperative movement is of "immense importance" (given that the state owns the means of production) from the standpoint of the transition to socialism, for it is the means that is *"simplest, easiest and most acceptable to the peasant."*[23]

Here, in a single phrase, we find rejected the one-sided importance which had been ascribed to state enterprises (in particular, to state farms), and the role of cooperation emphasized, especially as regards the peasantry, which was thenceforth more and more at the center of Lenin's preoccupations. Writing of the peasantry, he says: "If the whole of the peasantry had been organised in co-operatives, we would by now have been standing with both feet on the soil of socialism."[24]

The cooperatives whose development is thus identified

with creation of the conditions for transition to socialism may assume the widest variety of forms, but this cooperative movement must be voluntary in character, based on the conviction of the peasants themselves.

In formulating these propositions, Lenin was combating a tendency which was very strong in the Bolshevik Party, and which had developed especially strongly during "war communism." In that period, many Bolshevik leaders sought practically to integrate the cooperatives into the "Soviet organs," which in the circumstances meant not the *local soviets* (the organs of self-administration by the masses) but centralized administrative apparatuses (the Supreme Economic Council, the Commissariat of Food Supplies, the Commissariat of Agriculture).[25] In fact, this would have amounted to nationalizing the cooperatives. A majority of the "section for study of the co-operatives" at the Ninth Congress of the Bolshevik Party did, moreover, pronounce in favor of such a measure of nationalization. Only an intervention by Lenin at this congress led to the proposal being withdrawn. ("It is . . . impossible to speak of the nationalisation of the co-operatives as yet . . . First of all create a basis, and then—then we shall see.")[26]

In 1923 Lenin assigned a considerable role to cooperation. In his view, it was not merely a preparatory phase. "Co-operation under our conditions," he said, "nearly always coincides fully with socialism," for it makes possible the development of socialist economic relations. As we see, the question that Lenin is dealing with here is not that of the legal ownership of the means of production (which in this work appear as owned by the state), but the social production relations. This is why the "co-operative system" does not merely have a place in what Lenin often calls a "phase of transition to socialism," but is itself "the system of socialism."[27]

This work possesses a twofold significance: a general-theoretical one (which Lenin did not have time to develop), and a conjunctural one.

The general-theoretical significance of *On Co-operation* is that it shows Lenin making another break with one of the variants of the "statist" notions inherited from the Second

International. By explicitly affirming the socialist nature of the cooperatives under the dictatorship of the proletariat, Lenin links his doctrine with the quite explicit formulations found in Marx and Engels, which had so often been "overgrown" by simplistic conceptions of a statist character. In the political conditions of the time, the trimph of these conceptions could foster the reproduction of bourgeois social relations, under a specific legal covering, and enable nonproducers to dispose of the means of production by way of the state machine.

The "oblivion" into which the passages have fallen in which Marx and Engels gave great importance to cooperation and producers' associations, makes it necessary, no doubt, to remind the reader of them.

In *The Civil War in France,* Marx says that one of the great lessons of the Commune, resulting from the revolutionary boldness of the Communards, was that it promulgated practical measures "destroying . . . state functionarism." Among these were not only the political measures mentioned by Lenin in *The State and Revolution* (putting officials, whose numbers should be reduced, under control by the masses, who were to elect them, and fixing their rates of payment at the same level as workers' wages), but also economic measures, such as the transfer by the Commune of the means of production to associations of workers. In his introduction to *The Civil War in France*, written in 1891, Engels says that "by far the most important decree of the Commune instituted an organisation of large-scale industry and even of manufacture which was not only to be based on the association of the workers in each factory, but also to combine all these associations in one great union: in short, an organisation which, as Marx quite rightly says in *The Civil War*, must necessarily have led in the end to communism."[28]

A few years previously, writing about the period of transition to communism, Engels emphasized the fact that neither Marx nor himself "had ever doubted that in the case of transition to a communist economy it would be necessary to make extensive use of co-operative enterprises as an intermediate rung, provided that matters were organised in such a way that society (and so, to begin with, the state) retained ownership[29] of the means of production in order that the special interests of the co-operatives in contrast to the interest of society as a whole might not become consolidated."[30]

Thus, Lenin's *On Co-operation* links up with Marx's analyses and *carries further,* on this special but impórtant issue, the break with the ideas of the Second International already begun in *The State and Revolution.*

The situation of this work in the political conjuncture of late 1922 and early 1923 is equally important. *On Co-operation* gives concrete form to the implications of Lenin's conception of the NEP as it had begun to take shape toward the end of 1921. It does this by opening up a new path for the alliance between the workers and the peasants, thereby extending substantially the bearing of the passages in Marx and Engels which were particularly concerned with workers' cooperatives. The new conclusions to which Lenin thus arrived were the outcome of the experience of the first five years of the Russian Revolution, and of an analysis of the successes and failures recorded which brought out more and more clearly the right way to handle the contradictions that had developed between the proletariat and the peasantry on the basis of political and economic practices which were partly misconceived. These writings thus draw the lesson to be learned from past mistakes.

(b) The development of socialist economic relations and the struggle against the state machine

It was not accidental that Lenin was at one and the same time trying to find a path that would enable socialist economic relations to develop at the actual level of peasant production, and undertaking a struggle against the state machine.

In his writings of early 1923, Lenin mentions the need to carry out a set of tasks relating to the transformation of political and economic relations. He enumerates these tasks: struggle against a state machine inherited from tsardom, destruction of this machine and construction of a genuinely socialist one, launching joint work with the peasantry on a basis of trust, a fierce fight against megalomania, waste, boasting, and respect for hierarchy and the forms and usages of administrative procedure—all the features characteristic of a state machine which is "socialist only in name." In Lenin's view, these tasks could be accomplished only through reestablished and genuine unity between the working class and the peasantry, and by calling upon the advanced workers to learn, through practice and with a critical spirit, not fearing to condemn what might prove to be negative in past or present experience. Lenin thus denounced in advance many of the later attempts to "advance" by means of the same bureaucratic and statist methods as before.

The main axis of this political line of struggle against a state machine which he described as being the old tsarist one "anointed with Soviet oil," was the ideological and political leadership exercised by the proletariat over the peasantry. It was no longer a question of strangling the petty bourgeois element by means of coercion (though this must, of course, continue to be used against open violation of the rules of economic and political conduct laid down by the dictatorship of the proletariat), but of convincing the peasant masses and building along with them, step by step, a state of a really new type: "We must strive to build up a state in which the workers retain the leadership of the peasants, in which they retain the confidence of the peasants, and by exercising the greatest economy remove every trace of extravagance from our social relations.

"We must reduce our state apparatus to the utmost degree of economy. We must banish from it all traces of extravagance, of which so much has been left over from Tsarist Russia, from its bureaucratic capitalist state machine."[31]

The building of a new type of state, the development of relations of trust between the workers and the peasants, and the leading role of the working class implied the application of the mass line in new forms. This was necessary in order to build new political relations, which could only be consolidated, however, through transformation of the economic relations themselves, and, in the first place, of the production relations. As Marx wrote: "It is always the direct relationship of the owners of the conditions of production to the direct producers . . . which reveals the innermost secret, the hidden basis of the entire social structure, and with it the political form of the relation of sovereignty and dependence, in short, the corresponding specific form of the state."[32]

The link that Lenin established between transforming production relations in agriculture through cooperation and transforming the state was thus not at all fortuitous. Nevertheless, it is true (and I shall come back to this point) that Lenin does not take up in these works a whole series of questions concerned with the transforming of production relations in industry. Perhaps this was because, as Marx puts it, "mankind never sets itself tasks which it cannot solve," and the ideological and political conditions (the degree of acuteness of the contradictions) where transformation of production relations in industry was concerned, were not yet present at that time.

Even though Lenin does not tackle in its full magnitude the problem of revolutionary transformation of production relations in industry (that is, radical transformation of the production process), he does deal with some extremely important aspects of this problem (and this already in the spring of 1921), when he comes out in favor of a certain form of industrial development based on "the utmost local initiative," and of "small local industry."[33] He is not here rejecting the rapid development of large-scale industry, but he is sketching a line that was later to be put into effect in China under the two slogans of "walk on two legs"[34] and "two initiatives are better than one."[35] Lenin's writings are certainly far from being the equivalent of these slogans and their relation to the fight against the various forms of the division of labor inherited from class societies, but it is possible to perceive in them the start of such an orientation. His writings of 1923 confirm this, with their contrasting of the megalomania and unrealism of the state apparatuses with the modesty and earnestness of the initiatives coming from below, from the workers and peasants, thus stressing once again the need for a mass line for the revolutionary transformation of economic relations.

In any case, the beginning of such an orientation in Lenin's last writings was clear enough, the threat that this orientation represented to the state bourgeoisie then taking shape in the administrative and economic apparatuses was definite enough, and the capacity for pressure possessed by this "new bourgeoisie" was itself strong enough for *On Co-operation* and *Our Revolution*, which were written in January 1923, not to appear in *Pravda* until the end of May—an exceptionally long delay in the publication of anything written by Lenin.

(c) Mass line, cultural revolution, and transformation of economic relations

During the first months of the NEP, Lenin urgently stressed the need vigorously to apply a mass line once again. In his pamphlet *Instructions from the Council for Labour and Defence to Local Soviet Bodies*,[36] he wrote:

A number of capable and honest non-Party people are coming to the fore from the ranks of the workers, peasants and intellectuals, and they should be promoted to more important positions in economic work, with the Communists continuing to exercise the necessary control and guidance. Conversely, we must have non-Party people controlling the Communists. For this purpose, groups of non-Party workers and peasants, whose honesty has been tested, should be invited to take part, on the one hand, in the Workers' and Peasants' Inspection, and on the other, in the informal verification and appraisal of work, quite apart from any official appointment.[37]

This "instruction" clearly advocates the establishment of *control by the masses over the state apparatuses and over the Communists themselves*. This orientation is reiterated constantly thereafter in Lenin's writings and speeches, in his interventions at the Eleventh Congress of the Bolshevik Party (at the end of March and beginning of April 1922),[38] and in the works he wrote at the beginning of 1923.

In the last-mentioned writings, Lenin emphasizes particularly the role of direct contacts between workers and peasants. On this point, the following passage, taken from *Pages from a Diary*, deserves quotation: "It is our duty to establish contacts between the urban workers and the rural working people, to establish between them a form of comradeship which can easily be created. This is one of the fundamental tasks of the working class which holds power. To achieve this we must form a number of associations (Party, trade-union and private) of factory workers, which would devote themselves regularly to assisting the villages in their cultural development."[39]

In this passage, as in others, what is aimed at is many-sided organization of the masses, and activity by the workers among the peasantry so as to help the latter organize themselves, in order that they may not have to bow down before administrative apparatuses having nothing socialist about them, in order that they may control these apparatuses, and in order that they may gradually move in the direction of socialism of their own accord, thanks to the leading activity of the proletariat but without haste or coercion.

In the same period Lenin also returns to the theme of "cultural revolution" as an indispensable condition for the development of socialism. To be sure, what he has in mind, "for a start" (and, therefore, not as a final aim), is "real bourgeois culture," which, he thinks, will enable the masses to shake off "the cruder types of pre-bourgeois culture, i.e., bureaucratic culture or serf culture, etc." It is clear that when Lenin speaks of "bourgeois culture," he does this in order to brush aside the prefabricated notions of "proletarian culture" which were being advocated by "many of our young writers and Communists," and not in order to dismiss a genuine proletarian culture that would really "become part and parcel . . . of our social life, our habits."[40]

For Lenin, be it remembered, the term "cultural revolution" refers to two interwoven revolutionary processes. The first of these corresponds to the accomplishment, in the domain of way of life and education, of the democratic revolution: it is in this sense that Lenin speaks of getting rid of "pre-bourgeois culture, i.e., bureaucratic culture or serf culture, etc." The second process is that of a proletarian cultural revolution, the conditions for which Lenin was unable, at the time when he was writing, to explain, but the need for which he obviously feels when he calls upon the factory workers to help in the cultural development of the countryside, and when he says that the replacement of prebourgeois cultures by bourgeois culture is only "a start."

Lenin's conception of the relations between the superstructure and the infrastructure, which was radically different from the "mechanistic" views of many other Bolsheviks, especially Bukharin, explains the dialectical way in which he presents the problem of the class struggle in the superstructure, and the revolutionary transformation of the latter as a condition for transforming the economic basis.

(d) The revolutionary role of the peasantry

Starting with the conception of the NEP which he formulated toward the end of 1921—and so also with his critical review of the relations between the working class and the peasantry during the first years of the Russian Revolution— Lenin began to work out a new political line in relation to the peasantry, a line which treated these masses as the true ally of the proletariat not merely in the democratic stage of the revolution—as an ally capable of moving toward socialism, provided that it was shown the right road.

Some writings of Lenin's previous to *On Co-operation* clearly reveal this orientation. Thus, in his speech closing the Eleventh Party Congress (April 2, 1922), he said: "The central feature of the situation now is that the vanguard must not shirk the work of educating itself, of remoulding itself . . . The main thing now is to advance as an immeasurably wider and larger mass, *and only together with the peasantry,* proving to them by deeds, in practice, by experience, that we are learning, and that we shall learn to assist them, to lead them forward." [41]

The emphasis laid on advancing together with the peasantry, and only together with them was already present in several of Lenin's earlier writings. It goes far to explain the vehemence of his struggle against the Workers' Opposition whose theses embodied the danger of "putting the craft interest of the workers above their class interests,"[42] and thereby causing the proletariat to lose "its leading role" in the "direction of policy."[43] It was only in his writings of 1923, however, that Lenin set forth some of the conditions for a political alliance that could lead the peasantry, and with them Russia, toward socialism.

This was a step forward of immense significance, for it made possible a new definition not only of the relations between the proletariat and the Russian peasantry, but of the revolutionary role of the peasantry more generally, and thereby, a fresh appreciation of the international political situation, by recognizing that the center of gravity of the international revolution might be shifting from the West to the East, to countries inhabited by great masses of peasants.

It was therefore not accidental that, at the beginning of 1923, Lenin returned to the theme of the "peasants' war," and recalled what Marx had written in 1856 about a combination of a peasants' war with the working-class movement.[44] He saw more and more clearly the role that the peasant masses of Asia were destined to play in the development of the world revolution. In the last work that he wrote for publication (*Better Fewer, But Better*, March 2, 1923), Lenin explicitly declared:

> In the last analysis, the outcome of the struggle will be determined by the fact that Russia, India, China, etc., account for the overwhelming majority of the population of the globe. And during the past few years it is this majority that has been drawn into the struggle for emancipation with extraordinary rapidity, so that in this respect there cannot be the slightest doubt what the final outcome of the world struggle will be. In this sense, the complete victory of socialism is fully and absolutely assured.[45]

III. The predominance in the Bolshevik Party of an economistic interpretation of the NEP

The Bolshevik Party mainly ascribed to the NEP a significance different from that indicated in the preceding pages. The party did not see it as orientation that would make it possible to forge a political alliance of a new type, which could unite the proletariat with the broad masses of the peasantry so as to guide them on to the road of socialist construction. In fact (as will be shown in more detail in the next volume), the Bolshevik Party conceived and "practiced" the NEP as if it were above all an economic policy (in a very narrow sense of that expression) which had been imposed upon it as a result of an unfavorable relation of forces, and which it would therefore be necessary, as soon as circumstances had altered, to repudiate purely and simply, in order once again to put into effect measures regarded as being more in conformity with the requirements for building socialism. These measures would accord with the conception of a "frontal assault" upon capitalist and commodity relations, similar to that attempted under "war communism." For many of the Bolshevik leaders, indeed, "war communism" had not ceased to seem a "model" proletarian offensive, which had had to be abandoned for essentially conjunctural reasons which could therefore be regarded as merely temporary.

Thus, in 1928, the *Large Soviet Encyclopedia* stated that what was mistaken and utopian in "war communism" was the belief that the measures taken under pressure of war emergency could bring about "immediately," under the conditions of that time, a "centralized non-commodity economy." It was thus not the measures taken during the civil war that were to be seen as inadequate: only the moment when they were introduced was seen as inappropriate. The article on "war communism" consequently declared that "in building a consistent system of war communism [the expression is used without quotation marks—C.B.], the working class was at the same time laying the foundations for further socialist construction."[46]

What we see prevailing here, as elsewhere, is an economistic interpretation of the NEP. This interpretation signified that the Bolshevik Party had lost sight of (or even had never appreciated) the fact that Lenin's last writings opened the way for a new political strategy, and led necessarily to a realignment of the relations between the workers and the peasants and to a profound transformation in the relations between the masses and the political apparatuses whose bourgeois, and even "prebourgeois," character meant that they could not serve as instruments of real socialist construction.

The reasons for the prevalence of an economistic interpretation of the NEP were numerous. The most fundamental of them were political in character and were connected with the relation of class forces in Russia, especially inside the machinery of state. However, the development of an ideological struggle such as might have enabled this interpretation to be ousted by a revolutionary conception of the NEP, in conformity with the new indications given in Lenin's last writings, also came up against difficulties of a strictly ideological order. These difficulties were connected with certain hesitations in Lenin's own thinking, and crystallized around a small number of formulations, images, and metaphors which eventually helped to "conceal," to "disguise," what was radically new in those last writings of his. The images and metaphors in question had been used by Lenin for "pedagogical" purposes, but, by being taken literally, they were deprived of their real meaning.

Since the economistic interpretation of the NEP made itself increasingly felt after Lenin's death, we must examine how this interpretation was rooted in those images and metaphors which were used as pretexts for it. Otherwise, these metaphors may continue to hide the profound meaning of Lenin's last writings.

As we know, in 1921 Lenin acknowledged the "failure," as he himself called it, of the "methods of 'war communism.'" He drew from this the conclusion that political measures of a different type must be introduced as soon as possible. He did not shrink from saying that the setback suffered was due to the mistaken character of the policy which had been followed (even though it had been dictated by circumstances). As has already been observed, however, in his writings of 1921 the nature of the mistake made was not precisely analyzed: it did not clearly emerge whether the "methods of 'war communism' " were mistaken in principle, or whether it was only the conditions of the moment that doomed them to defeat. There was thus, in these writings, a "silence" which was rather unusual where Lenin was concerned. This silence was "filled" by means of metaphors and historical analogies.

In the report which he presented on October 29, 1921, to the Seventh Party Conference of the Moscow Gubernia, Lenin compared "war communism" to the assaults launched by the Japanese against Port Arthur during the Russo-Japanese War of 1905, and then compared the NEP to the siege of that town.[47] With this comparison was linked the metaphor of "withdrawal" and "retreat,"[48] which easily suggests that the measures taken during "war communism" were not mistaken in principle—it was only the moment when they were adopted that was badly chosen, from which it might be concluded that measures of "direct assault" (Lenin's image for "war communism") might become appropriate again when circumstances had grown more favorable.

We have seen that this interpretation was not in conformity with the conclusions toward which Lenin was actually moving. Nevertheless, the metaphor he used seemed to "authorize" those who were willing to make dogmatic use of his 1921 statement (and such dogmatization became frequent after Lenin's death) to resume, as soon as this should become possible, the methods of "direct assaults," involving the employment of state coercion against the working class as well as against the peasantry.

The distortion of what was essential in Lenin's writings of 1923 found apparent justification in dogmatic interpretations of other 1921 writings of his, in which the metaphor of "withdrawal" is coupled with that of a "new retreat."

This second metaphor fills, so to speak, a second "silence" in the speech of October 1921, namely, that which occurs when Lenin observes that the "retreat" effected in the spring has proved "inadequate." He merely notes a "fact," without explaining the reasons for it. They are, it seems, faced with a situation that has to be accepted and which, he says, dictates a "further retreat."

This image of the two successive "retreats" presents the transition from the first to the second variant of the NEP as a mere prolongation of one and the same withdrawal. Yet, the second "retreat" was something quite different from a "prolongation" of the first. What was described as a "retreat" was, in reality, the beginning of a change in strategy much more radical than that which had been announced some months earlier, since it tended toward an entirely new redeployment of class forces, and was thus calculated to prepare a new offensive which would itself be radically different from the first one.

What Lenin was proclaiming in the autumn of 1921—in a way that, at that moment, was not yet fully explicit, *even for himself*—and what was of decisive political importance, was renunciation of the dominant role accorded to "state capitalism" and an endeavor to build a real, lasting, and firm alliance with the peasantry. Lenin sketched out what was later to be the political line of the Chinese Communist Party, a line aimed at drawing the working peasantry on to the socialist road, and doing this not by means of coercion but by persuasion. This was the line which Lenin was to elaborate in his writings of late 1922 and early 1923.

Unfortunately, this *gigantic step forward* was presented by means of the misleading metaphor of "retreat."

The appearance of this metaphor in Lenin's report on the NEP was a sign that the magnitude of the political and theoretical break with the errors of the previous period was hardly beginning to be apparent even to Lenin himself. This explains why, in his speech of October 1921, Lenin used another formulation, surprising at first sight, when he said: "We must take our stand on the basis of existing capitalist relations."[49]

The formulation is surprising since one obviously cannot take one's stand anywhere else but on what exists, unless one chooses some imaginary basis. That is just the point, and is one of the profound meanings of this passage—what was involved was not a "return to the past" but a *return to reality*. To say that one is "retreating" to the basis of what exists is to say that one is not really retreating at all, but abandoning the imaginary basis of nonexistent socialist relations in order to take one's stand on real relations.

To say this was also to say that "war communism" had failed in the most profound sense, not because it had led to "economic difficulties" or because it "lacked adequate forces," but because it was not capable, as had been believed, of transforming economic relations; and, consequently, that they had let themselves be deceived by the outward appearances of political and legal relations to which they had supposed the social production relations could be "reduced," and had thus mistakenly identified socialist property, legal ownership by a state of the dictatorship of the proletariat, with socialist economic relations.

If we approach the matter from this angle, we see that the NEP was not really a retreat, but only apparently so. It corresponded to the abandonment of measures that were illusory from the standpoint of progress toward socialism (even if necessary in order to cope with the demands of war), because they could not affect the profound nature of economic relations. Abandoning such measures meant not a "retreat" but an "advance," for to take one's stand on real relations instead of on illusory ones is in fact to advance: and such an advance is necessary if the real social relations are actually to be transformed.

Why is all this said in the difficult, deceptive language, not customary with Lenin, of metaphors that require decoding?

First, because, as regards the strategic significance of the NEP, Lenin in 1921 had not yet broken completely with the earlier conception which "presented" the NEP as a "retreat" aimed at realizing a mere economic alliance with the peasantry (to whom temporary concessions were made). Consequently, we find, in several of Lenin's writings, this conception coexisting, at the level of certain formulations, with another, a new conception, which represents the real tendency then at work in Lenin's thinking, a conception in which the economic alliance between the proletariat and the peasantry is no longer merely an immediate aim, but the foundation of what is essential for the future: the political alliance between the proletariat and the peasantry, an alliance through which the peasants can be guided on to the socialist road. This combination of two contradictory conceptions, one only nascent while the other is being abandoned, explains why it happened that certain writings of Lenin's were for a long time seen as merely repeating what he had said previously about the economic alliance between the working class and the peasantry.

Actually, Lenin could not have said much more than he did say at that time, for the fundamental social and political reason that he was only at *the beginning of a break*—a break with a whole set of former theoretical and political conceptions, with a whole section of what, in the ideological and political "heritage" from the Second International, had not been jettisoned in Lenin's previous break in 1917—notably as regards the considerable role attributed to state centralization, and the "forgetting" of the transformation of economic relations which was made possible by the development of cooperation.

The significance of the break that then began could not, of course, become fully apparent except through the development of a new practice of class struggle to which it opened the way, thereby ensuring new relations between the working class, as the leading political force, and the peasantry and the petty bourgeoisie in general. Until this new practice had been sufficiently developed to make possible a theoretical reformulation, the *new strategy* heralded by the break could be expressed only in the language of the old one.

On the morrow of "war communism," however, the development of a new practice of class struggle under the leadership of the Bolshevik Party was held back by the ebbing of the political activity of the masses, who were at grips with the gravest difficulties in everyday life—hunger, cold, sickness, unemployment. This development was held back, also, by the changes which had taken place in the Bolshevik Party, so that the party's break with the conceptions of "war communism" and state capitalism was slow and only very partial. These changes also hindered Lenin in defining explicitly the new strategy he was proposing. Despite these hindrances, however, Lenin gradually marked out the main lines of this new class strategy. He was able to do this because of his exceptional political experience and his mastery of Marxism. The latter enabled him to link up his thinking with the lessons drawn by Marx and Engels from the history of the class struggle, lessons which had "fallen into oblivion" in the Second International.

Notes

1. In this chapter, which forms part of the balance sheet of five years of revolution, what is examined is only the changes in Lenin's *conception* of the NEP. The *actual consequences* of the NEP, which developed mainly after 1923, will be examined in the second volume of this work.
2. See Lenin's report on "concessions," presented on April 11, 1921, to the Communist fraction in the All-Russia Central Trade Union Council, in *CW*, vol. 32, p. 305.
3. Ibid., p. 215.
4. Ibid., pp. 404–405.
5. Ibid., p. 408.
6. Ibid., p. 410.
7. Ibid., p. 420.
8. *CW*, vol. 33, p. 23.
9. Ibid., p. 28.
10. *CW*, vol. 32, p. 484.
11. Ibid., pp. 484–485.
12. "In the transition from capitalism to socialism our chief enemy is the petty-bourgeoisie, its habits and customs" (*CW*, vol. 27, p. 294).
13. *CW*, vol. 27, pp. 335–336. The passage from his earlier work is

quoted by Lenin in his 1921 pamphlet on *The Tax In Kind* (*CW*, vol. 32, p. 331).

14. *CW*, vol. 32, p. 335.
15. Ibid., pp. 349–350.
16. Ibid., p. 352.
17. Ibid., p. 345. (My emphasis—C.B.)
18. Ibid., p. 352.
19. *CW*, vol. 33, pp. 81 ff.
20. Ibid., pp. 95–96.
21. Ibid., pp. 467–480, 487–502.
22. Ibid., p. 472.
23. Ibid., pp. 467–469.
24. Ibid., p. 474.
25. *K.P.S.S. v Rezolyutsiyakh*, vol. 1, p. 495.
26. *CW*, vol. 30, pp. 483–484.
27. *CW*, vol. 33, pp. 473–474.
28. Marx and Engels, *Selected Works*, vol. 2, pp. 186–187.
29. The place accorded here to state ownership of the means of production is determined by the actual existence of the state. It is because the latter exists *during the transition*, that Engels speaks here of cooperative enterprise as an "intermediate rung." This does not mean an "intermediate rung" on the way to state ownership of the production units, since the latter is obviously destined to disappear along with the state itself.
30. Marx and Engels, *Werke*, vol. 36, p. 426: letter from Engels to Bebel January 20–23, 1886. Engels's last phrase brings up a problem of great importance, which cannot, however, be dealt with merely through state ownership.
31. Lenin, *Better Fewer, But Better*, in *CW*, vol. 33, p. 501.
32. Marx, *Capital*, vol. III, p. 772.
33. Lenin, *CW*, vol. 32, p. 352.
34. Meaning that large-scale and small-scale industry must be developed at the same time, and that both the most up-to-date and the most established techniques must be used, including traditional techniques, which, moreover, can be gradually transformed.
35. Meaning a combination of central initiative and local initiatives.
36. *CW*, vol. 32, pp. 375 ff.
37. Ibid., p. 388.
38. *CW*, vol. 33, pp. 259 ff.
39. Ibid., p. 466.

40. Ibid., pp. 487–488.
41. Ibid., p. 326. (My emphasis—C.B.)
42. *CW*, vol. 32, p. 342.
43. Ibid., pp. 341–342. (My emphasis—C.B.)
44. *Our Revolution*, (January 16, 1923), in *CW*, vol. 33, p. 476.
45. Ibid., p. 500.
46. *Bolshaya Sovyetskaya Entsiklopediya*, vol. 12, p. 376.
47. *CW*, vol. 33, pp. 84–86.
48. Ibid., pp. 95–98.
49. Ibid., p. 98.

5. The tasks before the Bolshevik Party at the time of Lenin's death

It would be futile to try to state today what the Bolshevik Party "would have been able to do" at the time of Lenin's death, if the new strategy he proposed had been put into effect. This would be a foolish exercise, for history cannot be rewritten. One may, however, legitimately consider the significance of the tasks that Lenin then sought to assign to the Bolshevik Party, and the reasons why these tasks were fulfilled only partially.[1]

I. The transitional form of the dictatorship of the proletariat and the need to strengthen it

Lenin's last writings are dominated by one essential preoccupation—to set out the guidelines for preparing the elaboration of a new basic political line for the party, giving the NEP a content such as to make it possible to advance beyond the transitional form then borne by the dictatorship of the proletariat, and to strengthen it through a number of measures which go much further than mere matters of "economic policy," concerning, as they do, also ideological and political relations.

Inevitably, the guidelines we find in Lenin's last writings are still only very general in character. To become concrete, they would have had to pass into social practice, into a multitude of experiences necessitating activity by the masses, from which the party could draw lessons conducive to rectifications.

The transitional form of the dictatorship of the proletariat as it existed in 1923 was, as we have seen, the historical result of that extreme tension of forces caused by the military struggle against the White insurrection and the imperialist intervention. We know how serious were the political and economic effects of the period from which the Russian Revolution emerged at the beginning of 1921—effects which were still present in 1923.

The system of soviets, conceived as organizations animated by the masses, remained in a state of paralysis. The country's administration was dominated by apparatuses which were no longer under direct control by the working people. Consequently, the dictatorship of the proletariat was being exercised by the Bolshevik Party, which had merged with the most militant elements of the working class. The latter, as a result of the economic chaos and the quasi-paralysis of industry, was greatly reduced in numbers and partly "deproletarianized": instead of being made up of genuine workers who had participated as such in proletarian struggles and in the practice of industrial production, it consisted to a large extent of declassed petty bourgeois who were hostile to the dictatorship of the proletariat.

At the time, the strength of the dictatorship of the proletariat in Russia was due above all to the merging of the party with a few hundred thousand workers who were wholly devoted to the cause of Communism and to the presence at the head of the party of a leadership which had successfully survived the tests and trials of the insurrection and the civil war, and was implementing a policy based on Marxist theory in the most revolutionary form this had ever assumed in an organization guiding great masses of people. The strength of the dictatorship of the proletariat in Russia lay also in the capacity of the Bolshevik Party to criticize its own activities and rectify its mistakes.

In that period, the dictatorship of the proletariat brought

about a transformation of the social process of production and reproduction which, though revolutionary, was only partial. In industry this partial transformation affected the principal factories, insofar as these had been expropriated, and where their functioning was no longer subject first and foremost to the need to make profits, but was directed toward objectives laid down by the Soviet power. This transformation implied that the managers of the factories in question were subordinated to the proletariat through the medium of the Bolshevik Party, which appointed and dismissed them and supervised their activity with the help of the trade unions and the most active workers. This supervision was exercised very unevenly, but where it existed it effectively changed the relations between the working class, the managers of the state enterprises, and the means of production belonging to the latter.

Given the situation prevailing in the state sector, upon which the dictatorship of the proletariat was actually exercised to a partial extent only, and given, too, the enormous place occupied by petty peasant production and the role played by private capitalist production (a certain development of which was tolerated by the NEP), it must be said that the transitional form of the dictatorship of the proletariat which existed in 1923 was not based on a socialist economic foundation.

In order that no illusion should persist on that point, Lenin did not hesitate to say that "for a time we shall have to live in the midst of the capitalist system."[2]

The constituent elements of this "capitalist system" were numerous. In the first place, there were the capitalist relations which were reproduced, or could arise, in the private enterprises, on the peasant holdings, or in the enterprises which had been granted as "concessions" or "leased out." These relations showed themselves in the reproduction of commodity and money exchanges and wage relations, and in the functioning of a price system not controlled by the Soviet power and exercising a far-reaching influence upon the forms and ways of reproduction of the material and social conditions of production, including those in the state enterprises.

Indeed, one of the components of the "capitalist system" of which Lenin spoke was constituted by the relations which were reproduced in the state sector. In this sector, capitalist relations were still predominant, scarcely transformed by the fact of state ownership. Although the functioning of some state-owned factories was actually subjected to the requirements of the dictatorship of the proletariat, these factories were only scattered islets (whose survival depended, moreover, on the conditions of reproduction of the rest of the economy, which was subject to the laws of individual, commodity or capitalist production). In the main, production was carried on in the state sector under the same conditions as before, both as regards what was produced and as regards *the way it was produced* (the mode of production, in the strict sense of the expression). The forms, inherited from the past, in which the elements of production were combined, had not really been changed.

We know that a genuine social transformation of the relations and forms of production calls for a protracted class struggle, a struggle which must develop through stages whose succession is dictated by the development of the contradictions involved. It is the acuteness of these contradictions that determines the activity of the masses, and it is the correct guidance of this activity that enables production relations to be transformed, thereby making them more and more socialist. In 1923 this transformation had hardly been begun. The capitalist elements in the production relations were still deeply engraved in the totality of the processes of production and reproduction, in the forms of the division of labor inside the state-owned enterprises, and in the ways in which the latter were separated from each other. Consequently, commodity and wage relations were being reproduced, so that profit in money terms made its appearance again at the enterprise level: hence Lenin's remark about "the capitalist system."

It will be remembered that already in 1918, when the Bolshevik Party took a decision aimed at subjecting the workers in the state-owned factories to a discipline imposed by appointed managers, and paying the latter, as also the engineers and technicians who were put over the direct producers, salaries that were higher than the workers' wages, Lenin had pointed out that the relations that might thereby be reproduced were capitalist in character. He made the same appreciation of the "profit basis" on which state-owned enterprises were placed at the beginning of the NEP, for he saw that the management of these enterprises was being placed "to a large extent . . . on a capitalist basis."[3]

Thus, in 1923, the situation in Russia was marked by a profound contradiction between the dictatorship of the proletariat, which had been established and was being upheld through the activity of the most militant workers, soldiers, and peasants, closely linked with the Bolshevik Party and accepting its guidance, and a set of social and class relations which weakened the Soviet power and imposed upon it the transitional form it bore at this time.

By adopting the New Economic Policy, the Bolshevik Party, and its leadership in particular, took note of this contradiction, and of a certain number of others as well. However, the analysis made by the various leaders of the party of the system of contradictions then existing was far from being unanimous, as was to become strikingly apparent after Lenin's death. The most thorough analysis of these contradictions was Lenin's own. In 1923, though, this analysis was still to some extent expressed by means of formulations that were adapted to previous conceptions, and that, though historically unavoidable, made it hard to see the situation clearly. In these circumstances, the tasks which the Bolshevik Party had to carry out in order to consolidate the dictatorship of the proletariat still did not stand out clearly. This was all the more the case because within the apparatuses of the state and the party there were social forces which were pressing for the existent "capitalist system" not to be destroyed but, on the contrary, consolidated. As we shall see later on, these forces were very active in the years that followed.

The tasks incumbent upon the Bolshevik Party, if it was to

make Russia advance along the socialist road, the tasks which were indicated, in essence, by Lenin, were several, and concerned above all the transformation of ideological and political relations.

On the plane of ideological struggle, the party needed to help the masses to acquire an outlook other than one of acceptance of the existing economic and political relations and to undertake the transformation of these relations—which called for something quite different from a series of revolts without prospect of success. In the eyes of the party's leaders who were aware of the tasks connected with this ideological struggle, the latter appeared as demanding, above all, educational work (to be carried on especially by workers, among the peasantry), constant struggle against "precapitalist" habits and customs, and a form of revolutionary activity sometimes described as "cultural revolution" (though the content of this expression was not clearly defined).

On the plane of directly political struggle, what was needed was to restore life to the soviets, combat "bureaucracy," and reduce as far as possible the size of the state apparatus, while refraining from hasty measures which experience had shown resulted ultimately in causing the administrative apparatuses to grow bigger and increasing their independence in relation both to the masses and to political guidance by the party.

As regards economic relations, the Bolshevik Party agreed in 1923 that their transformation was a long-term task, but a unified view was not really arrived at as to the way in which this task should be carried out. The party leadership was far from being in complete agreement with Lenin's guidelines which meant renouncing future use of the methods of "war communism," and accepting the road of cooperation as the way to bring about the transition of the peasantry to socialism. The divergences that existed on this subject did not, however, entail immediate consequences, for the socialist transformation of economic relations was not then on the agenda.

For the moment, a relative unity of views prevailed in the party on the necessity of accepting, for the time being, the coexistence of a variety of forms of production, ranging from patriarchalism to the socialist form and including simple commodity production, capitalism, and state capitalism. It was almost unanimously agreed that, temporarily, a big place must be allowed to simple commodity production, especially in the countryside. There was much uncertainty, however, about the way in which this form of production could and should be linked with the others.

This uncertainty was to play a considerable role throughout the NEP period. The realization of these tasks, despite their importance, was itself subordinated to the realization of urgent political and economic tasks.

The most urgent political task was to unite the masses under the leadership of the Bolshevik Party. Without such unity no real step forward could be taken in any field whatsoever. Although, in 1923, the dictatorship of the proletariat was not under threat in the immediate sense, as it had been in the winter of 1920–1921, it could be consolidated only if the working people achieved unity for joint struggle, which was necessary if, in the middle and long runs, the task of eliminating bourgeois and prebourgeois social relations was to be accomplished. In order to secure unification of the masses for this struggle, it was above all essential to reestablish a real political alliance between the proletariat and the mass of the working peasants. The conditions for the reestablishment of this alliance were already given, to some extent, insofar as the broad masses of the peasantry saw the Bolshevik Party as alone capable of organizing resistance to the return of the landlords. To that extent, the peasants as a whole gave support to the Bolshevik Party. But in order to carry through new tasks, to go forward to socialism, this support was not enough: it had to be deepened and transformed into active backing by giving it a new political content. On the question of what, concretely, needed to be done in order to accomplish this essential task, there remained much uncertainty, especially as regards the conditions for political differentiation work among the peasantry, aimed at enabling the Bolshevik Party to obtain the active backing of the least well-off strata of the peasants, those who were most directly interested in a socialist transformation of the rural areas, while at the same time not losing the backing of a substantial fraction of the middle peasants. These problems, which had not been settled in 1923, were to be at the center of the divergences which developed in the Bolshevik Party in subsequent years.

In 1922 and 1923 the economic task which was still immediately and urgently incumbent upon the party was that of restoring production. At that time, the survival of the Soviet power still depended on its capacity to provide the working people with the means of life. If it failed to do this, there was no point in drawing up plans for the future. As Lenin told the Eleventh Party Congress: "The chief thing the people, all the working people, want today is nothing but help in their desperate hunger and need . . ."[4]

And in practice it was to this task that the Bolshevik Party at first applied itself—a task corresponding to the deepest and most crying needs of the people. In order to strengthen the trust that it was possible for the masses to feel for it, the Bolshevik Party had to show that it was capable of something more than merely leading political and military campaigns. The urgency of the tasks needing to be accomplished in the domain of production contributed to confer on the NEP the character of an essentially "economic" policy. It caused some of the Bolshevik leaders to lose sight of the political requirements for the struggle to increase production and feed the masses. Some, as we have seen, even showed willingness to agree to the state's giving up vital economic controls (such as the foreign trade monopoly), or sacrificing the immediate interests of the poorest peasants. Here, too, divergences were to appear at several points in the Bolshevik Party during the NEP period.

These divergences of view were to become all the greater because a number of ideological and political obstacles made it difficult to formulate the various tasks in a rigorous way and to appreciate how they determined each other. Something must be said on this subject, if we are to form a sufficiently clear picture of the situation in Soviet Russia at the moment of Lenin's death.

II.   *The ideological obstacles to accomplishing the Bolshevik Party's tasks*

The task of transforming social relations under the dictatorship of the proletariat was all the harder to tackle because, in this field, the Bolshevik Party lacked the benefit of any previous experience. To be sure, it had the experience of the revolutionary struggle against the bourgeois state, but the lessons of this experience could not be applied directly under the new conditions. As we know, the very exercise of power caused party members, including many leading members, to solve problems by using, first and foremost, the means provided by the state apparatus. However, even if this apparatus had been genuinely proletarian in character—which was far from being the case in 1923—giving priority to using this apparatus would not have made possible a revolutionary transformation of social relations, which always calls for action by the masses themselves. Recourse to the state apparatus makes it possible, under certain conditions, to defend transformations that have already been accomplished, but it cannot bring about fresh revolutionary transformations. Moreover, prolonged recourse to the state apparatus, without any effective intervention by the masses, tends to consolidate bourgeois and prebourgeois relations, engender passivity among the working people, and strengthen the positions of authority held by those who hold leading posts in the state apparatus. In 1923, however, this was not generally recognized by the Bolsheviks.

The exercise of power therefore required that the Bolshevik Party discover new methods for guiding the activity of the masses.[5] In this regard, too, however, the situation was complex. Insofar as the masses tended to trust the party, they were not very ready to take action, while, if they ceased to trust the party, their action might be directed against it. In his writings of 1923 Lenin emphasizes that the party must seek new forms of leadership of the people's struggles, and he suggests, as we have seen, organization of the masses in a variety of ways.

However, these guidelines were very general—they could hardly be otherwise at that time—and, above all, they did not make a very deep impression on the Bolshevik Party, whose members allowed themselves to become increasingly absorbed in tasks of management or administration.

The weakness of the efforts made to develop a mass line of a new type, adapted to the conditions of the dictatorship of the proletariat, had other ideological roots besides those which have just been mentioned. Among them was a certain form of *ouvriérisme* which had been inherited from the Second International. This *ouvriérisme* played a far from negligible role in causing the party to distrust the peasantry, and even those workers who had recently emerged from that class, which meant a very large proportion of the Soviet proletariat. In practice, this attitude hindered the development of the mass organizations, prevented broad and quasi-permanent consultation of non-party people, and was an obstacle to the initiation or consolidation of forms of activity adapted to the nature of the new contradictions, which could be handled correctly only on the basis of the experience of these contradictions acquired by the working people themselves.

In this field, very many Bolsheviks remained greatly under the influence of the positions taken up during "war communism" or during the first months of the NEP, when it was still considered possible to form an alliance with "state capitalism" against the small producer. The party consequently tended to forget that it was "but a drop in the ocean" and could therefore play its leading role "only when we express correctly what the people are conscious of."[6]

Other ideological limitations or obstacles, too, made it difficult for the Bolshevik Party to carry out some of its tasks. One of these was an inadequate appreciation of the class nature of the state apparatus. Even though Lenin had not hesitated to describe this apparatus as "bourgeois" and "tsarist," most of the Soviet leaders stressed mainly the "bureaucratic" character, or "bureaucratic distortion," of the Soviet state. Furthermore, they drew different practical conclusions from this characterization. For some, such as Stalin, the bureaucratic character of the state apparatus was mainly a cultural feature which would disappear as education progressed and which, in the meantime, could be partly combated by eliminating from the administrative and economic apparatuses the elements that had become most heavily "bureaucratized." For others, such as Trotsky, the bureaucratic aspects of the state apparatus (whose "abuses" should be "combated") were essentially bound up with the low level of the productive forces in Russia, and could therefore not be made to disappear until these forces had been sufficiently developed. Here, "bureaucracy" appeared as a social stratum which was assuming a determined and necessary function of constraint, a function which had to be exercised on the plane of production and distribution (the latter having to remain in conformity with "bourgeois right" so long as Russia had not made sufficient progress economically).

Trotsky's conception had not yet been very explicitly affirmed by 1923, but quickly became defined in the years that followed.

Lenin's writings, of course, contain some elements of analysis similar to those which have just been mentioned. Lenin, too, used the expressions "bureaucracy" and "bureaucratic distortion," but what is important is that he did not rest satisfied with these elements of analysis or of description, but strove to relate them to class relations and the class struggle. For almost all the party's members, including the leaders, however, the expression "bureaucracy" and "bureaucratic distortion" served as substitutes for class analysis. Thereby a mask was put upon the bourgeois political and ideological relations of which the "bureaucratic" phenomena were merely a manifestation. Consequently, the fight against these phenomena seemed not to be primarily a question of class struggle, but to depend exclusively on the development of the productive forces, of education, or of repression.

There was thus a connection between the Bolshevik Party's lack of a mass line aimed at smashing the bourgeois political and ideological relations in the state apparatus, and the dominant place occupied by the idea of "bureaucracy" in the way the effects of these relations were described.

The absence of a correct theoretical solution to two other important questions also restricted the party's capacity to carry out certain tasks that were needed for the consolidation of the dictatorship of the proletariat.

In the first place, there was the problem of the specific character of agrarian relations in the Soviet Russia of 1923. Without embarking here upon an analysis whose significance cannot fully emerge except in connection with an examination of the unsolved contradictions which developed between 1923 and 1929, it must be pointed out that two essential specific features of the dominant agrarian relations were not really taken into account theoretically by the Bolshevik Party.

One of these specific features was a consequence of the democratic revolution which had taken place in Russia under the leadership of the proletariat. As a result of this revolution, the payment of the rent and dues to which the peasants had previously been subjected was abolished without capitalist ground rent taking the place of these payments.

A second specific feature resulted from the renewal, in modified forms, of the prerogatives of the *mir* and of the general assemblies of its members.

These two features determined the particular forms of reproduction of the conditions of production in agriculture. Briefly, it can be said that as a result of these two features, the economic constraints obliging the peasants to market part of their produce and to increase production from one year to the next were extremely weak, and productive accumulation of private capital in agriculture was limited. It would have been necessary to take explicit account of these features to work out and carry through a coherent agricultural policy, and to guide correctly the class struggle in the countryside, but the Bolshevik Party's analyses lacked this explicit reckoning. The party tended to "apply" to the Soviet countryside the laws of reproduction appropriate to the development of a capitalist agriculture which did not possess the peculiarities that were present in Russia.

The second set of questions to which the Bolshevik Party was unable to provide a correct theoretical solution was that relating to the socialization of the means of production. Lenin had, indeed, frequently pointed out that nationalizing or statizing the means of production did not mean socializing them; he had shown that progress toward socialization required systematic accounting and control of all the means of production and social domination of their use; he had shown, too, that this accounting, control, and social domination could exist in reality only if they were the work of the working people themselves. Nevertheless, while formally agreeing with these theses, *the Bolshevik Party tended to identify accounting and control of the means of production by the state apparatus with the carrying out of these tasks by the masses themselves,* whereas it is impossible to arrive by that road at genuine socialization of the means of production.

The tendency to identify the activity of the state apparatus of the dictatorship of the proletariat with the activity of the masses was partly connected with a lack of sufficient clarity concerning the conditions in which the masses can effectively play the role that must be theirs in a genuine socialization of the means of production. Without such clarity, however, progress toward true socialization is impossible. On the one hand, the working people do not "spontaneously" move toward the carrying out of tasks of accounting and control of the means of production, tasks which demand time and organizational effort. On the other, if such effort is made to some extent, in a spontaneous way, it is not usually directed toward the utilization of the means of production in accordance with the overall interests of the dictatorship of the proletariat: rather, it serves narrower interests, such as those of the workers of each enterprise taken separately. This can result in transforming the means of production into the "collective property" of the workers in the various units of production (in fact, into a particular type of "capitalist ownership,"[7] which clearly does not lead to real socialization of the means of production). The question of accounting and control of the existing means of production, moreover, cannot be dissociated from that of the social division of labor and the conditions for transforming it. But these problems were not taken up in the Bolshevik Party, either because it seemed premature to formulate them (this was the case with Lenin) or because the illusion existed that they would solve themselves as the productive forces developed.

In 1923, therefore, a number of problems of decisive importance for the future of the dictatorship of the proletariat remained unsettled, even on the ideological plane. The situation is not, of course, surprising, since it is only on the basis of practice that theory can develop; but we must not forget that this situation existed, and that it could entail considerable political consequences.

However, the consequences of the existence of ideological obstacles to a transformation of social relations which could strengthen the dictatorship of the proletariat and advance toward socialism were not all equally apparent at once. Besides, from the theoretical standpoint, the Bolshevik Party was very far from lacking means to overcome such obstacles. The application of historical materialism, and the concrete analysis of the contradictions, successes, and failures experienced could have enabled the party to improve its theoretical knowledge and thus obtain a guide increasingly better adapted to the requirements of action. Concrete proof that such progress was possible is provided by the new theoretical developments found in Lenin's last writings.

It is impossible not to be struck by the gap which generally distinguishes, from the standpoint of rigor and lucidity of analysis, the writings of Lenin from those of the other Bolshevik leaders. In the fight against economism, against mechanistic forms of materialism, for a dialectical analysis of the realities of Russia and of the revolution, Lenin is almost constantly "ahead" of the party, including the great majority of the Central Committee: they have difficulty in bringing themselves to rectify earlier formulations, whereas Lenin does not hesitate to undertake rectifications whenever this seems to him to be necessary, even if it means his being at first in the minority and having to fight to make his views prevail. We have seen earlier how, where such vital questions were concerned as that of substituting the slogan of dictatorship of the proletariat for that of revolutionary-democratic dictatorship of the workers and peasants, the decision to launch the October insurrection, the question of a coalition government, the peace treaty of Brest-Litovsk, the absolute maintenance of the foreign trade monopoly—to mention only a few examples— Lenin had to fight for quite a long time before the Central Committee would follow him. On other points, mainly questions of organization, Lenin was not followed in this way,[8] or was obliged to agree to compromises. Subsequent history showed that, on essential matters, Lenin was the first to form a correct view, and this justifies us in saying that Lenin was usually "ahead" of the Bolshevik Party from the theoretical and political standpoint. For this reason, the use of the expression "the Leninist party" to describe the Bolshevik Party, is highly misleading: it was only belatedly, and not in every case, that the party came around to Lenin's positions, and even then it often did so without having assimilated what was new and vital in Lenin's thought. Hence, too, the considerable gap which frequently existed between the indications given by Lenin—especially as regards appealing to the initiative of the masses and respecting democratic centralism—and the actual practice of the Bolshevik Party.

Basically, the fact that Lenin remained at the head of the party despite the existence of the gaps, delays, and disparities which have been mentioned, testifies to the revolutionary character of the Bolshevik Party. Only a revolutionary party is capable of adopting and retaining a leader who is not just a sort of "arbiter" between different clashing conceptions but is, at one and the same time, the boldest Marxist theoretician with the best sense of reality. It was owing to the experience he had accumulated in the actual life of the Bolshevik Party, to his political and intellectual courage, and to his ability as a materialist dialectician that Lenin was usually "ahead" of his party, and it was because that party was a revolutionary Marxist party that Lenin was in fact its principal leader, who led the party forward, thanks to rigorous thinking and activity placed entirely at the service of the proletarian revolution.

If Lenin and the Bolshevik Party had to make progress, and did indeed make progress, in the domain of theory, this was because theory is always incomplete and must ceaselessly be enriched, which also means getting rid of erroneous ideas incompatible with a proletarian standpoint, which become exposed as such in the light of analysis of social practice. The fight to advance Marxist theory and the practice of a proletarian party is dictated by the class struggle, of which it is an effect. The discrepancies between Lenin's ideas and those that were dominant in the party, the gaps between his guidelines and the actual practice of the Bolshevik Party were also effects of the class struggle.

It was not accidental that in 1923 the gap was especially wide between some of the conclusions at which Lenin had arrived and the conceptions that were dominant in the party—and which were to make it very difficult to carry out a number of tasks needed for the consolidation of the dictatorship of the proletariat.

On the one hand, Lenin had only recently put forward his new conclusions. These were then available only in the form of notes or scattered remarks, and Lenin had not (and was not to have) the time to fight for the triumph of his new conclusions. On the other—and this was the social basis of the increasing difficulties Lenin encountered in trying to get his ideas accepted—the Bolshevik Party of 1923 had been penetrated by many bourgeois and petty bourgeois elements who had often come to the party by way of the administrative and economic apparatuses, in which they had made a "career," and where pressure was brought to bear in a multitude of ways to oppose the initiative of the masses, the strengthening of democratic centralism, and the adoption of conclusions enabling the proletarian character of the party's political line to be consolidated.

Ultimately, there were three kinds of ideological limitation which prevented the Bolshevik Party from accomplishing tasks which would have enabled it to go forward to a higher form of the dictatorship of the proletariat.

First, there were the previously existing theoretical lacunae connected with the lack of sufficient experience and the still-not-completely liquidated influence of the econ-omistic ideology inherited from the Second Inter-national—gaps not yet filled even though Lenin had al-ready opened up a path that made possible an advance toward a correct theoretical solution. The most typical of these was the substitution, for a class analysis of the "bureaucratic" phenomenon, of an "explanation" of it in terms of the de-velopment of the productive forces and the "cultural" level. Formulations of this sort are present, of course, in many of Lenin's writings, too, for, while fighting against the ideologi-cal heritage of the Second International, against what had constituted the pseudo-Marxism of a certain epoch of the working-class movement, he did not completely "liquidate" this inheritance—which continually reappears, moreover, as an effect of the bourgeois class struggle. These formulations, however, are merely a *residue* in Lenin, and not what is essential, for the essential in Lenin is the *new*.

Secondly, there were the mistaken ideas still present in the Bolshevik Party even after they had been rejected, in part at least, by Lenin himself. This was the case, for instance, with the role attributed to the methods of "war communism," which Lenin condemned as a matter of principle, but which the party generally regarded as having been not wrong in themselves, as means for making the transition to communist production and distribution, but only as inopportune as re-gards the time when they were introduced.

Finally, there were in the Bolshevik Party a certain number of mistaken ideas—for example, about the possible substitu-tion of action by the state apparatus for action by the masses in the revolutionary transformation of social relations—which were repudiated in words but often remained dominant in practice, because, under the influence of the class struggle, the repudiation of what was mistaken had remained superficial. Thus, almost everything that Lenin said about the class character of the "Soviet" state apparatus, which he described as "bourgeois" and even "tsarist" with respect to the class practices which were reproduced in it, was largely "forgotten." The party, instead of directing the struggle of the masses against this apparatus, confined itself to trying to combat "bureaucratic abuses" by multiplying the "controls" exercised by one part of the apparatus over another.

The ideological limitations on the consolidation of the dictatorship of the proletariat were in fact due to political relations, to the class struggle.

III. The political obstacles to accomplishing the Bolshevik Party's tasks

In 1923 the Bolshevik Party's ability to apply itself to the tasks that needed undertaking was limited, in the short run at least, by the obstacles constituted by certain of the political relations which had developed previously within the party, or between it, part of the masses, and the state apparatus.

One of these obstacles, a particularly serious one at a time when a new peasant policy needed to be launched, was the very weak representation of the party in the countryside, the inadequate contacts between the party and the peasant masses, so that the latter were mainly in contact with a state administrative apparatus whose characteristics are already known to us. Thus, when we read Lenin's pamphlet on *The Tax in Kind*, we see that a series of tasks which, in order to be carried out properly from the proletarian standpoint, should have been above all tasks for party activists ("generating the utmost local initiative," "assisting small industry," "directing the co-operatives"), were in fact to be carried out by employees and officials.[9] Already in this work, and, still more in his subsequent writings, Lenin raised the question of changing this situation; for example, through a large-scale transfer of Bolshevik leaders with jobs in the central administration to posts as leaders of counties or rural districts, so as to work there "on exemplary lines," in such a way as to "help to train new workers and provide examples that other districts could follow with relative ease."[10]

Lenin's suggestions show the extent to which the political relations existing at that time between the party and the peasant masses constituted an obstacle to the implementation of the NEP. This obstacle became still bigger when it became a matter of implementing the second variant of the NEP, which aimed at forming a new type of political alliance with the peasantry. What happened after Lenin's death showed that this obstacle had been removed only very partially, for the attempts made to remove it came up against the relations prevailing between the party and the state apparatus. These relations were such, indeed, that it was extremely difficult for the party to lead the struggle for a radical transformation of the bourgeois and prebourgeois social relations embodied in this apparatus. The contradictions were here all the greater because the party was the effective instrument of the dictatorship of the proletariat and was capable of taking decisions that struck at the bourgeoisie, including many bourgeois elements in the state apparatus and in the party itself, and yet, for all that, it was not capable—unless the masses went into action—of transforming the political relations embodied in the state apparatus.

The magnitude and character of the party purge carried out in 1921 and continued in 1922 showed that the party was capable at that time of ridding itself of bourgeois elements on a mass scale. The purge, together with voluntary withdrawals, affected a quarter of the party membership of 1921, and the chief charges brought against those who were expelled were careerism, corruption, and joining the party in order to carry on counter-revolutionary activities.[11] Only one-sixth of those party members classified as "workers" were expelled, whereas the proportion was two-fifths in the case of the peasant members (among whom there were quite a lot of kulaks) and one-third in that of the office workers, intellectuals, and others.[12] These figures show both the extent to which the composition of the party had deteriorated and the capacity it still possessed for eliminating dubious elements from its midst. All the same, because extensive help from the masses was not sought in the way Lenin had often suggested, the party purge remained very incomplete, and, above all, it failed to alter the bourgeois political relations existing within itself, as it needed to do if it was to be able effectively to lead the struggle against the bourgeoisie in the state apparatus itself. This was the reason for the development of a contradiction between the overall leading activity of the party and the fact that, in many cases, party members acted under the influence of officials who were bourgeois or representatives of the bourgeoisie. Lenin took note of this in 1922, in his political report to the Eleventh Party Congress, when he said that, where the bureaucratic machine was concerned, he doubted that the Communists were "directing," and even thought they were "being directed."[13]

Lenin's statement was not an exaggeration insofar as the expression "being directed" referred to the considerable influence which could be wielded by tens of thousands of officials hostile to the dictatorship of the proletariat and acting in defense of their own interests. This influence was sometimes manifested on a small scale, by giving a certain bias to the application in everyday life of the decisions taken by the party, and more especially by the party leadership. But this influence could also be exerted on the decisions of certain party leaders who were subject to the "arguments" and "logic" of the bourgeois elements present in the state's administrative and economic apparatuses.[14] This influence of theirs, however, was still limited at that time, insofar as the party leadership was made up of tried revolutionary fighters who took their decisions on the basis of the activity of a party which included many experienced cadres who had proved themselves in the fires of the civil war. Their influence was also restricted by the links uniting the party with the most militant elements of the proletariat, and by its leaders' ability to recognize their own mistakes.

Nevertheless, from day to day the party's activity was being countered by a body of officials who were basically hostile to the dictatorship of the proletariat, by the place such officials occupied at the top of the administrative machine, and by the bourgeois practices and methods they propagated. An idea of the scale of this hostility to the Soviet state is shown by the fact that only 9 percent of the "old" officials and 13 percent of the "new" ones declared themselves favorable to the Soviet regime when, in the summer of 1922, an inquiry was made among officials possessing an engineer's diploma.[15]

The influence of a body of officials largely hostile to the dictatorship of the proletariat could become even greater since some of the information which the Bolshevik leaders themselves were able to obtain regarding the real situation and the aspirations of the masses was acquired through the medium of a hostile state apparatus whose members had a bourgeois outlook.

Thus, the make-up of the state administrative and economic apparatuses, the way they operated, and their relations with the Bolshevik Party set limits to the tasks that the party could actually accomplish. These limits, however, could be transcended as long as their existence was not ignored, as long as the party continued to be sufficiently linked with the most advanced sections of the masses, as long as its leaders were capable of carrying out rectifications, and as long as party members were still able to voice their criticism through the practice of genuine democratic centralism.

In this respect the situation in the Bolshevik Party remained fundamentally sound, even though, since the Tenth Congress, the way the rule forbidding factions was applied, and the tendency to settle by administrative means the problems of party "unity," led to limitations of the members' freedom of expression, and even to the expulsion of some who expressed disagreement with the decisions of the Central Committee. It is known that some local or provincial organizations of the

Bolshevik Party made use of the purges to get rid of dissidents who were accused of ideological deviations.[16] At the time of the Eleventh Congress, several members of the Workers' Opposition were expelled in this way—a member of the Central Control Commission, which had been formed in order to combat "bureaucracy," declared that its task was to see that no one deviated from the line laid down by the party's Central Committee . . . [17]

The limitations imposed on the party members' opportunities to defend their views could hinder the party's ability to overcome its errors of judgment or its ideological weaknesses all the more seriously because political life outside the party continued to be practically suppressed. Those parties which had at first been regarded as "Soviet parties," and which had been able to function openly at certain periods, were no longer, de facto, allowed to exist. Mensheviks, SRs, and anarchists were often arrested by the GPU, even when they were not engaged in subversive activity. On several occasions Lenin himself intervened, especially when requested by Gorky and Kropotkin to check the "excesses" of repression.[18] The existence of this repression—which had had to be introduced when the dictatorship of the proletariat was really in danger through the counter-revolutionary activities of the bourgeois and petty bourgeois parties—limited the awareness that the Bolshevik Party was able to obtain of the contradictions that were developing.

The existence in 1923 of a system of repression which was to some extent pointless actually obstructed the leading role of the party, as well as the proper functioning of democratic centralism. It resulted from the acquisition of independence by the party's administrative apparatus. It showed that bourgeois political relations had developed inside the Bolshevik Party itself—something that Lenin noted on several occasions, as when he observed how the problem of relations between Soviet Russia and the non-Russian Soviet republics had been "settled."

These facts must be taken into consideration if one is to understand the obstacles that at the time made it more *difficult* for the Bolshevik Party to accomplish certain tasks involving the consolidation of the dictatorship of the proletariat. At the same time, one must not imagine that the situation in 1923 was comparable to repression on a quite different scale which was imposed at a later period. In 1923 there was nothing comparable, expecially not within the party. Even if the oppositions could not express themselves with the same facility as before the Tenth Party Congress, they could still make their voices heard. Their documents and critiques circulated, they were fairly widely known, and what they said was seriously taken into account in the working out of the party line. Outside the party, the interventions of the GPU did not cause a general concealment of opinions or of reasons for discontent—as is shown, for example, by the inquiry mentioned above, which revealed that nearly 90 percent of the officials questioned expressed a hostile attitude to the Soviet regime.

In short, in 1923, though there really were obstacles to the Bolshevik Party's fulfillment of some of the tasks needed for consolidating the dictatorship of the proletariat, these obstacles seemed to be of a kind that could be overcome. The obstacles of an ideological character were not the most serious ones, especially in the short run. They did not challenge the basic principles of revolutionary Marxism as it had been able to develop up to that time, and could therefore have been eliminated by means of experimentation and by drawing up a balance sheet of past errors in the light of Marxist theory. The obstacles of a political character constituted a more serious threat; but they left intact the proletarian character of the party, its leaders' will to fight for socialism, the devotion to the party of hundreds of thousands of militants, including a very high proportion of workers, and the support accorded to the party by broad masses of the people. Actually, what existed was a certain configuration of class relations which meant that, in the years to come, the dictatorship of the proletariat would be confronted by new problems with which the Bolshevik Party was not immediately ready to cope. Hence the special complexity of the struggles that developed after Lenin's death.

Notes

1. The policy that was actually followed can be analyzed only by examining the problems that arose after 1923 and the forms that the class struggle assumed at that time.
2. Lenin's report to the Eleventh Party Congress, in *CW*, vol. 33, p. 304.
3. *CW*, vol. 42, p. 376.
4. *CW*, vol. 33, p. 304.
5. This was what Lenin indicated when, after mentioning the need to combat the defects in the state apparatus, he declined to take the view that the methods for doing this were already known, and said: "We must first think very carefully how to combat its defects." (*CW*, vol. 33, p. 487.)
6. Lenin's report to the Eleventh Party Congress, in ibid., p. 304.
7. Insofar as the means of production are used in order to enable the workers of each enterprise to appropriate the value produced, these means of production function as capital. Under these conditions, the contradiction between labor and capital, "abolished" at the level of the unit of production, is maintained on the social scale. This is what Marx notes when writing about workers' cooperatives: he observes that the members are "their own capitalist" in that they "use the means of production for the employment of their own labour" (*Capital*, vol. III, p. 431).
8. In a letter of March 17, 1921, to the Bolshevik A. A. Joffe, Lenin wrote: "I cannot say how many times I have been in a minority on organisational and personal matters" (*CW*, vol. 45, p. 99).
9. *CW*, vol. 32, pp. 352–353.
10. Ibid., p. 356.
11. The other principal charges were passivity, religious practices, and drunkenness.
12. See Rigby, *Communist Party Membership*, p. 97.
13. *CW*, vol. 33, p. 289. It was in this report that Lenin compared the relationship between the Bolshevik Party and the state apparatus to that between a conquering and a conquered people, with the

former eventually becoming subject to the latter owing to the "superiority" of its culture. As we have seen, this comparison was taken up and developed by Bukharin.

14. This partly explains why Lenin had to wage such a struggle to protect the foreign trade monopoly.

15. Kritsman, *Geroichesky period,* p. 146.

16. See Rigby, *Communist Party Membership,* p. 98.

17. See Daniels, *The Conscience of the Revolution,* p. 167. Laid down *by the Central Committee,* be it noted, and not by the party congress: the traditional status of the latter as the party's highest political instance was thus undermined.

18. Liebman, *Leninism under Lenin,* p. 317.

Bibliography

Bolshevik party documents

1. Reports of party congresses

Sixth (1917). *Shestoi s'yezd R.S.D.R.P.(b.): protokoly.* Moscow: Gospolitizdat, 1958.
Seventh (1918). *Syed'moi ekstrennyi s'yezd R.K.P.(b.), mart 1918 goda: stenograficheshy otchet.* Moscow: Gospolitizdat, 1920 and 1962.
Eighth (1919). *Vos'moi s'yezd R.K.P.(b), mart 1919 goda: protokoly.* Moscow: Gospolitizdat, 1959.
Ninth (1920). *Devyaty s'yezd R.K.P.(b.), mart-aprel' 1920 goda: protokoly.* Moscow: Gospolitizdat, 1921 and 1960.
Tenth (1921). *Desyaty s'yezd R.K.P.(b.): stenograficheshy otchet, 8–16 marta 1921 goda.* Moscow: Gospolitizdat, 1921 and 1963.
Eleventh (1922). *Odinnadtsaty s'yezd R.K.P.(b.), mart-aprel' 1922 goda: stenograficheshy otchet.* Moscow: Gospolitizdat, 1961.
Twelfth (1923). *Dvenadtsaty s'yezd R.K.P.(b.): stenograficheshy otchet, 17–25 aprelya 1923 goda.* Moscow: Krasnaya Nov', 1923.

2. Reports of party conferences

Seventh (April 1917). *Sed'maya (aprel'skaya) vserossiiskaya i Petrogradskaya obshchegorodskaya konferentsiya R.S.D.R.P.(b.), aprel' 1917 goda: protokoly.* Moscow: Gospolitizdat, 1958.
Eighth (December 1919). *Vos'maya konferentsiya R.K.P.(b.), dekabr' 1919 goda: protokoly.* Moscow: Gospolitizdat, 1961.

3. Resolutions and decisions

K.P.S.S. v rezolyutsiyakh i resheniyakh s'yezdov, konferentsii i plenumov Ts. K., vol. 1. Moscow: Gospolitizdat, 1953.

532   *Charles Bettelheim*

Collections of statistics

Narodnoye Khozyaistvo SSSR v 1958 g. Moscow: 1959.
Narodnoye Khozyaistvo SSSR v 1970 g. Moscow: 1971.
Narodnoye Khozyaistvo SSSR, 1922-1972 gg. Moscow: 1972.

Books and articles

Anfimov, A. M. *Rossiiskaya derevnya v gody pervoi mirovoi voiny.* Moscow: 1962.
Antonov-Saratovsky, V. P., ed. *Sovyety v epokhu voyennogo kommunizma, 1918-1921.* 2 vols. Moscow: Komm Akademiya, 1928.
Anweiler, O. *Die Rätebewegung in Russland, 1905-1921.* Leiden: E. J. Brill, 1958. (Available in English: *The Soviets.* New York: Pantheon, 1974.)
Avrich, Paul. *Kronstadt 1921.* Princeton: Princeton University Press, 1970.
Baudelot, Christian, and Establet, Roger. *L'école capitaliste en France.* Paris: Maspero, 1971.
Begaux-Francotte, Colette. "La *prokuratura* soviétique." *Revue du Centre d'études des pays de l'Est* (Brussels), nos. 1 and 2 (1970).
Bettelheim, C. *Cultural Revolution and Industrial Organization in China.* New York: Monthly Review Press, 1974.
――――. *Economic Calculation and Forms of Property.* New York: Monthly Review Press, 1976. (Originally published as *Calcul économique et formes de propriété.* Paris: Maspero, 1970.)
――――. *Planification et croissance accélérée.* Paris: Maspero, 1964.
――――. *The Transition to Socialist Economy.* Hassocks, Sussex: Harvester Press, 1975. (Originally published as *La Transition vers l'économie socialiste.* Paris: Maspero, 1968.)
Bolshaya Sovyetskaya Entsiklopediya (first edition). Vols. 11 and 12. Moscow: 1928.
Bolsheviks, The, and the October Revolution: Central Committee Minutes, August 1917-February 1918. London: Pluto, 1974.
Brinton, Maurice. *The Bolsheviks & Workers' Control, 1917 to 1921: The State and Counter-Revolution.* London: Solidarity, 1970.
Broué, P. *Le Parti bolchévique.* Paris: Editions de Minuit, 1963.
――――. *Problèmes politiques et sociaux.* Paris: la Documentation française (no. 74), 1971.

Bukharin, N. *Economics of the Transformation Period.* New York: Bergman, 1971.

————. *Proletarskaya revolyutsiya i kultura.* Petrograd: Priboy, 1923.

Bukharin, N., and Preobrazhensky, E. *The ABC of Communism.* Edited by E. H. Carr. London: Penguin, 1969.

Bunyan, J., and Fisher, H. *The Bolshevik Revolution, 1917–1918.* Stanford: Stanford University Press, 1934.

Carr, E. H. *The Bolshevik Revolution, 1917–1923.* 3 vols. London: Penguin, 1966.

————. *Foundations of a Planned Economy.* Vol. 2. London: Macmillan, 1971.

————. *Socialism in One Country.* Vol. 1. London: Macmillan, 1964.

Carr, E. H., and Davies, R. W. *Foundations of a Planned Economy.* Vol. 1. London: Macmillan, 1969.

Chayanov, A. V. *The Theory of Peasant Economy.* Homewood: American Economic Association, 1966.

Collins, D. N. "A Note on the Numerical Strength of the Russian Red Guards in October 1917." *Soviet Studies* (October 1972).

Daniels, R. V. *The Conscience of the Revolution.* Cambridge: Harvard University Press, 1960.

Dobb, Maurice. *Soviet Economic Development since 1917.* London: Routledge, 1948.

Dubrowski, S. *Die Bauernbewegung in der russischen Revolution 1917.* Berlin: 1929.

Ekonomicheskoye rassloyenie krestyanstva v 1917 i 1919 gg. Moscow: Statistika, 1922.

Engels, F. *The Peasants' War in Germany.* Moscow: Foreign Languages Publishing House, 1956.

Entsiklopedichesky Slovar'. Edited by B. A. Vvedensky. 2 vols. Moscow: 1963.

Fainsod, Merle. *How Russia Is Ruled.* Cambridge: Harvard University Press, 1953.

Ferro, Marc. *The Russian Revolution of February 1917.* London: Routledge, 1972.

Fotiyeva, L. A. *Iz vospominaniy o V. I. Lenine.* Moscow: Politizdat, 1964.

Gierek face aux grévistes de Szezecin, 24 janvier 1971. Paris: SELIO, 1972.

Gins, G. K. *Sibir', soyuzniki i Kolchak.* Peking: Izd. Obshchestva Vozrozhdeniya Rossii, 1921.

Grosskopf, Sigrid. "Appropriation, utilisation et partage des terres à l'époque de la N.E.P." *Cahiers du monde russe et soviétique* (October-December 1973).

Grosskopf, S. *Le Problème des céréales en Russie et la N.E.P., Mémoire.* Paris: Ecole Pratique des Hautes Etudes (VIe Section), September 1970.

Grumbach, M. *Contribution à l'étude du développement du capitalisme en Russie, Thèse de 3e cycle.* Paris: Ecole Pratique des Hautes Etudes (VIe section), 1973.

Haupt, G. "Ouvrages bibliographiques concernant l'histoire de l'U.R.S.S." *Cahiers du monde russe et soviétique,* no. 3 (April-June 1960).

Haupt, G., and Marie, J.-J. *Makers of the Russian Revolution.* London: Allen and Unwin, 1974.

Kollontai, A. *The Workers' Opposition.* London: Solidarity, n.d.

Kondrat'ev, N. D., and Oganovsky, N. P. *Perspektivy razvitiya sel'skogo khozyaistva S.S.S.R.* Part I. Moscow: Novaya Derevnya, 1924.

Kritsman, L. *Geroichesky period velikoi russkoi revolyutsii.* Moscow: Gosizdat, n.d.

Krzhyzhanovsky, G. M. *Desyat' let khozyaistvennogo stroitel'stva SSSR 1917–1927.* Moscow: 1928.

Labry, R. *Une Législation communiste: recueil des lois, décrets, arrêtés principaux du gouvernement bolcheviste.* Paris: Payot, 1920.

Lefort, Claude. *Eléments d'une critique de la bureaucratie.* Geneva: Droz, 1971.

Lenin, V. I. *Collected Works.* 4th ed., in English. Moscow: Foreign Languages Publishing House, 1960–1970.

————. *Polnoye Sobranie Sochinenii.* 5th ed., vol. 45. Moscow: 1964.

————. *Sochineniya.* 3rd ed. Moscow: 1935.

Leninsky Sbornik. Vols. 7 and 11. Moscow: 1928 and 1929.

Lewin, Moshe. *Lenin's Last Struggle.* London: Faber, 1969.

Liebman, M. *Leninism under Lenin.* London: Jonathan Cape, 1974.

Limon, D. L. "Lénine et le contrôle ouvrier." *Autogestion* (December 1967).

Lindenberg, Daniel. *L'Internationale Communiste et l'école de classe.* Paris: Maspero, 1972.

————. "Sur la préhistoire de l'école soviétique." *Politique aujourd'hui* (September 1971).

Lozovsky, A. *Rabochy Kontrol'*. Moscow: 1918.
Luxemburg, Rosa. *The Russian Revolution*. New York: Workers' Age, 1940.
Malaya Sovyetskaya Entsiklopediya. Moscow: 1929.
Mao Tse-tung. *On Khrushchev's Phoney Communism and Its Historical Lessons for the World*. Peking: Foreign Languages Press, 1964.
—————. *Selected Works*. 4 vols. Peking: Foreign Language Press, 1961–1967.
Marx, K. *Capital*. Vol. III. Moscow: Foreign Languages Publishing House, 1959.
—————. *Contribution to the Critique of Political Economy*. London: Lawrence and Wishart, 1971.
—————. *Grundrisse*. London: Penguin, 1973.
—————. *Le Capital: un chapitre inédit*. Edited by R. Dangeville. Paris: Collection 10/18, 1971.
Marx, K., and Engels, F. *The German Ideology*. Moscow: Progress, 1964.
—————. *The Holy Family*. Moscow: Foreign Languages Publishing House, 1956.
—————. *The Russian Menace to Europe*. Edited by P. W. Bienstock and B. F. Hoselitz. London: Allen and Unwin, 1953.
—————. *Selected Correspondence*. Moscow: Foreign Languages Publishing House, 1956.
—————. *Selected Works in Three Volumes*. Moscow: Progress, 1969–1970.
Medvedev, Roy. *Let History Judge*. London: Macmillan, 1972.
Narkiewicz, Olga A. *The Making of the Soviet State Apparatus*. Manchester: Manchester University Press, 1970.
Osipov, V., et al. *Saratovskaya partiinaya organizatsiya v gody vosstanovleniya narodnogo khozyaistva*. Saratov: 1960.
Partiya v tsifrovom osvechenii. Moscow and Leningrad: Giz, 1925.
Political Economy: A Textbook Issued by the Institute of Economics of the Academy of Sciences of the U.S.S.R. London: Lawrence and Wishart, 1957.
Polyakov, Yu. A. "Sotsialno-ekonomicheskie itogi agrarnykh preobrazovanii oktyabrskoi revolyutsii." *Istoriya sovyetskogo krestyanstva i kolkhoznogo stroitelstva v SSSR* (Moscow), 1963.
Popov, P. *Proizvodstvo khleba v R.S.F.S.R.* Moscow: Gosizdat, 1921.
Pravda o Kronshtadte. Prague: 1921.

Preobrazhensky, E.; Rakovsky, C.; and Trotsky, L. D. *De la bureaucratie*. Paris: Maspero, 1971.

Rakovsky, Christian. "Power and the Russian Workers." *New International* (November 1934).

Rigby, T. H. *Communist Party Membership 1917–1967*. Princeton: Princeton University Press, 1968.

Sadoul, Jacques. *Notes sur la Révolution bolchévique*. Paris: Maspero, 1971.

Schapiro, Leonard. *The Communist Party of the Soviet Union*. 2nd ed. London: Methuen, 1970.

Schram, Stuart R. *Mao Tse-tung Unrehearsed*. London: Penguin, 1974.

Serge, Victor. *Memoirs of a Revolutionary*. London: Oxford University Press, 1963.

Shanin, T. *The Awkward Class*. Oxford: Clarendon, 1972.

Sharapov, G. *Razreshenie agrarnogo voprosa v Rossii posle pobedy oktyabr'skoi revolyutsii, 1917–1920*. Moscow: 1961.

Sobranie uzakonenii i rasporyazhenii Rabochego i Krestyanskogo Pravitelstva (1917–1918, 1919, 1920, 1922, 1923). Moscow: 1918–1924.

Sorlin, P. *The Soviet People and Their Society*. London: Pall Mall, 1969.

Sosnovsky, L. S. *Dyela i Lyudi*. Vol. 1. Moscow: Krasnaya Nov', 1924.

Sotsialnyi i natsionalnyi sostav V.K.P.(b): itogi vsesoyuznoi partiinoi perepisi 1927 goda. Moscow: 1927.

Sovyety, syezdy sovyetov i ispolkomy. Moscow: NKVD, 1924.

Stalin, J. V. *Economic Problems of Socialism in the U.S.S.R.* Moscow: Foreign Languages Publishing House, 1952.

————. *Leninism*. London: Lawrence and Wishart, 1940.

————. *Works*. Moscow: Foreign Languages Publishing House, 1952–1955.

Strong, Anna Louise. *The Stalin Era*. New York: Mainstream, 1956.

Sweezy, Paul M., and Charles Bettelheim. *On the Transition to Socialism*. New York: Monthly Review Press, 1971.

Syezdy Sovyetov R.S.F.S.R. v postanovleniyakh. Moscow: 1939.

Trotsky, L. D. *Kak vooruzhalas' revolyutsiya*. Moscow: 1923.

————. *Leon Trotsky Speaks*. New York: Pathfinder, 1972.

————. *Military Writings*. New York: Pathfinder, 1971.

————. *The Revolution Betrayed*. London: New Park Publications, 1957.

————. *Sochineniya*. Vol. 15. Moscow: 1927.

Ustinov, M. "K voprosu o formakh zemlepolzovaniya." *Bolshevik*, no. 19–20 (1927).

Vanag, N. N. *Finantsovy kapital v Rossii nakanune mirovoi voiny.* Moscow: 1925.

————. "K metodologii izucheniya finansovogo kapitala v Rossii." *Istorik marksist,* no. 12 (1929).

Volin, L. *A Century of Russian Agriculture.* Cambridge: Harvard University Press, 1970.

Vserossiiskaya peripis' chlenov R.K.P. 1922 goda. Moscow: 1922.

White, James D. "Moscow, Petersburg and the Russian Industrialists." *Soviet Studies* (January 1973).

Znamensky. "Iz istorii razvitiya sovetskogo apparata v Tambovskoi Gubernii." *Sovetskoye Stroitelstvo, Sbornik I.* Moscow: Komm. Akademiya, 1925.

Principal journals and periodicals

In Russian

Derevyenskaya Kommuna
Ekonomicheskaya Zhizu
Istoricheskiye Zapiski
Izvestiya
Izvestiya Tsentralnogo Komiteta R.K.P.
Narodnoye Khozyaistvo
Partiinaya Zhizn
Pravda
Sovyetskoye Stroitelstvo
Voprosy Istorii

In French

Annales d'histoire économique et sociale
Bulletin communiste
Cahiers du monde russe et soviétique
Etudes soviétiques
Problèmes économiques et sociaux (Documentation française). No. 74 (1971).

In English

Slavic Review
Soviet Studies

Index

Management, collective, rejected, 406; *see also*
Technicians
Mao Tse-tung, 48n, 129n, 326n
on correct ideas, 198
going against the tide, 414
on having several parties,
289n–90n
on leadership, 62
on need for an army, 290n–91n
Martov, Y. O., 121, 266
Marx, Karl, 115, 470
and cooperation, 489–90
defines capitalist class, 44
economism and, 43, 473–74
and educational system, 169
and indicators of social conditions, 137
Jacobinism and, 343
on necessity of revolution, 177
and ownership of means of
production, 21, 22
on Paris Commune, 164
and peasant war and working-
class movement, 496
and political forms, 251
and production relations, 21,
163, 208n–9n, 333, 334,
459, 492
and productive forces, 24, 52n
on proletariat, 359
reestablishing contact with
thought of, 49n
and Russia, 214, 215, 218, 245,
246n
state and, 460–61
on workers' cooperatives, 529n
Marxism, 190
abandoned, 11
in Bolshevik Party, 292, 342,
345, 410–11

bourgeois ideology and, 50n
and constitution of proletariat
as dominant class, 190,
191
"democratic" parties and development of, 270
dialectical development of, 119
as economism, 16, 46
emerging conceptions in
conflict with, 159
fresh vigor in, 47–48, 49n
and ideological obstacles to
transforming social rela-
tions, 519
of Kautsky, 470
of Lenin, *see* Lenin, Vladimir
Ilich
and political obstacles to dictatorship of proletariat,
528
proletarian revolution and revolutionary, 113, 114
revisionism and, 19–20; *see
also* Revisionism
sclerotic, 47
struggle for primacy of, in labor
movement, 114–18
theses of, congealed, 20–32
Mass line, 191–93, 493–95, 515,
517
Mdivani, B., 427
Means of production, 529n
bourgeois loss of power and
loss of control over, 136
collective control over, 44
in *mir*, 244
owned by poor peasants, 244
See also State ownership
Mensheviks, 24, 190
changes in trade unions and,
184